Exploring Microsoft Excel's Hidden Treasures

Turbocharge your Excel proficiency with expert
tips, automation techniques, and overlooked features

David Ringstrom, CPA

BIRMINGHAM—MUMBAI

Exploring Microsoft Excel's Hidden Treasures

Copyright © 2022 Packt Publishing

All rights reserved. No part of this book may be reproduced, stored in a retrieval system, or transmitted in any form or by any means, without the prior written permission of the publisher, except in the case of brief quotations embedded in critical articles or reviews.

Every effort has been made in the preparation of this book to ensure the accuracy of the information presented. However, the information contained in this book is sold without warranty, either express or implied. Neither the author, nor Packt Publishing or its dealers and distributors, will be held liable for any damages caused or alleged to have been caused directly or indirectly by this book.

Packt Publishing has endeavored to provide trademark information about all of the companies and products mentioned in this book by the appropriate use of capitals. However, Packt Publishing cannot guarantee the accuracy of this information.

Group Product Manager: Alok Dhuri
Publishing Product Manager: Shweta Bairoliya
Senior Editor: Nithya Sadanandan
Technical Editor: Pradeep Sahu
Copy Editor: Safis Editing
Project Coordinator: Manisha Singh
Proofreader: Safis Editing
Indexer: Hemangini Bari
Production Designer: Shyam Sundar Korumilli
Marketing Coordinator: Deepak Kumar and Rayyan Khan
Business Development Executive: Puneet Kaur

First published: August 2022

Production reference: 0290822

Published by Packt Publishing Ltd.
Livery Place
35 Livery Street
Birmingham
B3 2PB, UK.

ISBN 978-1-80324-394-8

www.packt.com

– For Erin, Rachel, and Lucas—and Ringo too

Contributors

About the author

David Ringstrom exclaimed "Well, this is a stupid program, you can't do anything with it" the first time that he launched Lotus 1-2-3 in 1987, unaware that pressing the slash key displayed the menu. That moment sealed his fate as he is now a nationally recognized spreadsheet expert. In 1991, David started a spreadsheet consulting practice that he still runs today. David has taught over 2,000 webinars and published hundreds of articles, all on Excel, and he imparts spreadsheet skills to thousands of college students each year. He is the author or coauthor of five books and the technical editor of over 40 books. He is a certified public accountant and a graduate of Georgia State University and has served in the United States Navy.

> *Thank you to my training and consulting clients for decades of Excel questions that inspired this book. I'm grateful to my family for their unending support. A special thank you goes to my editors Nithya Sadanandan and Manisha Singh, and technical reviewers John Christovassilis and Alan Murray, for bearing with my creative process and enhancing this book. Also special thanks to all of the Packt team working behind the scenes to bring this book to life!*

About the reviewers

John Christovassilis has a double major Bachelor of Science in computer science and physics (Queen Mary, Univ. of London), a Master of Science in information security (Royal Holloway, Univ. of London), and a Master of Science in airport planning and management (Loughborough Univ.). He is a **Microsoft Certified Trainer (MCT)**, **Microsoft Certified Professional (MCP)**, **Microsoft Office Specialist (MOS)** Master Instructor, and is ITIL Foundation certified. John is a data analysis expert, having produced Excel reports with detailed metrics, macros, complex formulas, functions, charts, pivot tables, and so on for 25+ years. He also has 15+ years' experience consulting, managing, and delivering custom learning and technical training solutions to clients worldwide.

Alan Murray is a Microsoft MVP, Excel trainer, and author. He has been helping people in Excel for over 20 years. He loves training and the joy he gets from knowing he is making people's working lives easier. Alan runs his own blog, Computergaga (https://computergaga.com), and writes for multiple other websites. His YouTube channel (Computergaga) has over 600 videos and over 40 million views. He organizes a free monthly Excel meetup in London where anyone can come learn Excel, chat, and enjoy each other's company.

Table of Contents

Preface	xv

Part 1: Improving Accessibility

1

Implementing Accessibility — 3

Technical requirements	3	Merge Cells feature	17
Making Excel more accessible	4	Minimizing the use of watermarks, headers, and footers	19
Finding worksheet functions	4	Working carefully with color	23
Microsoft Search box	7	Using the Table feature	24
Help tab of Excel's Ribbon	9		
On-demand PivotTables and charts	10	Accessibility Checker feature	25
Implementing accessibility within spreadsheets	14	Accessibility Reminder add-in	26
		Examples of inaccessible spreadsheets	28
Assign worksheet names	14	Summary	30

2

Disaster Recovery and File-Related Prompts — 33

Technical requirements	33	Accessing prior AutoSave versions	42
Undo and Redo	34	Resolving the disabled AutoSave	43
The AutoRecover feature	35	Permanently disabling AutoSave	44
Excel for Windows AutoRecover	36	The Always create backup setting	45
Excel for macOS AutoRecover	38	Repairing damaged workbooks	46
AutoSave with OneDrive	39	Removing excess formatting	48
Saving files to OneDrive	40		

Warning prompts when opening workbooks 49	Trusted documents 51
Protected View 49	CSV prompt 53
	Summary 54

3

Quick Access Toolbar Treasures 55

Technical requirements 56	**Commands Not in the Ribbon** 68
Exploring the Quick Access Toolbar 56	Enhanced commands 68
Customizing Excel's Ribbon 59	**Workbook-specific toolbars** 70
Understanding the nuances of Quick Access Toolbar shortcuts 59	**Creating shortcuts for Excel macros** 71
Repositioning the Quick Access Toolbar commands 60	**Transferring your Quick Access Toolbar between computers** 74
Removing Quick Access Toolbar commands 61	**Restoring legacy features** 75
Resetting the Quick Access Toolbar 62	The Full screen feature 75
The Alt-Number Pad nuance 63	Full-screen mode 76
Adding Ribbon commands to the toolbar 64	Restoring the Full Screen feature 78
Center text 65	The Share Workbook feature 78
Locking/unlocking worksheet cells 66	Show Changes 79
PDF shortcuts 67	**Summary** 81

4

Conditional Formatting 83

Technical requirements 84	A Date Occurring 91
Formatting versus Conditional Formatting 84	Duplicate Values 93
Highlight cell rules 86	**Top and bottom rules** 94
Greater Than 87	**Data Bars** 95
Less Than 88	**Color Scales** 97
Between 88	**Icon Sets** 98
Equal To 89	**Custom rules** 101
Text That Contains 90	IS functions 101
	CELL function 103

Logical tests	105	**Troubleshooting Conditional Formatting**	**111**
Managing rules	**106**	No formatting appears	111
Editing existing rules	106	Changing the order of the rules	113
Applies to ranges	107	Wingdings font	114
Creating a Conditional Formatting legend	108	**Summary**	**115**
Removing Conditional Formatting	109		

Part 2: Spreadsheet Interactivity and Automation

5

Data Validation and Form Controls — 119

Technical requirements	**120**	Custom rules	146
Introducing Data Validation	**120**	**Protecting Data Validation cells**	**150**
Settings tab	124	**Auditing Data Validation cell inputs**	**151**
Input Message tab	125	**Enabling the Developer tab**	**151**
Error Alert Message tab	125	**Exploring Form Controls**	**152**
Removing Data Validation	129	The INDEX function	154
Implementing Data Validation rules	**131**	Combo Box Form Control	154
Any value	131	**Checkboxes and Option Buttons**	**156**
Whole Numbers	131	Creating Checkboxes	156
Decimal	132	Creating Option Buttons	157
List	132	Managing Form Controls	158
Date	141	**Summary**	**159**
Time	143		
Text length	145		

6

What-If Analysis — 161

Technical requirements	**162**	Setting the scene for a scenario	165
The PMT function	**162**	Creating scenarios	166
The CUMIPMT function	**163**	Showing scenarios	168
Understanding the Scenario Manager feature	**164**	Scenario reports	169
		Merging scenarios	173

The Goal Seek feature	174	Improving calculation performance	182
The Data Table feature	177	Projecting amounts with the Forecast Sheet feature	183
Creating a Data Table with one input	177	Introducing the Solver feature	185
Creating a Data Table with two inputs	179	Summary	189
Creating a Data Table with three inputs	180		

7

Automating Tasks with the Table Feature — 191

Technical requirements	192	Self-resizing charts	217
Excel's unwritten rule	192	**Other Table techniques**	**218**
What is a Table?	194	Customizing Table Styles	219
The Format as Table command	196	Transferring Table Styles to other workbooks	221
The Insert | Table command	198	Modifying or removing custom Table Styles	222
Table characteristics	199	Copying and pasting Tables	223
Removing Tables	**203**	Keyboard and mouse shortcuts	225
Table automation opportunities	**204**	**Troubleshooting Tables**	**227**
Calculated Columns	205	The Include new rows and columns in Table option	227
Self-resizing formulas	207	Fill formulas in Tables to create Calculated Columns	229
Using structured references to write formulas	208	Deleting rows prevents Table expansion	230
Filtering	210	**Summary**	**232**
Slicers	**211**		
PivotTable integrity improvements	214		

8

Custom Views — 233

Technical requirements	233	Creating a Custom Views Quick Access Toolbar shortcut	240
Introducing Custom Views	234	Hiding and unhiding worksheets	242
Creating multipurpose worksheets	235	Unhiding worksheets with a macro	243
Creating a base view	236	Hiding and unhiding worksheets with Custom Views	246
Creating a Quarters Only view	238	Creating a Summary Only view	247
Creating an Executive Summary view	238	**Automating filtering**	**247**
Page Layout view conflict	239		

Applying print settings on demand	251	Table feature conflicts	255
Updating a Custom View	253	Worksheet protection conflicts	257
Removing all Custom Views from a workbook	253	Workbook protection	260
Custom Views conflicts	255	Summary	262

9

Excel Quirks and Nuances 263

Technical requirements	264	Excluding weekend dates from charts	274
Compatibility Checker feature	264	Sparklines	276
Compatibility Mode	266	Circular references	279
Save As versus Convert command	267	Enable iterative calculation option	280
Double-click trick for navigating within worksheets	269	Inquire add-in	282
Enter Mode Versus Edit Mode	271	Summary	285

Part 3: Data Analysis

10

Lookup and Dynamic Array Functions 289

Technical requirements	290	The XMATCH function	303
The VLOOKUP function	290	The UNIQUE function	304
The IFNA function	292	The SORT function	305
The MATCH function	293	The FILTER function	309
The SUMIF function	296	The Spilled Range Operator	312
The SUMIFS function	296	The dynamic amortization table	313
The XLOOKUP function	297	The SEQUENCE function	315
The if_not_found argument	298	The EOMONTH function	316
The match_mode argument	298	The PPMT function	317
Combining results into a single column	300	The SUMIF function	317
The search_mode argument and returning results to multiple columns	300	The #SPILL! errors	318
Matching on multiple column criteria	301	The RANDARRAY function	319
Returning results from multiple cells	302	Summary	321

11

Names, LET, and LAMBDA — 323

Technical requirements	323	Introducing the LAMBDA function	344
Simple volume calculations in Excel	324	Developing a LAMBDA formula	344
Multiplication	324	Naming Parameters and defining the calculation	345
Decision-making functions	325	Evaluating a LAMBDA function	346
Naming worksheet cells	328	Creating reusable LAMBDA functions	346
Name Box	328	Moving LAMBDA functions between workbooks	348
Create from Selection	331		
Define Name	332	Going deeper with LAMBDA functions	350
Name Manager	334	Optional LAMBDA Parameters	351
Using **Names** within formulas	338	LAMDBA conflicts and errors	352
Introducing the LET function	339	The Advanced Formula Environment add-in	354
Handling formula errors	340	The XBOXVOLUME function	356
The IFERROR function	341		
The ISERROR function	341	Custom VBA worksheet functions	358
Eliminating repetitive calculations	342	Summary	361
Variables restrictions	342		

12

Power Query — 363

Technical requirements	363	Transforming reports	377
Introducing Power Query	364	Setting a locale or region	382
Creating a list of worksheets	365	Adding supplemental formulas to **Power Query** results	383
The HYPERLINK function	369		
Making **Power Query** results into a clickable index	370	Updating a **Power Query** connection with new data	384
Refreshing **Power Query Connections**	371	Breaking **Power Query Connections**	384
Updating the worksheet index	372	Extracting data from PDF files	386
Updating source data connections	374	Unpivoting data	393
Automatic report cleanup	375	Appending and merging data from multiple sources	394
Analytical obstacles	376		

Connecting to databases and installing ODBC drivers	402	Establishing ODBC connections	404
		Installing ODBC drivers and creating data sources	405
Establishing an Access database and SQL Server connections	402	Summary	406

Index 407

Other Books You May Enjoy 420

Preface

I coined the phrase *Either you work Excel, or it works you!* over a decade ago to describe how the average user gets pushed around when building and using spreadsheets. Even advanced Excel users can fall prey to what I call the *death by a thousand cuts* experience, where tasks are accomplished slightly inefficiently or in a repetitive fashion. The cumulative effect of both is that you accomplish less, maybe think Excel is too hard, or perhaps tell yourself you're not smart enough to use spreadsheets. I've heard it all over the years, and so I have included numerous automation and productivity tips in this book to dispel all of those myths and issues.

I quickly exceeded the budgeted page count on every chapter. I am truly grateful to Packt for graciously allowing me to cover each topic in the depth that I felt was warranted. There's always more that I could have written, but I aimed for a balance of being informative without being overwhelming.

You'll see a couple mentions of programming code in this book, but almost all of the automation that I discuss involves code-free solutions. I want to empower you to create resilient spreadsheets that have better data integrity and require much less of your time.

Who this book is for

In this book David Ringstrom, CPA has distilled knowledge and questions asked from thousands of webinars and decades of spreadsheet consulting engagements into a concise guide aimed squarely at intermediate, advanced, and even Excel power users -- and those who aspire to such levels. David teaches and consults with accountants, business managers, CFOs, analysts, business owners, insurance specialists, human resource managers, grant managers, budget officers, controllers, the list goes on. If you spend a significant amount of time working in Excel, this book is assured to help boost your productivity. David coined the phrase "Either you work Excel, or it works you!" and has devoted his career to help anyone that uses Excel work smarter, faster, and agilely. The more time that you spend in Excel, the more time this book will save you. Don't let your data bog you down, this curated collection of code-free automation techniques, keyboard shortcuts, and overlooked features will empower you to become the Excel user you've always dreamed of becoming.

What this book covers

Chapter 1, Implementing Accessibility, will focus on accessibility from two perspectives. First, I'll discuss features in Excel that make it easier to unearth features and worksheet functions, so that you can utilize more of the program, no matter what your abilities are. Second, I'll discuss accessibility from the perspective of accommodating users that have disabilities, while showing that making spreadsheets more accessible to those that require assistive technologies actually makes spreadsheets easier for *all* users.

Chapter 2, Disaster Recovery and File-Related Prompts, focuses on bolstering your defenses against spreadsheet crashes and missteps. You'll see how to build in layers of backups. You'll understand various warning prompts that can appear when you open an Excel workbook, and choose which prompts you wish to suppress to minimize distractions.

Chapter 3, Quick Analysis Toolbar Treasures, discusses how to create shortcuts for virtually any Excel command. You'll also see how to unearth legacy features you may have thought were no longer available. You'll also be able to create custom toolbars that travel with specific workbooks, so that others can benefit as well.

Chapter 4, Conditional Formatting, gives you a deep dive on Excel's **Conditional Formatting** feature, which enables you to apply color and graphics to your data based upon conditions that you specify. You'll get the lowdown on all of the built-in rules, and also see how to create custom rules to suit your needs.

Chapter 5, Data Validation and Form Controls, empowers you to add ease-of-use and internal control features to your workbooks. **Data Validation** enables you to assign data entry rules to specific cells in your workbooks, as well as on-screen documentation. Data Validation is easy to implement, but enterprising users can easily circumvent the functionality if desired. Conversely, **Form Controls** enable you create data entry features that cannot be easily defeated.

Chapter 6, What-If Analysis, is one of several chapters focusing on automation. What-If Analysis features are problem solving tools that allow you to calculate a missing input, swap different sets of inputs into a spreadsheet, forecast date-based amounts into the future, and swap different sets of inputs simultaneously through a single formula.

Chapter 7, Automating Tasks with the Table Feature, focuses on one of the best features in Excel for eliminating repetitive tasks and improving data integrity. The **Table** feature streamlines filtering tasks, automates formula management, and makes Excel features and formulas self-updating when new data is added to a **Table**.

Chapter 8, Custom Views, brings more automation opportunities into the foreground. The **Custom Views** feature empowers you to create multipurpose worksheets by hiding and unhiding columns and rows in one fell swoop, applying filter settings, managing print settings, as well as hiding/unhiding worksheets.

Chapter 9, Excel Quirks and Nuances, focuses on certain rough edges in Excel, such as clarifying the difference between **Enter mode** and **Edit mode** so that you can avoid frustration when working in certain fields in Excel's dialog boxes. Navigation nuances, compatibility issues, circular references, and a suite of auditing tools that are only available to certain Excel users are discussed as well.

Chapter 10, Lookup and Dynamic Array Functions, is all about worksheet functions, and mostly focusses on new additions in Microsoft 365 and Excel 2021. Lookup functions can transform how you write spreadsheets, and also vastly improve data integrity. Dynamic array functions are a new class of worksheet function that can automate manual tasks such as sorting, filtering, and removing duplicates. Unlike traditional functions that can only return results to a single cell, dynamic array functions are able to spill results into as many cells as needed. You'll even see how traditional worksheet functions can take on dynamic array characteristics.

Chapter 11, Names, LET, and LAMBDA, begins with covering the concept of naming cells and ranges in worksheets as groundwork for the LET and LAMBDA functions. The LET function in **Microsoft 365** and **Excel 2021** allows you to assign names within a formula to inputs and calculations that you can reference elsewhere in the formula, so as to eliminate repetitive portions of calculations. The LAMBDA function in **Microsoft 365** allows you to create custom worksheet functions that you can then transfer to other workbooks.

Chapter 12, Power Query, covers the code-free automation opportunities available to transform reports and data from Excel workbooks, database, PDF files, and other sources into self-updating data sets.

To get the most out of this book

You will be able to carry out just about every task in this book in **Microsoft 365 for Windows**. I do mention a couple of features that are in beta testing that may not be available on your computer just yet, but that should appear in the coming months. Throughout the book I note which features or techniques are not available in **Excel for macOS**, **Excel for the Web**, and **Excel Mobile**. It's rare, but you will run across a couple of things that you can only do in **Excel for macOS** but not in **Excel for Windows**. Much of the book is relevant to users as far back as **Excel 2013**, but certain features and functions will require **Microsoft 365**. Some **Ribbon** tabs may have different names or slightly different configurations in older versions of Excel.

Software/hardware covered in the book	Operating system requirements
Microsoft 365, Excel 2021, Excel 2019, Excel 2016, Excel 2013	Windows or macOS
Excel for the Web	Windows, macOS, ChromeOS
Excel Mobile	IOS or Android

If you run across a feature or function that is missing from your version of **Microsoft 365**, choose **File | Account | Check for Updates** and install any updates that are available. The **About** section of this window will show if you are in the **Current** or **Monthly Enterprise** channels, which means new features and updates get pushed to your computer as often as monthly, or if you're in the **Semi-Annual Enterprise** channel which means new updates and features will appear in January and July of each year.

Download the example workbooks

Every example that you see in this book is included in the example workbooks that you can download from GitHub at: `https://github.com/PacktPublishing/Exploring-Microsoft-Excels-Hidden-Treasures`. Any updates to the example workbooks will be uploaded to the GitHub repository. We also have code bundles from our rich catalog of books and videos available at: `https://github.com/PacktPublishing/`. Check them out!

Download the color images

We also provide a PDF file that has color images of the screenshots and diagrams used in this book. You can download it here: `https://packt.link/k7VcU`.

Conventions used

There are a number of text conventions used throughout this book.

`Code in text`: Indicates code words in text, database table names, folder names, filenames, file extensions, pathnames, dummy URLs, user input, and Twitter handles. Here is an example: "Enter `=COLUMN()` in any worksheet cell to return the column position within a worksheet, or in this case `=COLUMN(DS1)` to return the position without physically scrolling to that column."

A block of code is set as follows:

```
html, body, #map {
  height: 100%;
  margin: 0;
  padding: 0
}
```

When we wish to draw your attention to a particular part of a code block, the relevant lines or items are set in bold:

```
[default]
exten => s,1,Dial(Zap/1|30)
exten => s,2,Voicemail(u100)
exten => s,102,Voicemail(b100)
exten => i,1,Voicemail(s0)
```

Bold: Indicates a new term, an important word, or words that you see onscreen. For instance, words in menus or dialog boxes appear in **bold**. Here is an example: "**Find in Document** is an alternative to the **Find** command located on the **Find & Replace** menu on the **Home** tab of Excel's ribbon."

> Tips, Nuances, and Quirks Appear like this.

Get in touch

Feedback from our readers is always welcome.

General feedback: If you have questions about any aspect of this book, email us at `customercare@packtpub.com` and mention the book title in the subject of your message.

Errata: Although we have taken every care to ensure the accuracy of our content, mistakes do happen. If you have found a mistake in this book, we would be grateful if you would report this to us. Please visit `www.packtpub.com/support/errata` and fill in the form.

Piracy: If you come across any illegal copies of our works in any form on the internet, we would be grateful if you would provide us with the location address or website name. Please contact us at `copyright@packt.com` with a link to the material.

If you are interested in becoming an author: If there is a topic that you have expertise in and you are interested in either writing or contributing to a book, please visit `authors.packtpub.com`.

Share Your Thoughts

Once you've read *Exploring Microsoft Excel's Hidden Treasures*, we'd love to hear your thoughts! Scan the QR code below to go straight to the Amazon review page for this book and share your feedback.

`https://packt.link/r/1803243945`

Your review is important to us and the tech community and will help us make sure we're delivering excellent quality content.

Part 1: Improving Accessibility

The Merriam-Webster dictionary offers five different definitions for the word "accessibility". This part will focus on two of the five definitions, "being in reach" and "easily used or accessed by people with disabilities." The first chapter addresses both definitions by showing you resources in Excel that can bring more features and functions within your reach, as well as illustrating how adapting spreadsheets for those that have disabilities actually makes things easier for *everyone*. There are not many things worse to an Excel user than having your work suddenly vanish from the screen, so the second chapter shares ways that you can defend against Excel crashes and better understand some of Excel's messaging. The third chapter is all about streamlining access to Excel features by way of built-in as well as customizable shortcuts, including showing you the way to revive features you may have thought were lost to time. The fourth chapter is on making data more accessible by overlaying colors and/or shapes with conditional formatting.

The following chapters are included in this part:

- *Chapter 1, Implementing Accessibility*
- *Chapter 2, Disaster Recovery and File-Related Prompts*
- *Chapter 3, Quick Analysis Toolbar Treasures*
- *Chapter 4, Conditional Formatting*

1
Implementing Accessibility

There's nothing quite like breaking your arm to energize your interest in accessibility. I should know because about a month and a half into drafting this book, I broke my right arm in a mountain biking accident. Fortunately, I was able to type even before the surgery that was needed to put my arm back together, so I didn't have to do a deep dive into voice dictation and other measures. Regardless, even before my accident, I had planned to lead off this book with a discussion on accessibility because I'd realized that anything that makes a spreadsheet easier for people that are color-blind or require assistive technologies also makes the spreadsheet easier for *all users*. Further, it's not just spreadsheets that can feel inaccessible. You may sometimes feel that Excel itself is impenetrable. Over the course of the entire book, my goal is to demystify as many aspects of Excel as will fit in the pages I have available.

In this chapter, I'll discuss design strategies that will improve accessibility for all users, and point out certain Excel features that can improve accessibility within workbooks, but also within the program itself.

This chapter will delve into the following areas:

- How to make Excel more accessible regardless of your abilities
- Implementing accessibility within spreadsheets
- Using Excel's Accessibility Checker feature
- Accessing Excel's Accessibility Reminder add-in
- A brief overview of spreadsheets that are inaccessible because of design strategies

Technical requirements

The example workbook that I used in this chapter is available for download from GitHub at `https://github.com/PacktPublishing/Exploring-Microsoft-Excels-Hidden-Treasures/tree/main/Chapter01`.

Making Excel more accessible

Although this entire book is centered on making Excel more accessible, I'd like to lead off with some features that can help make Excel feel more approachable. I'll first show you how to determine whether Excel offers a worksheet function suitable for the calculation or data transformation that you're considering. I'll then show how you can transform staid lists of data into helpful reports and charts with just a couple of mouse clicks. After that, I'll show you hidden ways to initiate Excel tasks with a plain English statement, and then offer a quick overview of Excel's help resources. Let's begin by looking at worksheet functions.

Finding worksheet functions

Depending upon your version, Excel has over 500 worksheet functions, which can feel overwhelming. Fortunately, Excel offers some tools you can use to decide whether a worksheet function that you need exists:

- **Insert Function**: This command appears on Excel's formula bar, the **Formula** tab of the **Ribbon**, or you can press *Shift + F3* to display the dialog box shown in *Figure 1.1*:

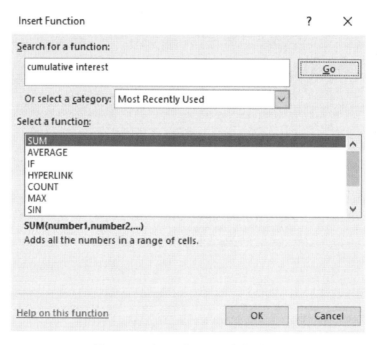

Figure 1.1 – Insert Function dialog box

Let's say that you want to compute the total interest on a loan. I explain how to build an amortization schedule in *Chapter 10, Lookup Functions and Dynamic Arrays*, but there's a worksheet function you can use instead. Enter `cumulative interest` in the **Search for a function** field and then press *Enter* or click **Go**. The **Select a function** list will display `CUMIPMT` and `CUMPRINC`. Function descriptions appear beneath the **Select a function** list. For instance, `CUMIPMT` "returns the cumulative interest paid between two periods." Click **OK** to accept this selection and display the **Function Arguments** dialog box shown in *Figure 1.2*:

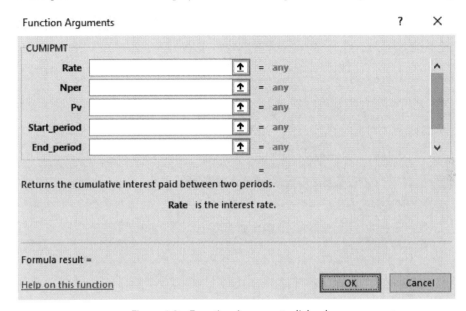

Figure 1.2 – Function Arguments dialog box

> **Nuance**
>
> The **Search for a function** field is rather specific. For instance, typing `total interest` in that field won't surface the `CUMIPMT` function, but `cumulative interest` does. Similarly, `car payment` won't make the `PMT` function available for selection, but `loan payment` will. If you can't find what you're looking for, try an internet search such as `Microsoft Excel total interest`. Also, notice that the **Or select a category** list is set to **Most Recently Used**. This does not mean that functions you type into worksheet cells will appear on the recent version. This list only contains functions that you've searched for within the **Insert Function** dialog box.

I will explain the CUMIPMT function in *Chapter 6, What-If Analysis*, but I'm mentioning it here to point out two nuances in the **Function Arguments** dialog box. CUMIPMT has *six* arguments, but only *five* can be displayed in the **Function Arguments** dialog box at a time. You can use the scrollbar on the right to see the sixth argument, which is **Type**. The second nuance is related to the documentation in the **Function Arguments** dialog box. The valid choices for the **Type** field are **0** for payments made at the end of a loan period or **1** for payments made at the beginning. The explanation that appears when you scroll down to the **Type** field does not provide this information, which in this context at least makes the **Function Arguments** dialog box inaccessible. Conversely, when you type the CUMIPMT function out directly into a cell, Excel will display a drop-down list detailing the two options when you get to the sixth argument. In general, the **Function Arguments** dialog box is a useful tool, but as with many aspects of Excel, it does have its quirks and nuances.

- **Function ScreenTip**: A Function ScreenTip appears any time you click inside the parentheses of an Excel formula, as shown in *Figure 1.3*:

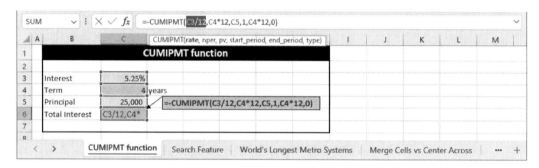

Figure 1.3 – Function ScreenTip

There are some subtleties to be aware of with regard to Function ScreenTips:

- Click on any argument name to select that part of the formula. In *Figure 1.3*, I chose **rate** within the Function ScreenTip.

- Click on the function name itself to display help documentation on the function.

- You can move the Function ScreenTip when it obscures column letters or other information that you wish to see. Grab any corner of the Function ScreenTip with your left mouse button and drag the tip to a new location. This is only a temporary change, as the Function ScreenTip will snap back to its normal location when you start editing the next formula.

> **Nuance**
>
> When working inside a formula, you can press *F9* to convert a part of a formula to its calculated value. Once you've done so, either press *Ctrl + Z* to undo the change or press *Esc* to leave the formula and discard your change. You can generally undo up to your last 100 actions when working in Excel, but you can only undo *one* action within a worksheet cell or the formula bar. A safer approach is to choose **Formulas | Evaluate Formula** when verifying formula calculations, but keep in mind that you cannot make any edits within the **Evaluate Formula** dialog box.

Now let's see ways that you can unearth Excel commands that are either new to you or whose location you've forgotten.

Microsoft Search box

The **Microsoft Search** box was known as the **Tell Me** feature in earlier versions of Excel and appears in Excel's title bar. In *Figure 1.4*, I selected a cell within my chart data and then typed `Create a chart` in the **Search** field:

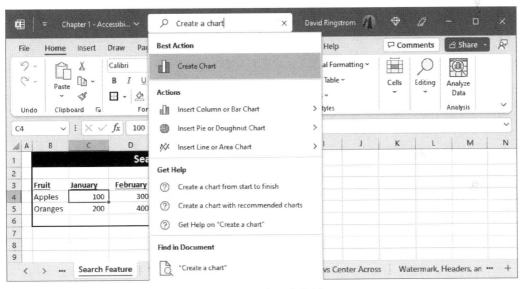

Figure 1.4 – Search field

Depending upon your request, the **Microsoft Search** box will offer you a variety of options, including commands for conducting actions:

- **Best Action**: Based upon Excel's interpretation of your request, this is the action that you'll want to conduct.
- **Actions**: This section presents alternatives to the Best Action.

- **Get Help**: This section suggests help topics related to the keyword or phrase that you entered.
- **Find in Document**: Choose this option to search your document for the term or phrase that you entered. This is an alternative to choosing **Home** | **Find & Select** | **Find** or pressing *Ctrl + F* (⌘ + *F* in Excel for macOS).
- **Files**: Recent workbooks you used that Excel determined may be relevant to the keyword or phrase that you entered.

The **Microsoft Search** box makes Excel more accessible, as it brings commands to you upon request. This turns the normal Excel experience on its head where users don't remember where a command resides or whether a particular feature even exists.

> **Nuance**
>
> The **Microsoft Search** box is an effective means for finding commands in Excel, but it does a poor job with worksheet functions. The **Insert Function** command discussed earlier in this chapter is a more effective approach for unearthing functions. Further, not every command in the menu appears, even when you type it by name. For instance, typing `Text to Columns` shows alternatives but not the feature itself, which appears on the **Data** tab. Like many aspects of Excel, blind spots abound.

If you're sensitive to changes in Excel's user interface, you can collapse the **Microsoft Search** box down to an icon:

1. Choose **File** | **Options** | **General**.
2. Click **Collapse the Microsoft Search box by default** in the **User Interface options** section and then click **OK**.

A magnifying glass icon stays in place in the title bar, which you can click any time you wish to use the **Microsoft Search** box, or you can type *Alt + Q* in Excel for Windows. As shown in *Figure 1.5*, you can also access another version of the **Microsoft Search** box by right-clicking on any cell in Excel for Windows:

Making Excel more accessible   9

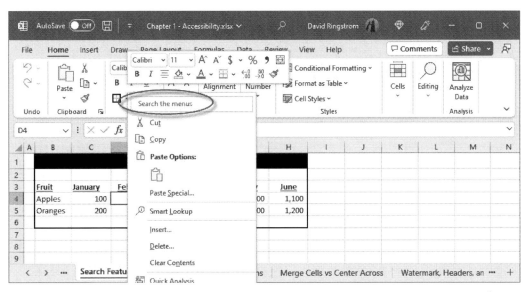

Figure 1.5 – Context menu-based search option

You can enter search terms into the context menu in the same fashion as the **Microsoft Search** box at the top of the screen. Now, let's see how you can get more help in Excel.

Help tab of Excel's Ribbon

The **Help** tab first appeared in **Excel 2019** and is designed to provide immediate access to several support resources.

Figure 1.6 – Help tab

As shown in *Figure 1.6*, the **Help** tab of the **Ribbon** has the following commands:

- **Help**: Click this command or press *F1* to display the **Help** task pane, which you can use to search for help on any aspect of Excel.

> **Nuance**
> Your device must be connected to the internet before you can use any command on the **Help** menu.

- **Contact Support**: This section requires you to enter a search term and then click **Get Help**. Relevant articles will appear, below which a **Contact Support** button enables you to create an online chat session with a Microsoft support agent. If you cancel the chat session, Microsoft will follow up with you via email.

- **Feedback**: This command enables you to send a smile to Microsoft for something you like about Excel, a frown for something you don't like, or to send a suggestion.

> **Nuance**
>
> You may be surprised to learn that the Excel development team at Microsoft takes user feedback seriously. The **Suggestion** option enables you to not only suggest changes in Excel but also vote on requests by others. For instance, as of this writing, 276 votes were enough to get Microsoft to commit to adding **Center Across Selection** to the **Home | Merge & Center** drop-down menu. I'll explain how to access **Center Across Selection** later in the *Using Center Across Selection instead of merged cells* section. The bottom line is, given the hundreds of millions of Excel users around the globe, it truly takes a handful of voices to effect change in Excel. If something is frustrating you about Excel, it's probably bothered others as well, so take a moment to vote on someone else's suggestion or post your own.

- **Show Training**: This command supplies instant access to a free video-based library of training materials that often includes downloadable templates so that you can follow along.

- **What's New**: This command enables you to figure out whether any new features have been added to your version of Microsoft 365 recently.

- **Community**: This command links to a Microsoft-sanctioned online forum where you can ask and answer questions about Excel. Always be sure to search the forum before posting a new question because often you will find that your question has already been asked and answered.

- **Excel Blog**: This command opens a page with up-to-date news about Excel from the development team and is a straightforward way to keep up with new features that have been added recently or that are in development.

Let's now look at ways to convert a list of data into an instant analysis.

On-demand PivotTables and charts

Excel offers three different approaches that allow any user to quickly transform a list of data into easy-to-understand reports or charts:

- **Recommended PivotTables**: This feature can create an instant report out of a list of data:

    I. Select any cell within the list on the **World's Longest Metro Systems** worksheet of this chapter's example workbook.

Making Excel more accessible   11

II. Choose **Insert | Recommended PivotTables**.

III. Choose any report from the **Recommended PivotTables** task pane shown in *Figure 1.7*:

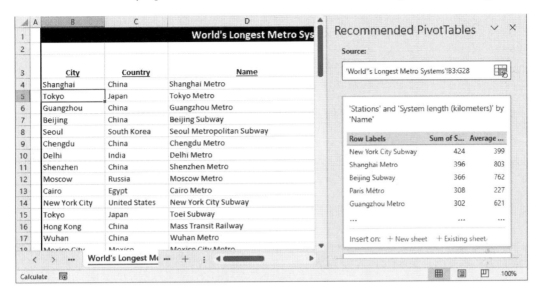

Figure 1.7 – Recommended PivotTables task pane

> **Nuance**
>
> **Recommended PivotTables** appears as a dialog box in **Excel 2021** and earlier. Your version of Microsoft 365 may still have the dialog box as well. New features are pushed out to users in waves, so there can be a delay of 6 months or more before the latest changes to Excel make it to your device.

Any reports that you generate by way of **Recommended PivotTables** are merely a starting point. You can add or remove fields as needed by way of the **PivotTable Fields** task pane, which appears when you click within any **PivotTable**.

- **Recommended Charts**: This artificial intelligence feature analyzes your data and makes suggestions as to which Excel charts are best suited to your needs:

  I. Select any cell within the list on the **World's Longest Metro Systems** worksheet of this chapter's example workbook.

  II. Click **Insert | Recommended Charts**.

III. Choose a report from the **Recommended Charts** tab of the **Insert Chart** dialog box shown in *Figure 1.8*, and then click **OK**. In Excel for macOS, chart recommendations appear in a drop-down menu instead of a dialog box, and no rationale for why the chart is appropriate is offered.

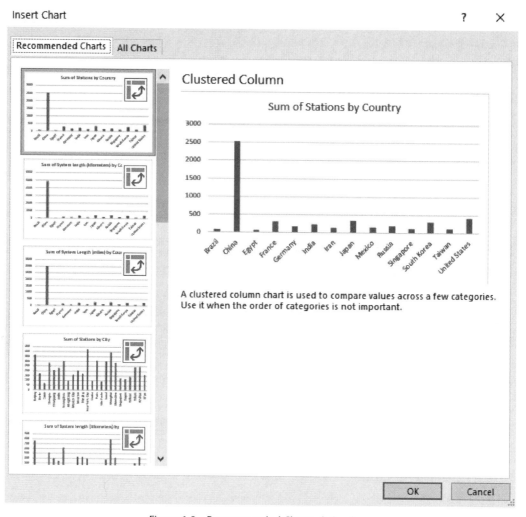

Figure 1.8 – Recommended Charts dialog box

- **Analyze Data**: This feature can be thought of as **Recommended Charts** on steroids. The feature debuted as **Insights** and was renamed **Ideas** before being dubbed **Analyze Data**. You can not only create reports but also find unusual aspects within a list:

    I. Select any cell within the list on the **World's Longest Metro Systems** worksheet of this chapter's example workbook.

II. Click **Home | Analyze Data**.

III. Choose a report or chart from the **Analyze Data** task pane, or as shown in *Figure 1.9*, enter a plain English question such as `stations per mile` to create a chart that will show the distribution of stations by system length in miles. Depending upon the question you ask, **Analyze Data** will either create a chart, **PivotChart**, or **PivotTable**.

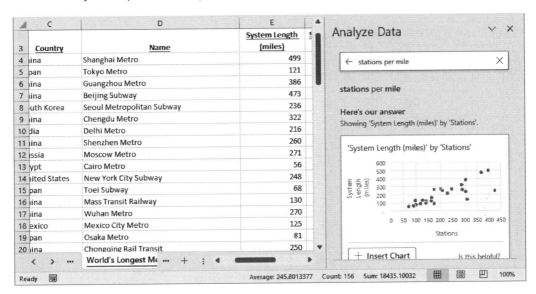

Figure 1.9 – Analyze Data task pane

> **Nuance**
>
> Presently, **Analyze Data** only works with datasets that have 1.5 million cells or less. The feature works best when your list is formatted as a **Table**, which I discuss how to do in *Chapter 7, Automating Tasks with Tables*. Dates in the `yyyy-mm-dd` format, such as `2024-01-01` for January 1, 2024, will be treated as text, although you can convert these to dates by using the `DATEVALUE` or `VALUE` functions, or by using the **Text to Columns** feature. To use this feature, select the dates that you wish to convert, choose **Data | Text to Columns**, click **Next** twice, choose **Date**, and then specify `YMD` from the corresponding list, and then click **OK**. Generally, the **Text to Columns** feature is used to separate a column of data into two or more columns, but it also works as a handy data transformation tool, especially when dates or numbers are formatted or stored as text.

Now that we've discussed some ways to make Excel more accessible, let's see how to improve accessibility within individual workbooks.

Implementing accessibility within spreadsheets

The good news about spreadsheet accessibility is that a few minor changes to how you work can have a significant impact on both users that require assistive technology and those that don't. Keeping accessibility top of mind makes spreadsheets easier for *everyone*. Even better, the techniques are surprisingly simple. As you'll see, techniques such as naming your worksheets, avoiding merged cells, limiting the use of watermarks, headers, and footers, using color conscientiously, and converting lists to **Tables** are huge boons to able and disabled users alike.

Assign worksheet names

Every new Excel workbook starts out with at least one worksheet, and the first sheet has a default name of **Sheet1**. Three ways that you can add more worksheets are as follows:

- Click **New Sheet**, which appears as a + to the right of the worksheet tabs in modern versions of Excel, or as a miniature worksheet tab in older versions of Excel
- Choose **Home** | **Insert** drop-down menu | **Insert Sheet**
- Press *Shift + F11*

The second sheet in a workbook has a default name of **Sheet2**, the third **Sheet3**, and so on. Many times, users focus on the content within the sheets and don't take the time to label the worksheets themselves. As you'll see in the *Check Accessibility feature* section, Microsoft flags default sheet names as an accessibility issue, plus the default names make it harder for everyone to locate specific data in a workbook. Here's how to rename a worksheet tab:

1. Use any of these three techniques:

    - Double-click on the worksheet tab
    - Right-click on a worksheet tab, and then choose **Rename**
    - In Excel for Windows, press *F6* to select the current worksheet tab, press *Shift + F10* to display the context menu, and then type R to choose **Rename**

2. Type up to 31 characters and then press *Enter*.

> **Nuance**
>
> The following characters cannot be used within a worksheet tab name:
>
> \, /, *, [,], and ?
>
> Excel will ignore these characters if you try to type them, just as it ignores any characters beyond the first 31 that you try to type. Most other punctuation is allowed.

Worksheet names should be as specific as possible to make it easier for users to find the data they're looking for. You can navigate between worksheets in several ways:

- In Excel for Windows, press *F6* to select the current worksheet tab and then use the *left* or *right arrow* keys to navigate to a new sheet, and then press *Enter*.
- Right-click on the navigation arrows at the bottom left-hand corner of the Excel window to display the **Activate** dialog box shown in *Figure 1.10*. Type the first letter of a sheet name to move purposefully through the list.

Figure 1.10 – Activate dialog box

> **Nuance**
>
> The **Activate** dialog box only shows visible worksheets in a workbook. Choose **Home | Format | Hide & Unhide | Unhide Sheet** to unhide any hidden worksheets, or right-click on any worksheet tab and choose **Unhide Sheet**. If **Unhide Sheet** is disabled, then most likely there are no hidden worksheets in the workbook. It is possible to use the Visual Basic Editor to set a worksheet to `xlSheetVeryHidden`, which means the worksheet cannot be unhidden through Excel's user interface.

- Choose **Review | Navigation** in Microsoft 365 to display the **Navigation** pane shown in *Figure 1.11*:

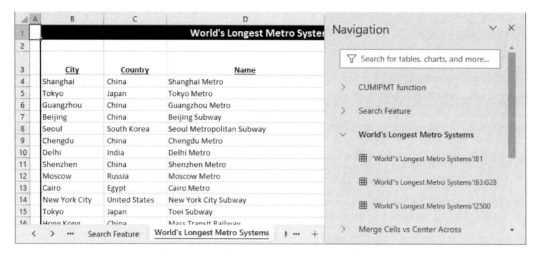

Figure 1.11 – Navigation pane in Microsoft 365

Notice that three ranges are listed on the **World's Longest Metro Systems** worksheet:

- **B1**: The first non-blank cell on the worksheet
- **B3:G28**: A cluster of text, values, and/or formulas
- **Z500**: A random cell that I typed a tip into

The **Navigation** pane lists every contiguous block of non-blank cells, as well as individual non-blank cells, so you can easily determine where data appears in each worksheet.

> Nuance
>
> The **Navigation** task pane is only functional when you have an internet connection. As of this writing, the **Navigation** task pane is still in beta testing, so it may or may not be available to you as you read this, but in the worst-case scenario, it will be available in the coming months.

In Excel for Windows, press *Ctrl + PgUp* to move one worksheet to the left at a time or *Ctrl + PgDn* to move one worksheet to the right at a time, or in Excel for macOS, press *Fn + ^ + ↓* to move one worksheet to the right at a time or *Fn + ^ + ↑* to move one worksheet to the left.

> **Quirk**
>
> You cannot assign the name History to an Excel worksheet. The **Track Changes** feature in Excel creates a **History** worksheet, and so that name is a reserved word that you cannot use in Excel. You can use the word History with a space at the beginning or end, but be mindful in doing so, as users may not realize that the tab name has an extra space and could end up frustrated when trying to write formulas by typing the sheet name directly.

Let's now explore a divisive feature that I find Excel users either absolutely love or absolutely hate.

Merge Cells feature

If there's ever a reality TV series where we get to vote features out of Excel, **Merge Cells** is first on my list. I realize that these are fighting words for some users who rely heavily on merged cells, but from an accessibility standpoint, merged cells should be avoided whenever possible. First, merged cells can wreak havoc with assistive technology such as screen readers. Second, merged cells also wreak havoc with ordinary tasks you may try to conduct in Excel. Few things in life set my teeth on edge quite like the prompt shown in *Figure 1.12*. This prompt can appear even when you're making a change that is seemingly unrelated to merged cells because the action will affect rows or columns that intersect with the merged cells:

In the vein of *not that you would but you could*, here's an example of how to merge cells:

1. Select cells B4:G5 on the **Merge Cells vs. Center Across** worksheet of this chapter's example workbook and then choose **Home | Merge & Center**.
2. The prompt shown in *Figure 1.13* appears because we're trying to merge more than one row of data at a time. If you click OK, Excel will merge and center cells B4:G5 but will discard the data from row 5. You can click **Undo** or press *Ctrl + Z* (⌘ + Z) if you click through the prompt accidentally, or click **Cancel** to stop the merge process.

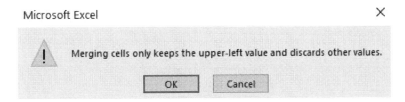

Figure 1.13 – Merged cells error prompt

3. Click the **Merge & Center** drop-down menu and then choose **Merge Across** to merge cells B4 : G4 and B5 : G5 separately and keep the data from each row, as shown in *Figure 1.14*:

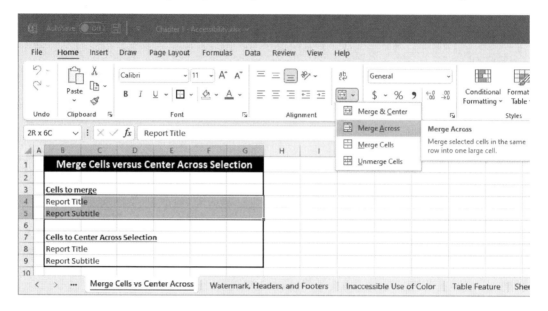

Figure 1.14 – Merge Across

4. Optional: Choose **Home** | **Center** to center data within the merged cells, or press ⌘ + E in Excel for macOS.

To unmerge cells, simply select a range that includes one or more sets of merged cells and then choose **Home** | **Merge & Center** or choose **Home** | the **Merge & Center** drop-down menu | **Unmerge Cells**. As you'll see in the *Using the Table feature* section later in this chapter, converting a range of cells to a **Table** automatically unmerges any cells within the list as well.

Merged cells are often used to center headings across reports, which you can easily conduct in a different manner to make the spreadsheet more accessible to users of every stripe.

Using Center Across Selection instead of merged cells

A hidden but highly effective alternative to merging cells is named **Center Across Selection**. This helpful feature is buried in the **Format Cells** dialog box. Let's say that you want to center the headings in cells B8 : B9 of *Figure 1.14* across columns B : G:

1. Select cells B8 : G9.
2. Click the **Alignment Settings** button on the **Home** tab of the **Ribbon**, press *Ctrl + 1* (⌘ + *1*), or choose **Home** | **Format** | **Format Cells**.

3. Activate the **Alignment** tab if needed.
4. Choose **Center Across Selection** from the **Horizontal** list as shown in *Figure 1.15*, and then click **OK**:

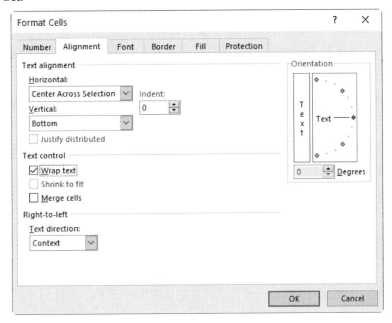

Figure 1.15 – Center Across Selection

The text is now centered across columns B : G. If you change your mind about centering the text, simply select cells B8 : G9 and choose **Home | Align Left**. **Center Across Selection** eliminates all of the frustrations that can arise when you merge cells but provides the same effect.

Let's now look at aspects of Excel that can make certain information inaccessible for viewing, or even editing.

Minimizing the use of watermarks, headers, and footers

Information placed within watermarks, headers, or footers can present a particular challenge for users using assistive technology because the information doesn't appear within the worksheet itself. However, it's easy for *any* user to overlook information stored in these locations because such information is only displayed in certain contexts in Excel. Further, because there isn't a *Watermark* command in Excel, it can be tricky for others to know how to remove or edit an existing watermark. A watermark is an identifier, such as a company logo, or a message, such as the words DRAFT or CONFIDENTIAL, that can be overlaid over a worksheet. One approach involves the **WordArt** feature:

1. Choose **Insert | WordArt**, or **Insert | Text | WordArt**.

Implementing Accessibility

2. Click on the worksheet to create a floating object and change the text as needed, as shown in *Figure 1.16*:

Figure 1.16 – WordArt

3. Optional: Use the button above the text that looks like an arrow pointing in a circle, as shown in *Figure 1.17*, to rotate the watermark:

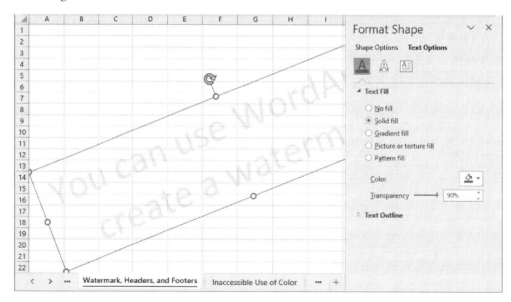

Figure 1.17 – Format Shape task pane and rotation arrow

4. Optional: Change the transparency of the text by right-clicking on the image and choosing **Format Shape** | **Text Options** | **Text Fill** and then adjust the **Transparency** setting, as shown in *Figure 1.17*.

> **Nuance**
>
> Objects that float above the worksheet, such as WordArt and textboxes, can be tricky to format, as you have to pay attention to what is selected. If you see handles around the edge of the object, as shown in *Figure 1.17*, your formatting changes will affect the object as a whole. If you don't see the handles, then most likely your formatting changes will affect some or all of the text within the object.

This sort of watermark will float above the worksheet, which means it can obscure text beneath it or confuse screen-reading technology. To remove the watermark, you can click once on the image and then press the *Delete* key on your keyboard.

A second approach involves placing the watermark in the header of a worksheet. The **Header** feature enables you to specify text that you wish to display at the top of a printed page or images that you wish to display within the body of the worksheet. The **Footer** feature enables you to specify text that appears at the bottom of a printed page. The challenge with headers and footers is that the user may be unaware of information stored in these sections unless they choose **File** | **Print** or **View** | **Page Layout**. **Page Layout** mode enables you to add a header or footer by clicking on the left, center, or right header and footer fields. A **Header & Footer** tab then appears in the **Ribbon** that contains commands that make it easy to craft headers and footers. Choose **View** | **Normal** when you're ready to exit **Page Layout** mode.

> **Nuance**
>
> **Page Layout** mode is not compatible with the **View** | **Freeze Panes** feature. An alert message will appear if you try to enter **Page Layout** mode on a worksheet with frozen panes. If you click **OK**, you will enter **Page Layout** mode but your worksheet panes will no longer be frozen.

Alternatively, you can use these steps to add a watermark to a header without disrupting frozen worksheet panes, as well as add text to a header or footer:

1. Choose **Page Layout** | **Print Titles**.
2. Click the **Header/Footer** tab in the **Page Setup** dialog box.
3. Click **Custom Header** or **Custom Footer**.

> **Nuance**
>
> Images that you place in the **Header** section will appear near the top of your printout, while images that you place in the **Footer** section will appear near the bottom of the page. You cannot place an image in the center of the printed page in this fashion unless the image is large enough to span the entire printed page.

4. Select a section and then click the **Insert Picture** button, which is the second button from the right, as shown in *Figure 1.18*:

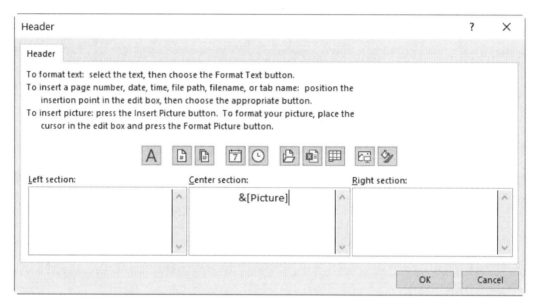

Figure 1.18 – Header dialog box

5. Make a choice from the **Insert Pictures** dialog box, which asks whether you want to choose a file from your local drive or an online resource.

6. Once you select an image, a **&[Picture]** placeholder will appear in the section you chose, as shown in *Figure 1.18*.

7. Optional: Click **Format Picture**, which is the last button on the right, to change the size of the picture. You may also wish to click on the **Picture** tab and change **Color** to **Washout** in the **Image control** section.

8. Click **OK** as needed to close any open dialog boxes.

9. Choose **File** | **Print** to display a print preview, because if you choose **View** | **Page Layout** to enter **Page Layout** mode, any frozen worksheet panes will become undone. You can return to the **Page Setup** dialog box and change the settings if needed, such as shrinking the dimensions to prevent an image from overrunning the printed page.

To remove headers or footers, choose **Page Layout** | **Print Titles**, activate the **Header/Footer** tab, and then choose (**none**) from the top of the corresponding drop-down list.

> **Nuance**
>
> **Page Layout** | **Background** offers a third approach for creating a watermark. The difference is that the image will repeat throughout Excel's entire grid, and there is no way to edit the image. If you add an image in this fashion, the **Background** command toggles to **Delete Background**.

Any worksheet that has vital information in a watermark, header, or footer, such as CONFIDENTIAL or INTERNAL USE ONLY, should be considered inaccessible because assistive technology cannot access those areas of Excel. Any such information should also be repeated in cell A1, where it can be accessed by assistive technology but also be readily visible to all users of the worksheet.

Let's now see how color can have an impact on the accessibility of your spreadsheets.

Working carefully with color

Accessibility standards call for colors to have sufficient contrast between background fill and fonts used within cells. One sure-fire way to ensure proper contrast is to use a black background with white text or light shades of gray. Black text on a white background is accessible as well. Conversely, let's say blue text on a red background can be difficult for anyone to read, much less anyone with vision impairments or color-blindness.

Further, standards call for any indicators in a spreadsheet that are represented by color-only to also have supportive text, as shown in *Figure 1.19*. As much as 8% of the world's male population and 0.5% of the female population is color-blind. That means if you work with say nine other people, there's a good chance at least one person may be color-blind.

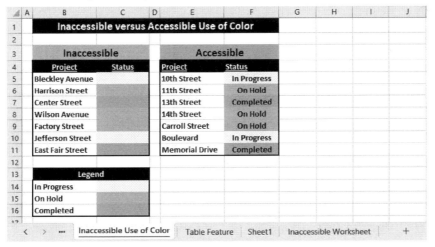

Figure 1.19 – An inaccessible list versus an accessible list

The list on the left only uses color to find the status of each project, such that anyone, no matter the level of vision they have, may find themselves struggling to make sense of the data, at least at first. Conversely, the list on the right pairs the color and text together, so that all users can decide the status of each project at once. I discuss how to automate color coding based upon cell contents in *Chapter 4, Conditional Formatting*, along with an approach where you can combine color coding with cell icons to provide an additional means for identifying types of data.

Let's now see how the **Table** feature can improve accessibility within a worksheet.

Using the Table feature

I talk extensively about the **Table** feature in *Chapter 7, Automating Tasks with Tables*, so I won't go into much detail here, but the **Table** feature is one of the best ways to improve the accessibility of a worksheet. First, you cannot use merged cells within a **Table**; any commands or options related to merged cells are disabled when your cursor is within a **Table**.

> **Nuance**
>
> When you convert a range of cells into a **Table**, any merged cells within the list will be automatically unmerged because merging cells is not compatible with the **Table** feature.

Enabling the **Header Row** and **First Column** options, as shown in *Figure 1.20*, can particularly improve accessibility for all:

Figure 1.20 – Table options

The **Header Row** allows you to place meaningful titles in the top row of a list. The titles move up into the worksheet frame when you scroll down past the first row of a **Table**. **Filter** arrows appear automatically in the **Header Row** to enable users to easily collapse the list down to just records of their choice. **First Column** makes the text in the first column bold but can also be used to help users of assistive technology know that they're starting out in the first column rather than landing unexpectedly in the middle of a **Table**. Finally, assigning a meaningful name to the **Table** by way of **Table Design | Table Name** helps all users understand at once what type of data is contained within the Table. It is best to also supply a description of the data above the Header Row. As I discuss later in the book, **Table Names** supply an effortless way for all users of the spreadsheet to be able to jump directly to a list of data by selecting the **Table Name** from the **Name** box.

Leaving the default **Table Names** in place, such as **Table1**, **Table2**, **Table3**, and so on, quickly makes it difficult to know what data is where and cuts off the ability to move purposefully to a list of data anywhere in the workbook.

Let's now see how you can easily find potential accessibility challenges in any workbook.

Accessibility Checker feature

The **Accessibility Checker** feature, available in Microsoft Excel and other Microsoft Office programs, can review your workbooks and supply feedback on changes you can make to improve the accessibility of your spreadsheets. You can launch the **Accessibility Checker** feature in one of three ways:

- Choose **Review | Check Accessibility**.
- In Excel for Windows, choose **File | Info | Check for Issues | Check Accessibility**.
- Click the **Accessibility** button in Excel's status bar, which displays the message **Accessibility: Investigate**, as shown in *Figure 1.21*, when one or more potential accessibility issues have been noted, or **Accessibility: Good to Go** when no issues have been found.

Any of these choices will display in the **Accessibility** task pane shown in *Figure 1.21*:

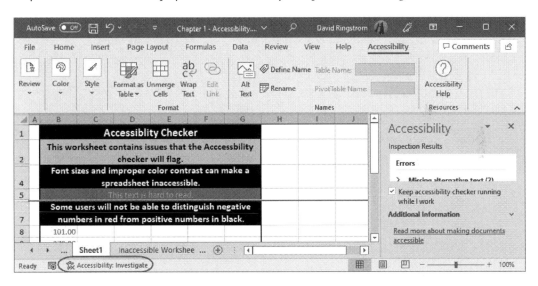

Figure 1.21 – Accessibility Checker

The **Accessibility Checker** feature has three levels of feedback and a **Ribbon** tab::

- **Errors** are content that will be exceedingly difficult or impossible for disabled users to use. Situations can include negative numbers formatting in red and information rights restrictions.

- **Warnings** are triggered by content that will be difficult for disabled users to use. Situations can include worksheets with default names, and insufficient contrast between font color and cell fill color, such as dark gray letters on light gray cell fill.

- **Tips** are triggered by content that could be better organized to improve the ease of use for disabled users.

> **Nuance**
> **Accessibility Checker** is an imperfect feature and may flag issues that seem immaterial while blithely ignoring blatant accessibility issues that you can see in plain sight. Similarly **Spell Check** won't inform you if you've used the word `principle` when you should have used `principal`. With both spelling and accessibility issues, you must trust but verify that everything is in order. The **Accessibility Checker** does offer a **Ribbon** comprised of tools that can help adjust formatting, assign names, along with other accessibility features.

Now, let's look at a hidden tool in Excel that you can use to annotate accessibility issues that you plan to clear up in your workbooks.

Accessibility Reminder add-in

The **Accessibility Reminder** add-in is a free tool that makes it easy to add comments to spreadsheets to call attention to accessibility issues. To install this add-in, follow these steps:

1. Choose **Insert | Get Add-ins**.
2. Type `Accessibility` in the **Search** field and then press *Enter*.
3. Click the **Add** button next to **Accessibility Reminder** and then click **Continue**.

   A new **Accessibility Reminder** tab appears in the **Ribbon**, as shown in *Figure 1.22*.

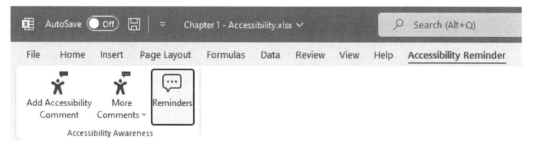

Figure 1.22 – Accessibility Reminder **Ribbon** tab

The **Accessibility Reminder** tab offers three commands:

- **Add Accessibility Comment**: Adds a generic comment that the file has accessibility issues.

- **More Comments**: Allows you to choose between adding three types of comments: **Low Vision**, **Screen Reader**, and **Custom**. The **Custom** comment defaults to the same text as **Add Accessibility Comment**, but you can create a message of your choosing on the **Customize** tab of the **Accessibility Reminder** task pane.
- **Reminders**: Displays an **Accessibility Reminder** task pane that has three sections, as shown in *Figure 1.23*:

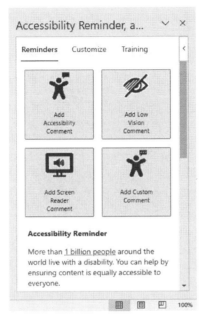

Figure 1.23 – Accessibility Reminder task pane

- **Reminders**: This section has four buttons that mirror the functionality of the **Add Accessibility Comment** and **More Comments** commands on the **Accessibility Reminder** tab of the **Ribbon**.
- **Customize**: This section allows you to create a custom comment that you add to worksheets by choosing the **Custom Comment** option from the **Ribbon** or the **Reminders** section of the task pane.
- **Training**: This section has three buttons:
- **Launch Training**: This command connects you to video-based training that discusses accessibility across the entire Microsoft 365 suite
- **Watch Video**: This command links you to application-specific video-based training, which includes Excel
- **View Features**: This command takes you to a comprehensive listing of accessibility discussions and resources

Implementing Accessibility

> **Tip**
>
> More accessibility training is available at www.section508.gov, which is a website kept by the US General Services Agency. **Section 508** refers to the area of the United States Code that codifies the accessibility standards for documents that, by law, all federal government departments must follow.

Examples of inaccessible spreadsheets

The United States Supreme Court Justice William Rehnquist once noted, "*I may not be able to define pornography, but I know it when I see it.*" Much the same can be said about inaccessible spreadsheets; often you know them when you see them. Although I have laid out some guidelines in this chapter, the 17 billion cells available within every Excel worksheet supply lots of room for users to create all kinds of chaos. Spreadsheets are always more accessible when you orient your data vertically, going down columns whenever possible, and in as few sheets as possible. Doing so enables you to use a wide variety of features in Excel that can make quick work of tasks. Psychologically though, many users feel compelled to orient their data horizontally, meaning going across rows. The further to the right that your data extends, the less accessible it is for everyone that uses the spreadsheet. Granted, sometimes, such spreadsheets are generated by an accounting program, such as the report shown in *Figure 1.24*:

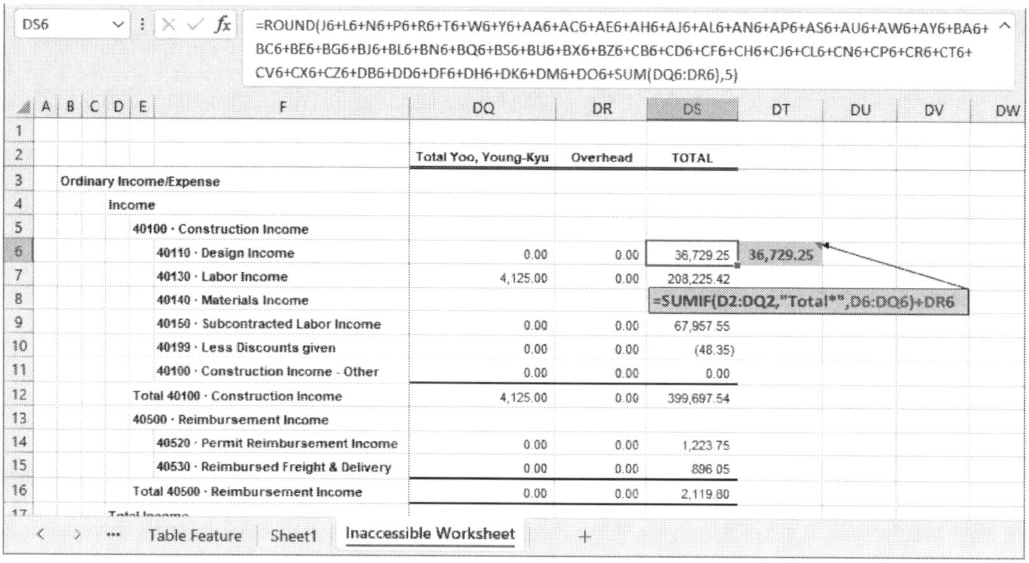

Figure 1.24 – An inaccessible accounting report

Three things make this report inaccessible:

- Account numbers appear in columns D, E, and F, which can stymy users that wish to use lookup functions such as VLOOKUP, XLOOKUP, and SUMIF, which I discuss in *Chapter 10, Lookup Functions and Dynamic Arrays*.
- The data in the spreadsheet starts in column A and ends in column DS, which means it spans *123 columns*. In *Chapter 12, Power Query*, I show how to unpivot this report, meaning transposing the data from going horizontally across rows to instead running vertically down columns.

> **Nuance**
> Enter =COLUMN() in any worksheet cell to return the column position within a worksheet, or in this case, =COLUMN(DS1), to return the position without physically scrolling to that column.

- Cell DS6 on the **Inaccessible Worksheet** tab contains the formula =ROUND(J6+L6+N6+P6+R6+T6+W6+Y6+AA6+AC6+AE6+AH6+AJ6+AL6+AN6+AP6+AS6+AU6+AW6+AY6+BA6+BC6+BE6+BG6+BJ6+BL6+BN6+BQ6+BS6+BU6+BX6+BZ6+CB6+CD6+CF6+CH6+CJ6+CL6+CN6+CP6+CR6+CT6+CV6+CX6+CZ6+DB6+DD6+DF6+DH6+DK6+DM6+DO6+SUM(DQ6:DR6),5), which is completely inaccessible for most Excel users. Conversely, cell DT6 contains the formula =SUMIF(G2:DQ2,"Total*",G6:DQ6)+DR6. The SUMIF function has three arguments:

    - **Range** – This argument specifies the range of cells Excel should search, in this case, G2:DQ2.
    - **Criteria** – This argument specifies the criteria that Excel should match on. In this case, "Total*" enables SUMIF to perform a partial match and add up the values from every column where the values in row 2 begin with the word Total. The asterisk is known as a wildcard character for performing partial matches such as this.
    - **Sum_range** – The range of cells that should be summed when matching criteria is found, in this case, cells G6:DQ6.

    Notice that the formula includes +DR6 because cell DR2 contains the word Overhead, and so it would be excluded based upon the criteria specified in the SUMIF function.

Inaccessible spreadsheets are a fact for many Excel users, but throughout this book, you'll discover ways to turn the tide and improve their usability. I'll leave you with one last rule of thumb, which is to use as few worksheets in a workbook as possible. For instance, stick with a single worksheet that has a month or period column that you fill in on each row, instead of creating 12 monthly worksheets to house data by period. In general, resist the urge to recreate the same sheet over and over, such as separate worksheets for each vehicle, department, project, or what have you, and instead, make minor modifications to keep the data to a single worksheet. Doing so treats Excel more like a database and unlocks many ways to use your data more effectively.

Choose **Review | Workbook Statistics** to determine of worksheets in a workbook, as shown in *Figure 1.25*. A double-digit number of worksheets doesn't automatically make a workbook inaccessible, but inaccessible workbooks typically have double-digit worksheet counts or sometimes more.

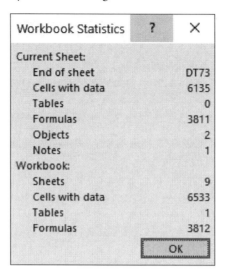

Figure 1.25 – Workbook Statistics dialog box

> **Nuance**
>
> The **Workbook Statistics** dialog box includes both hidden and visible sheets, along with the number of filled cells, the number of **Tables**, formulas, and objects. Objects are anything that floats above the worksheet, such as the **WordArt** that we created earlier.

Let's now look at what you've learned in this chapter.

Summary

It's easy to dismiss accessibility as something akin to eating your vegetables, or exercising; you know you should do both, but you'll get to it tomorrow. Accessibility improves everyone's experience, not just those that use assistive technology. If your boss asks you to perform an analytical task in Excel, and you don't know where to start, suddenly, Excel is inaccessible. Fortunately, the **Insert Function** command lets you easily lay your hands on any of the hundreds of worksheet functions available within Excel. Similarly, the **Microsoft Search** box puts even the most hidden Excel commands at your fingertips. When you need to go further, the **Help** tab of the Ribbon connects you to an extensive array of resources that include online documentation, training videos, online chat support, and user-to-user support by way of an Excel community forum.

You also learned how artificial intelligence is making Excel more accessible by way of features such as **Recommended PivotTables**, **Recommended Charts**, and **Analyze Data**. All these features can help you get past that *I don't know where to start* phase of analyzing a dataset.

Accessibility extends far beyond goodwill for disabled users. Any time you implement even simple accessibility techniques, such as naming **Tables** and worksheets, avoiding the use of merged cells, limiting the use of critical information within watermarks, headers, and footers, ensuring proper color contrasts, and using the **Table** feature within your spreadsheets, you improve the ease of use of the workbook for every single user that touches it.

It can feel overwhelming to try to find all the accessibility issues in a workbook, especially if you have a legal mandate to do so. Fortunately, the **Check Accessibility** feature supplies instant feedback on issues that can cause a workbook to be considered inaccessible. The free **Accessibility Reminder** add-in makes it easy to document accessibility issues you wish to clean up and supplies links to more training materials.

Accessibility is subjective, particularly in large workbooks, but just remember, if you're struggling with a workbook that you authored yourself, it's highly unlikely that others will be able to make any sense of it. The good news is that accessibility runs through this book as an unspoken theme, and as you progress through the book, you'll become ever more empowered to work with Excel, as opposed to Excel pushing you around or, worse, stopping you in your tracks.

In the next chapter, I'll be discussing how to implement disaster recovery techniques, including what to do when terrible things happen to good spreadsheets.

2
Disaster Recovery and File-Related Prompts

In this chapter, I'll show you various ways that you can minimize or, hopefully, mitigate spreadsheet disasters. The only saving grace I've observed when losing a spreadsheet is that the work goes faster the second time around—cold comfort indeed. Fortunately, there are steps you can take to bolster your defenses against spreadsheet crashes no matter whether you're saving your files locally to your computer or online to the cloud. In addition, repeatedly clicking through prompts can take a toll on your workday and your wrists. In this chapter, I'll discuss how several prompts that serve as speed bumps can work when you are opening spreadsheets.

In this chapter, you'll learn about the following topics:

- **Undo** and **Redo**
- The **AutoRecover** feature
- **AutoSave** with **OneDrive**
- **OneDrive** version history
- The **Always create backup** setting
- Warning prompts when opening workbooks

By the end of the chapter, you'll have new levels of defense against spreadsheet disasters. This will include both proactive and reactive responses to spreadsheet mishaps. Also, you'll have new tricks in your toolbox to eliminate certain repetitive tasks and prompts in Excel.

Technical requirements

Everything that I share in this chapter will work as described in Excel for Windows. A couple of the techniques work differently in Excel for macOS, or not at all. I'll point out these distinctions within my discussion of each feature.

The different workbooks and the CSV file that I used in this chapter are available for download from GitHub at `https://github.com/PacktPublishing/Exploring-Microsoft-Excels-Hidden-Treasures/tree/main/Chapter02`.

Undo and Redo

No matter how assiduous we are about saving our work, often, we're just one keystroke or mouse click away from a spreadsheet catastrophe. For instance, Excel can, and does, crash without notice, making your work suddenly vanish from the screen. However, that's an extreme example—it's much more likely that you'll delete the wrong data or accidentally paste over the wrong area of your worksheet. In such instances, pressing *Ctrl + Z* (or ⌘ + Z in Excel for macOS) will put things back. If you want to undo up to the last 100 actions in your workbook, you can click on the **Undo** drop-down menu, as shown in *Figure 2.1*, and select a series of consecutive actions to reverse:

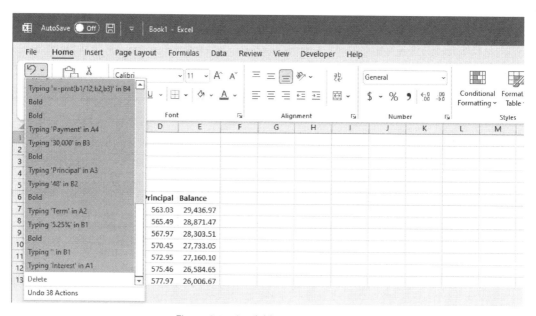

Figure 2.1 – Available actions to undo

One hidden benefit of **Undo** is the ability to redo the actions that you've undone. This means that you can roll a spreadsheet back up to 100 steps to see how things looked at that point, and then roll the spreadsheet forward again. As shown in *Figure 2.2*, the **Redo** command displays a list of actions that you can redo. Also, you can redo actions by pressing *Ctrl + Y* (⌘ + Y) or the *F4* key (*Fn + F4* on some keyboards):

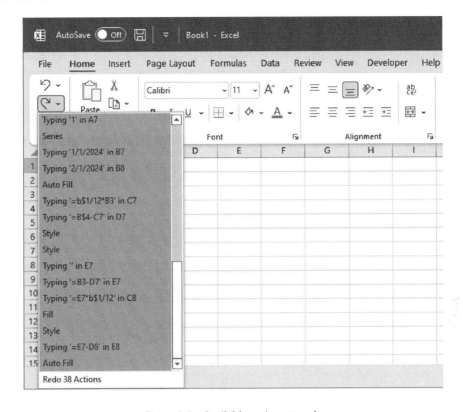

Figure 2.2 – Available actions to redo

Undo is a helpful safety net in Excel, but bear in mind that certain actions in Excel circumvent your ability to undo any previous actions:

- Deleting a worksheet
- Running a macro in Excel
- Saving and closing a document, and other actions that involve Excel's **File** menu

Therefore, it is important to have secondary measures in place that can give you fallback positions, such as Excel's **AutoRecover** feature.

The AutoRecover feature

Both the Windows and macOS versions of Excel offer an **AutoRecover** feature that automatically creates backup copies of your workbooks while you work. Excel for Windows offers customization and additional functionality not offered in Excel for macOS, so I'll discuss both versions separately.

Excel for Windows AutoRecover

In Excel for Windows, you can specify the interval you wish Excel to use for creating backup copies of your work. The default value is every **10** minutes, but in my experience, this means backups get made in between 20 to 25 minutes. I don't know about you, but I can complete a lot in Excel tasks in that amount of time, so I like to shorten the interval:

1. Choose **File | Options | Save**.
2. Make sure that the **Save AutoRecover information** checkbox is turned on.
3. Change the **Save AutoRecover information** setting from every **10** minutes to every **2** minutes instead, as shown in *Figure 2.3*:

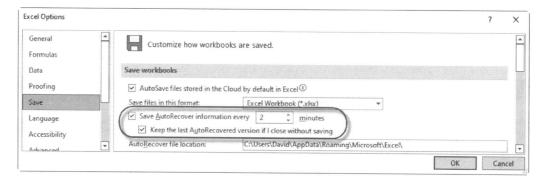

Figure 2.3 – The AutoRecover settings

4. Ensure that the **Keep the last AutoRecovered version if I close without saving** checkbox has been enabled.
5. Click on **OK**.

Making these changes will now protect you in two different ways. First, let's say that Excel crashes or that you close your workbook and inadvertently click on **Don't Save** instead of **Save**. The most recent backup will reside in an `Unsaved Workbooks` folder on your computer for a few days. Files seem to stay in this folder anywhere from 3 or 4 days to, sometimes, a little longer. It is a *temporary* archive, so make sure that you access any files you need from this folder before they vanish.

> **Tip**
> You can extend your access to **AutoRecover** files if you change the **AutoRecover** file location to a folder that a cloud-based file service such as **OneDrive**, **Dropbox**, or **Google Drive** syncs with. Typically, these services allow you to restore deleted files for 30 days or longer. Keep in mind that the **AutoRecover** files do not have meaningful names, but you might be able to identify files you wish to restore based on the date/time stamp.

Now, let's see how you can access backups that **AutoRecover** makes while you're actively working on your spreadsheet.

Accessing interim backups

AutoRecover in Excel for Windows offers another level of protection: you can access up to five backups made while you're actively working on a spreadsheet. To access these backups, perform the following steps:

1. Click on **File | Info**.
2. Any available backups appear as timestamps adjacent to the **Manage Workbook** button, as shown in *Figure 2.4*:

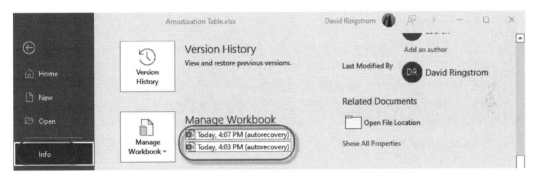

Figure 2.4 – AutoRecover backups

3. Click on any timestamp to open the backup along with your live file.

Keep in mind that these backups only exist until you close the file that you're working on. If you purposefully or accidentally close the workbook without saving it, the last backup will remain in the **Unsaved Files** folder for a few days, as discussed in the previous section.

As the saying goes, often, the best defense is a good offense. So, let's see how to make Excel for Windows less prone to crashing.

Removing temporary files

When temporary files used by Microsoft Windows accumulate in the background, Excel can become more prone to crashing. Typically, this happens when hundreds or thousands of temporary files pile up. Windows doesn't always clear these out on its own. To periodically remove these files, perform the following steps:

1. Open a **My Computer** or **Windows Explorer** window.
2. Right-click on your hard drive and choose **Properties**.

3. Click on **Disk Cleanup**.

4. Select **Temporary Files** from the list (this is not to be confused with **Temporary Internet Files**, which you can also delete), and then click on **OK**.

Alternatively, you can use a more hands-on approach:

1. Close as many open programs as possible, including browser windows.

2. Type `%temp%` or `%tmp%` into the address bar of a **My Computer** or **File Explorer** window. Then, press *Enter*.

3. Select any file within your `Temp` folder. Then, press *Ctrl + A* to select all the files and folders.

4. Press the *Delete* key to remove the files. Some files will be in use and unable to be deleted, so skip any files that are in use or require administrator permission.

> **Tip**
> The goal isn't to empty the `Temp` folder completely but to keep the number of files ideally in the dozens rather than the hundreds or thousands instead. The more temporary files you have, the greater the odds that Excel will unceremoniously crash on you.

As you can see, Excel for Windows offers a variety of disaster recovery options. Unfortunately, it's a different story in Excel for macOS.

Excel for macOS AutoRecover

The **AutoRecover** capability is far more limited in Excel for macOS. You can enable or disable the feature, but you can't set a time interval, nor can you access any unsaved files. Additionally, you cannot access any of the backups that Excel makes while you're working on your spreadsheet. The best you can hope for with **AutoRecover** on the Mac is that, if Excel crashes, then it will present a panel that allows you to recover any documents that you were working on.

You can use the following steps to manage your **AutoRecover** settings:

1. Choose **Excel | Preferences | Sharing and Privacy | Save**.

2. As shown in *Figure 2.5*, click on **Enable AutoRecover** to turn the feature on. Alternatively, clear the checkbox to turn it off, and then close the **Excel Preferences** dialog box:

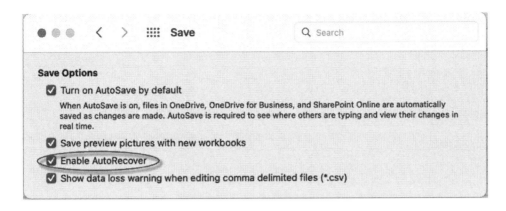

Figure 2.5 – The Excel for macOS AutoRecover preference

Given the limited functionality of **AutoRecover**, you'll most certainly want to explore using **AutoSave with OneDrive** to give yourself more options on how to revert to prior versions of a document.

AutoSave with OneDrive

Older versions of Excel used to have a built-in **AutoSave** command that would periodically backup Excel workbooks. This feature fell by the wayside in the massive overhaul with **Excel 2007**. Fortunately, **AutoSave** is back for documents saved to Microsoft's **OneDrive** and **SharePoint Online** services. If you have a **Microsoft 365** subscription, then you already have a **OneDrive** account. Beyond that, anyone can get 5 GB of free storage by simply creating a free Microsoft account. If you need more space, home users can buy 100 GB of storage for $19.99/year, while **OneDrive for Business** starts at $5/user/month. Learn more or subscribe at www.onedrive.com.

Typically, files that you save to **OneDrive** are saved every few seconds, which means that it is much harder to lose your work. As shown in *Figure 2.6*, you can toggle **AutoSave** on or off on a workbook-by-workbook basis by way of the slider in the **Quick Access Toolbar**:

Figure 2.6 – The AutoSave toggle

> **Nuance**
>
> **AutoSave** is not available for files that you save to competing cloud-based platforms, such as Google Drive or Dropbox. You can only use **AutoSave** for spreadsheets saved to one of Microsoft's cloud-based platforms.

Saving files to OneDrive

If you toggle **AutoSave** on for a given document, you'll be prompted to upload the file to **OneDrive**. As shown in *Figure 2.7*, you'll choose the platform you wish to use, and then you'll be prompted to name the file:

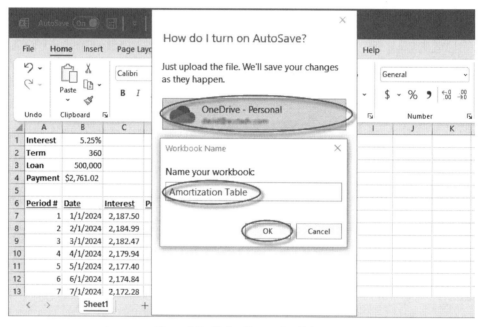

Figure 2.7 – Uploading to OneDrive

> **Nuance**
>
> Excel's title bar always displays the name of your workbook. If you save your document to **OneDrive** or **SharePoint Online**, typically, you'll either see the word **Saving** or **Saved** after the filename. **Saving** means that you've made changes to the spreadsheet that have not been saved yet. **Saved** means that a new version has been saved that incorporates your changes. The **Saving/Saved** indicator only appears for files saved to the Microsoft Cloud. Sometimes, other messages will appear, such as **Awaiting Upload** or **Last Modified**. You can still press *Ctrl* + *S* (⌘ + *S*). Alternatively, click on the **Save** icon adjacent to **AutoSave** if you want to be particularly sure that your work gets saved.

The upload approach that I just discussed doesn't allow you to choose a folder to save the file in, so your workbook will appear at the root level of your **OneDrive** account. Fortunately, you can have complete control when you use this approach:

1. Choose **File** | **Save As**.
2. Choose **OneDrive** or **SharePoint Online**, as shown in *Figure 2.8*:

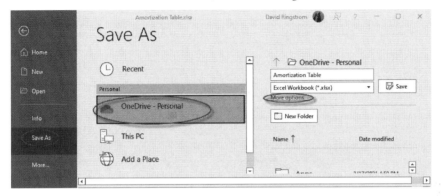

Figure 2.8 – Using Save As with OneDrive

3. Click on **More options** to display the **Save As** dialog box.
4. Choose or create a folder for your spreadsheet, assign a name, and then click on **Save**.

However, let's say that you assigned a filename in *Figure 2.7* but now wish to rename or move the file elsewhere. To do so, perform the following steps:

1. Click on the *filename* in the title bar at the top of your Excel screen.
2. Optionally, assign a new filename, as shown in *Figure 2.9*—this renames the file in **OneDrive**, as opposed to making a new copy.
3. Optionally, click on the button beneath **Location** to display a dialog box that you can use to move the file to a different folder within **OneDrive**. This is similar to how the **Save As** dialog box works:

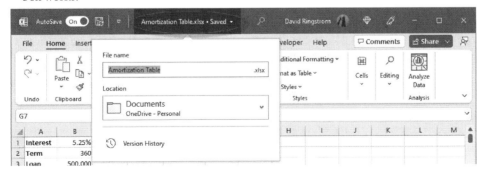

Figure 2.9 – Renaming and/or relocating a spreadsheet

Keep in mind that when you use **AutoSave**, not only are your most recent changes saved but copies of your previous work are saved, too. Let's see how to determine what's available to you via **AutoSave**.

Accessing prior AutoSave versions

When you save files to your hard drive, typically, you only have access to the last copy you saved. Later in this chapter, in the *Always create backup* section, I'll discuss a way that you can add one more level of backup. Of course, **AutoSave** goes much farther and allows you to retrieve multiple versions of your work. Here's how to access **AutoSave's Version History** feature:

1. Click on the *filename* in the title bar at the top of your Excel screen.
2. Choose **Version History**, as shown in *Figure 2.9*.
3. A **Version History** task pane appears on the right-hand side of Excel, as shown in *Figure 2.10*:

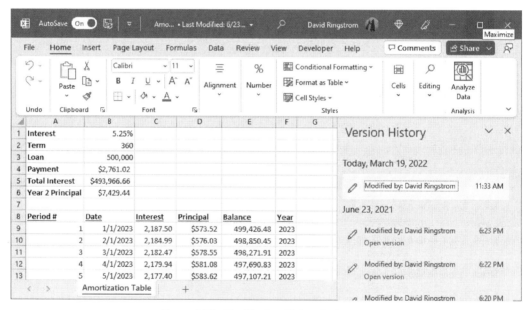

Figure 2.10 – The Version History task pane

4. Click on **Open Version** beneath the backup copy you wish to retrieve.
5. As shown in *Figure 2.11*, you can click on **Restore** in Excel's **Message Bar** to replace the most recent backup with this version. Or you can choose **Save As** in the **File** menu to save a copy of the backup to the location of your choice:

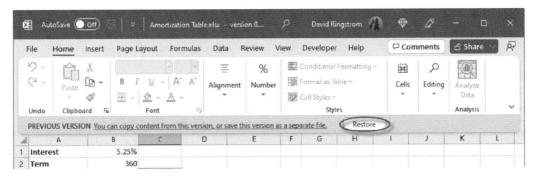

Figure 2.11 – The Restore button

> **AutoSave Limitations**
>
> Although the feature names are similar, **AutoSave** and **AutoRecover** function differently. As discussed previously, **AutoRecover** allows you to revert to up to five different versions of your file during the current work session. Conversely, **AutoSave** periodically backs up your file, but not every interim backup will be accessible. **AutoSave** is best used for reverting to how the file looked during previous work sessions. An ideal scenario would be to be able to use **AutoSave** and **AutoRecover** together, but **AutoRecover** only works for files saved locally to your computer, while **AutoSave** only works for files saved to the cloud.

Typically, **AutoSave** will be a set-and-forget feature, but sometimes, circumstances might arise where **AutoSave** is inexplicably disabled.

Resolving the disabled AutoSave

By default, any documents that you have saved to **OneDrive**, **OneDrive for Business**, or **SharePoint Online** will have **AutoSave** enabled automatically. However, sometimes, you might encounter situations where the **AutoSave** command has been disabled. Here are a few scenarios that can disable **AutoSave** for specific documents:

- You haven't saved the document yet, or you saved it to your local hard drive or network.
- Sometimes, **AutoSave** is initially disabled for workbooks you open by way of **Microsoft Teams** or **SharePoint Online**. Usually, you can turn **AutoSave** on once you open the file.
- The workbook is saved in the Excel 97–2003 workbook format (.xls format).
- The legacy **Share Workbook** feature, which I discuss in *Chapter 3*, *Quick Access Toolbar Treasures*, might be enabled. You must disable this feature to use **AutoSave**.
- The file has a workbook-level password. Choose **Review | Protect Workbook** and remove the password.

- The **Refresh Data When Opening the File** setting is enabled in one or more **Tables** and/or **PivotTables**. I discuss this feature in *Chapter 12, Power Query*, which you must disable in order to use **AutoSave**.

There are more scenarios that can prevent **AutoSave** from working, but the preceding list identifies the most common culprits.

> **Nuance**
>
> Enabling **AutoSave** for a given spreadsheet will disable the **Save As** command in Excel's **File** menu. You will be able to choose **Save As Copy** to make an offline copy of the spreadsheet, but remember, any changes you make to the copy will not sync with **OneDrive** or **SharePoint Online**.

Of course, if you prefer to maintain control over when your documents are saved, you can turn off the default **AutoSave** setting.

Permanently disabling AutoSave

If you wish, you can disable the **AutoSave** feature for future workbooks:

1. Choose **File** | **Options**.
2. Choose the **Save** section.
3. Clear the checkbox for **AutoSave files stored in the Cloud by default in Excel**, as shown in *Figure 2.3*.
4. Click on **OK**.

The steps are slightly different in Excel for macOS:

1. Choose **Excel** | **Preferences**.
2. Choose the **Save** section.
3. Clear the checkbox for **Turn on AutoSave by default**, as shown in *Figure 2.5*.
4. Close the **Preferences** dialog box.

Excel will no longer automatically save documents stored in **OneDrive** or **SharePoint Online** unless you toggle the **AutoSave** command on for specific workbooks. In older versions of Excel, we could remove the **AutoSave** command from the **Quick Access Toolbar** section:

1. Right-click on the **AutoSave** command.
2. Choose **Remove from Quick Access Toolbar**.

Microsoft 365 no longer allows you to remove **AutoSave** as it has been decoupled from the **Quick Access Toolbar** section. I'll discuss this in more detail in *Chapter 3, Quick Access Toolbar Treasures*.

AutoSave can provide robust disaster recovery protection, but not everyone saves their files to **OneDrive** or **SharePoint Online**. Fortunately, there's a way to add in a small amount of additional protection for spreadsheets that you can save to your hard drive, a local network, or another storage medium.

The Always create backup setting

You can instruct Excel for Windows to create an automatic fallback position for critical workbooks. There are a few caveats:

- You must enable this setting on a workbook-by-workbook basis.
- Your backup copy is the most previously saved copy of your workbook.
- Excel creates a file that has a .XLK extension that it will not recognize when you open your backup file, which we'll discuss.
- The backup file must reside in the same folder as the original document, as there is no provision for saving backup files elsewhere.
- This feature is not available in Excel for macOS.

Let's see how to establish an automatic backup for key workbooks:

1. Choose **File | Save As | Browse** or **More Options**.
2. Click on **Tools** in the **Save As** dialog box, to the left-hand side of the **Save** button.
3. Click on **General Options**.
4. Click on the **Always Create Backup** checkbox, as shown in *Figure 2.12*, and then click on **OK**.
5. Click on **Save**:

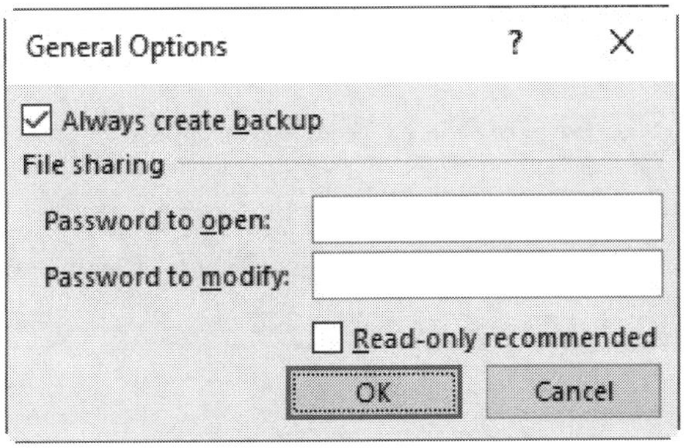

Figure 2.12 – The Always create backup setting

Let's say that your workbook is named Budget.xlsx and is saved in your **Documents** folder. Every time you save your budget, the previous version of the workbook will be renamed Copy of years. You Budget.xlk and will also be saved inside your **Documents** folder. Each time you save the Budget.xlsx file, Excel updates the back-up copy of your workbook. I can attest that this feature has saved me from losing critical workbooks numerous times over the years. You never know when a file will get corrupted while you're saving.

You can open the .xlk backup file in the same fashion as a normal Excel file, but be aware that Excel will warn you that the workbook could be corrupted or unsafe, as shown in *Figure 2.13*:

Figure 2.13 – A misleading error prompt

It's a weird quirk in Excel that it doesn't recognize the .xlk extension as a valid Excel file. Rest assured, you can safely click on **Yes** to open the backup file and then resave it as a normal Excel workbook.

> **Tip**
>
> Often, I incorporate version numbers into my workbook names that I periodically increment. For instance, I might use 2024 Cash Flow Projection 1.01.xlsx as the initial filename for a spreadsheet. Whenever I'm about to make major changes to the workbook, I increment the filename to 1.02, 1.03, and so on to build in fallback positions.

Sometimes, despite our best efforts, Excel workbooks can still get corrupted or start displaying odd behaviors. Let's see what actions we can take when such situations arise.

Repairing damaged workbooks

The prompt that no one ever wants to see in Excel is the one that says a workbook has been corrupted and cannot be opened. Of course, there are varying degrees of workbook corruption. Low levels of damage can result in odd behaviors or prompts as you work on the document, while more severe damage can render the workbook inaccessible. In such situations, you might be able to repair the workbook in Excel for Windows. Make sure that you close the affected file because you cannot repair files that are currently open in Excel. Once you've done so, perform the following steps:

1. Choose **File | Open**.
2. Click on the arrow on the right-hand side of the **Open** button and choose **Open and Repair...**, as shown in *Figure 2.14*:

Repairing damaged workbooks 47

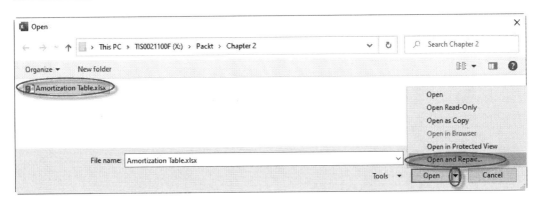

Figure 2.14 – The Open and Repair command

3. Click on **Repair**, as shown in *Figure 2.15*:

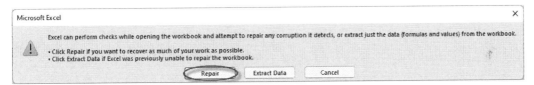

Figure 2.15 – The Open and Repair dialog box

4. Hopefully, Excel will display a second prompt that informs you that the repair was successful, as shown in *Figure 2.16*:

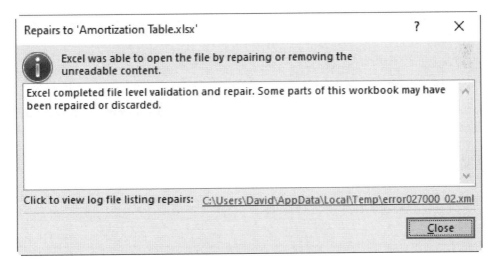

Figure 2.16 – A successful repair

If the repair doesn't work, carry out the preceding steps again, but this time, click on **Extract Data** in *Figure 2.15* instead of **Repair**. When it works, **Extract Data** discards all formatting in the workbook—meaning fonts, colors, number formatting, borders, and more—and only keeps the formulas and the data. In my experience, if the first option fails, **Extract Data** will fail too, but it never hurts to try.

If the **Repair** option within Excel doesn't work, the next steps that I will try are listed as follows:

- Opening the damaged workbook in Excel for macOS, which can sometimes open files that the Windows version can't.
- Download and install the free **LibreOffice** suite. Sometimes, the **Calc** app within **LibreOffice** can open damaged Excel workbooks.

> **Tip**
> Additionally, you can use **LibreOffice** if you need to open a **Lotus 1-2-3** file so that you can convert it into an Excel workbook.

- Write a formula in a new workbook that links back to the damaged workbook. If the workbook is named `Damaged File.xlsx` and is stored in `E:\Documents`, then enter `='[E:\Documents\Damaged File.xlsx'!A1` into cell **A1** of a blank worksheet. Copy the formula down and across to fill the approximate area you feel the damaged worksheet spans. Note that you can reference a sheet name if you know it, or you can omit the sheet name to pull data from the first worksheet only.

Now, let's see a proactive step that you can take to improve the stability of your workbooks, especially those that have been passed around among multiple users.

Removing excess formatting

Sometimes, you can forestall the need to repair an Excel workbook by removing excess formatting. Such formatting arises when users select an entire column and apply number formatting, fonts, colors, and more to more than one million cells. When you start doing things a million times here and a million times there, it's easy for a workbook to become bloated and unstable. Whenever possible, only apply formatting to the specific cells that are needed. Fortunately, you can overcome past transgressions from yourself or others. **Microsoft 365 Apps for Enterprise** offers an **Inquire Add-in** that includes a **Clean Excess Cell Formatting** feature that can slim down bloated workbooks.

> **Nuance**
> **Microsoft 365 Apps for Enterprise** is considered the business version of Excel, as opposed to the **Home and Family** version of **Microsoft 365**. If you're not clear about which version of Excel you have, choose **File**, and then **Account**. If **Microsoft 365 Apps for Enterprise** appears on the right-hand side, then you have access to the **Inquire Add-in** option.

Here's how to enable the **Inquire add-in** option in **Microsoft 365 Apps for Enterprise**:

1. Choose **File | Options**.
2. Choose **Add-Ins**.
3. Click on the arrow adjacent to **Excel Add-Ins** and choose **COM Add-Ins**. Then, click on **Go**.
4. If available, click on **Inquire** and then click on **OK** to add an **Inquire** tab to the **Ribbon**.
5. Choose **Inquire | Clean Excess Cell Formatting**, click on **OK**, and then click on **Yes**.

> **Tip**
> If your version of Excel doesn't offer the **Inquire** add-in, you can download and install the free **XLStylesTool** tool from the **Windows App store** to remove excess styles from your workbooks.

Now that we've explored a variety of disaster recovery options, let's see how to manage the plethora of prompts that can slow your work down every time you open certain workbooks.

Warning prompts when opening workbooks

In 1999, the Melissa virus infected countless computers around the world. The virus spreads itself in the form of infected **Microsoft Word** documents. Over the years, Microsoft added several levels of defense to their products to prevent a recurrence of a similar virus. The trade-off is that users are often subject to warning prompts every time they open a spreadsheet.

In this section, I'll discuss the most frequent prompts that appear and how you can manage the risks of working with spreadsheets of unknown provenance. First, let's discuss the **Protected View** feature in Excel for Windows.

Protected View

Protected View first appeared in **Excel 2007**. It is designed to allow you to safely open and review a document in a sandbox environment that prevents it from making any changes to your computer. As shown in *Figure 2.17*, you can view but not edit the document when it is in **Protected View**:

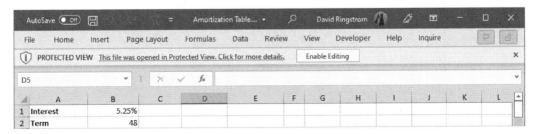

Figure 2.17 – The Protected View prompt

By default, **Protected View** is triggered every time you open a spreadsheet originating from the internet or an email attachment. **Protected View** disables the following elements of a workbook:

- Macros (programming code embedded within an Excel workbook)
- External data connections, such as database queries
- Workbook links, meaning formulas that link to other spreadsheets
- Dynamic data exchange links, an obsolete means of transferring data between programs
- Hyperlinks, a clickable navigation link to another document or perhaps a web page

In short, **Protected View** disables any connection to the outside world from within the workbook, which also prevents you from being able to edit the workbook, too. Once you determine that a workbook is safe to access, you can click on **Enable Editing**, as shown in *Figure 2.17*, to use the workbook in a normal fashion.

As with any computer security, sometimes, you might find that an ounce of prevention is much harder to swallow than the cure. For instance, if you frequently export files from, say, a cloud-based accounting software, you could be required to click on **Enable Editing** many times a day. If you are cautious about the spreadsheets that you download, you can consider disabling **Protected View**:

1. Choose **File | Options | Trust Center.**
2. Click on **Trust Center Settings** on the right-hand side of the **Trust Center Setting** section.
3. Click on **Protected View** on the left-hand side of the **Trust Center** dialog box.
4. Optionally clear the **Enable Protected View for files originating from the Internet** checkbox, as shown in *Figure 2.18*

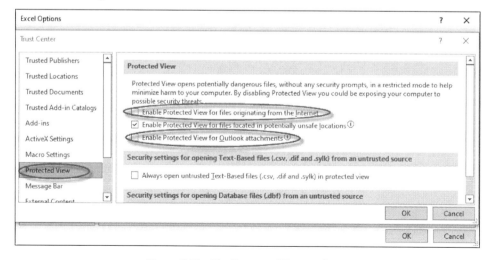

Figure 2.18 – The Protected View options

5. Optionally, clear the **Enable Protected View for Outlook attachments** checkbox if you frequently encounter the **Protected View** prompt when opening email attachments.

> **Warning**
> Do not clear the checkbox for **Enable Protected View for files located in potentially unsafe locations**, as doing so can put your computer at risk.

6. Click on **OK** twice to close the **Trust Center** and **Excel Options** dialog boxes.

You can still utilize **Protected View** situationally if you want to inspect a file of unknown provenance before editing it in Excel for Windows:

1. Choose **File | Open**.
2. Click once on the file in question.
3. Click on the arrow on the right-hand side of the **Open** button.
4. Choose **Open in Protected View**, as shown in *Figure 2.14*.

This allows you to safely review a file in a protected manner.

Trusted documents

Sometimes, you will run into security warning prompts when you open an Excel workbook. In *Chapter 12, Power Query*, I will show you how to use **Power Query** to pull data into Excel from other data sources, including text files, Excel workbooks, databases, PDF files, and more. Although it is unlikely, malicious actors can perpetuate mischief on your computer by way of specially crafted queries. Because of this potential risk, the **Enable Content** prompts, shown in *Figure 2.19*, can present another speed bump that can prevent you from getting work done on a spreadsheet.

Similar versions of this prompt appear when you open files that contain macros, which are programming code used to automate tasks in Excel, or workbook links, which retrieve data from other workbooks:

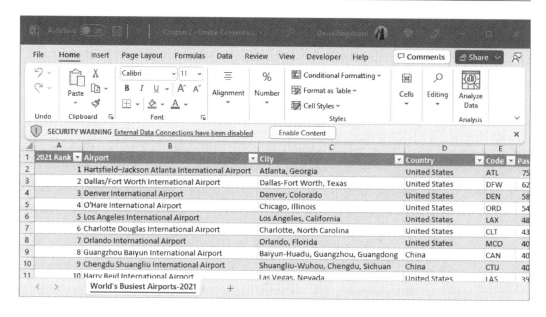

Figure 2.19 – The Enable Content prompt

If you poke around in the **Trust Center** settings in Excel, you can disable all of these prompts across the board. However, doing so presents a higher level of risk than simply disabling **Protected View**. When you disable **Protected View**, the **Enable Content** prompts still appear, creating a gauntlet of prompts. Additionally, the **Enable Content** prompt can be triggered by workbook links and workbooks that have macros. If you've created the external connections, workbook links, or macros, then there's no risk, and you can safely turn these prompts off by creating a trusted document.

> **Nuance**
>
> If you click on the **Enable Content** button in Excel's **Message Bar**, you will relegate yourself to having to click on that button each time you open your file. Do not click on **Enable Content** if you wish to suppress the prompt; instead, use that prompt as a tickler to carry out the steps in the next section.

If you wish to suppress the **Enable Content** prompt for a specific workbook, carry out these steps when that button is present on screen:

1. Choose **File** | **Info**.
2. Click on **Enable Content** | **Enable All Content**.

If your **Enable All Content** command displays (**Make this a trusted document**), you'll no longer encounter the security warning when this document. Otherwise you must continue to click Enable Content each time.

If you change your mind about granting trusted document status, you can clear your trusted document list:

1. Choose **File | Options | Trust Center.**
2. Click on the **Trust Center Settings** button on the right-hand side of the **Excel Options** dialog box.
3. Click on **Trusted Documents** on the left-hand side of the **Trust Center** dialog box.
4. Click on **Clear**.
5. Confirm that you wish to clear your list of trusted documents.
6. Click on **OK** twice to close the **Trust Center** and **Excel Options** dialog boxes.

Clearing your trusted documents list is an all-or-nothing proposition. You cannot revoke trusted document status for a single workbook. Further, trusted document status is on a per-computer basis, so your co-workers will need to mark documents as trusted, too, if they wish to suppress the security warning prompts.

CSV prompt

There's one other prompt that comes to mind that can slow down your day-to-day work if you periodically save files in the **comma-separated value** (CSV) file format. To open a **CSV** file, perform the following steps:

1. Choose **File | Open | Browse**.
2. Change the **File Type** setting to **Text Files (*.prn, *.txt, *.csv)**.
3. Select a **CSV** file, and then click on **Open**.
4. Some CSV files will open directly in Excel; if not the Text Import Wizard will appear. In that case, perform the following actions:
    I. Accept the default of **Delimited** on the first screen of the wizard, and then click on **Next**.
    II. Turn off the **Tab** option and turn on **Comma** on the second screen of the wizard. Then, click on **Finish**.

As shown in *Figure 2.20*, Excel might alert you that you run the risk of losing data. This is because **CSV** files are text-based and cannot store formulas, data connections, charts, or any aspect of an Excel workbook other than numbers and letters.

If you find this prompt distracting, click on **Don't show again** to permanently disable it:

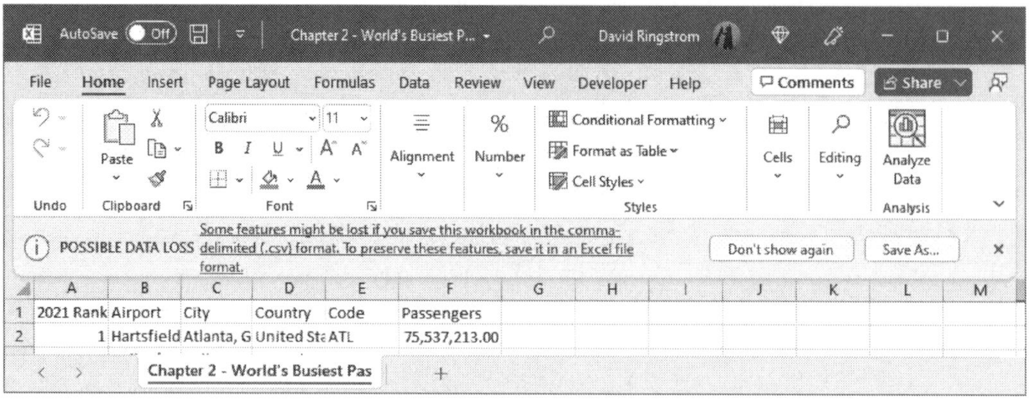

Figure 2.20 – Data loss warning

Perform the following steps if you ever wish to restore this prompt:

1. Choose **File** | **Options** | **Save**.
2. Enable the **Show Data Loss Warning When Editing Comma Delimited Files (.csv)** checkbox, and then click on **OK**.

Excel for macOS users will use these steps:

1. Click on **Excel** | **Preferences** | **Save**.
2. Enable the **Show Data Loss Warning When Editing Comma Delimited Files (.csv)** checkbox, and then close the **Preferences** dialog box.

You should now be able to work more efficiently in Excel by suppressing the well-meaning but often unnecessary prompts while you work in Excel.

Summary

In this chapter, you learned about several ways to set up a series of defenses against mishaps in your Excel spreadsheets. **Undo** and **Redo** allow you to quickly respond at that moment, unless an Excel command or feature removes that safety net without notice. The **AutoRecover** and **AutoSave** commands enable you to for keeping backup copies of your work offline or in the cloud, respectively. The **Always Create Backup** setting provides an additional fallback position for critical workbooks that are saved locally.

Also, you saw how to dispatch the flurry of warning prompts that can appear when you open an Excel workbook that contains data connections, workbook links, or macros. Well-intentioned security prompts can interrupt your workflow or worse, stymy your work if you don't understand the prompt.

We'll continue our quest for improved productivity in *Chapter 3*, *Quick Access Toolbar Treasures*, where I'll show you how to streamline common tasks with icons and custom keyboard shortcuts.

3
Quick Access Toolbar Treasures

The **Quick Access Toolbar** is a customizable row of icons that you can configure at the top of your screen. In this chapter, I'll show you how to create a keyboard shortcut for practically any feature in Excel, including certain features that Microsoft has removed from the menu interface known as the **Ribbon**. Of course, the **Quick Access Toolbar** isn't just about keyboard shortcuts if you prefer to use your mouse to carry out tasks.

In this chapter, you'll learn about the following topics:

- Unhiding the **Quick Access Toolbar** if needed
- A tricky keyboard shortcut nuance
- **Reposition or removing** commands from the toolbar
- Time-saving commands
- Accessing commands that aren't in the **Ribbon**
- Creating workbook-specific toolbars
- Creating shortcuts for Excel macros
- Migrating **Quick Access Toolbar** icons between computers
- Restoring legacy features in Excel

As you progress through this chapter, you'll be able to add commands that Microsoft never put on the **Ribbon** or has removed from the **Ribbon**. You will discover new keyboard shortcut possibilities and condense repetitive tasks down to a single mouse click or keystroke. You will also get a brief introduction to Excel's **Macro Recorder** feature, which can start you down the path of creating your own automation in Excel.

Technical requirements

Everything in this chapter works in Excel for Windows. I will note which features and techniques are not available in Excel for macOS. Additionally, I will demonstrate the new **Show Changes** feature, which, presently, is only available in **Excel for the Web** instead of Excel Online but can be used to review changes to workbooks that have been edited in Excel for Windows or macOS. You can download the examples for this chapter from `https://github.com/PacktPublishing/Exploring-Microsoft-Excels-Hidden-Treasures/tree/main/Chapter03`.

Exploring the Quick Access Toolbar

The **Quick Access Toolbar** debuted in **Excel 2007** and has been a mainstay of Excel's **Ribbon** up until the upcoming *visual refresh* that Microsoft is slowly rolling out to **Microsoft 365** users as of this writing. As shown in *Figure 3.1*, the **Undo** and **Redo** commands have traditionally appeared on the **Quick Access Toolbar**:

Figure 3.1 – The traditional location of Undo and Redo

As you can see in *Figure 3.2*, the **Undo** and **Redo** buttons are moving to the **Home** tab of Excel's **Ribbon** as part of the update to Excel's user interface. Oddly, in these new Excel builds, the **Quick Access Toolbar** is automatically hidden if you haven't customized it previously. These changes will occur unbidden by you once Microsoft pushes the update out to your computer:

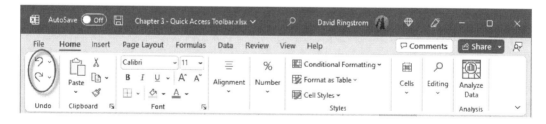

Figure 3.2 – Undo and Redo appear on the Home tab and the Quick Access Toolbar is hidden

> **Tip**
> If you're not sure which version of Excel you're using, choose **File | Account**. You'll either see a mention of **Microsoft 365** on the right-hand side of the **Account** screen, or you'll see something such as **Excel 2021**, **Excel 2019**, and so on. Microsoft refers to the latter as *single-purchase* versions of Excel, which means the user interface is frozen in time and will not change until you upgrade to a newer version of Excel.

Here are the steps to restore a hidden **Quick Access Toolbar**:

1. Right-click on the **File** menu.
2. Choose **Show Quick Access Toolbar**, as shown in *Figure 3.3*:

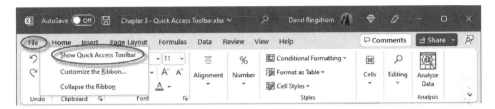

Figure 3.3 – Unhiding the Quick Access Toolbar

3. The **Customize Quick Access Toolbar** button will either appear adjacent to the **Save** command, as shown in *Figure 3.4*, otherwise your **Quick Access Toolbar** will be positioned below the ribbon, as shown in *Figure 3.5*:

Figure 3.4 – The Quick Access Toolbar beneath the Ribbon

4. Click on **Customize Quick Access Toolbar** to display a menu that allows you to do the following:

    - Select **Undo** and/or **Redo** if you wish to add the commands back to the **Quick Access Toolbar**. You can, of course, use *Ctrl + Z* (⌘ + *Z* in Excel for macOS) to undo and *Ctrl + Y* (⌘ + *Y*) to redo instead. However, it's hard to overcome muscle memory if you're conditioned to clicking these commands with your mouse. I can attest that having to activate the **Home** tab to click on these commands gets old fast. Other commands you might find helpful include the following:

        - **Email** – This attaches the current workbook to a blank email with a single mouse-click or keyboard shortcut, which means your email software will launch if needed.

- **Quick Print** – This sends the print range of the current worksheet directly to your default printer.

- **Print Preview and Print** – This launches Excel's **Print Preview** screen, which is also known as the **Backstage View** in Excel for Windows.

- Choose **More Commands** to add additional commands to your toolbar, which we'll do throughout the chapter.

- Click on **Show Above the Ribbon** or **Show Below the Ribbon** to reposition the toolbar. This command toggles between the two based on the toolbar's current position.

- If available, choose **Show Command Labels**, shown in *Figure 3.5*, to display the command name adjacent to the icon when the toolbar is displayed below the **Ribbon**, as shown in *Figure 3.6*. This feature is available in the *visual refresh* version of **Microsoft 365**:

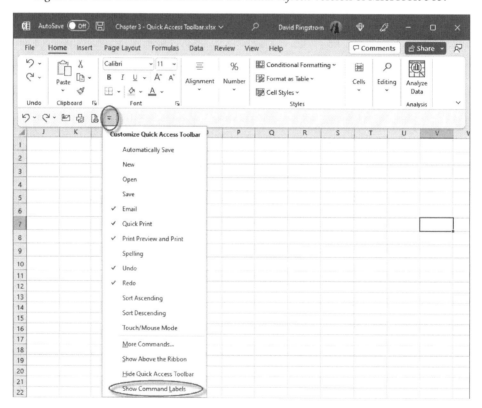

Figure 3.5 – The Show Command Labels option

At this point, we've ensured that your **Quick Access Toolbar** is visible, and you've seen how to add popular commands, reposition the toolbar, and possibly enable command labels. Now, let's customize Excel's menu interface known as the **Ribbon**.

Customizing Excel's Ribbon

You can customize the menu interface in Excel in a similar fashion to the **Quick Access Toolbar**. To do so, perform the following steps:

1. Choose **File** | **Options** | **Customize Ribbon**.
2. Choose a tab that you wish to customize from the right-hand column or click on **New Tab** to add a blank tab to your Ribbon. Click on **Rename** if you wish to change the name of any tab in the **Ribbon**.
3. Each **Ribbon** tab is broken down into groups, such as **Clipboard**, **Font**, **Alignment**, and more in the **Home** tab. You cannot add commands to any of the built-in groups, but you can click on **New Group** to add a custom group to an existing **Ribbon** tab or click on **New Tab** to create a new tab.
4. Add commands to new groups and tabs by making selections from the left-hand column and then clicking on **Add**.
5. Click on **OK** to close the **Excel Options** dialog box once you've finished your customizations.

The **Quick Access Toolbar** offers one-click access to commands with your mouse, but there's an additional dimension to the toolbar in Excel for Windows.

Understanding the nuances of Quick Access Toolbar shortcuts

In Excel for Windows, every command on your **Quick Access Toolbar** is assigned an alphanumeric keyboard shortcut. (Excel for macOS does not offer this feature.) These keyboard shortcuts entail pressing the *Alt* key and a shortcut code determined by the position of a command in your **Quick Access Toolbar**. I'll discuss how to reposition commands on the toolbar in the *Repositioning and removing icons* section a little later. As shown in *Figure 3.6*, when you tap the *Alt* key, onscreen tips will show you the keyboard shortcut associated with each command:

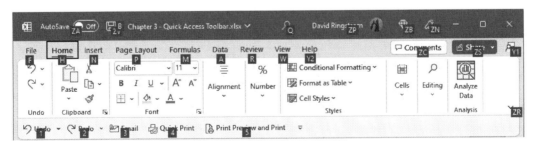

Figure 3.6 – The Quick Access Toolbar shortcut tips

The shortcut naming convention works as follows:

- The first nine shortcuts are assigned from **1** to **9**, meaning you press *Alt + 1* to access the first command, *Alt + 2* for the second, and so on.

- The 10th through 18th shortcuts are assigned from **09** to **01**, meaning you press *Alt + 09* to access the 10th command, *Alt + 08* for the 11th, and so on. The first character is zero.

- The 19th through 44th shortcuts are labeled **0A** through **0Z**, meaning you press *Alt + 0A* to access the 19th command, *Alt + 0B* for the 20th, and so on.

- The 45th command and beyond will not be accessible via your keyboard. Depending upon your screen resolution and the number of commands that you add, you might have to click on a button at the end of the toolbar to see commands that can't be displayed on the screen.

The shortcuts are predicated on the order that the commands appear in your toolbar. This means you'll probably want to have your most frequently used icons in the first nine positions. There are never any commitment issues with **Quick Access Toolbar** icons. You can move commands around at will or remove them from the toolbar. You can even reset the entire toolbar along with the Ribbon if you find that you're not happy with the state of either.

Repositioning the Quick Access Toolbar commands

You can change up the order of your **Quick Access Toolbar** commands at will:

1. Click on the **Customize Quick Access Toolbar** button represented by an *arrow* (or *three dots* in Excel for macOS), and then choose **More Commands…**.

2. The column on the right-hand side the order of your existing commands, which you can change by using these steps:

    - **Excel for Windows**: Click on any command, and then use the *Up* or *Down* arrows located to the right of the list to reposition the commands. You cannot drag commands in this version of Excel.

    - **Excel for Mac**: Drag the commands into a new position within the column. There are no *Up* or *Down* buttons in this version of Excel.

3. Once you've completed your changes, perform the following steps:

   - **Excel for Windows**: Click on **OK** to close the **Excel Options** dialog box
   - **Excel for macOS**: Click on **Save** and then close the **Excel Preferences** dialog box

Now that you have seen how to reorganize your **Quick Access Toolbar**, let's look at how to remove unwanted commands.

Removing Quick Access Toolbar commands

You can remove commands from the toolbar in one of three ways:

- **Customize Quick Access Toolbar menu**: If you've added a popular command, such as **Undo** or **Redo**, display the **Customize Quick Access Toolbar** menu and then unclick the commands that you wish to remove.
- **Quick Access Toolbar**: Right-click on any command on the toolbar and choose **Remove from Quick Access Toolbar**.
- **Excel Options Dialog Box**: Choose **File | Options | Quick Access Toolbar** (or, in Excel for macOS, choose **Excel | Preferences | Ribbon & Toolbar | Quick Access Toolbar**). Click on any command in the column on the right-hand side and then click on **Remove** in Excel for Windows (or the **left-arrow** button in Excel for macOS).

> **Tip**
> Clicking on the **Customize Quick Access Toolbar** button and then choosing **More Commands** is simply a secondary way to access the **Quick Access Toolbar** section of the **Options** dialog box.

As we move through this chapter, I'm going to show you even more commands that you can add to your **Quick Access Toolbar**. Feel free to experiment because you can always reset the entire toolbar in one fell swoop.

Resetting the Quick Access Toolbar

Resetting the toolbar means removing any customizations you've made and restoring the toolbar back to how it looked when Excel was first installed on your computer. Here are the steps:

- **Excel for Windows**: Click on **Reset | Reset Only Quick Access Toolbar** in the **Excel Options** dialog box, as shown in *Figure 3.7*. Then, click on **OK**:

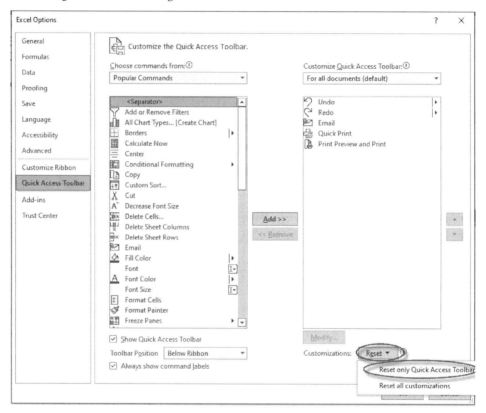

Figure 3.7 – Resetting the Quick Access Toolbar

- **Excel for macOS**: Click on the *three-dot* button at the bottom of the second column of Excel's **Preferences** dialog box, and then choose **Reset Only Quick Access Toolbar**.

> **Nuance**
>
> The **Reset** menu also includes a **Reset All Customizations** command that will reset both the **Quick Access Toolbar** section and Excel's **Ribbon**, if you've made customizations to both. If you customized the **Ribbon** but want to keep your **Quick Access Toolbar** settings, you'll need to export the **Quick Access Toolbar** first, and then import the `.exportUI` file again after you've reset the **Ribbon** and **Quick Access Toolbar**.

Understanding the nuances of Quick Access Toolbar shortcuts

We'll start adding more commands to your **Quick Access Toolbar** in a moment, but first, I want to share a keyboard-related nuance in Excel for Windows.

The *Alt*-Number Pad nuance

In Excel for Windows, you can access the first nine commands by tapping on the *Alt* key and typing any number from *1* to *9* using the top of your keyboard. If your keyboard has a physical number pad, you can also tap the *Alt* key and press any number from *1* to *9* on your number pad.

Notice that I said to *tap* the *Alt* key. This is where muscle memory can get the best of us. We're accustomed to holding down the *Ctrl* key, so it's easy to do the same with the *Alt* key. Two different outcomes can arise when you hold down the *Alt* key while typing *1* to *9* on your keyboard, instead of tapping the *Alt* key:

- When you type any number from *1* to *9* via the keys above the letters on your keyboard, the command tied to the **Quick Access Toolbar** icon that you selected will execute
- When you type any number from *1* to *9* via the number pad, Excel will insert a symbol into your spreadsheet, as shown in *Figure 3.8*:

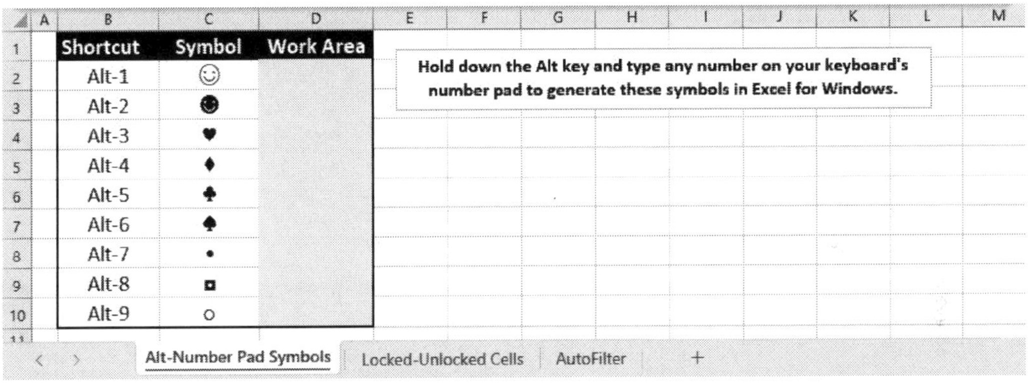

Shortcut	Symbol
Alt-1	☺
Alt-2	☻
Alt-3	♥
Alt-4	♦
Alt-5	♣
Alt-6	♠
Alt-7	•
Alt-8	◘
Alt-9	○

Hold down the Alt key and type any number on your keyboard's number pad to generate these symbols in Excel for Windows.

Figure 3.8 – Symbols accessible by holding the Alt key and using the number pad

Most of these symbols are rather goofy, but the one that I do find helpful is *Alt* + *7*, which creates a bullet symbol. It is much easier to hold down the *Alt* key and press the number *7* on the number pad than it is to locate a bullet in the traditional fashion in Excel:

1. Choose **Insert | Symbol**.

2. Choose a bullet symbol:

   - **Excel for Windows**: Select or type in `Wingdings` and then press *Enter* in the **Font** field, shown in *Figure 3.9*. Scroll several rows down, as needed, to locate the bullet symbol on the 8th row (or any other row). Double-click to insert the symbol (or single-click on any symbol, and then click on **Insert**). Click on **Cancel** to exit the **Symbol** dialog box:

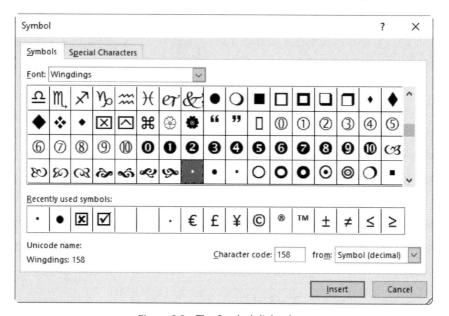

Figure 3.9 – The Symbol dialog box

   - **Excel for macOS**: Type `bullet` into the **Search** field, click on the symbol of your choice to insert it into the current worksheet cell, and then close the **Symbol** dialog box.

Now that we've covered the nuances of the **Quick Access Toolbar** keyboard shortcuts, let's reclaim a little bit of your day by adding time-saving commands to your toolbar.

Adding Ribbon commands to the toolbar

It might feel redundant to add commands from the Ribbon to your **Quick Access Toolbar**, but doing so provides two benefits. First, the **Quick Access Toolbar** is always visible when the **Ribbon** is displayed, which means you don't have to activate a specific **Ribbon** tab. Second, adding commands to the toolbar assigns keyboard shortcuts to commands such as Home | Center, that were deemed not to warrant a built-in shortcut.

Center text

A long-time quibble I've had with Excel for Windows is that you can't press *Ctrl + E* to center text the way that you can in Microsoft Word, PowerPoint, or Outlook. There wasn't a shortcut assigned to *Ctrl + E* for decades until the **Flash Fill** feature debuted in Excel 2013. with *Ctrl + E* now activates Flash Fill in Excel for Windows, while in Excel for macOS ⌘ + *E* centers text, and Flash Fill doesn't have a shortcut. Fortunately, you can create your own keyboard shortcut for centering text in Excel for Windows:

1. Right-click on the **Center** command in the **Home** tab of Excel's **Ribbon**.
2. Choose **Add to Quick Access Toolbar**.

> **Nuance**
> The **Add to Quick Access Toolbar** option is disabled (grayed-out) whenever a particular command already appears on your **Quick Access Toolbar**.

3. Tap the *Alt* key to reveal the keyboard shortcut.

That's all there is to it, which means you can now create shortcuts for any frequently used commands. Sometimes, I temporarily add shortcuts to the toolbar in to keep from repetitively accessing the **Ribbon** tab for a particular command or drop-down menu. For instance, you can use these steps to create a shortcut for the **Top and Double Bottom Border** command:

1. Choose the **Home | Borders** drop-down menu.
2. Right-click on **Top and Double Bottom Border**.
3. Choose **Add to Quick Access Toolbar**.

Now you can add the top and double bottom borders, or any border of your choice, to cells with a keyboard shortcut or a single mouse click.

> **Nuance**
> You can't add every command in a drop-down menu in this fashion. For instance, right-clicking on the **Fill**, **Font Color**, or **Shapes** commands and choosing **Add to Quick Access Toolbar** will add the entire gallery to the toolbar instead of a single command. While you cannot add individual cell colors to the toolbar, you can create a macro to apply cell colors. Refer to the *Creating shortcuts for macros* section later in this chapter.

Sometimes, adding a command from the **Ribbon** unlocks some hidden functionality, such as the ability to quickly determine whether a cell is marked as locked or not.

Locking/unlocking worksheet cells

Every cell in a worksheet is marked as locked until you unlock one or more cells by using one of the following techniques:

- **Format Cells dialog box**: Choose **Home** | **Format** | **Format Cells** | **Protection** to display the **Protection** tab of the **Format Cells** dialog box. Clear or click on the **Locked** checkbox depending upon whether you want to unlock or lock a particular cell.

- **Lock Cell command**: Choose **Home** | **Format** | **Lock Cell**. The downside to this approach is that when you click on **Lock Cell**, the locked or unlocked status is toggled but then the menu vanishes, so you can be left unsure whether you made the change you intended.

> **Tip**
> In *Chapter 4, Conditional Formatting*, I will discuss how to use **Conditional Formatting** to color-code cells that you have unlocked prior to protecting a worksheet.

Either of these approaches can turn tedious if you need to repetitively unlock numerous non-adjacent cells, but you can condense the steps to a keyboard shortcut or a mouse click:

1. Choose **Home** | **Format** and then right-click on **Lock Cell**.
2. Choose **Add to Quick Access Toolbar**.

   When added to the **Quick Access Toolbar** section, the **Lock Cell** command not only toggles the locked/unlocked status of cells but also enables you to determine whether a cell has been marked as locked or unlocked.

3. Click on cell **B3** of the **Locked-Unlocked** worksheet in this chapter's example workbook.
4. The **Lock Cell** icon has shading behind it when a cell is marked as locked, as shown in *Figure 3.10*:

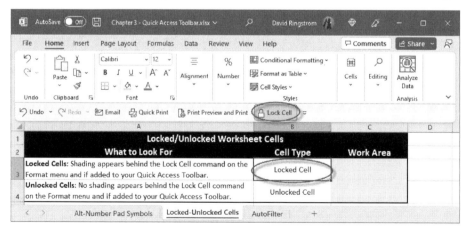

Figure 3.10 – The Lock Cell command indicating a locked cell

5. Click on cell **B4** and notice that shading vanishes because I unlocked the cell, as shown in *Figure 3.11*:

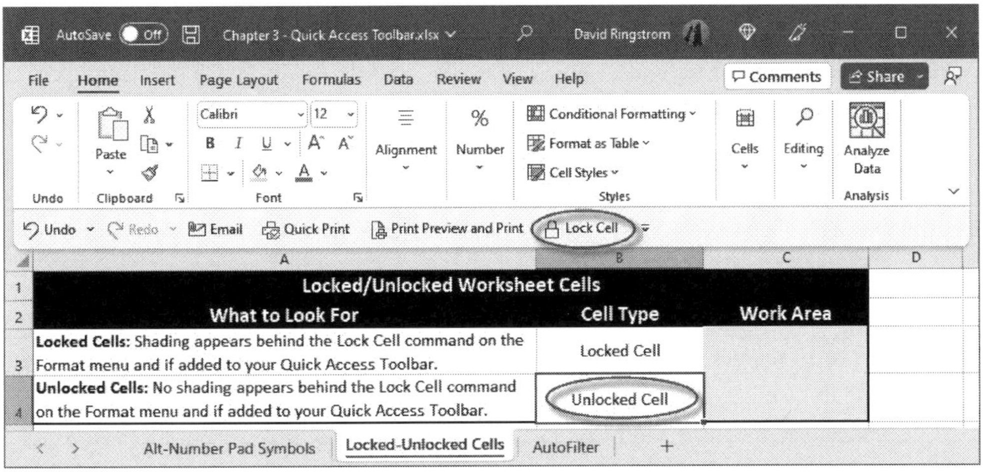

Figure 3.11 – The Lock Cell command indicating an unlocked cell

As you can see, adding the **Lock Cell** command to your toolbar gives you an easy way to monitor and change the locked/unlocked status of cells as you move through a worksheet. Now, let's see how to add commands from Excel's **File** menu to your **Quick Access Toolbar**.

PDF shortcuts

Although you can right-click on **Ribbon** commands in Excel for Windows, you can't right-click on commands within Excel's **File** menu, which means you'll have to go through Excel's **Options** dialog box. You might be surprised to learn that Excel for Windows offers two different commands that enable you to convert spreadsheets into **PDF** files with just a mouse click or a keystroke:

1. Access the **Quick Access Toolbar** section of the **Excel Options** dialog box.
2. Click on **Choose Commands From | File Tab**.
3. Optionally, choose one or both commands:

    - **Email as PDF Attachment** – This command converts the current workbook into a **PDF** file and attaches it to a blank workbook email in your email software, such as **Outlook**.

    - **Publish as PDF or XPS** – This command displays a **Publish as PDF or XPS** dialog box that enables you to save all or part of your workbook as a **PDF** file.

4. Optionally, browse through the **File Tab** commands or other ribbon tab lists to locate commands that you might wish to add to your toolbar.
5. Click on **OK** to close the **Excel Options** dialog box.

> **Tip**
> Click on the **Options** button in the **Publish as PDF or XPS** dialog box to control the page numbers that get sent to the PDF file and allows you to choose from **Selection**, **Active Sheets**, and **Entire Workbook** options. The command defaults to **Active Sheets**.

At this point, you've seen how to add almost any command from Excel's Ribbon or the **File** menu to your **Quick Access Toolbar**. Now, let's go even deeper by exploring the **Commands Not in the Ribbon** collection.

Commands Not in the Ribbon

One of my favorite areas to explore in Excel is the **Commands Not in the Ribbon** listing in the **Quick Access Toolbar** section of Excel's **Options** dialog box. Sometimes, you can find enhanced versions of built-in commands that streamline tasks or enable hidden functionality. In addition, you might be able to unearth and restore commands that Excel has removed from the Ribbon.

Enhanced commands

First, let's look at versions of commands that offer functionality that you can't accomplish through Excel's **Ribbon**. I'll show you how to add and then use the **AutoFilter** command in Excel for Windows, which enables you to filter a list based upon a single cell's contents with one click:

1. Access the **Quick Access Toolbar** section of the **Excel Options** dialog box.
2. Click on **Choose Commands From | Commands Not in the Ribbon**.
3. Click once on **AutoFilter** in the left-hand column. Then, click on **Add** (or double-click on **AutoFilter** to skip the **Add** button).
4. Click on **OK** to close the **Excel Options** dialog box.

> **Tip**
> Right-click on the **Clear** command in the **Data** tab of the Ribbon, and choose **Add to Quick Access Toolbar** to create a shortcut for removing filters from a list while keeping the filter arrows in place.

5. Activate the **AutoFilter** tab of this chapter's example workbook.
6. Click on any cell within the list, and either click on the **AutoFilter** icon in your **Quick Access Toolbar** or tap *Alt* and type in the corresponding shortcut key to filter the list for that item.

> **Nuance**
>
> You can only use the **AutoFilter** command with one cell at a time; if you select two or more cells, no action will be taken. You do not have to turn the **Filter** arrows on in advance; **AutoFilter** will turn the feature on if needed. You can use **AutoFilter** in multiple columns, but you can only filter based on one cell's contents at a time. Finally, **AutoFilter** does not work within the **Table** feature, which I will discuss in *Chapter 7, Automating Excel Tasks with the Table Feature*. In that situation, clicking on **AutoFilter** will simply toggle the **Filter** arrows on and off.

Now, let's look at some other commands in the **Commands Not in the Ribbon** list that you might find helpful:

- **Close All** – Back in the day, if you held down the *Shift* key in **Excel 2003** or earlier, the **Close** command on the **File** menu would change to **Close All**. This offered an easy way to close all open workbooks but still leave Excel open. That *Shift* key trick hasn't worked in any subsequent versions of Excel, but you can add **Close All** to your **Quick Access Toolbar** to give yourself an easy way to close all open spreadsheets at once.

> **Tip**
>
> You will be asked whether you want to save any open workbooks when you click on **Close All**. The confirmation dialog box has a **Save All** button that you can click on to save all open workbooks. However, sometimes, you don't want to save anything. Rather than clicking on **Don't Save** repeatedly, hold down the *Shift* key and click on **Don't Save** to convert the **Don't Save** button into a hidden **Don't Save All** command. The wording on the button won't change but all open workbooks will be closed at once.

- **Custom Views** – In *Chapter 8, Custom Views*, I talk about many ways that you can use **Custom Views** to automate hiding and unhiding worksheets, applying filters and print settings, and more. Adding **Custom Views** from the **Commands Not in the Ribbon** section provides a drop-down list from which you can choose to change views on the fly, eliminating the need to choose **View** | **Custom Views**, choose a view, and then click on **Show**.

> **Tip**
>
> **Custom Views** is a feature that is particularly useful for hiding and unhiding swaths of worksheets in large workbooks, but you will likely only use it for a small percentage of your workbooks. Rather than putting **Custom Views** on my main **Quick Access Toolbar**, I instead like to create workbook-specific toolbars, which I'll discuss in the next section.

- **Freeze Panes** – This command enables you to freeze or unfreeze worksheet panes with a single click or keyboard shortcut. Typically, to freeze panes, you must choose **View** | **Freeze Panes** | **Freeze Panes** (Excel for macOS only requires **View** | **Freeze Panes**).

> **Nuance**
>
> You can right-click on **Freeze Panes** in the **Ribbon** and choose **Add to Quick Access Toolbar**, but that version of the command will require you to interact with the drop-down menu. The **Freeze Panes** command under **Commands Not in the Ribbon** toggles frozen panes on or off with a mouse click or a keyboard shortcut.

- **Print Preview Full Screen** – In **Excel 2010**, Microsoft grafted the **Print Preview** screen into **Backstage View** on the File menu in Excel for Windows. Add this command to your **Quick Access Toolbar** if you miss the classic full-screen print preview that was available up through **Excel 2007**.

I could go on and on about all the goodness buried within the **Commands Not in the Ribbon** section, but I'll stop here. Let's look at how to create **Quick Access Toolbars** that will travel with an individual workbook next.

Workbook-specific toolbars

So far in this chapter, every change we've made to the **Quick Access Toolbar** has been a global change, meaning the commands will be available in every workbook that you open. You can also create toolbars that are specific to individual workbooks, which means that anyone else who opens the workbook will be able to access the custom toolbar. If you add **Custom Views** in the fashion I described in the previous section, most of the time, you'll end up with a blank list consuming space on your toolbar. This technique requires Excel for Windows, as it is not possible in Excel for macOS. Here's how to create a workbook-specific **Quick Access Toolbar**:

1. Access the **Quick Access Toolbar** section of the **Excel Options** dialog box.
2. Choose a workbook name from the **Customize Quick Access Toolbar** list above the second column, on the right-hand side, as shown in *Figure 3.12*:

Figure 3.12 – Workbook-specific Quick Access Toolbar

3. Add any commands you wish to have available when this workbook is active.
4. Click on **OK** to close the **Excel Options** dialog box.

Your default icons will always appear when you activate a workbook that has a custom **Quick Access Toolbar**, followed by any commands that are specific to that workbook. In turn, workbook-specific commands will vanish when you access another workbook.

At this point, I've helped you unlock hundreds of potential commands that you can add to your **Quick Access Toolbar**. However, if Excel doesn't have a command to automate a particular repetitive task, you might be able to add custom features to Excel by recording a macro.

Creating shortcuts for Excel macros

Excel macros are programming code written in **Visual Basic for Applications** (**VBA**). This is a programming language that can automate repetitive tasks in Excel. I could devote a whole book to exploring the concept of macros, but I only have a small amount of space available. Allow me to share a technique that uses Excel's **Macro Recorder** to change the cell color of one or more cells to yellow, which we'll then tie to a **Quick Access Toolbar** icon. Let's begin:

1. Select cell **A1** of a blank worksheet.
2. Choose **View** | **Macros** | **Record Macro…**.
3. Assign a name, such as `YellowHighlight`, in the **Macro Name** field of the **Record Macro** dialog box, as shown in *Figure 3.13*:

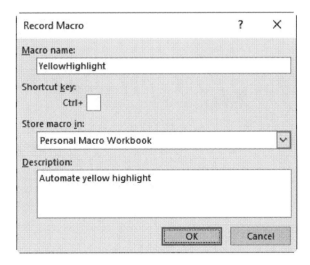

Figure 3.13 – Macro Recorder

> **Nuance**
>
> You cannot use spaces or punctuation when naming Excel macros. The first character of a macro name must be a letter or underscore. You can use numbers in the second position and beyond. Be mindful of using Excel feature names, such as **Merge**, if you were to create a macro for merging cells. You can inadvertently run afoul of using a reserved word in Excel's programing language. When in doubt, an easy workaround is to add a prefix, such as Run, so that your macro is named RunMerge. Doing so will ensure that you avoid the inscrutable error prompts that arise when your macro name inadvertently uses a reserved word.

4. Choose **Personal Macro Workbook** from the **Store Macro In** list, as shown in *Figure 3.13*.

> **Tip**
>
> Any macros that you place in the **Personal Macro Workbook** section will be available for use in any Excel workbook on your computer. It's a great way to automate rote tasks. The **Macro Recorder** feature cannot create macros that involve decision-making, but it is a way to streamline repetitive tasks such as assigning cell colors or applying another formatting that could require multiple steps. The macro recorder is also a stepping stone toward learning more about VBA so that you can write macros that handle more complex tasks or enlist the help of someone with the necessary expertise to do so.

5. Enter Automate yellow highlight into the **Description** field, as shown in *Figure 3.13*.
6. Click on **OK** to start recording your macro.
7. Choose **Home** | **Fill Color**, and choose a color, such as yellow, from the gallery.
8. Choose **View** | **Macros** | **Stop Recording**.

> **Nuance**
>
> Be sure not to click on any other cells while recording this macro; otherwise, you'll potentially create a macro that is tied to specific worksheet cells. If you select cell **A1** before you record the macro and only change the color of the cell and then stop recording, you'll create a macro that can be used for any cell or cells that you select.

At this point, you can run your macro manually:

1. Move your cursor to a new cell (or select several cells at once if you're feeling colorful).
2. Click on the top portion of **View** | **Macros** (or choose **View** | **Macros** | **View Macros**).
3. Double-click on the name of your macro (or click once on the macro name and click on **Run**).

Clearly, this is about the same number of steps, if not more, as choosing a color from the **Fill** gallery. That's why you'll want to create a **Quick Access Toolbar** icon for your macro:

1. Access the **Quick Access Toolbar** section of the **Excel Options** dialog box.
2. Click on **Choose Commands From | Macro**.
3. Double-click on the name of your macro to add it to the **Quick Access Toolbar**, or click once on the macro name and click on **Add**.
4. Optionally, in Excel for Windows, click on the **Modify…** button at the bottom to choose an icon for your command and change the caption to `Yellow Highlight` if you wish, as shown in *Figure 3.14*. The caption field is for display purposes only, which means that spaces are permitted:

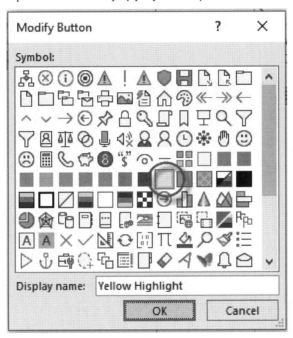

Figure 3.14 – The Modify Button dialog box

> **Nuance**
>
> You can only use the **Modify** button in conjunction with macros that you add to the toolbar. *Figure 3.14* shows a yellow square icon that can be a great option for this macro. You will always see a yellow square on your toolbar if your **Quick Access Toolbar** appears below the **Ribbon**. If your toolbar appears above the **Ribbon**, you will see a white square unless your **Office Theme** is set to **White** or **Use System Setting**. To change the **Office theme**, choose **File**, **Account**, and then select from the **Office Theme** list. You'll see the theme change immediately so that you can revert before you leave the screen if needed.

> **Nuance**
>
> Macros can save a lot of time in Excel, but there's a catch. After you run a macro in Excel, you cannot undo any prior tasks that you carried out during that Excel session. In *Chapter 2, Disaster Recover and File-Related Prompts*, I will show you how to access backup files that Excel might have created earlier in your work session if you need to return to a previous point in your workbook and are unable to undo your past actions.

At some point in the future, **Microsoft 365** might enable us to sync our Excel settings and preferences between two or more computers that we use, much in the way that web browsers can sync our bookmarks. Until that time arrives, you'll have to manually port your settings between computers.

Transferring your Quick Access Toolbar between computers

You can export your toolbar settings to a special file that you can then import into Excel on another computer. You're out of luck in this regard if you use Excel for macOS, but with Excel for Windows, users can conduct the following steps:

1. Access the **Quick Access Toolbar** section of the **Excel Options** dialog box.
2. Click on **Import/Export | Export All Customizations**, as shown in *Figure 3.15*:

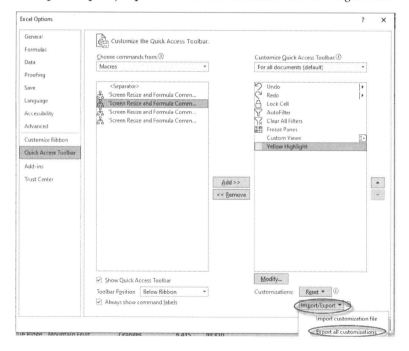

Figure 3.15 – Exporting customizations

3. Optionally, specify a location and/or a new filename.
4. Click on **Save**.
5. Transfer the `.exportUI` file to your new computer, such as via email, or archive the file into a folder of your choice to create a backup of your current customizations.

   Carry out these commands on any other Windows computer where you wish to apply the customizations (or restore the settings on your current computer):
6. Access the **Quick Access Toolbar** section of the **Excel Options** dialog box.
7. Choose **Import/Export | Import Customization File**.
8. Browse and select the `.exportUI` file.
9. Click on **Open**.

All the customizations will be applied to Excel on this computer. If you find that you're not happy with the outcome, see the *Resetting the Quick Access Toolbar* section from earlier. Now, let's see how you can unearth legacy features that Microsoft has removed from Excel's **Ribbon**.

Restoring legacy features

The term *legacy feature* is an epithet Microsoft uses for features that they consider have outlived their useful life. Microsoft rarely removes a feature outright from the software. Typically, deprecated commands get buried in the **Commands Not in the Ribbon** list, much like storing things in a basement or cellar. Let's see how to bring back a couple of features that you might have thought were long gone.

> Nuance
>
> Microsoft did remove the **Workspace** feature in **Excel 2013** and later. Workspaces were a collection of two or more workbooks and their onscreen layout. You still saved each workbook individually, but you could open the collection of workbooks in one fell swoop by opening the workspace file, which had a `.XLW` extension. You can still open workspace files in Excel, but you cannot create new workspaces. The workspace feature was a cousin of the **Binder** feature, which last appeared in Office 2000, and would allow you to create collections of Office documents, meaning Excel workbooks, Word documents, and more.

The Full screen feature

In **Excel 2013**, Microsoft also removed **View | Full Screen** from the **Ribbon**. The **Full Screen** command hides the **Ribbon**, **Formula Bar**, and **Status Bar** sections, which means the worksheet grid completely fills the screen. Let me define a couple of terms to avoid confusion:

- **Ribbon** – Microsoft's name for the tabbed menu interface, which was first introduced in **Excel 2007**.

- **Formula Bar** – A screen element that typically appears above the worksheet grid and below the **Ribbon** that you can turn on or off with **View | Formula Bar**.

- **Status Bar** – Typically, the bottom row of an Excel screen, most often with the word **Ready** at the far left. The **Status Bar** feature gives you information about Excel and your worksheets. There are no built-in options for disabling the **Status Bar** feature if you'd like to add one more row to your worksheet grid, but you can use a bit of VBA code to turn the status bar off or back on:

    I. Press *Alt + F11* to display Excel's **Visual Basic Editor**.

    II. Choose **View** and then **Immediate Window** or press *Ctrl + G (⌘ + G)*.

    III. Type `Application.DisplayStatusBar = False` and then press *Enter* in the **Immediate Window** to permanently hide the status bar. If you change your mind, type `Application.DisplayStatusBar = True` into the **Immediate Window** to restore the status bar.

Full Screen mode makes it easy to see more data on the screen at once and lessens the need to scroll the worksheet. You can press *Escape* at any point to exit **Full Screen**.

Microsoft initially replaced **Full Screen** with the **Autohide Ribbon** command that has since been renamed **Full-screen mode**. As you'll see, **Full-screen mode** behaves differently from **Full Screen**, so let's contrast the two features, because you can resurrect **Full Screen**.

Full-screen mode

Carry out the following steps to enter **Full-screen mode**:

1. Click on the *down arrow* in the right-hand corner of the **Ribbon,** as shown in *Figure 3.16*:

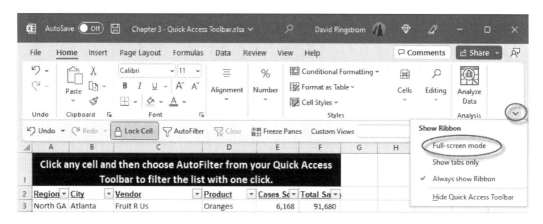

Figure 3.16 – The Full-screen mode command

2. Choose **Full-screen mode**.

> **Nuance**
>
> Your version of Excel might instead have a *down arrow* in the corner of the **Ribbon** that collapses the interface. You can expand the **Ribbon** by double-clicking on any of the tabs. In this case, you'll click on **Ribbon Display Options**, which is the fourth button in the upper-right corner of Excel. Then, you'll choose **Auto-Hide Ribbon** in lieu of **Full-Screen Mode**.

3. Excel hides the **Ribbon** and the status bar but keeps the formula bar and a blank bar across the top of the screen. Click anywhere on the bar to display the **Ribbon**, which will then, frustratingly, obscure the first few rows of your spreadsheet, as shown in *Figure 3.17*:

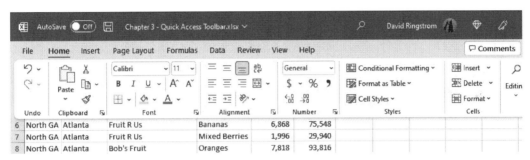

Figure 3.17 – Full-screen mode obscures the worksheet rows

4. Unlike the classic **Full Screen** mode, you cannot just press *Escape* to exit **Full-screen mode** or **Auto-Hide Ribbon**. Instead, you must do the following:

   A. Click on the bar at the top of the screen to display the **Ribbon**.

   B. Click on the **Show Ribbon** button on the right-hand side of the screen (or the **Ribbon Display Options** button at the top of the screen), and then choose **Always Show Ribbon** (or **Show Tabs and Commands**).

The **Show Ribbon/Auto-Hide Ribbon** menus include a **Show Tabs Only** (**Show Tabs**) option that hides the body of the **Ribbon** plus the status bar while keeping the **Ribbon** tabs and formula bar in place. Click on any tab to display the **Ribbon**, which, again, will obscure a few rows of your worksheet.

I think this approach is unnecessarily clunky, particularly when compared to the classic **Full Screen** feature. For instance, you cannot access the **Show Ribbon** or **Ribbon Display Options** menus with your keyboard, so you *have* to use your mouse to enter or exit **Full-Screen Mode**. Now, let's see how to **Full Screen**.

Restoring the Full Screen feature

You can add **Full Screen** to your **Quick Access Toolbar** in Excel for Windows, but unfortunately not Excel for macOS. Here are the steps to use:

1. Access the **Quick Access Toolbar** section of the **Excel Options** dialog box.
2. Choose **Commands From | Commands Not in the Ribbon**.
3. Depending upon your version of Excel, the command is either named **Full Screen (Toggle Full Screen View)** or **Toggle Full Screen View**. You can scroll down the list or click on any command in the list and type g to move near the **Full Screen (Toggle Full Screen View)** command or u to move near **Toggle Full Screen View**.
4. Double-click on **Full Screen (Toggle Full Screen View)** or **Toggle Full Screen View** to skip the **Add** button.
5. Click on **OK** to close the **Excel Options** dialog box.

Now, you're ready to use **Full Screen**:

1. Click on **Full Screen** (or **Toggle Full Screen View**) or tap the *Alt* key and type in the number that appears on the command.
2. Excel hides the **Ribbon**, the formula bar, and the status bar, which lets you see at least two more rows of your worksheet versus **Full-screen mode**.
3. Press *Escape* at any point to exit **Full Screen** mode and restore the **Ribbon**, formula bar, and status bar.

Now you can see much more of your worksheet during the times that you don't need to access the **Ribbon**. Now, let's look at restoring the classic **Share Workbook** feature.

The Share Workbook feature

Historically, **Review | Share Workbook** enabled you to work on a workbook simultaneously with other users. The catch was that all users had to have access to the location of the workbook, which, often, excluded remote users. Microsoft refers to the replacement feature as **co-authoring**, but you won't see the term **co-authoring** in Excel's user interface—it's simply named **Share** and appears in the upper-right corner. The **Share** command allows you to co-author workbooks saved to **OneDrive** with anyone anywhere around the world. If you're unwilling or unable to use **OneDrive**, you can use the **Share Workbook** feature instead:

1. Access the **Quick Access Toolbar** section of the **Excel Options** dialog box.
2. Choose **Commands From | Commands Not in the Ribbon**.
3. Click once on any command in the first column.

4. Type the letter t to jump to the start of the commands that begin with the letter **T**, which will also show you commands that start with the letter **S**.
5. Double-click on **Share Workbook (Legacy)**, or click once on **Share Workbook (Legacy)** and then click on **Add**.
6. Click on **OK** to close the **Excel Options** dialog box.

> **Nuance**
> You can add the **Protect and Share (Legacy)** command along with the classic **Track Changes (Legacy)** command in the same fashion.

Review | Track Changes was removed from the **Ribbon** in **Excel 2016**, although, you can restore the feature by way of the **Quick Access Toolbar**. With that said, **Excel for the Web** has a feature called **Show Changes** that can display changes made in a desktop version.

Show Changes

Show Changes is available in the Excel for the Web, but it can be used to track changes to workbooks that you have edited in any other version of Excel that supports the **co-authoring** feature that I discussed in the previous section. The first step is to save your workbook to **OneDrive**.

> **Tip**
> **Microsoft 365** users receive storage space on **OneDrive** as part of their subscription. Alternatively, you can create a *OneDrive Basic 5 GB* account for free at www.onedrive.com.

To save a spreadsheet to **OneDrive** from within Excel, perform the following steps:

1. Choose **File**, and then select **Save As**.
2. Choose **OneDrive** on the **Save As** screen. You might be prompted to authenticate your account.
3. Assign a name to the file, and then click on **Save**.

Another approach that you can take is to enable **AutoSave** in the upper-left corner of any Excel screen. When you toggle **AutoSave** on, Excel will walk you through saving the file to **OneDrive**. I discuss **AutoSave** in more detail in *Chapter 2, Disaster Recovery and File-Related Prompts*.

> **Nuance**
> **Excel for the Web** only allows you to access Excel workbooks that have a .xlsx file extension that is 25 MB in size or less, plus workbooks cannot contain any macros. Excel for the Web will inform you if you attempt to open a file that violates any of these restrictions.

Microsoft is slowly creating a divide between users that subscribe to **Microsoft 365** versus those that use a *single-purchase* version of Excel—any version of Excel that has a year number in its name. For instance, any tracked changes will be erased when you open a workbook edited in one of those versions in Excel for the Web. To view changes in a workbook, perform the following steps:

1. Log into **Office Online** at `https://office.com`.
2. Choose a recent workbook from the **Recent** list, or click on the **Excel** icon along the left-hand side to view a **Recent** list that only shows **Excel** workbooks.
3. Choose **Review | Show Changes** to display the **Changes** task pane, as shown in *Figure 3.18*, which lists all changes made in the last 60 days:

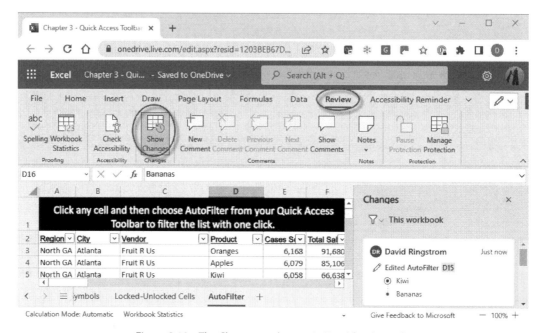

Figure 3.18 – The Changes task pane in Excel for the Web

4. Optionally, click on the **Filters** button near the top of the task pane to filter the changes by **Range** or by **Sheet**.
5. Optionally, if you wish to collapse the task pane, click on the right arrow on the upper-right edge of the task pane. Then, you can click on the resulting left arrow that appears to expand the task pane again.
6. Click on the close button represented by an **X** icon in the upper-right corner of the task pane once you have reviewed the changes in your workbook.

Microsoft is using **Excel for the Web** and Excel Mobile as test platforms for new features such as this, so it's likely, at some point in the future, we'll see this **Show Changes** feature make its way into the desktop versions of Excel. For instance, Excel Mobile has offered the ability to convert pictures of text and numbers into editable data for several years now. As of this writing, that feature is being beta tested in the desktop versions of **Microsoft 365**.

Summary

In this chapter, first, you saw how the **Quick Access Toolbar** is evolving in **Microsoft 365** and how to unhide the toolbar if needed. The **Quick Access Toolbar** allows you to create up to 44 custom keyboard shortcuts in Excel for Windows, but if you're not aware of the nuance, you might be baffled why, let's say, a heart or spade appears in your worksheet cell instead of carrying out a command. We always *hold down* the *Ctrl* key when executing a shortcut such as *Ctrl + Z*, but we must use an alternate behavior for the *Alt* key. Remember to *tap* the *Alt* key if you want to your number pad to execute a shortcut. You have complete control over the order of your icons, which enables you to prioritize the keyboard shortcuts.

We explored ways to create shortcuts for **Ribbon** commands that don't have shortcuts, and we dug into the **Commands Not in the Ribbon** area to unearth commands that can streamline repetitive tasks. You can add commands to your default **Quick Access Toolbar**, or you can create workbook-specific **Quick Access Toolbars**.

Sometimes, there just is not a command for a task that you want to streamline, so we explored how to use the **Macro Recorder** feature to automate rote tasks. If you invest a lot of time curating your **Quick Access Toolbar**, you will likely want to back it up, perhaps transfer it to a new computer, or share your handiwork with a colleague. The transfer is easy to accomplish in Excel for Windows. Some of the techniques I shared in this chapter are not available in Excel for macOS, but the **Quick Access Toolbar** can still be a valuable resource on that platform.

Then, we looked at how to restore legacy features in Excel—Microsoft's term for features they wish to retire but that you might wish to keep using. As you saw with **Full Screen**, replacement functionality Microsoft adds to Excel isn't necessarily better than what it replaces. Sometimes, the replacement functionality, such as for Track Changes, doesn't even exist in the desktop version yet, as evidenced by the **Show Changes** feature in Excel for the Web.

In *Chapter 4, Conditional Formatting*, I'll show you how you can enliven data in your workbooks with color, cell formatting, and even in-cell charts and icons.

4
Conditional Formatting

In this chapter, I'll show you the wonders of Excel's **Conditional Formatting** feature that can help you enliven your data with color, charts, or icons. You can, of course, use all three at once, but usually, less is more when it comes to data visualization. **Conditional Formatting** is a live overlay for worksheet cells that dynamically applies formatting such as font color, cell color, borders, and number formatting, based upon the cell contents matching specific criteria. The built-in **Conditional Formatting** rules eliminate the need to manually color-code data, and you can extend this functionality in limitless ways by crafting custom rules. Along the way, I'll point out nuances that frustrate even the most experienced spreadsheet users.

In this chapter, I'll cover the following:

- Formatting versus **Conditional Formatting**
- **Highlight Cell Rules**
- **Top and Bottom Rules**
- **Data Bars**
- **Color Scales**
- **Icon Sets**
- Wingdings symbols
- Custom rules
- Managing **Conditional Formatting** rules
- Removing **Conditional Formatting**
- **Conditional Formatting** nuances

By the end of the chapter, you'll see numerous ways that **Conditional Formatting** can identify and illustrate data based on criteria that you specify. Twenty years ago, Excel had a limit of no more than three **Conditional Formatting** rules per worksheet, but now there is no practical limit to the number of rules that you can apply to a worksheet.

Technical requirements

Everything in this chapter will work the same in Excel for macOS and Excel for Windows.

At the time of writing, Microsoft has made some changes to the **Conditional Formatting** feature in **Excel for the Web** that will most likely make their way into the desktop versions of Excel. Excel for the Web has emerged as a proving ground for user interface changes that Microsoft is contemplating.

The workbook that I used in this chapter is available for download from GitHub at `https://github.com/PacktPublishing/Exploring-Microsoft-Excels-Hidden-reasures/tree/main/Chapter04`.

Formatting versus Conditional Formatting

In Excel, you can apply a wide variety of formatting to cells by way of the **Format Cells** dialog box. As you'll see, Conditional Formatting utilizes a subset of the **Format Cells** dialog box, which means you can apply almost all of the same formatting with **Conditional Formatting**. Let's compare the two:

1. Choose **Home** | **Format** | **Format Cells**, or press *Ctrl + 1* (⌘ *+ 1* in Excel for macOS).
2. As shown in *Figure 4.1*, the **Format Cells** dialog box has six tabs that allow you to control every aspect of formatting within a worksheet cell:

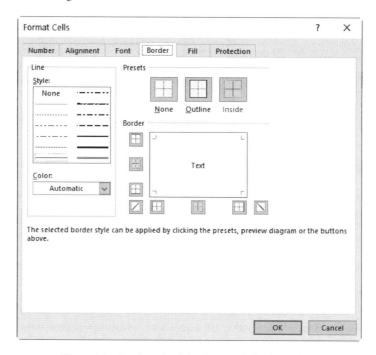

Figure 4.1 – Border tab of the Format Cells dialog box

3. **Optional**: click on each tab to review the available formatting.
4. Click **Cancel** to close the **Format Cells** dialog box.

Let's now have a look at the **Conditional Formatting** version of the **Format Cells** dialog box:

1. Choose **Home | Conditional Formatting | New Rule | Use a Formula to Determine Which Cells to Format**, and then click the **Format…** button.
2. The abbreviated version of the **Format Cells** dialog box appears, with four tabs instead of six, as shown in *Figure 4.2*. Note how this version of the **Border** tab has fewer styles than the **Border** tab shown in *Figure 4.1*. Also, certain styles, such as diagonal, cannot be applied.

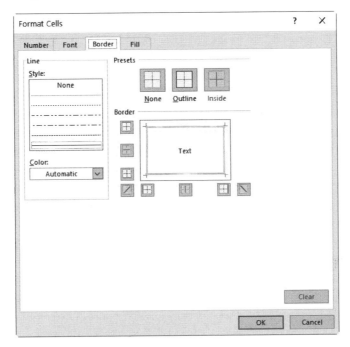

Figure 4.2 – **Conditional Formatting** version of the Format Cells dialog box

3. **Optional**: Click on each tab to review the available formatting.
4. We'll make use of this dialog box later in the chapter, so for now, click **Cancel** twice to close the **Conditional Formatting** dialog boxes.

As you can see, **Conditional Formatting** allows you to apply one or more of the following formats to any range of cells in your worksheet:

- Number formatting
- Underline

- Strikethrough
- Font colors
- Bold
- Italics
- Certain cell borders
- Background colors
- Cell patterns
- Fill effects

Conversely, you cannot apply any of the following formats to cells with **Conditional Formatting**:

- Font names
- Font sizes
- Superscript or subscript
- Alignment aspects, such as centering
- Cell border styles and positions
- Protection settings, such as unlocking or hiding cell contents

You can, however, go beyond the **Format Cells** dialog box by conditionally applying **data bars**, **color scales**, and **icon sets**. Further, you can apply as many **Conditional Formatting** rules to a range of cells as you wish. Let's see how to apply **Conditional Formatting** to a range of cells, starting with the highlight cells rules.

> **Nuance**
>
> Long-time Excel users may recall that Excel 2003 and earlier had a limit of three **Conditional Formatting** rules per cell. There's no limit to the number of rules that you can apply in Excel 2007 and onward.

Highlight cell rules

The **Home** | **Conditional Formatting** | **Highlight Cells Rules** submenu offers eight different options. I'll discuss the first seven here and then cover the **More Rules** command later in the chapter in the *Custom rules* section. I'll demonstrate the **Greater Than** and **Less Than** rules, and then briefly discuss the other rules, since all are applied in the same fashion. The **Greater Than-Less Than-Between** worksheet in the example workbook has three rules applied to cells **D6:D25**. Let's first apply the **Greater Than** rule to the **Work Area** section of the worksheet.

Greater Than

As you may expect, the **Greater Than** rule allows you to apply formatting to cells that contain numbers or dates that are greater than a specific value. Let's assign a color to every road that is greater than **8,000 miles**:

1. Select a range of cells, such as **J3:J22**, on the **Greater Than-Less Than-Between** worksheet in this chapter's example workbook, as shown in *Figure 4.3*.

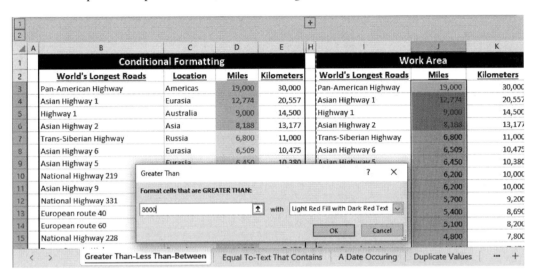

Figure 4.3 – Greater Than **Conditional Formatting** rule

2. Choose **Home | Conditional Formatting | Highlight Cells Rules | Greater Than**.
3. Enter 8000 in the **Format cells that are GREATER THAN** field, as shown in *Figure 4.3*. A preview of the default formatting **Light Red Fill with Dark Red Text** should appear in cells **J6:J9**.
4. Click **OK** to close the **Conditional Formatting** dialog box and accept the default formatting of **Light Red Fill with Dark Red Text**.

> **Nuance**
>
> Unlike most formatting that you apply to cells, **Conditional Formatting** is a live layer of formatting. If you change cell **J3** to be a number less than 8,000, you'll see that the formatting vanishes. Conversely, cell **J10** will be formatted in red if you change its value to greater than 8,000.

Now, let's apply the **Less Than** rule to the same set of cells.

Less Than

The **Less Than** rule allows you to apply formatting to cells that contain numbers or dates that are less than a specific value. Let's assign a second color to roads that are less than 4,000 miles long:

1. Select a range of cells, such as **J3:J22**, of the **Greater Than-Less Than-Between** worksheet, as shown in *Figure 4.4*.

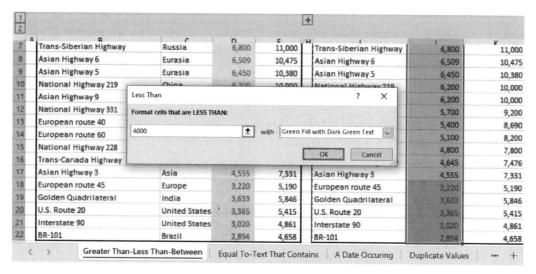

Figure 4.4 – Less Than **Conditional Formatting** rule

2. Choose **Home | Conditional Formatting | Highlight Cells Rules | Less Than**.
3. Enter 4000 in the **Format Cells that are LESS THAN** field, as shown in *Figure 4.4*.
4. Choose **Green Fill with Dark Green Text** from the **with** dropdown, as shown in *Figure 4.4*.
5. Click **OK** to close the **Conditional Formatting** dialog box.

Let's apply one final rule to this worksheet, which will format cells that are between 4,000 and 8,000 miles long.

Between

The **Between** rule allows you to apply formatting to cells that contain numbers or dates that are between two values. Let's assign a third color:

1. Select a range of cells, such as **J3:J22**, of the **Greater Than-Less Than-Between** worksheet.
2. Choose **Home | Conditional Formatting | Highlight Cells Rules | Between**.
3. Enter 4000 and 8000 in the **Format Cells that are BETWEEN** fields, as shown in *Figure 4.5*.

Highlight cell rules

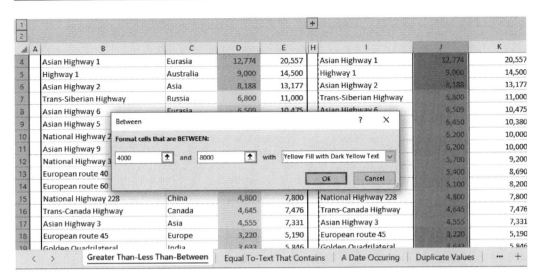

Figure 4.5 – Between Conditional Formatting rule

4. Choose **Yellow Fill with Dark Yellow Text** from the **with** dropdown, as shown in *Figure 4.5*.
5. Click **OK** to close the **Conditional Formatting** dialog box.

> **Nuance**
>
> The **Between** rule includes the values that you enter in the **Conditional Formatting** dialog box. This means that if you change cell **J9** to 8000, it will become formatted in yellow instead of red. Enter 7999 instead of 8000 in the respective value fields if you want amounts *greater than or equal to 8,000* to be formatted in red.

You may have noticed that cells **B2:H4** contain a legend that documents the **Conditional Formatting** rules. This helps users understand the color scheme that is in place. I'll describe how to create a legend like this in the *Managing conditional formatting* section later in this chapter. Now that you see that you can apply multiple levels of **Conditional Formatting** to a range of cells, let's see how to go beyond the default formatting choices from the **with** dropdown list and pick your own formatting when we apply the **Equal To** rule.

Equal To

The **Equal To** rule formats cells that are equal to the value that you specify, which can be text, numbers, or dates:

1. Select a range of cells, such as **H3:H22** of the **Equal To-Text That Contains** worksheet.
2. Choose **Home** | **Conditional Formatting** | **Highlight Cells Rules** | **Equal To**.

3. Enter Asia in the **Format cells that are EQUAL TO** field, as shown in *Figure 4.6*.

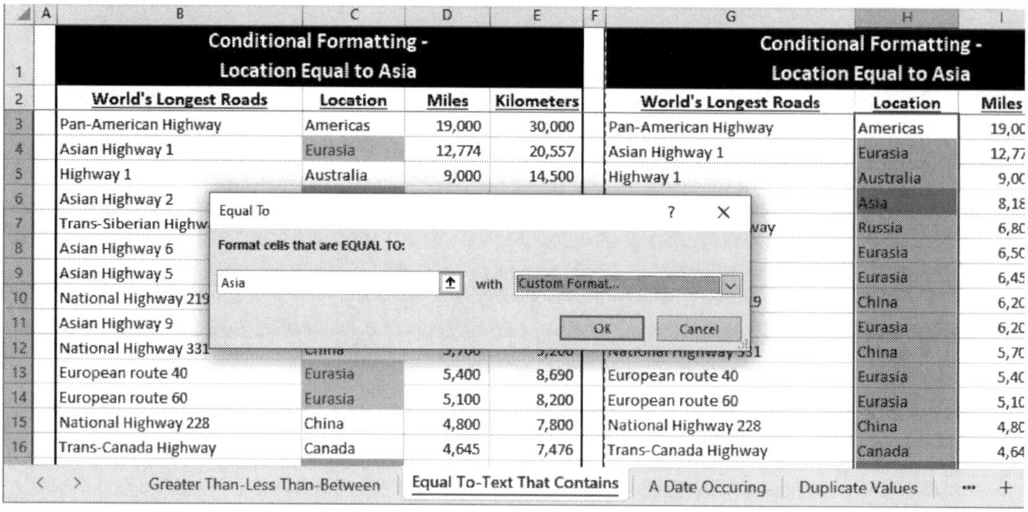

Figure 4.6 – Equal To **Conditional Formatting** rule

> **Nuance**
>
> **Conditional Formatting** is not case sensitive, which means that you can enter asia, ASIA, or even aSiA in the **Format cells that are EQUAL TO** field to format all cells that contain Asia.

4. Choose **Custom Format…** from the **with** dropdown to display the **Format Cells** dialog box, as shown previously in *Figure 4.2*.
5. Choose a color from the **Fill** tab, such as a shade of blue, along with any other formatting you want, such as **Bold** from the **Font** tab.
6. Click **OK** twice to close the **Format Cells** and **Conditional Formatting** dialog boxes.

Now, let's apply a second rule to this set of cells by applying the **Text That Contains** rule, which will also illustrate how easy it is to create a conflict between **Conditional Formatting** rules.

Text That Contains

The **Text That Contains** rule allows you to format cells that are full or partial matches on the text that you enter:

1. Select a range of cells, such as **H3:H22** of the **Equal To-Text That Contains** worksheet.
2. Choose **Home | Conditional Formatting | Highlight Cells Rules | Text That Contains**.
3. Enter Asia in the **Format cells that contain the text:** field, as shown in *Figure 4.7*.

Highlight cell rules

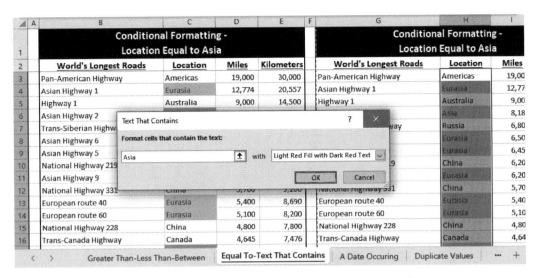

Figure 4.7 – Text That Contains **Conditional Formatting** rule

> **Nuance**
>
> The **Text That Contains** rule can be applied to numbers as well. For instance, you can select cells **I3:I22** and enter 5 in the **Format cells that contain the text:** field to format all cells that contain the digit **5**.

4. Click **OK** to close the **Conditional Formatting** dialog box and accept the default formatting of **Light Red Fill with Dark Red Text**.

> **Nuance**
>
> Note how both **Asia** and **Eurasia** are formatted in red, even though you previously set the cells that contain Asia to be in blue. In this case, the **Text That Contains** rule is being applied *before* the **Equals** rule, which results in the **Asia** and **Eurasia** cells being formatting in red, while the **Asia** cells are also marked in bold. I'll show you how to resolve this in the *Troubleshooting conditional formatting* section at the end of the chapter.

Now, let's see how to apply formatting to ranges of dates.

A Date Occurring

The **A Date Occurring** rule allows you to format dates within a timeframe that you specify. The following choices are available:

- **Yesterday**
- **Today**

- **Tomorrow**
- **In the last 7 days**
- **Last week**
- **This week**
- **Next week**
- **Last Month**
- **This month**
- **Next month**

The **A Date Occurring** worksheet in this chapter's example workbook has three rules applied to cells **B2:B63** that dynamically assign different colors to dates that fall in last week, this week, and next week. Here are the steps if you'd like to follow along in the work area:

1. Select cells **H2:H63** on the **A Date Occurring** worksheet.
2. Choose **Home | Conditional Formatting | Highlight Cells Rules | A Date Occurring**.
3. Choose **Last week** from the **Format cells that contain a date occurring:** dropdown, as shown in *Figure 4.8*, and then click **OK** to accept the default formatting.

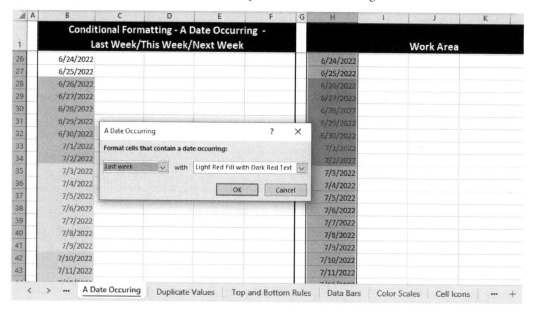

Figure 4.8 – A Date Occurring Conditional Formatting rule

4. Choose **Home | Conditional Formatting | Highlight Cells Rules | A Date Occurring**.

Highlight cell rules

5. Choose **This week** from the **Format cells that contain a date occurring:** dropdown, choose **Yellow Fill with Dark Yellow Text** from the **with** dropdown, and then click **OK**.
6. Choose **Home | Conditional Formatting | Highlight Cells Rules | A Date Occurring**.
7. Choose **Next week** from the **Format cells that contain a date occurring:** dropdown, choose **Green Fill with Dark Green Text** from the **with** dropdown, and then click **OK**.

Since **Conditional Formatting** is a live layer, the date formatting that you see today may shift when you open the workbook tomorrow and certainly if you open the workbook again next week.

> **Nuance**
>
> Any **Conditional Formatting** rule that allows you to enter a numeric value accepts dates as well. This means that you can use one or more other rules instead of **A Date Occurring** if you need to format dates in a fashion that is not possible with the previous choices.

Now, let's see how to identify duplicates within a list.

Duplicate Values

Duplicate Values is my favorite way to quickly identify duplicate or unique values within a list. As you'll see, you can then filter the list based on color to work with a subset of the data. Here's how to apply the rule:

1. Select a range of cells, such as cells **E4:E18**, of the **Duplicate Values** worksheet in *Figure 4.9*.

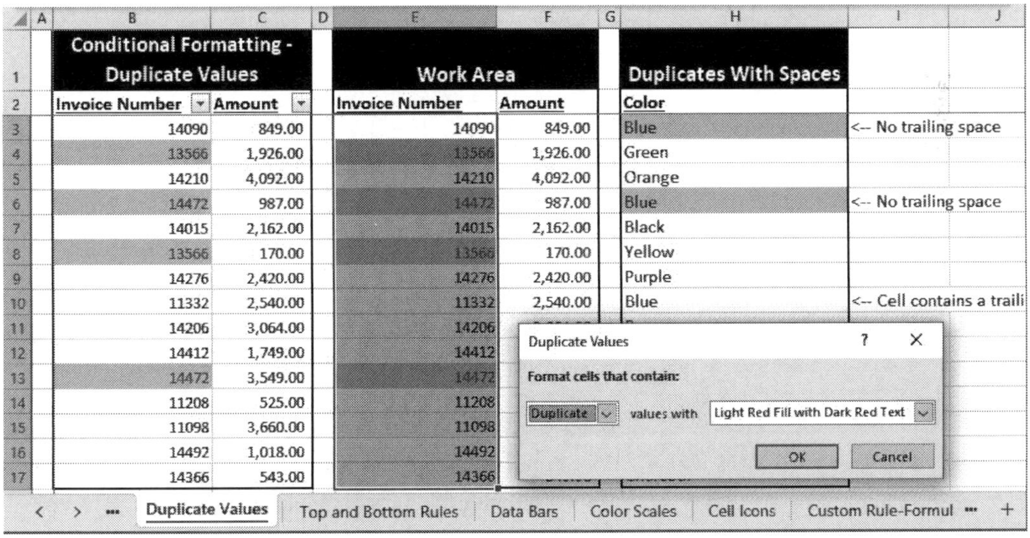

Figure 4.9 – **Conditional Formatting**

2. Choose **Home | Highlight Cells Rules | Duplicate Values**.

3. Accept the default choice of **Duplicate** from the **Format cells that contain:** dropdown or choose **Unique**.

4. Optionally assign formatting of your choice and then click **OK**.

> **Tip**
>
> I will discuss ways to create new lists that are free of duplicates in *Chapter 10, Lookup and Dynamic Array Functions*.

5. **Optional**: Right-click any of the duplicate cells and then choose **Filter | Filter by Selected Cells Value**.

6. **Optional**: Change the value of cell **E5** to `13566a` to see the color-coding will vanish from cells **E5** and **E9** because the cells will no longer be duplicates.

7. **Optional: Data | Reapply** or **Home | Sort & Filter | Reapply** to apply the filter again, which will hide rows **5** and **9**.

8. Choose **Data | Filter** or **Home | Sort & Filter | Reapply** to turn the filter feature off and display all the rows again.

> **Nuance**
>
> The word **Blue** appears three times in cells **H3:H17** of the **Duplicate Values** worksheet, but the **Duplicate Values Conditional Formatting** rule I applied only formatted the first two instances. This is because the third instance has the word *Blue* with a trailing space. Users often inadvertently bump the space bar when entering data, which can create inconsistencies. Excel's `TRIM` function offers an easy way to eliminate extraneous spaces.

Now that we have reviewed all the **Highlight Cells** rules, let's take a brief look at the **top and bottom** rules.

Top and bottom rules

The top and bottom rules allow you to identify values based on their relative positions within a list. Four out of the six reference **10 Items** or **10%**, but you can enter any number or percentage that you wish. To apply any of these rules, do the following:

1. Select a range of cells that you wish to format, such as cells **H3:H22**, of the **Top and Bottom Rules** worksheet in this chapter's example workbook.

2. Choose **Home | Conditional Formatting | Top/Bottom Rules** and then select a rule:

   - **Top 10 Items**: Formats the 10 largest values in the list unless you specify a different value

- **Top 10%**: Formats 10% of the largest values in the list unless you specify a different value

> **Nuance**
> The percentage is based on the number of items on your list. If your list has 90 items and you specify **Top 10%**, the **Conditional Formatting** feature will multiply **90** by **10** to determine that the **9** largest values should be formatted.

- **Bottom 10 Items**: Formats the 10 smallest values in the list unless you specify a different value
- **Bottom 10%**: Formats 10% of the largest values in the list unless you specify a different value
- **Above Average**: Formats cells that exceed the average, meaning that in a list that contains the numbers 1 to 10 that amounts 6 through 10 would be formatted
- **Below Average**: Formats cells that are less the average, meaning that in a list that contains the numbers 1 to 10 that amounts 1 through 5 would be formatted

3. **Optional**: Enter a number or percentage if the rule allows.
4. **Optional**: Assign formatting of your choice.
5. Click **OK** to close the **Conditional Formatting** dialog box.

Now, let's look at using **Data Bars** to illustrate your data with in-cell charts.

Data Bars

Data Bars are charts that appear within cells to provide a sense of proportionate scale within a column of numbers. As you'll see, numbers can appear in the cell with the charts, or you can hide the numbers. Cells **D3:D22** of the **Data Bars** worksheet in the example workbook for this chapter show how numbers and **Data Bars** can coexist in the same cell. To create this type of formatting, do the following:

1. Select a range of cells that contain numbers, such as **K3:K22** of the **Data Bars** worksheet.
2. Choose **Home | Conditional Formatting | Data Bars** and select from the **Gradient Fill** or **Solid Fill** sections.

> **Tip**
> Most **Conditional Formatting** rules in the desktop versions of Excel offer live previews as you craft a rule, or when you hover your mouse over a particular data bar, color scale, or icon set.

3. As shown in *Figure 4.10*, the **Data Bars** are commensurate with the size of the numbers in a cell in comparison to the other numbers in the list. Thus, the largest values will have the longest **Data Bars**, and the smallest values will have the shortest **Data Bars**.

	A	B	C	D	E	F	G H	I	
1			Conditional Formatting - Data Bars						
2		World's Longest Roads	Location	Miles	Show Bar Only	Kilometers		World's Longest Roads	Lo
3		Pan-American Highway	Americas	19,000		30,000		Pan-American Highway	Amer
4		Asian Highway 1	Eurasia	12,774		20,557		Asian Highway 1	Euras
5		Highway 1	Australia	9,000		14,500		Highway 1	Austr
6		Asian Highway 2	Asia	8,188		13,177		Asian Highway 2	Asia
7		Trans-Siberian Highway	Russia	6,800		11,000		Trans-Siberian Highway	Russi
8		Asian Highway 6	Eurasia	6,509		10,475		Asian Highway 6	Euras
9		Asian Highway 5	Eurasia	6,450		10,380		Asian Highway 5	Euras
10		National Highway 219	China	6,200		10,000		National Highway 219	China
11		Asian Highway 9	Eurasia	6,200		10,000		Asian Highway 9	Euras
12		National Highway 331	China	5,700		9,200		National Highway 331	China
13		European route 40	Eurasia	5,400		8,690		European route 40	Euras
14		European route 60	Eurasia	5,100		8,200		European route 60	Euras
15		National Highway 228	China	4,800		7,800		National Highway 228	China
16		Trans-Canada Highway	Canada	4,645		7,476		Trans-Canada Highway	Cana
17		Asian Highway 3	Asia	4,555		7,331		Asian Highway 3	Asia
18		European route 45	Europe	3,220		5,190		European route 45	Europ
19		Golden Quadrilateral	India	3,633		5,846		Golden Quadrilateral	India

Figure 4.10 – Data Bars Conditional Formatting

Alternatively, you can show amounts in one column and data bars in the second column:

1. Select cells **L3:L22** of the **Data Bars** worksheet, which contains the same numbers present in cells **K3:K22**.
2. Choose **Home | Conditional Formatting | Data Bars | More Rules…**.
3. Click the **Show Bar Only** checkbox and then click **OK**.

Data Bars are one of many tools you can use in Excel to create a dashboard, which is a spreadsheet that presents a large amount of information in as small a space as possible, typically with graphics that can be comprehended immediately. For instance, cells **O3:P14** illustrate how a mix of positive and negative values are presented, as shown in *Figure 4.11*.

Color Scales

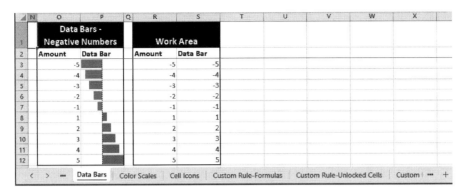

Figure 4.11 – **Data Bars** presenting negative and positive amounts

Next, let's look at how to apply color scales by way of **Conditional Formatting**.

Color Scales

Color Scales are an easy way to create a heat map within your data, and assign colors based on a number's proportionate scale within a list. Here are the steps:

1. **Optional**: Sort the amounts in ascending or descending order.
2. Select a range of cells that contain numbers, such as cells **I3:I22** in the **Color Scales** worksheet of this chapter's example workbook.
3. Choose **Home | Conditional Formatting | Color Scales**, and then choose a **Color Scale** grouping to create a heat map, such as cells **D3:D22** in *Figure 4.12*.

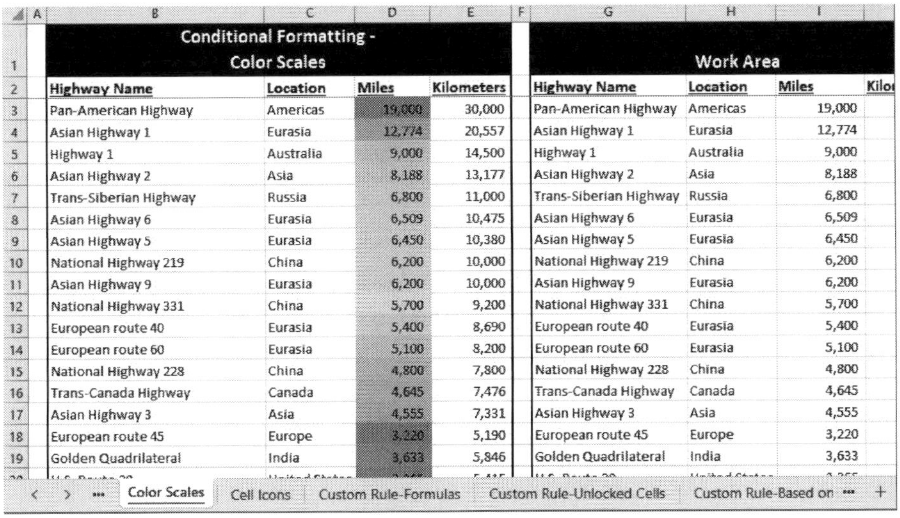

Figure 4.12 – Color scales **Conditional Formatting**

> **Nuance**
> As with data bars, you can choose **More Rules** to fine-tune the presentation of the formatting.

Now, let's look at the **Icon Sets** rule, which offers yet another way to graphically present your data.

Icon Sets

Icon Sets, also known as **Cell Icons**, are in-cell graphical indicators that provide a sense of scale or value relative to other numbers in your list. As with Data Bars, you can choose to show numbers and icons in the same cell or hide the numbers and only show the icons. By default, **Icon Sets** group amounts based upon percentages, but you can edit the rule to use percentiles instead. Here are the default percentages that Excel uses and how they're calculated:

- **67th percent**: This calculation takes the form *smallest value from the list plus .67 multiplied by (largest value minus smallest value)*. This is illustrated by the formula =MIN(D8:D27)+0.67*(MAX(D8:D27)-MIN(D8:D27)) in cell **C2** of the **Cell Icons – Percent** worksheet. The MIN function returns the smallest value in a range, while the MAX function returns the largest. As shown in cell **D2**, this calculates as **72.03%**, which means any amounts that are greater than the largest value in the list multiplied by **72.03%** will be formatted with the first icon in the set.

- **33rd percent**: This calculation takes the form *smallest value from the list plus .33 multiplied by (largest value minus smallest value)*. This is illustrated by the formula =MIN(D8:D27)+0.33*(MAX(D8:D27)-MIN(D8:D27)) in cell **C3**. As shown in cell **D3**, this calculates out to **43.21%**, which means any amounts that are less than the largest value in the list multiplied by **43.21%** will be formatted with the third icon in the set.

- **34th through 66th percent**: In this case, any amounts greater than **43.21%** of the largest value and less than **72.03%** of the largest value are formatted with the second icon in the set.

> **Nuance**
> **Icon Sets** that have four icons base these calculations on 25%, 50%, and 75%, while **Icon Sets** that have five icons use 20%, 40%, 60%, and 80% to determine the brackets.

To apply **Cell Icons** based upon percentages, do the following:

1. Select a range of cells, such as **I8:I27**, on the **Cell Icons** worksheet.
2. Choose **Home | Conditional Formatting | Icon Sets** and then choose an **Icon Sets** (e.g., directional, shapes, indicators, or ratings).
3. Cells **D8:D27** in *Figure 4.13* give a sense of what **Cell Icons** look like when applied to a range of cells with the **Percent** grouping default.

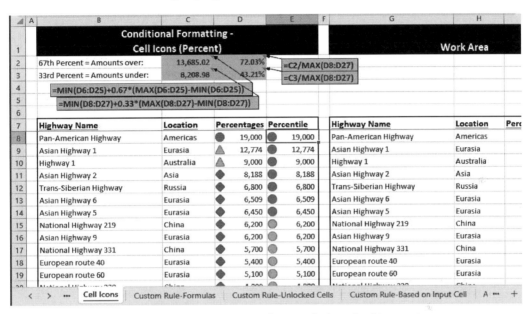

Figure 4.13 – Percentage and percentile-based cell icons

Alternatively, you can apply **Icon Sets** based upon percentiles to group the amounts into thirds, as shown in cells **E3:E28** of *Figure 4.13*:

1. Select a range of cells, such as **J8:J27**.
2. Choose **Home | Conditional Formatting | Icon Sets | More Rules….**

3. Choose **Percentile** from the **Type** dropdowns within the **Edit Formatting Rule** dialog box, as shown in *Figure 4.14*.

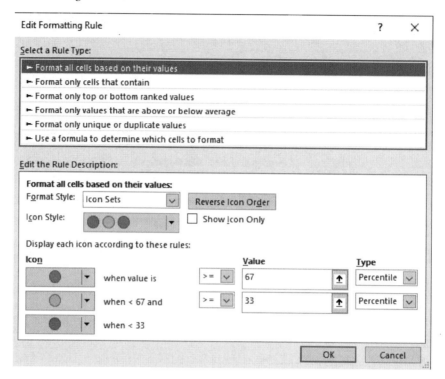

Figure 4.14 – Editing Icon Sets rule to use percentiles

4. Click **OK** to close the **Edit Formatting Rule** dialog box.

> **Nuance**
>
> You're not limited to grouping by thirds, as you can adjust the values in the **Edit Formatting Rule** dialog box as needed. You can also choose an **Icon Set** that has four icons to divide the amounts into quarters, or choose five icons if you wish to illustrate quintiles.

5. **Optional**: Right-click on any **Cell Icon**, and then choose **Filter** and **Filter by Cell Icon** to collapse the list down to just an amount with a particular icon.

> **Nuance**
>
> You can also filter by choosing **Data | Filter** or **Home | Sort & Filter | Filter**. Click the filter arrow for the column that contains your Cell Icons, choose **Filter by Color**, and then choose an icon. It's easy to overlook this functionality, since the menu doesn't toggle to **Filter by Cell Icon**.

Now that we have explored all the built-in **Conditional Formatting** rules, let's see how you can take things further by creating your own rules.

Custom rules

Custom **Conditional Formatting** rules give you the ability to test for any condition that can be expressed as a logical test. Excel offers an array of IS functions that test for various conditions and return TRUE or FALSE. The CELL function also returns the equivalent of TRUE or FALSE. You also use the *logical_test* portion of what you would enter in an IF formula to create a TRUE or FALSE calculation as well. Let's see create a rule that will mark a cell in red if a user overwrites a formula with a static value, also known as a constant in Excel.

IS functions

Examples of IS functions include ISBLANK, ISNUMBER, and ISTEXT. Each IS function has a single reference argument where you reference a cell that you wish to test, and the function returns TRUE or FALSE. Let's create a custom **Conditional Formatting** rule that will make a cell turn red if the user types over a formula:

1. Select a range of cells, such as **J10:L57**, on the **Custom Rules – Formulas** worksheet.
2. Choose **Home | Conditional Formatting | New Rule… | Use a formula to determine which cells to format**.
3. Enter =ISFORMULA(J10)=FALSE in the **Format values where this formula is true** field.

> **Nuance**
> Press the *F2* (or *Fn + F2*) key if you want to be able to use the arrow keys to move left or right within a field such as **Format values where this formula Is true**. Fields such as these default to **Enter mode**, which means the cursor moves around in the worksheet, and cell references are inserted into the field when you touch the arrow keys. **Edit mode** is particularly helpful when you have a formula that extends beyond the visible portion of the field.

4. Click the **Format** button and choose a color from the **Fill** tab, such as bright red.
5. Click **OK** twice to close the dialog boxes.

To test the functionality, enter the number 1 into any cell in the **J11:L57** range. The cell should turn red, as shown in the case of cell **E11** in *Figure 4.15*. In the case of this worksheet, you can press *Ctrl + '* and then *Enter* to restore the formula, at which point the red formatting should vanish.

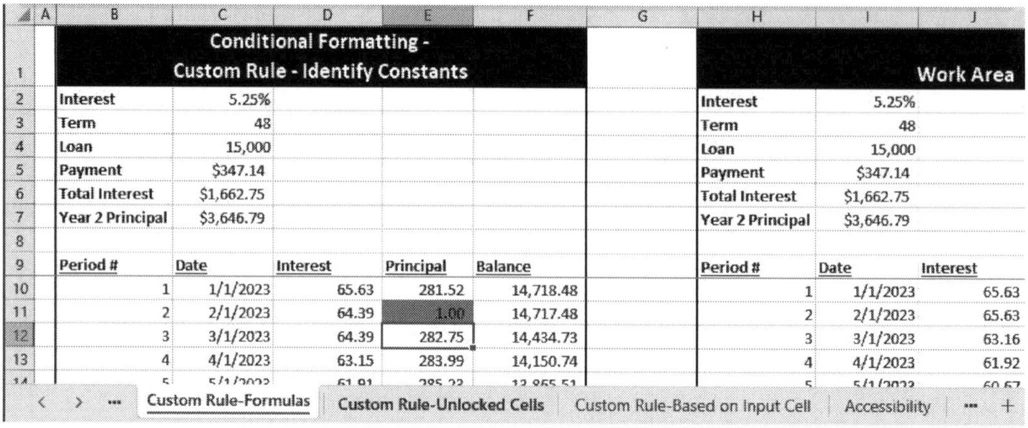

Figure 4.15 – A custom Conditional Formatting rule identifying an overwritten formula

> **Nuance**
>
> **Conditional Formatting** is easy to erase by simply copying and pasting over a cell. For instance, enter the number 1 into cell **N1** and then press *Ctrl + C* (⌘ + C) to copy the value to the clipboard. Navigate to any cell formatted with **Conditional Formatting**, such as J11, and then press *Enter* to paste the value. Note how the formula is now overwritten, and there's no color coding because pasting from other cells overwrites **Conditional Formatting**.

The best practice is to protect worksheets that contain formulas by choosing **Review | Protect Sheet**, optionally entering a password, and then clicking **OK**. In *Chapter 3, Quick Access Toolbar Treasures*, I discussed how to unlock cells that you want the user to be able to change. Let's now see how to create a **Conditional Formatting** rule that will identify the unlocked cells in a worksheet.

CELL function

The CELL function returns information about a worksheet cell, such as the column width or the filename where the cell is located in. The function can also determine whether a worksheet cell is marked as locked or unlocked. The function has two arguments:

- **Info_type**: A text-based value that describes the type of information that you wish to return. In this context, we'll use the `"protect"` *info_type* value to determine whether a cell is locked or unlocked. This info type is only available in the desktop versions of Excel, as it is not available in **Excel for the Web**, **Excel Mobile**, or **Excel Starter**. Other *info_type* values include but are not limited to `"width"` to return a column width or `"filename"` to return the file path, filename, and worksheet name that the cell is located in.

> **Nuance**
>
> In **Microsoft 365** and **Excel 2021**, you can use the formula `=@CELL("width",A1)` to return just the column width. The @ symbol, known as the **implicit intersection operator**, returns the first result from a dynamic array (see *Chapter 10, Lookup and Dynamic Array Functions*). You may also run across @ in array formulas created in older versions of Excel, and in structured reference formulas.

- **Reference**: This optional argument allows you to provide the address of a cell that you're seeking information about.
- The `"protect"` *info_type* value causes the CELL function to return **0** (zero) if a cell is marked as unlocked or **1** if the cell is marked as locked. Now, let's use the CELL function within a **Conditional Formatting** rule.

Creating a custom Conditional Formatting rule

As I've mentioned earlier in this chapter, **Conditional Formatting** is a live overlay, so any formatting that you sent will turn on when a cell is marked as unlocked or vanish when the cell is marked as locked. Here are the steps:

1. Select cell **H1** of the **Custom Rule-Unlocked Cells** worksheet. Typically, you'd start with cell **A1**, but I've already applied a **Conditional Formatting** rule to cells **A1:F57**.
2. Press *Shift + End + Home* (*Ctrl + Shift + Fn* + right arrow on Excel for macOS) to select the remaining used range of the worksheet, or manually select the cells that you wish to audit.
3. Choose **Home | Conditional Formatting | New Rule… | Use a formula to determine which cells to format**.

4. Enter =CELL("protect",H1)=0 in the **Format values where this formula is true** field, as shown in *Figure 4.16*.

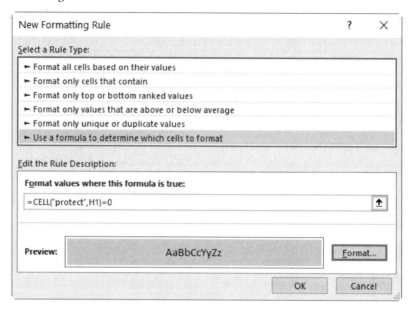

Figure 4.16 – A custom Conditional Formatting rule

5. Click the **Format** button and choose a color from the **Fill** tab, such as light green.
6. Click **OK** twice to close the dialog boxes.

As shown in *Figure 4.17*, the unlocked cells are now shaded. Sometimes, I leave the **Conditional Formatting** in place so that the user knows which cells they can change; other times, I erase the **Conditional Formatting** after I've audited the **Locked** status of the cells, which I'll cover in the upcoming *Removing conditional formatting* section.

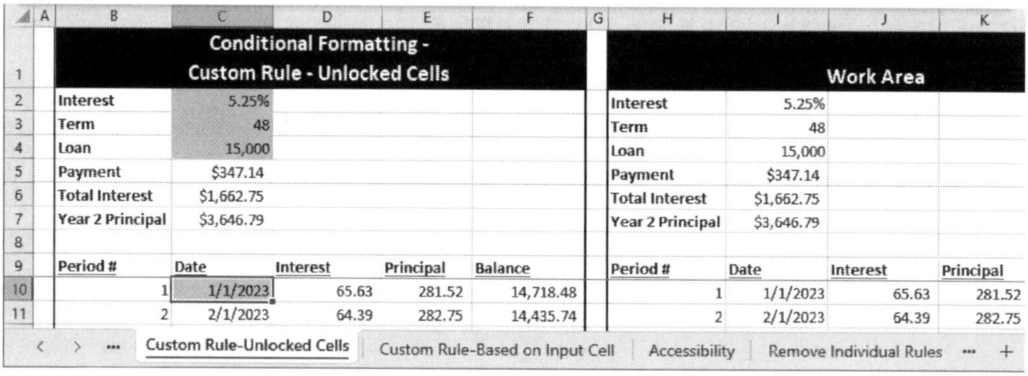

Figure 4.17 – Unlocked cells are marked with shading

Up until this point, we've created **Conditional Formatting** that is based upon the cell where the **Conditional Formatting** is applied. Let's now see how to format cells within a worksheet based upon an input cell.

Logical tests

The IF function in Excel has three arguments, **logical_test**, **value_if_true**, and **value_if_false**. The latter two arguments are used to display information or perform calculations. In the case of **Conditional Formatting**, you'll only need the equivalent of the *logical_test* argument. The custom rule you create will be applied when the test returns TRUE and will not be applied when your test returns FALSE.

> **Nuance**
>
> It's easy to think that you need to enter an IF formula into the **Format values where this formula is true** field, but remember that **Conditional Formatting** needs is a logical test.

Let's say that you want to create a rule where you format cells where an amount is greater than or equal to a particular value. Here are the steps to take:

1. Activate the **Custom Rule-Based on Input Cell** worksheet within this chapter's example workbook.

2. Designate a cell as the input to drive the **Conditional Formatting**, such as cell **H3** in *Figure 4.18*, and enter an amount, such as 7,500.

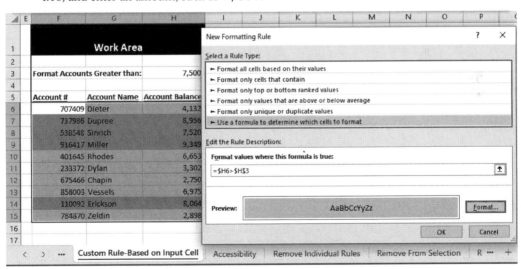

Figure 4.18 – A custom rule based upon an input cell

3. Select the range of cells that you wish to format, such as cells **F6:H15**.

4. Choose **Home | Conditional Formatting | New Rule… | Use a formula to determine which cells to format**.

5. Enter =$H6>$H$3 in the **Format values where this formula is true** field.

> **Nuance**
>
> The $ signs can make or break a **Conditional Formatting** rule. In this case, you *do not* want dollar signs around H6 because you want the formatting to be based upon the contents of cells **F6:H15**. If you used $H$6, then the rule would format rows **6** through **15** based upon the contents of cell **H6** alone. Conversely, you *do* want $ around **H3** to create an absolute reference to column **H** and row **3**. If you omit the $, then your **Conditional Formatting** will be based upon the location of other cells relative to their position from cell **H3**.

6. Click the **Format** button and choose a color from the **Fill** tab, such as light green.
7. Click **OK** twice to close the dialog boxes.
8. Enter 5,000 in cell **H3** and note that more rows become highlighted.

Now that we've laid our hands on many aspects of applying or creating **Conditional Formatting** rules, let's now see how to manage the rules that we've applied to our spreadsheet.

Managing rules

Nothing about **Conditional Formatting** is set in stone, so you can always make changes as needed. I'll discuss a few ways that you can manage existing rules in this section and provide even more options in the upcoming *Troubleshooting conditional formatting* section. In this section, I'll show you how to change the color applied to a rule and adjust the range of cells that **Conditional Formatting** is applied to. I'll also show you how to create a legend that can document the color scheme in use, and then we'll look at how to remove rules from a range of cells all the way through an entire worksheet.

Editing existing rules

Sometimes, you may decide that you want to change a color that a **Conditional Formatting** rule applies. Let's change **Fill Color** for the first rule that we created at the start of this chapter:

1. Activate the **Greater Than-Less Than-Between** worksheet, and then click on cell **D3**.
2. Choose **Home | Conditional Formatting | Manage Rules**.
3. Double-click on the **Cell Value > 8000** rule, or click once on the rule and then click **Edit** to display the **Edit Formatting Rule** dialog box.

4. This dialog box allows you to change any aspect of the **Conditional Formatting** rule except for the range of cells that the rule applies to. Click the **Format** button and choose a shade of blue from the **Fill** tab.

5. Click **OK** to close the **Format Cells** dialog box.

6. Note that you now have a blue fill with red text. Click the **Format** button again, activate the **Font** tab, and then choose **Automatic** from the **Color** dropdown.

7. Click **OK** twice to close the dialog boxes.

As I mentioned, the **Edit Formatting** dialog box enables you to change every aspect of a rule other than which cells the rule applies to. We'll use the **Conditional Formatting Rules Manager** to adjust the cells to be formatted.

Applies to ranges

As shown in *Figure 4.19*, the **Applies to** column of the **Conditional Formatting Rules Manager** dialog box enables you to see which cells are being formatted. You can review this column to make sure that **Conditional Formatting** is being applied to the cells that you expect.

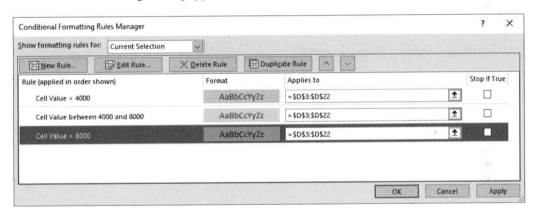

Figure 4.19 – The Applies to column shows where Conditional Formatting is applied

Let's see how easy it is for this range of cells to become compromised:

1. Activate the **Greater Than-Less Than-Between** worksheet.
2. Type 6450 into a blank cell, such as **M9** and then press *Enter*.
3. Copy cell **M9** and paste it into cell **J9**, which will erase the **Conditional Formatting** in that cell.
4. Choose **Home | Conditional Formatting | Manage Rules**.
5. The **Applies to** field for the rules that apply to column **D** will show two ranges, such as $D$3:$D$8,$D$10:$D$22, because cell **D9** no longer contains **Conditional Formatting**.

6. To restore your **Conditional Formatting**, click the button to the right of the **Applies to** field and reselect the range, or close the **Conditional Formatting Rules Manager** dialog box and choose **Home | Format Painter** to transfer the **Conditional Formatting** from an existing cell to any cells where the formatting has been removed. Either action will restore the contiguous range that you had previously.

Sometimes, rules can get so compromised that the path of least resistance is to remove them and start over. Or, rules get duplicated over and over, especially when applied to a single cell – I recently cleaned up a workbook for a client where a handful of **Conditional Formatting** rules had morphed into over 2,500 rules. Much more often though, I find myself using **Conditional Formatting** situationally, where I identify duplicates or unlocked cells and then remove the formatting.

Creating a Conditional Formatting legend

Let's see how to create the **Conditional Formatting** legend that appears in cells **B2:E4** of the **Accessibility** worksheet. The first step is identifying the fill color assigned to the first level of **Conditional Formatting**:

1. Select cell **H6** of the **Greater Than-Less Than-Between** worksheet.
2. Choose **Home | Conditional Formatting | Manage Rules**.
3. Double-click on the **Cell Value > 8000** rule, or click once on the rule and then click **Edit**.
4. Click the **Format** button in the **Edit Formatting Rule** dialog box.
5. Activate the **Fill** tab of the **Format Cells** dialog box.
6. Click the **More Colors** button.
7. Select the characters in the **Hex** field and then press *Ctrl + C* (⌘ + C), or right-click on the selection and choose **Copy**.
8. Click **OK** four times to close the series of dialog boxes.
9. Select cells **G2:I2** and then choose **Home | Format | Format Cells**, or press *Ctrl + 1* (⌘ + 1).
10. Activate the **Fill** tab and then click **More Colors**.
11. Activate the **Custom** tab and then paste the **Hex** code you copied from *Step 7*.
12. Click **OK** twice to close the **Format Cells** dialog box.
13. **Optional**: Repeat the same steps to capture the font color used by **Conditional Formatting**, as well by activating the **Font** tab instead of the **Fill** tab.

> **Nuance**
>
> The **Hex** code enables you to exactly match a color from elsewhere in the worksheet or from a color palette chart. An alternative to Hex codes is the **RGB** model, which is short for **Red Green Blue**, a series of 1-to-3-digit numbers that can be used to match colors as well.

Making the Conditional Formatting legend accessible

In *Chapter 1, Implementing Accessibility*, I discuss how a good number of Excel users cannot see colors due to color blindness or other conditions. Since **Conditional Formatting** is mostly color based, it's easy to solve one problem, say categorizing data, while creating a new problem, such as making the data inaccessible to a subset of users. As shown in *Figure 4.20*, the **Accessibility** worksheet in the example workbook shows one approach you can take, where cells **D6:D25** have both color and cell icon **Conditional Formatting** applied, while the legend includes words that describe the shapes. This approach combines techniques covered earlier in this chapter.

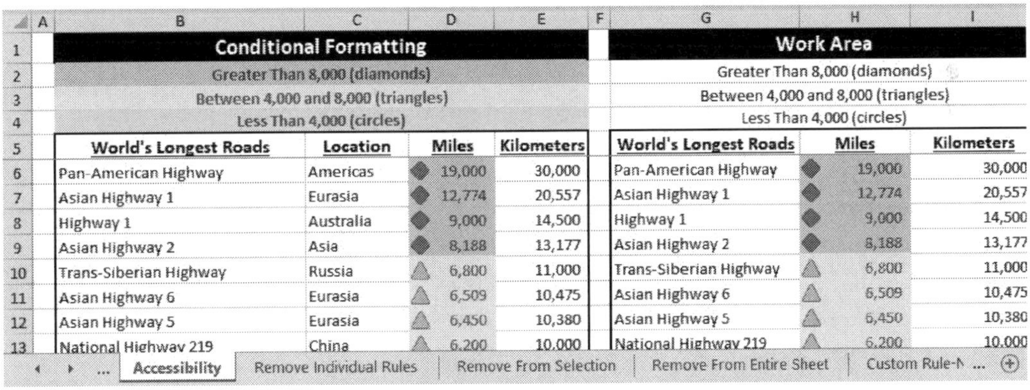

Figure 4.20 – An accessible Conditional Formatting legend

Removing Conditional Formatting

Let's first use the **Conditional Formatting Rules Manager** to remove individual rules:

1. Activate the **Remove Individual Rules** worksheet.
2. Choose **Home | Conditional Formatting | Manage Rules**.
3. Choose **This Worksheet** from the **Show formatting rules for** list if necessary.

4. Click once on any rule within the list and then click **Delete Rule**, as shown in *Figure 4.21*.

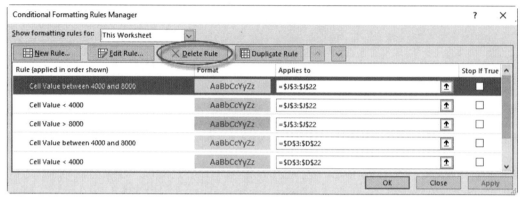

Figure 4.21 – Removing individual Conditional Formatting rules

> **Nuance**
>
> Excel does not ask you to confirm the deletion of a rule. It's easy to delete a rule that you intended to keep when selectively removing rules. Click **Apply** periodically to confirm deletions that you're certain of. You can also click **Undo** or press *Ctrl + Z* (⌘ + Z) to restore rules that you just deleted by way of the **Conditional Formatting Rules Manager**.

5. Repeat as desired and then click **OK** to close the **Conditional Formatting Rules Manager** dialog box.

Conversely, you can remove rules from a portion of a worksheet or an entire worksheet. Keep in mind that **Conditional Formatting** is worksheet-specific, so there's no way to remove all the **Conditional Formatting** from an entire workbook in one fell swoop unless you write some programming code to do so. Here's how to remove **Conditional Formatting** from specific areas of a worksheet:

1. Select cells **G3:G22** on the **Remove From Selection** worksheet.
2. Choose **Home | Conditional Formatting | Clear Rules | Clear Rules from Selected Cells**.

On the other hand, if you say to yourself that *everything must go*, here are the steps to remove all **Conditional Formatting** from a worksheet:

1. Activate the **Remove From Entire Sheet** worksheet.
2. Choose **Home | Conditional Formatting | Clear Rules | Clear Rules from Entire Worksheet**.

There are two other commands on the **Clear Rules** submenu that will generally be disabled. To enable either of these rules, place your cursor within a table or PivotTable that has **Conditional Formatting** to access the **Clear Rules from This Table** or **Clear Rules from This PivotTable** commands respectively.

> **Tip**
> In recent years, the Excel for the Web (https://www.office.com) has become a platform where Microsoft tests new features revisions and enhancements to existing features. For instance, **Excel for the Web** has a task-pane interface that replaces the dialog boxes that you've seen in this chapter. It's a good bet that this overhauled interface, along with new features like **Show Changes**, will make its way into the desktop versions of Excel at some point.

Now, let's see what to do when **Conditional Formatting** makes mockery of you by not presenting the formatting that you're expecting.

Troubleshooting Conditional Formatting

Generally, you can select a range of cells and apply **Conditional Formatting** to all cells at once. However, when crafting custom rules, you may need to apply **Conditional Formatting** to a single row of your list first, and then use the **Format Painter** command on the **Home** menu to apply the formatting to the remaining cells in your list. As noted earlier in this chapter, the positioning of the $ signs to indicate an absolute or mixed cell reference can make or break how a **Conditional Formatting** formula works. If you are applying more than one rule to an area of your worksheet, then choose **Conditional Formatting** and **Manage Rules** to display the list of rules being applied. In some cases, you may need to change the sequencing of the rules in the list to eliminate a conflict.

No formatting appears

This situation will generally only arise when you have created a custom **Conditional Formatting** rule. One exception that comes to mind is the **Duplicate Values** rule, as no formatting will appear if there are no duplicate values. Here are a couple of things to check when your custom rule doesn't format cells in the manner that you're expecting:

- As shown in *Figure 4.22*, make sure that you have set a format to apply when creating a custom rule. It's easy to get caught up in getting a custom rule right and then clicking **OK** without assigning any actual formatting.

Most other **Conditional Formatting** commands either provide automatic formatting or offer a drop-down list to choose formatting from.

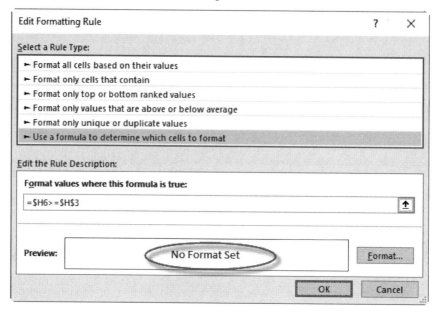

Figure 4.22 – A custom Conditional Formatting rule with no formatting instructions

- The next thing to check is the positioning of dollar signs within your custom rules. Remember that if you click on a worksheet cell while crafting a rule, Excel will create an absolute reference to that cell, such as **$A$2**. In the *Logical tests* section earlier in this chapter, we used the formula =H6>$H$3. You could unwittingly write this as =H6>$H$3, which would mean that your cells would only get formatted when an amount in cell **H6** is greater than or equal to cell **H3**. Indeed, you can also end up with the opposite effect, where formatting intended for a certain cell gets applied to all cells in the **Applied to** range for the rule.

- A third thing to try is to apply the rule to a single row instead of multiple rows at once. Once you get the rule working for a single rule, use **Home | Format Painter** to transfer the rule from the first row to the other rows that you wish to format.

As you've seen in this chapter, there is more nuance than usual in Excel when it comes to Conditional Formatting. For instance, on the **Equal To-Text That Contains** worksheet, we ran into a situation where our second **Conditional Formatting** rule overwrote the first. In other cases, you may change your mind and want to alter an aspect of an existing rule, or you may want to remove **Conditional Formatting** from all or part of a worksheet. You'll see how to do all three tasks in this section. You can always come back and modify the rules that you have applied to your worksheet.

Changing the order of the rules

If you carried out the steps in the *Equal To* and *Text That Contains* sections of this chapter, you found that the second rule overwrote the first. The goal is to have the word **Asia** formatted in blue with bold text, and then any other words that contain **Asia** to be formatted in red. The situation that arose is that all the cells that match either rule are formatted in red due to the order that the rules are being applied in. When conflicts like this arise, often the first step is to change the order of the rules:

1. Activate the **Equal To-Text That Contains** worksheet.
2. Choose **Home | Conditional Formatting | Manage Rules**.
3. Choose **This Worksheet** from the **Show formatting rules** list to display all rules in use in the current worksheet.

> **Nuance**
>
> The **Show formatting rules list** displays a list of every worksheet in the workbook that has **Conditional Formatting** applied. In the example workbook for this chapter, you'll see every worksheet in this list except for the **IF Function-Wingdings** worksheet because that one does not have any **Conditional Formatting** applied.

4. Click once on the **Cell Value contains "Asia"** rule to select it.
5. Click the **Up** arrow that appears to the right of the **Duplicate Rule** button, as shown in *Figure 4.23*.

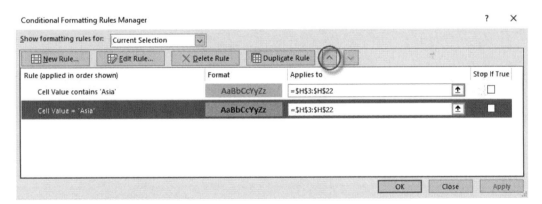

Figure 4.23 – Changing the order of Conditional Formatting rules

6. Click **Apply** to see the effect of this change and note how the cells that contain **Asia** are formatted blue, albeit with a red font instead of black. This is because a portion of the second rule is still being applied.
7. Click the **Stop If True** checkbox for the **Cell Value contains 'Asia'** rule and then click **Apply** again.

8. At this point, only the cells that contain **Asia** should be formatted in blue with a bold, black font, while the cells that contain **Eurasia** should be formatted in red.

> **Nuance**
>
> The **Apply** button allows you to see the effect of your changes before you close the **Conditional Formatting Rules Manager** dialog box. Any changes that you make in this dialog box are not permanent until you click **OK** or **Apply**. No changes are saved when you click **Cancel**, so if you inadvertently click **Delete** or make a change that you wish to undo, clicking **Cancel** will restore the rules you deleted and/or discard any other changes you may have made, if you haven't clicked **Apply** yet.

Wingdings font

You can create your own types of cell icons by using the **Wingdings** font in conjunction with an `IF` function. This allows you to go beyond **Conditional Formatting** to create any sort of symbology that you choose. I'll share a brief example:

1. Click on a blank cell in an Excel worksheet, such as cell **G1** in *Figure 4.24*.

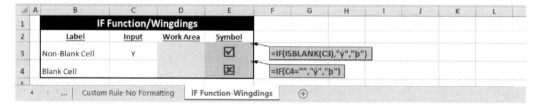

Figure 4.24 – The IF function and Wingdings

2. Choose the **Symbol** command from the **Insert** menu in Excel.
3. Choose **Wingdings** from the **Font** list.
4. Choose a symbol, such as the **checkmark** (þ) icon shown in *Figure 4.24*, click **Insert**, and then click **Close**.
5. Move your cursor to another blank cell, such as cell **G2**, and then repeat *steps 1–4* to pick a second symbol, such as the **x** (ý) icon shown in *Figure 4.24*.

6. Type a formula, such as =IF(ISBLANK(C3),"y","n"), in a cell where you want the symbols to appear, such as cell **D3** in *Figure 4.24*.

7. Copy the character in cell **G1** from the formula bar and paste it into the IF function in place of Y. Replace N with the second symbol from cell **G2**. Your formula may now look something like =IF(ISBLANK(C3),"ý","þ").

8. Assign the **Wingdings** font to cell **D3** by typing Wingdings in the font listing on the **Home** tab of Excel's ribbon.

9. You can now copy the formula down as many rows as needed.

10. When cells **C3** or **C4** contain any value, cells **D3** and **D4** will display þ; otherwise, an ý icon will appear.

You can change the font size to make the icons larger if you wish. This enables you to go beyond the **Icon Sets** rules in Excel if you need additional flexibility.

Summary

In this chapter, you learned how you can use **Conditional Formatting** to identify data in worksheet cells based upon criteria that you specify. Excel offers several built-in rules that are easy to apply, such as when you want to identify the top or bottom values in a list, or dates within a given period. However, these rules only scratch the surface of **Conditional Formatting's** potential. You can now use **Conditional Formatting** to provide a visual cue to users that attempt to overwrite a formula with a static value. You can also easily identify unlocked cells in a worksheet, which makes it less likely that you'll inadvertently leave key input cells locked and inaccessible when the worksheet is protected. You also now know how to craft rules that will format certain cells based upon the value of an input cell.

Custom **Conditional Formatting** rules can be tricky to perfect because a single misplaced $ can cause a formula to behave in an unexpected fashion. In other cases, it's easy to slip up and craft the rule but omit the formatting. Sometimes, it's simply a matter of changing the order in which rules get applied.

In the next chapter, I'll walk you through creating data entry rules and documentation for your spreadsheets with the Data Validation and Form Controls features.

Part 2: Spreadsheet Interactivity and Automation

This chapter will empower you with interactivity and automation techniques. Data validation provides interactivity, documentation, and internal control, but can be bypassed by savvy users. The Form Controls feature provides more controlled interactivity when necessary. Many users fail to notice the potential of Excel's What-If Analysis features, which can eliminate manual guesswork in a flash. The Table feature offers more automation potential than I could fit into the chapter. Custom Views is one of my favorite code-free automation solutions in Excel that can save you time in several ways. The final chapter, *Excel Quirks and Nuances*, explains how to avoid getting snared by tricky pitfalls in Excel.

The following chapters are included in this part:

- *Chapter 5, Data Validation and Form Controls*
- *Chapter 6, What-If Analysis*
- *Chapter 7, Automating Tasks with the Table Feature*
- *Chapter 8, Custom Views*
- *Chapter 9, Excel Quirks and Nuances*

5
Data Validation and Form Controls

I often describe Excel spreadsheets as having an American *Wild West* atmosphere where anything goes. Type anything you want, anywhere you want. Many users combat this by protecting certain worksheet cells as I'll discuss later in this chapter. However, **worksheet protection** only restricts whether a cell can be edited or not.

Data Validation allows you to restrict the type of data that can be entered into specific cells. In addition, **Data Validation** enables you to create on-demand documentation that appears on screen when a user clicks on a cell.

Even better, **Data Validation** can provide immediate feedback if a user doesn't comply with the rule. Determined users can circumvent **Data Validation**, so we'll offer two defenses. The first is a means to audit invalid entries. The second approach will enable you to raise the bar by using **Form Controls** to restrict inputs.

In this chapter, the following topics will be covered:

- Introducing **Data Validation**
- Implementing **Data Validation** rules
- Protecting **Data Validation** cells
- Auditing **Data Validation** cells
- Enabling the **Developer** tab
- Exploring **Form Controls**
- **Checkboxes** and **Option Buttons**

By the end of the chapter, you'll have tools you can use to *user-proof* your spreadsheets in ways that will both improve the integrity and the accessibility of your spreadsheets. **Data validation** and **Form Controls** are internal control measures that are often overlooked by spreadsheet developers.

Technical requirements

Everything in this chapter will work the same in **Excel for Windows** and **macOS**. You will need to enable the **Developer** tab of Excel's **ribbon**, which we'll describe in the *Exploring Form Controls* section.

The workbook that we used in this chapter is available for download from GitHub at https://github.com/PacktPublishing/Exploring-Microsoft-Excels-Hidden-Treasures/tree/main/Chapter05.

Introducing Data Validation

The **Data Validation** feature allows you to create rules that limit the type of data that can be entered in one or more worksheet cells. The rules can limit users from entering numbers, list items, dates, or times, and you can create custom rules. You can also craft a data entry prompt that appears when the user clicks on a cell that contains **Data Validation** and follow up invalid entries with an error prompt. Let's begin by comparing cells **C4** and **C5** on the **Data Validation** worksheet of this chapter's example workbook as follows:

1. Select cell **C4** as shown in *Figure 5.1*.

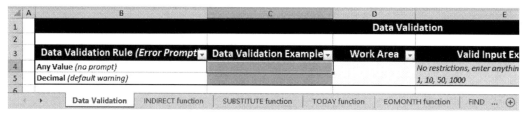

Figure 5.1 – Example data for this chapter

2. Choose **Data** | **Data Validation** to display the **Data Validation** dialog box shown in *Figure 5.2*.

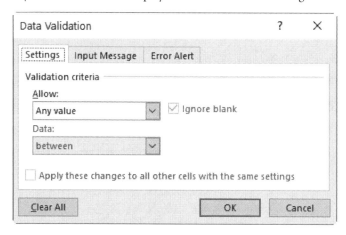

Figure 5.2 – The Settings tab of the Data Validation dialog box

3. Notice how the **Allow** field on the **Settings** tab of the dialog box is set to allow **Any value**. This means that you can type anything you wish into cell **C4**, which is the default for all cells in a worksheet until you enable another **Data Validation** rule.

4. Activate the **Input Message** tab and notice the **Title** and **Input message** fields shown in *Figure 5.3*. You can use these fields to create a data entry prompt.

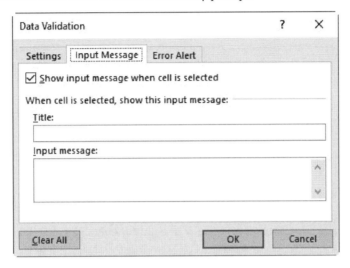

Figure 5.3 – The Input Message tab of the Data Validation dialog box

5. Activate the **Error Alert** tab and notice the **Title** and **Error message** fields shown in *Figure 5.4*, along with a **Style** list that enables you to control how restrictive a **Data Validation** rule is. The input fields allow you to craft a custom error alert that appears when invalid input is entered.

Figure 5.4 – The Error Alert tab of the Data Validation dialog box

6. Click **OK** to close the **Data Validation** dialog box. You can enter anything you want into cell **C4** because no **Data Validation** rule is set.
7. Next, type the word `Excel` into cell **C5** and press *Enter*. Notice that the generic **Data Validation** error prompt shown in *Figure 5.5* appears.

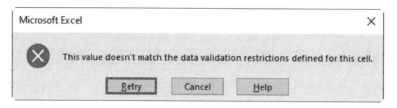

Figure 5.5 – Generic Data Validation error prompt

- At this point you have a few options as follows:
    - Click **Retry**, type a number greater than zero, and then press *Enter*
    - Click **Cancel** or press *Esc* to dismiss the error prompt and discard the invalid input
    - Click **Help** to display generic help related to **Data Validation**, although I can tell you in advance that the help documentation will rarely, if ever, explain the rule that has been implemented

> **Tip**
> The buttons that you see in *Figure 5.5* relate to the **Stop** style, which is the most restrictive. Data validation also offers **Warning** and **Information** styles that allow users to bypass the rule if desired.

There was no way for you to know in advance that I had created a rule that requires a numeric input for cell **C5** because I did not fill in the **Input Message** or **Error Alert** tabs when I created the rule. Conversely, the data entry prompt shown in *Figure 5.6* appears when you click on cell **C6**, and the warning prompt shown in *Figure 5.7* appears when you type text, such as `Excel`, and then press *Enter*.

Introducing Data Validation

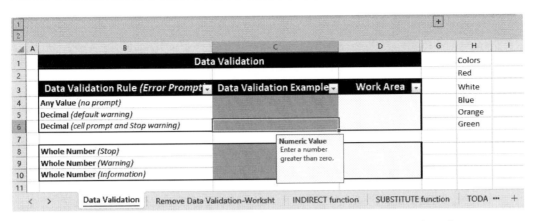

Figure 5.6 – A Data Validation input message appears when a cell is selected

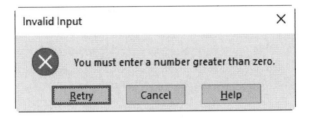

Figure 5.7 – A descriptive **Data Validation** error prompt

The following steps describe how to recreate the **Data Validation** rule in cell **C6**:

1. Select cell **D6** and then choose **Data | Data Validation**.
2. Select **Decimal** from the **Allow** list and **Greater than** from the **Data** list.
3. Enter 0 (zero) in the **Minimum** field.
4. Activate the **Input Message** tab, type `Numeric Value` in the **Title** field, and `Enter a number greater than zero.` in the **Input message** field.
5. Activate the **Error Alert** tab, type `Invalid Input` in the **Title** field, and `You must enter a number greater than zero.` in the **Error message** field.
6. Click **OK** to close the **Data Validation** dialog box.
7. Optional: try typing numeric and non-numeric values into cell **D6**.

> **Nuance**
>
> Keep in mind that any data that has already been entered into cells that you apply **Data Validation** to is grandfathered into the rules, meaning Excel will not alert you to invalid entries, so it's always best to apply **Data Validation** to blank cells when possible.

Now let's walk through each tab of the **Data Validation** dialog box to understand the full range of options.

Settings tab

The **Allow** list on the **Settings** tab of the **Data Validation** dialog box enables you to assign the following rules to one or more cells:

- **Any value**: No restrictions are placed – this is the default for all worksheet cells
- **Whole number**: Inputs are restricted to whole numbers only
- **Decimal**: Inputs are restricted to numbers with or without decimals
- **List**: Inputs are restricted to items from a specified list
- **Date**: Inputs are restricted to date values
- **Time**: Inputs are restricted to time values
- **Text length**: Inputs are limited based upon a specified number of characters
- **Custom**: Formulas that return TRUE or 0 (zero) indicate valid inputs, whereas FALSE, 1, or an error such as #VALUE! indicates an invalid input

You can further limit each rule, except for **List** and **Custom**, with one of the following restrictions:

- **Between**: **Minimum** and **Maximum** fields allow you to specify a range of valid values.
- **Not between**: **Minimum** and **Maximum** or **Start** and **End** fields allow you to specify a range of invalid values.
  - **Equal to**: A **Value** field enables you to specify text, value, date, or time that the user must enter.
  - **Not equal to**: A **Value** field enables you to specify text, value, date, or time that the user cannot enter.
  - **Greater than**: A **Minimum** or **Start** field allows you to specify the lower end of a range of values. The minimum or start value provided *will not* be a valid choice in the cell.
  - **Less than**: A **Maximum** or **End** field allows you to specify the upper end of a range. The maximum or end value provided *will not* be a valid choice in the cell.
  - **Greater than or equal to**: A **Minimum** or **Start** field allows you to specify the lower end of a range of values. The minimum or start value provided *will* be a valid choice in the cell.
  - **Less than or equal to**: A **Maximum** or **End** field allows you to specify the upper end of a range. The maximum or end value provided *will* be a valid choice in the cell.

The following settings are optional:

- **Ignore blank:** This checkbox appears no matter what type of **Data Validation** you are creating, but it is typically only applicable to lists that are dependent on other cells. We'll provide an example of this in the *Creating dependent lists* subsection later in this chapter.
- **Apply these changes to all other cells with the same settings**: This checkbox is disabled until you apply **Data Validation** to a cell. Its purpose is to allow you to apply subsequent **Data Validation** changes to all cells that have the same restriction applied.

Now let's look at the **Input Message** tab.

Input Message tab

The **Input Message** tab enables you to craft an onscreen message that appears when a user clicks into a cell that has a **Data Validation** rule. I recommend that you always fill in this tab immediately after you complete the **Settings** tab to avoid the confusion that you may have experienced in the initial example in this chapter. The **Input Message** tab has two fields and one checkbox as follows:

- **Title**: You may enter up to **32** characters in this field to create a heading for the input prompt that will appear when you click on a cell that contains **Data Validation**, such as `Numeric Value` as shown in *Figure 5.6*.
- **Input Message**: Enter up to **255** characters in this field to create the body of the message that appears when you click on a cell, such as `Enter a number greater than to zero.` as shown in *Figure 5.6*.

> **Nuance**
>
> The **Input message** and **Error message** fields will initially accept more than **255** characters but only the first **255** characters will be kept when you click **OK** to close the **Data Validation** dialog box.

- **Show input message when cell is selected**: This checkbox enables you to suppress inputs that appear in the **Title** and **Input** message fields if you want to suppress the prompt without erasing the fields. Typically, you'll leave this checkbox selected.

Now let's review the **Error Alert** tab.

Error Alert Message tab

The **Error Alert** tab enables you to craft an error prompt message, such as in *Figure 5.7*, that appears when a user's input conflicts with the **Data Validation** rule for a given cell. As with the **Input Message** tab, you should always complete this tab immediately after setting a rule in **Settings**.

The **Error Alert** tab has three fields and one checkbox as follows:

- **Style**: As you'll see in the following section, you can choose between **Stop**, **Warning**, and **Information** styles. *Figure 5.7* illustrates the **Stop** style in use, which is the most restrictive.

- **Title**: You may enter up to **32** characters in this field to create a heading for the input prompt that will appear when you click on a cell that contains **Data Validation**, such as `Invalid Input` as shown in *Figure 5.7*.

- **Error alert**: Enter up to **255** characters in this field to create the body of the message that appears in the error prompt, such as `You must enter a number greater than zero.` as shown in *Figure 5.7*.

- **Show error alert after invalid data is entered**: This checkbox enables you to suppress the error prompt in *Figure 5.7*. Doing so enables users to enter anything that they want in the cell even if a **Data Validation** rule is in place. Typically, you would leave this checkbox enabled since it is the error prompt that enforces **Data Validation** rules.

Now let's look at the **Error Alert** styles.

Error Alert styles

The **Error Alert** styles control enforcement of **Data Validation** rules by determining which buttons appear in the error prompt as well as which icon appears. Cells **C8:C10** on the **Data Validation** worksheet require that a whole number greater than zero be entered. Let's see all three styles in use.

Stop style

Type `-1` in **C8** and press *Enter* to trigger the prompt shown in *Figure 5.8*. The **Stop** style causes the following buttons to appear in the error prompt dialog box:

- **Retry**: Allows the user to make another attempt at entering valid data, in this case, a number greater than or equal to 0

- **Cancel**: Discards any entry that the user may have made into the cell and keeps the original contents, if any

- **Help**: Displays help documentation regarding the **Data Validation** feature, but not the rule itself

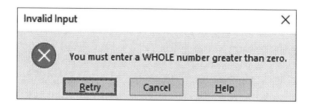

Figure 5.8 – Stop style error alert

Introducing Data Validation

Use the following steps to recreate the rule in cell **C8**:

1. Select cell **D8** and then choose **Data | Data Validation**.
2. Select **Whole Number** from the **Allow** list and **Greater than** from the **Data** list.
3. Enter 0 (zero) in the **Minimum** field.
4. Activate the **Input Message** tab, type `Numeric Value` in the **Title** field, and then type `Enter a number greater than zero.` in the **Input message** field.
5. Activate the **Error Alert** tab, type `Invalid Input` in the **Title** field, and then type `You must enter a number greater than zero.` in the **Error message** field.
6. Accept the default style of **Stop** and then click **OK** to close the **Data Validation** dialog box.
7. Enter `1.5` into cell **D8** and then press *Enter*. Notice how the prompt shown in *Figure 5.8* can cause one problem and create a new one. The value `1.5` *is* a number greater than zero, but our rule requires a whole number. Click **Cancel** or press *Esc* to close the error prompt.
8. Click on cell **D8** and then choose **Data | Data Validation**.
9. Activate the **Input Message** tab and update the **Title** and **Input message** fields to read `Whole Number` and `Enter a whole number greater than zero.`, respectively.
10. Activate the **Error Alert** tab and update the **Error alert** field to read `You must enter a WHOLE number greater than zero.`

> **Tip**
>
> The only formatting option available in the **Error alert** field is to type certain words in upper case, so entering `You must enter a WHOLE number greater than zero.` is a way to emphasize the rule.

11. Click **OK** to close the **Data Validation** dialog box.
12. Enter `1.5` into cell **D8** and press *Enter* to see how the documentation communicates the rule more clearly.

Now let's look at the more permissive **Warning** style.

Warning style

Type `1.5` in cell **C9** to trigger the prompt shown in *Figure 5.9*, which gives the user the option to override the **Data Validation** rule by choosing between the following buttons:

- **Yes**: Allows the user to bypass the **Data Validation** rule
- **No**: Rejects the invalid input and enables the user to try again, in the same fashion as how the **Retry** button works when the **Stop** style is in use

- **Cancel**: Discards any entry that the user may have made into the cell and keeps the original contents, if any
- **Help**: Displays help documentation regarding the **Data Validation** feature, but not the rule itself

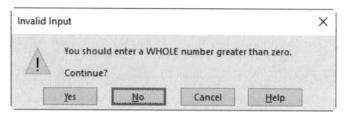

Figure 5.9 – Warning style error alert

Use the following steps to recreate the rule shown in cell **C9**:

1. Select cell **D9** and then choose **Data | Data Validation**.
2. Select **Whole Number** from the **Allow** list and **Greater than** from the **Data** list.
3. Enter 0 (zero) in the **Minimum** field.
4. Activate the **Input Message** tab, type `Numeric Value` in the **Title** field, and then type `Enter a whole number greater than zero.` in the **Input message** field.
5. Activate the **Error Alert** tab, type `Invalid Input` in the **Title** field, and then type `You should enter a WHOLE greater than zero.` in the **Error message** field.
6. Choose **Warning** from the **Style** list and then click **OK**.

> **Tip**
> As shown in *Figure 5.9*, the **Warning** style causes the phrase **Continue?** to appear beneath the **Error alert** that you specify. So in this context, it's best to word the alert as a suggestion as opposed to a directive when using the **Stop** style.

7. Enter `1.5` into cell **D9**, press *Enter*, and then click **Yes** to override the **Data Validation** rule.

Now we'll move on to the **Information** style, which is the least restrictive.

Information style

Type `1.5` in **C10** to trigger the prompt shown in *Figure 5.10*. The **Information** style is the most permissive and presents the following buttons for the user to choose from:

- **OK**: Accepts the user's entry even if it does not conform to the **Data Validation** rule
- **Cancel**: Discards any entry that the user may have made into the cell and keeps the original contents, if any.

- **Help**: Generic help regarding **Data Validation**

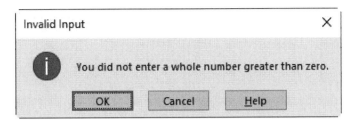

Figure 5.10 – Information style error alert

Use the following steps to recreate the rule shown in cell **C10**:

1. Select cell **D9** and then choose **Data | Data Validation**.
2. Select **Whole Number** from the **Allow** list and **Greater than** from the **Data** list.
3. Enter 0 (zero) in the **Minimum** field.
4. Activate the **Input Message** tab, type `Numeric Value` in the **Title** field, and then type `Enter a whole number greater than zero.` in the **Input message** field.
5. Activate the **Error Alert** tab, type `Invalid Input` in the **Title** field, and then type `You did not enter a whole number greater than zero.` in the **Error message** field.

> **Tip**
> In this context, the **Error alert** should be informational since the user can simply click **OK** to dismiss the error prompt.

6. Choose **Information** from the **Style** list and then click **OK**.
7. Enter `1.5` into cell **D10**, press *Enter*, and then click **OK** to override the **Data Validation** rule.

Let's see how to remove **Data Validation** from one or more cells.

Removing Data Validation

There are a couple of ways to purposefully remove **Data Validation**, and at least one accidental method. To purposefully remove **Data Validation**, you need to perform the following steps:

1. Select a range of cells, such as **C12:C14**, and then choose **Data | Data Validation**.
2. Click **Clear All** at the bottom of the **Data Validation** dialog box.
3. Click **OK** to close the **Data Validation** dialog box.

You can now enter any sort of data you wish into these cells.

> **Nuance**
>
> The **Clear All** command does not ask you if you're sure you want to remove **Data Validation**. If you click **Clear All** and then change your mind, click **Cancel** instead of **OK** to keep the **Data Validation** in place.

The second way to remove **Data Validation** enables you to act on an entire worksheet if you wish, as follows:

1. Activate the **Remove Data Validation** worksheet.
2. Choose any cell, such as **A1**, and then choose **Home | Find & Select | Data Validation**.
3. Excel selects the cells that have **Data Validation** rules applied, in this case, cells **A2:A16** and **E2:E4**, as shown in *Figure 5.11*.

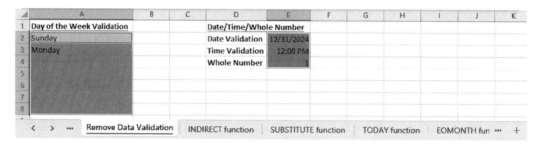

Figure 5.11 – Multiple cells with Data Validation rules assigned

4. Choose **Data | Data Validation**.
5. The cells that you selected in *step 3* have more than one type of **Data Validation** assigned, so Excel displays the prompt shown in *Figure 5.12*. Click **OK** to erase **Data Validation** from all of the selected cells or click **Cancel** to keep the rules in place.

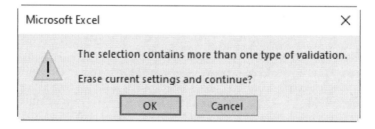

Figure 5.12 – Multiple validation type warning

> **Nuance**
> Another way to remove **Data Validation** rules from selected cells is to choose **Home | Clear | Clear All**. Keep in mind that doing so will also remove all other formatting, hyperlinks, and cell contents from the selected cells as well.

Now that we've explored the **Data Validation** dialog box, let's work our way through the various rules that you can apply to cells within your worksheets.

Implementing Data Validation rules

As you can see, **Data Validation** rules limit the types of entries that users can make within worksheet cells. This section will discuss each of the **Data Validation** rules that you can assign to worksheet cells.

Any value

As I discussed earlier in the chapter, **Any value** means that the user can type any value that they wish. Clearing **Data Validation** rules as we did in the preceding section resets the cell(s) to allow any value. Every cell in a worksheet defaults to **Any value**.

> **Tip**
> You can choose to fill in the **Input Message** tab for any cell while leaving the validation rule set to **Any value**. This allows you to create documentation that appears on demand when a user clicks on a worksheet cell, and it is an alternative to adding a note or comment to a cell. In this context, you would leave the **Error Alert** tab blank since there's no rule in place that would trigger an error prompt.

The next rule on the **Allow** list is **Whole Number**.

Whole Numbers

As I discussed earlier in the chapter, the **Whole Number** rule restricts users from entering whole numbers into a cell. Valid inputs are further constrained by the choice you make from the **Data** list.

> **Nuance**
> Make sure that you change the **Input message** and **Error alert** fields accordingly when you choose **Greater than or equal to** versus **Greater Than**, or **Less than or equal to** versus **Less than**. Also, make sure that you make it clear that a whole number is expected, as opposed to a numeric input.

The next rule on the **Allow** list is **Decimal**.

Decimal

As I discussed earlier in this chapter, the **Decimal** rule is suitable for cells where you want to allow a numeric input but not necessarily limit the input to whole numbers only. The **Decimal** rule accepts any number that meets the constraints you specify in the **Data** list and the resulting input fields that appear.

> **Nuance**
>
> You must use decimal values such as `.10` in the **Data Validation** dialog box, but users can enter decimals or percentages, meaning `.10` or `10%` in the worksheet itself. In most places in Excel, values such as `.10` and `10%` are interchangeable, except in the **Data Validation** dialog box.

Now let's see how to use **Data Validation** to create in-cell drop-down lists.

List

The **List** rule allows you to limit users to making a choice from a list and causes a drop-down arrow to appear when the cell is selected. You can interact with the list in the following three ways:

- Use your mouse to click the drop-down arrow shown in *Figure 5.13* to display the list. Choosing an item from the list enters that value into the worksheet cell.

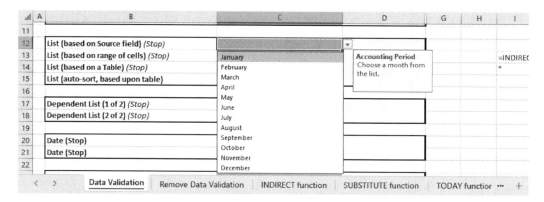

Figure 5.13 – In-cell drop-down list

- Press *Alt-Down* (*Option-Down*) to display the list by using your keyboard, use the *Down* (or *Up*) arrow key to navigate the list, and then press *Enter* once you make a selection.
- Bypass the drop-down menu by typing a value directly into the worksheet cell, but be mindful that the **List** rule is case-sensitive. If you want to choose **January** from cell **C12**, you must type `January` with a capital **J**, as all lower-case `january` will be rejected as an invalid input.

> **Nuance**
>
> In older versions of Excel, the in-cell drop-down list shows up to eight items on the list and then requires you to scroll to see the ninth item and beyond. As of this writing, Microsoft is beta testing an update for the **List** rule that displays as many options as will fit on screen as well as automatic in-cell filtering as you type, which makes it far easier to enter the correct data when typing into a cell.

Lists can be embedded in the **Source** field in the **Data Validation** dialog box, or you can store the list in a range of worksheet cells.

Storing a list in the Source field

Let's now store a list of all 12 months in the **Data Validation** dialog box as follows:

1. Click on cell **D12** of the **Data Validation** worksheet and then choose **Data | Data Validation**.
2. Choose **List** from the **Allow** field and then enter all 12 months separated by commas in the **Source** field, as shown in *Figure 5.14*. The **Source** field can contain up to **256** characters, which includes any separators, such as commas.

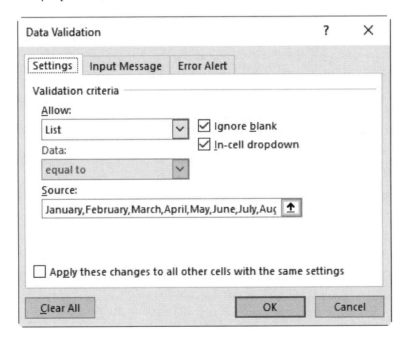

Figure 5.14 – Data Validation Source field

3. Activate the **Input Message** tab, enter `Accounting Period` in the **Title** field, and enter `Choose a month from the list.` in the **Input message** field.

4. Activate the **Error Alert** tab, enter `Invalid Input` in the **Title** field, and enter `You must make a choice from the list. Inputs are case sensitive.` in the **Error message** field.

5. Click **OK** to close the **Data Validation** dialog box.

> **Nuance**
>
> In *Chapter 9, Excel Quirks and Nuances*, I discuss **Enter** mode versus **Edit** mode for fields such as the **Source** field in the **Data Validation** dialog box. This means if you use the left or right arrow keys within the **Source** field, you'll insert a cell reference from the worksheet. Conversely, if you press *F2* (*Fn* + *F2* on some keyboards), you'll switch to **Edit** mode, which allows you to navigate within the field by using the left and right arrow keys.

Let's now see how you can also use the **Source** field to reference a list that you've stored in the worksheet.

Storing lists in worksheet cells

When you click the drop-down arrow in cell **C13**, you can choose from a list of colors that appear in cells **H2:H6**. The following steps show you how to recreate this rule:

1. Click on cell **D13** of the **Data Validation** worksheet and then choose **Data | Data Validation**.

2. Choose **List** from the **Allow** field and then enter or select H2:H6 in the **Source** field, as shown in *Figure 5.15*.

> **Tip**
>
> Excel adds dollar signs ($) to create an absolute reference when you select a range of cells. You can include dollars signs if you're entering the range address, such as $H$2:$H$6 or simply H2:H6. Similarly, you can type the equal sign or omit it.

3. Fill in the **Input Message** and **Error Alert** tabs, and then click **OK** to close the dialog box.

Implementing Data Validation rules   135

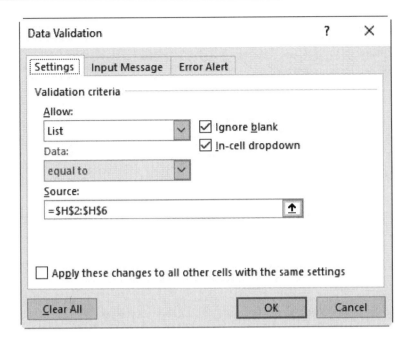

Figure 5.15 – Worksheet-based Data Validation list

Any changes that you make to cells **H2:H6** will be immediately reflected in the drop-down list in cell **C13**. However, any new colors that you add in cell **H7** and beyond will not appear until you edit the **Source** field to include the new items, as follows:

1. Type a new color, such as `Brown`, in cell **H7**.
2. Display the drop-down list in cell **D13** and notice how **Brown** does not appear on the list.
3. Choose **Data | Data Validation**, click in the **Source** field, enter or select H2:H7, and then click **OK**.
4. Display the drop-down list in cell **D13** and notice how **Brown** now appears on the list.

> **Nuance**
> Some users try to minimize resizing lists by selecting a bigger range, such as cells **H2:H22**, to allow for expansion. Doing so can result in a series of blanks at the bottom of your **Data Validation** list that may confuse the user. Any blank items that the user chooses from the bottom of the list will be considered valid input.

A better way to make lists expand automatically is to convert the list into a **Table**.

Creating a self-updating list

The **Data Validation** list in cell **C14** is based on a **Table** in cells **J1:J6**, which makes the list self-updating. To test this, perform the following steps:

1. Display the drop-down list in cell **C14** and notice how the last color listed is **Green**.
2. Type **Brown** in cell **J7** and then press *Enter*.
3. Display the drop-down list in cell **C14** and notice how the last color listed is now **Brown**.

The following steps show you how to create a **List** rule that is based on a **Table**:

1. Click on any cell within **L1:L6**.
2. Choose **Insert | Table** or press *Ctrl + T* (⌘ + T in Excel for macOS).
3. Make sure that the **My table has headers** checkbox is selected if the first item in your list is a header, such as the word **Colors** in cell **L1**, and then click **OK**.
4. Select cell **D14** and then choose **Data | Data Validation**.
5. Choose **List** from the **Allow** field, and then enter or select L2:L6 in the **Source** field. Do not include the list heading in cell **L1** unless you want the user to be able to select that from the list.

> **Nuance**
>
> In *Chapter 7, Automating Tasks with the Table Feature*, I discuss using **Table** Names with Excel features, such as **PivotTables**, **PivotCharts**, **charts**, and so on. The **Data Validation** feature does not recognize **Table Names** as valid references, so you must select the second cell through the last cell of the **Table** instead.

6. Complete the **Input Message** and **Error Alert** tabs and then click **OK**.
7. Add a new color in cell **L7**, such as Brown. The **Table** expands automatically to include the latest item.
8. Display the drop-down list in cell **D13** and notice how **Brown** appears at the bottom of the list.
9. You can manually sort the **Table** to make the items appear in alphabetical order, or in **Microsoft 365** and **Excel 2021**, you can create a self-expanding list that sorts itself automatically.

Creating a self-updating list

Cell **N2** of the **Data Validation** worksheet contains the =SORT(Colors[Colors]) formula. This references the **Colors Table** that starts in cell **J1**. The SORT function is a dynamic array function that I discuss in *Chapter 10, Lookup and Dynamic Array Functions*, but in short, it automatically sorts data that you reference, which includes additional data that gets added to the **Table**. This enables you to create a self-updating **Data Validation** list that sorts itself automatically.

Let's first test this functionality as follows and then we'll show you how to implement it:

1. Add a new color to the list in column **J**.
2. Display the drop-down list in cell **C15** and notice that the new colors appears in alphabetical order.

Now let's recreate the functionality as follows:

1. Enter the word `Colors` into cell **P1**.
2. Type `=SORT(` into cell **P2**, select from cell **J2** down to the bottom of the **Table**, close the parenthesis, and then press *Enter*. This creates the dynamic list that **Data Validation** will reference.
3. Click on cell **D15** and then choose **Data | Data Validation**.
4. Choose **List** from the **Allow** field, type `P2#` into the **Source** field or click on cell **P2**, and then add the **spilled range operator** (#), which creates a resizable cell reference. As I will discuss in *Chapter 10, Lookup and Dynamic Array Functions*, the **spilled range operator** can only be used when referencing the results of a dynamic array function, such as `SORT`.

> **Tip**
> As discussed earlier, converting the source data for a **Data Validation** list makes the list self-updating. That technique works in any version of Excel. The automatic sorting capability is only available in **Microsoft 365** and **Excel 2021**.

5. Complete the **Input Message** and **Error Alert** tabs and then click **OK**.
6. Add a new color to column **J** and notice how the list in cell **D15** expands and sorts automatically.

There's one more dimension to **Data Validation** lists that I want to share with you, which is creating a secondary list with choices predicated on the selection you make from a primary list.

Creating dependent lists

The example workbook does not contain a demonstration of this following technique, but I'll walk you through the steps. We'll use **Names** and the `INDIRECT` and `SUBSTITUTE` worksheet functions to create a dependent list in cell **D18** that will be driven by the choice you make in cell **D17**. I discuss **Names** in detail in *Chapter 11, LET and LAMBDA*, so I won't go into much detail here. Let's first assign the **Names**.

Assigning Names

Creating dependent lists requires each item on the primary list to have a **Name** assigned as follows:

1. Select cells **R2:R4** and then choose **Formulas | Define Name**.

2. Type `Recommended_for_promotion` as shown in *Figure 5.16* and then click **OK**.

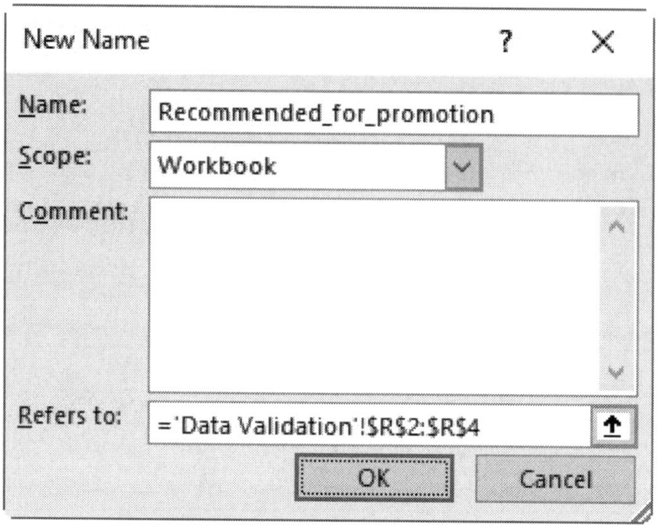

Figure 5.16 – The New Name dialog box

> **Tip**
> **Names** cannot contain spaces, so make sure to place an underscore between each word. Also, make sure to double-check your spelling; otherwise, this technique won't work. **Names** are not case-sensitive.

3. Select cell **S2:S4** and then choose **Formulas | Define Name**.
4. Type `Not_recommended_for_promotion` and then click **OK**.

Let's now walk through the `INDIRECT` function.

The INDIRECT function

Cell **C3** of the **INDIRECT function** worksheet contains the `=INDIRECT(B3)` formula, as shown in *Figure 5.17*. Cell **C3** will return **December** when you type `F13` in cell **B3** and then press *Enter*. This works the same way as typing `=F13`, but the difference is that you would have to replace `=F13` with `=F6` to reference **May** while `INDIRECT` allows you to type **F6** in cell **B3**. In this context, `INDIRECT` converts the text in cell **B3** to a valid cell reference.

Implementing Data Validation rules   139

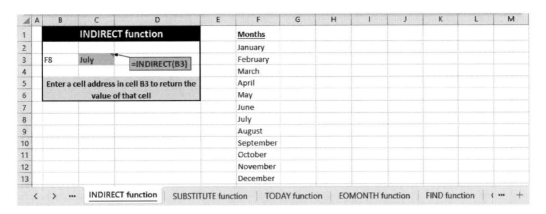

Figure 5.17 – The INDIRECT function

The INDIRECT function has the following two arguments:

- Ref_text: The text that you want to convert to a cell reference or **Name**.
- A1: An optional argument where you specify TRUE for an **A1 reference** style or FALSE for an **R1C1 reference** style. In our case, we'll omit this argument because we want to use the default style where we reference cells based on the column letter and row number, meaning **B3**, rather than the **R1C1** reference style of R3C2, meaning third row and second column.

INDIRECT is going to enable us to dynamically reference the Names of the two dependent lists. Now let's see how to use the SUBSTITUTE function to replace spaces with underscores.

The SUBSTITUTE function

As shown in *Figure 5.18*, cell **D4** contains the =SUBSTITUTE(B4," ","_") formula, which replaces any spaces in cell **B4** with underscores.

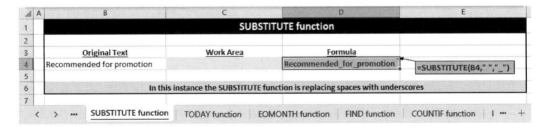

Figure 5.18 – The SUBSTITUTE function

The SUBSTITUTE function has the following four arguments:

- Text: The text to be searched.
- Old_text: The existing text you wish to remove.

- `New_text`: The replacement text you wish to use instead.
- `Instance_num`: This optional argument lets you indicate a specific instance of `old_text` to replace. The formula in cell **D4** omits this argument.

With that background in mind, let's now create dependent **Data Validation** lists.

Assembling the lists

Let's now create the primary and secondary lists as follows:

1. Click on cell **D17** on the **Data Validation** worksheet and choose **Data | Data Validation**.
2. Choose **List** from the **Allow** field and then enter or select `R1:S1` in the **Source** field, as shown in *Figure 5.19*.

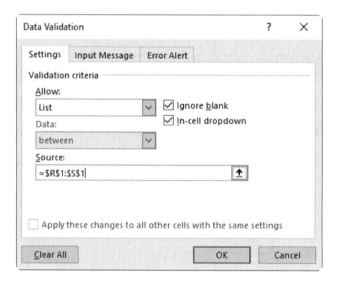

Figure 5.19 – Row-based Data Validation list source

3. Complete the **Input Message** and **Error Alert** tabs and then click **OK**.
4. Select cell **D18** and choose **Data | Data Validation**.
5. Choose **List** from the **Allow** field, and then enter `=INDIRECT(SUBSTITUTE($D$17,"","_"))` in the **Source** field, as shown in *Figure 5.20*.

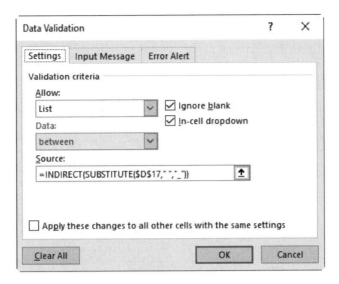

Figure 5.20 – INDIRECT/SUBSTITUTE functions

6. Complete the **Input Message** and **Error Alert** tabs and click **OK**.

The choices available in cell **D18** are now contingent upon the choice that you make in cell **D17**.

> **Nuance**
>
> An invalid entry can remain in cell **D18** if you set cell **D17** to Recommended for promotion and make a selection in **D18** but then change cell **D17** to Not recommended for promotion without also updating **D18**. You can enter the =ISNA(MATCH(D17,INDIRECT(SUBSTITUTE(D17," ","_")),0)) formula in a custom **conditional formatting** rule to make cell **D18** change colors if the entry in the cell does not appear on the corresponding list. We discuss **conditional formatting** and the MATCH function in *Chapters 4, Conditional Formatting,* and *10, Lookup and Dynamic Array Functions,* respectively.

Now let's see how to use the **Date** rule.

Date

The **Date** rule requires a user to enter a date in cells where the rule is in use. For instance, valid inputs in cell **C20** of the **Data Validation** worksheet are any dates between January 1, 2024 and December 31, 2024. The following steps show you how to recreate this functionality:

1. Select cell **D20** and then choose **Data | Data Validation**.

2. Choose **Date** from the **Allow** list and then choose **Between** from the **Data** list.
3. Enter 1/1/2024 in the **Start Date** field and 12/31/2024 in the **End Date** field.
4. Complete the **Input Message** and **Error Alert** tabs and then click **OK**.

You can also create dynamic validation rules with functions such as TODAY and EOMONTH.

The TODAY function

The =TODAY() formula in cell **C3** of the **TODAY function** worksheet returns today's date. This function does not have any arguments, nor does the NOW function in cell **C4**, which returns the current date and time. TODAY and NOW are often interchangeable unless you're comparing a date to the result of the NOW function – the decimal portion that NOW returns that represents the current time can cause the comparison to fail.

Now let's see how to use EOMONTH.

The EOMONTH function

The =EOMONTH(C4,0) formula in cell **D4** on the **EOMONTH function** worksheet returns **12/31/2024** since cell **C4** contains **12/1/2024**. EOMONTH is short for *end of month*, and has the following two arguments:

- Start_date: A static or calculated date.
- Months: The number of months in the future or past for which you want to calculate a month-end date. For instance, use 0 for the current month, 1 for the last day of the following month, -1 for the last day of the previous month, and so on.

Now let's use TODAY and EOMONTH to create a dynamic **Data Validation** rule.

Formula-based Date rule

Cell **C21** of the **Data Validation** worksheet requires an input that is greater than or equal to the first day of the following month. The following steps show you how to recreate this functionality:

1. Click on cell **D21** and choose **Data | Data Validation**.
2. Choose **Date** from the **Allow** List and **Greater than** from the **Data** list.
3. Enter the =EOMONTH(TODAY(),0) formula in the **Start Date** field, as shown in *Figure 5.21*.
4. Complete the **Input Message** and **Error Alert** tabs and then click **OK**.

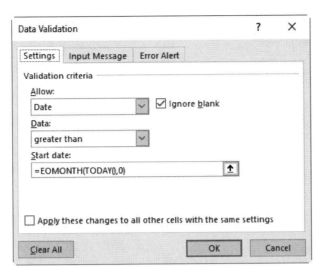

Figure 5.21 – Dynamic Date rule

> **Nuance**
>
> Pay particular attention to whether you want to use **greater than** or **greater than or equal to** when using date inputs. For instance, if you used =EOMONTH(TODAY(),0)+1 with the **greater than** rule, then the user would not be able to enter the first day of a month as a valid choice. Conversely, **greater than or equal to** would work in that case, because adding **1** to the **EOMONTH** calculation returns the first day of the following month.

This brings us to the **Time** rule.

Time

Cell **C23** of the **Data Validation** worksheet requires an input of a time that is between 8:00 AM and 5:00 PM (08:00 to 17:00). The following steps show you how to recreate this functionality:

1. Select cell **D23** and then choose **Data** | **Data Validation**.
2. Choose **Time** from the **Allow** list and accept the default of **Between** in the **Data** list.

3. Enter 8:00 AM (or 08:00) in the **Start time** field and 5:00 PM (or 17:00) in the **End time** field, as shown in *Figure 5.22*.

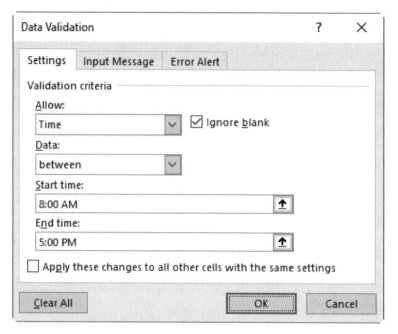

Figure 5.22 – Time restriction rule

> **Tip**
>
> Excel recognizes inputs such as 8 a and 5 p as valid time inputs as well. Inputs such as 8 and 17 are not valid.

4. Complete the **Input Message** and **Error Alert** tabs, and then click **OK**.

> **Nuance**
>
> Time values from **12:00 PM** and onward are tricky. If you type 3:00 in cell **C16**, Excel will interpret the input as **3:00 AM** and will display the error alert. When completing the **Input Message** and **Error Alert** tabs, remind the user to include **AM** or **PM** in their time entries to avoid frustration.

This brings us to the **Text length** rule, which controls the number of characters that can appear in a cell.

Text length

Cell **C25** of the **Data Validation** worksheet allows inputs of up to **10** characters. To recreate this functionality, perform the following steps:

1. Select cell **D23** and then choose **Data | Data Validation**.
2. Choose **Text length** from the **Allow** list and then **Less than or equal to** in the **Data** list.
3. Enter 10 in the **Maximum** field as shown in *Figure 5.23*, complete the **Input Message** and **Error Alert** tabs, and then click **OK**.

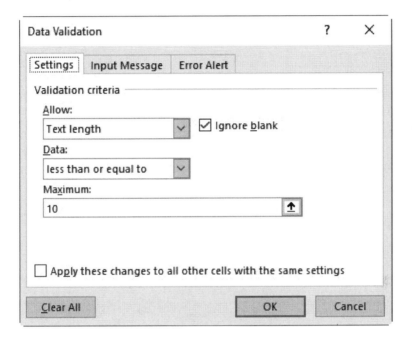

Figure 5.23 – Text length restriction

> **Nuance**
>
> This rule is best suited to situations where you only allow entering a few characters because there is no onscreen feedback as to how many characters the user has typed. For instance, if you set the restriction to less than or equal to 50 characters, it will be difficult at best for the user to know how many characters they've typed. One solution is to first enter the text into any blank cell, such as **H25** in this case, and then use the =LEN(H25) formula to return the number of characters.

Now that we've reviewed the built-in rules, let's see how you can craft your own **Data Validation** rules to suit any purpose.

Custom rules

Custom **Data Validation** rules allow you to craft formulas that determine whether the user has made a valid entry in a cell or not. Formulas used in custom rules must evaluate to TRUE or 0 (zero) for the input to be considered valid. Formulas that evaluate to FALSE, 1, an error such as #N/A and #VALUE, and so on are invalid inputs and will trigger the **Error Alert** prompt. Let's use FIND to create a rule that requires names to be entered in *last name, first name order*, and then we'll use COUNTIF to create a custom rule that prevents duplicate inputs.

The FIND function

Cell **D4** of the **FIND function** worksheet contains the =FIND(",",B4) formula, which returns **10** because cell **B4** contains **Ringstrom, David**, as shown in *Figure 5.24*. This means a comma was found in the tenth position of cell **B4**. Conversely, the =FIND(",",B5) formula in cell **D5** returns #VALUE! because cell **B5** contains **David Ringstrom**, which does not contain a comma.

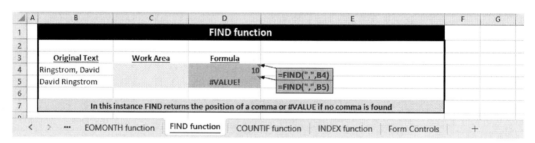

Figure 5.24 – The FIND function

The FIND function has the following three arguments:

- Find_text: Text that you want to search for
- Within_text: Text to be searched
- Start_num: Optional starting position within the text to start the search from

The function either returns the position where find_text is found or returns #VALUE! to indicate that find_text could not be found.

Let's now look at the COUNTIF function.

The COUNTIF function

Cell **E3** of the **COUNTIF function** worksheet contains the =COUNTIF($B$3:$B$11,D3) formula, which returns 3 because the value in cell **D3** appears three times in cells **B3:B11**, as shown in *Figure 5.25*.

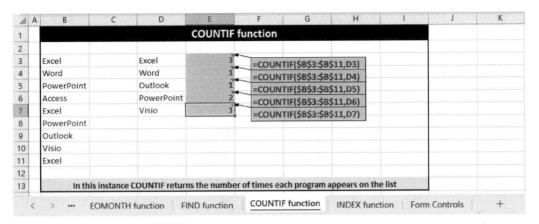

Figure 5.25 – The COUNTIF function

The COUNTIF function has the following arguments:

- Range: The address of two or more cells where you count the number of specific instances of an item
- Criteria: The item that you wish to count to see how many times it appears in the range of cells

Let's now apply the FIND function in a **Data Validation** rule.

Entering names in last name, first name order

Cell **C27** of the **Data Validation** worksheet contains a rule that requires you to enter a name in *last name, first name* order. The following steps show you how to recreate this rule:

1. Select cell **D27** of the **Data Validation** worksheet and then choose **Data | Validation**.

2. Choose **Custom** from the **Allow** list and enter =FIND(",",D27) in the **Formula** field, as shown in *Figure 5.26*.

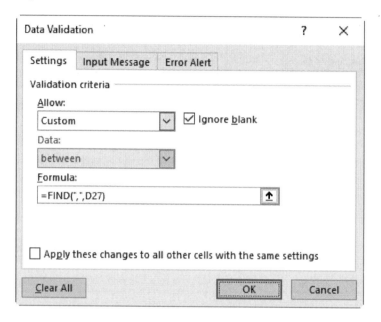

Figure 5.26 – Last name, first name Data Validation rule

3. Complete the **Input Message** and **Error Alert** tabs, and then click **OK**.

> **Nuance**
>
> When creating a rule like this, it is best to have placeholder text in the cell while crafting the rule. For instance, if you leave cell **D27** blank and create a custom rule with the =FIND(",",D27) formula, Excel will display a prompt that states **This formula currently evaluates to an error. Do you want to continue?** This can make it difficult to determine whether you have an actual error in your formula or if this prompt is appearing because the cell is blank.

Preventing duplicate entries

Cells **C29:C33** of the **Data Validation** worksheet contain a rule that prevents duplicate values from being entered in this part of the worksheet. The following steps show you how to put such a rule in place:

1. Select cells **D29:D33** and then choose **Data | Validation**.
2. Choose **Custom** from the **Allow** list and then enter =COUNTIF($D$29:$D$33,D29)=1 in the **Formula** field, as shown in *Figure 5.27*.

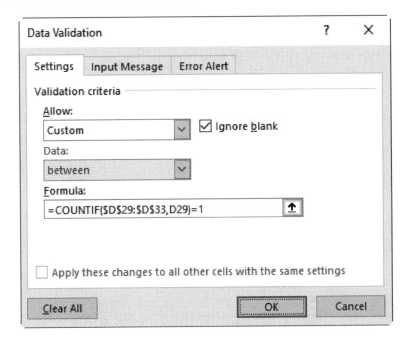

Figure 5.27 – Preventing duplicate entries rule

3. Complete the **Input Message** and **Error Alert** tabs and then click **OK**.

In *Chapter 4, Conditional Formatting*, I showed you how you can color-code duplicate entries in a list. You can pair that functionality with **Data Validation** to identify and block duplicate entries on the fly. In this case, COUNTIF determines how many times a cell value appears within **D29:D33**. **Data Validation** displays an **Error Alert** prompt if the result is anything other than **1**; otherwise, the input is accepted without issue. Blank cells are not evaluated in this context.

> **Nuance**
>
> Pay close attention to the absolute versus relative references in =COUNTIF($C$19:$C$23,C19)=1. Notice that the *range* portion of the formula is an absolute reference. If you omit the $ signs, then **Data Validation** will use a different range on every row, which will cause your **Data Validation** restrictions to not work correctly. Conversely, make sure not to use any $ with the *criteria*; otherwise, that cell will be used as the input for all other cells, which again may cause the rule to malfunction.

Now that we've explored **Data Validation** from every angle, let's see how to protect the rules that you implement in your spreadsheets.

Protecting Data Validation cells

A downside of **Data Validation** is that users can purposefully or inadvertently remove rules from cells by copying and pasting. Excel doesn't ask, *are you sure?*; it simply erases any **Data Validation** settings. The following steps show you how to protect your **Data Validation** rules:

1. Select any cell on the **Data Validation** worksheet, and then choose **Home** | **Find & Select** | **Data Validation** to select all cells that have **Data Validation** rules assigned.
2. Press *Ctrl+1* (⌘*+1*) or choose **Home** | **Format** | **Format Cells** | **Protection**.
3. As shown in *Figure 5.28*, clear the **Locked** checkbox and then click **OK**.

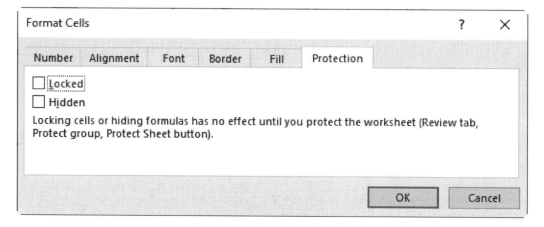

Figure 5.28 – Unlocking cells

4. Choose **Review** | **Protect Sheet**, optionally enter and confirm a password, and then click **OK**.

> **Tip**
>
> You must use the **Protect Sheet** command to protect your **Data Validation** settings. Unlocking the cells is only a precursor step that on its own does not offer any protection.

This offers *partial* protection of your **Data Validation** settings because users cannot erase the rules by pasting data into a cell, although invalid inputs will still be pasted.

Auditing Data Validation cell inputs

The **Circle Invalid Data** command in Excel enables you to identify cells where a user bypassed **Data Validation** settings by pasting information into a cell. The following steps show you how to perform the audit:

1. Choose **Review** | **Unprotect Sheet** and enter the password to unprotect the worksheet if necessary.
2. Choose **Data** | **Data Validation** drop-down menu | **Circle Invalid Data**, as shown in *Figure 5.29*.

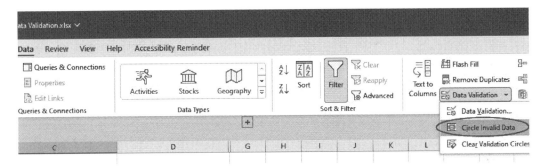

Figure 5.29 – The Circle Invalid Data command

Red circles will appear around any cells where the user has entered invalid data. No feedback will be offered if all cells comply. Keep in mind, though, that the red circles vanish when you save the file, or when you choose **Data** | **Data Validation** drop-down menu | **Clear Validation Circles**.

Now that you have a sense of the limitations of **Data Validation**, let's explore a more robust alternative known as **Form Controls**. We'll first need to unhide a hidden tab within Excel's ribbon.

Enabling the Developer tab

The menu across the top of the Excel screen is known as the **ribbon**. As you may have noticed, certain tabs appear and disappear from the ribbon based on context. For instance, a **Table Design** tab appears when you click on a **Table** in your workbook and vanishes when you click on any cell that is not part of a **Table**. The hidden **Developer** tab has commands related to creating macros, working with XML files, and creating **Form Controls**. You must enable the **Developer** tab if you wish to create **Form Controls**, as follows:

1. Choose **File** | **Options** | **Customize Ribbon**.

2. Click the **Developer** checkbox on the right-hand side, as shown in *Figure 5.30*, and then click **OK**.

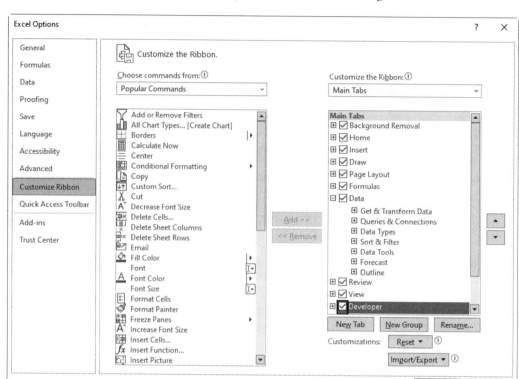

Figure 5.30 – Enabling the Developer tab

Now that you have enabled the **Developer** tab in Excel's ribbon, we can compare **Form Controls** to **Data Validation** when additional control or different interactivity is warranted.

Exploring Form Controls

Form Controls are objects that you can use to add interactivity to an Excel worksheet. Unlike **Data Validation**, users can't circumvent **Form Controls** by pasting over the data. *Figure 5.31* shows the **Developer | Insert** command and displays three of the types of **Form Controls** that are available.

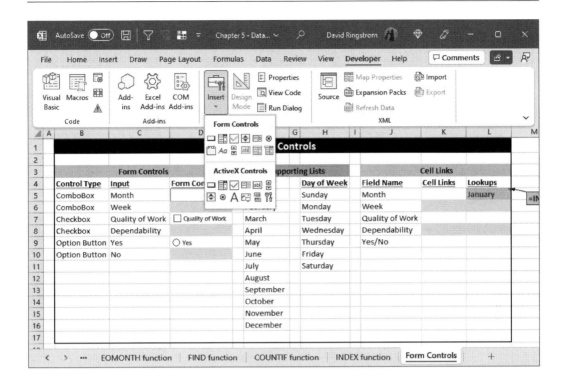

Figure 5.31 – Insert command and Form Controls

I'll demonstrate the following **Form Controls**:

- The **Combo Box** in cell **D5**
- The **Checkbox** in cell **D7**
- The **Option Button** in cell **D9**

I don't have space to go very deep on **Form Controls**, but mastering the preceding three types will give you a good sense of how **Form Controls** work.

> **Nuance**
>
> As you can see in *Figure 5.31*, Excel offers both **Form Controls** and **ActiveX Controls**. Typically, **Form Controls** will enable you to create the interactivity that you're seeking. **ActiveX Controls** are similar but more sophisticated. For instance, you must enable **Design Mode** on the **Developer** tab to work with **ActiveX Controls** and click the **Properties** command to display a panel of settings related to the control. In addition, **ActiveX Controls** cannot be displayed in Excel for macOS.

Form Controls float above the worksheet, but you can capture the choice that the user made in a worksheet cell that you designate as the **cell link**. The cell link often contains a position number that you may want to translate back to an actual choice. Let's see how to accomplish that with the INDEX function.

The INDEX function

Cell **C4** of the **INDEX function** worksheet contains the =INDEX($E$4:$E$7,B4) formula that returns **Summer**, since cell **B4** contains **3**, as shown in *Figure 5.32*. This means that the INDEX function is returning the third value from cells **E4:E7**. Cell **C5** contains the =INDEX($E$4:$E$7,B5) formula that returns **#REF!** because E4:E7 is a four-cell range while **B5** contains 5. It is impossible to return a fifth value from a four-cell range.

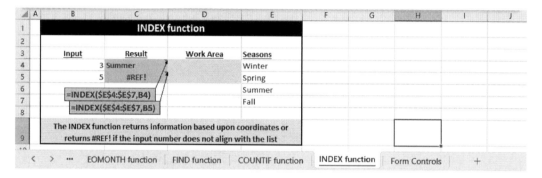

Figure 5.32 – The INDEX function

I discuss the INDEX function in more detail in *Chapter 10, Lookup and Dynamic Array Functions*, particularly how it is often paired with the MATCH function. We don't need MATCH in this context because our **Form Controls** will provide a position number instead.

Now let's create a **Combo Box**, which functions like a **Data Validation** list.

Combo Box Form Control

A **Combo Box** is a combination of a data entry field and a drop-down list. The catch is you cannot type directly into the field itself; you must instead make a choice from the list. This will frustrate users that rely on keyboard shortcuts, as a mouse or touchscreen is required to access a **Combo Box**.

Cell **D5** of the **Form Controls** worksheet has a **Combo Box** that is tied to the list in cells **G5:G16**. When you click on the drop-down arrow, notice that you can see all 12 months on the list without needing to scroll in the fashion required by **Data Validation** in older versions of Excel. The position of the choice that you make is stored in cell **L5**, and the =@INDEX(F5:F16,K5) formula returns the name of the month that you chose.

> **Nuance**
>
> The @ sign is known as the implicit intersection operator in Excel. I included it in the formula because in **Microsoft 365** and **Excel 2021** when cell **K5** is blank, the INDEX function will either display all 12 months in cells **L5:L16**, or return a #SPILL! error. The @ sign instructs Excel to always display the first item in the array, which will either be **January**, or the item from the list that corresponds to the index number returned by the **Combo Box**. In **Microsoft 365** and **Excel 2021**, INDEX is now a dynamic array function that can return multiple values. I discuss the concept of dynamic arrays in much more detail in *Chapter 10*.

Let's now create a **Combo Box** based on cells **H5:H11** so that you can understand the process, as follows:

1. Choose **Developer | Insert** and then choose the **Combo Box** control, which is the second icon on the first row of the **Form Controls** section, as shown in *Figure 5.31*.
2. Hold down your left-click mouse button and drag a rectangle in cell **D6** to create the **Combo Box**.

> **Tip**
>
> If your mouse gets out from under you, you may end up with a large arrow on your screen. If this happens, right-click on the arrow and then grab the handles with your mouse to pull the arrow into a **Combo Box** such as cell **D5**. In **Excel for Windows**, you can hold down the *Alt* key while you drag within a cell to make a **Combo Box** snap to the exact size of the underlying worksheet cell. Unfortunately, there is no equivalent key in **Excel for macOS**.

3. Right-click on the **Combo Box**, choose **Format Control | Protection**, and then clear **Locked**. If you don't, the form control will be frozen on screen if you protect the worksheet.
4. Activate the **Control** tab and then enter or select H5:H11 in the **Input range** field, as shown in *Figure 5.33*.

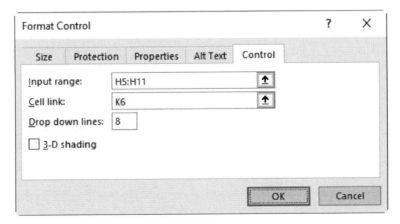

Figure 5.33 – The Format Control dialog box

5. Enter or select K6 in the **Cell link** field.
6. Optional: Adjust the **Drop down lines** field if needed.
7. Click on **OK**.
8. Click on any cell other than **D6** to deselect the **Combo Box**, and then notice how a position number appears in cell **K6** when you make a choice from the **Combo Box**.
9. Enter =@INDEX(H5:H11,K6) in cell **L6** to return the name of the day of the week that you chose.

> **Tip**
> It's typically best to store cell links on a separate worksheet from the **Form Controls** so that you don't inadvertently compromise the cells when making edits to your form. If the cell links reside on a worksheet that you will be protecting, make sure to unprotect the cell link cells; otherwise, you will encounter an error when you attempt to use your form control because Excel cannot update locked cells. See the *Protecting Data Validation cells* section if you're unclear as to how to unlock cells.

As you can see, **Combo Box** controls are like **Data Validation** lists but cannot be overridden by pasting data into them. Let's now see how to add **Checkboxes** and **Option Buttons** to a worksheet.

Checkboxes and Option Buttons

Checkboxes and **Option Buttons** enable you to allow the user to make choices within a spreadsheet. Users can tick as many **Checkboxes** as they would like, whereas **Option Buttons** (sometimes referred to as **radio buttons**) allow a single choice within a group. Let's compare the differences between **Checkboxes** and **Option Buttons**.

Creating Checkboxes

Cell **D7** of the **Form Controls** worksheet contains a **Checkbox** that is linked to cell **K7**. When you click the **Checkbox**, Excel puts the word **TRUE** in cell **K7**. If you click the **Checkbox** again, Excel puts the word **FALSE**. If you wish to reset the **Checkbox**, simply erase cell **K7**.

Now let's see how to add a **Checkbox** to cell **D8** as follows:

1. Choose **Developer | Insert** and then click the **Checkbox** command, which is the third command on the first row under **Form Controls**, as shown in *Figure 5.31*.
2. Click in cell **D8** to create the **Checkbox**.
3. If needed, right-click on the **Checkbox** to display the handles around the outside, and then use the arrow keys to nudge the **Checkbox** into the desired position.

4. When the handles are present, click once on the text and make any edits, such as entering `Dependability`. (You can also right-click on the text when you first insert the **Checkbox** and select **Edit Text**, but this option eventually disappears once the text has been customized.) Remove all text if you only want a **Checkbox** as opposed to a **Checkbox** and a label.

5. Right-click on the **Checkbox** and choose **Format Control** | the **Protection** tab and clear the **Locked** checkbox.

6. Activate the **Control** tab, enter or select K8 in the **Cell Link** field, and then click **OK**.

Users can make as many choices from **Checkboxes** as are applicable. Conversely, **Option Buttons** function more like a list, meaning the user can only choose one **Option Button** at a time.

Creating Option Buttons

Cell **D9** of the **Form Controls** worksheet contains an **Option Button** that is linked to cell **K9**. When you click on the **Option Button**, Excel puts the number **1** in cell **K9**. Until you add another **Option Button**, the only way to clear this option is to erase cell **K9**.

Now let's add a second **Option Button** as follows:

1. Choose **Developer** | **Insert** and then click the **Checkbox** command, which is the third command on the first row under **Form Controls**, as shown in *Figure 5.31*.

2. Click in cell **D10** to create the **Option Button**.

3. If needed, right-click on the **Option Button** to display the handles around the outside, and then use the arrow keys to nudge the control into the desired position.

4. When the handles are present, click once on the text and make any edits, such as entering No. Remove all text if you only want an **Option Button** as opposed to an **Option Button** and a label.

5. Right-click on the **Checkbox** and choose **Format Control** | the **Protection** tab and clear the **Locked** checkbox.

6. Activate the **Control** tab, and notice that **Linked Cell** is already set to **K9** as **Option Buttons** automatically share the same linked cell, and then click **OK**.

7. Click any cell other than **D10** to deselect the **Option Button** and then click on the **Option Button** in cell **D10**. Number **2** should appear in cell **K9**, indicating that you chose the second **Option Button**.

If you wish to have more than one set of **Option Buttons** on a worksheet, you'll need to place a **Group Box** form control around the **Option Buttons** so that Excel knows which buttons comprise a set. The **Group Box** control appears under **Developer** | **Form Controls**.

Managing Form Controls

Since **Form Controls** float above the worksheet, you can choose to temporarily hide them if you wish, as follows:

1. Choose **Home | Find & Select | Selection Pane**.
2. Click on the icon to the right of any object in the **Selection** task pane to hide it, as shown in *Figure 5.34*. The icon is a toggle, so you can unhide objects in the same fashion. Furthermore, you can double-click the name of the object in the **Selection** pane and provide a more meaningful name so that you can better keep track of the various objects on a worksheet.

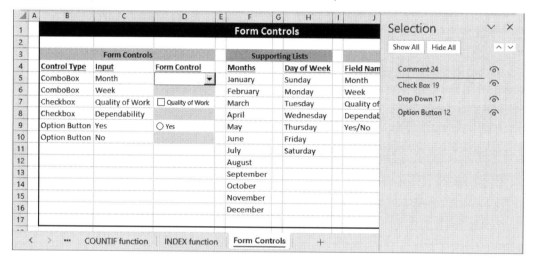

Figure 5.34 – The Selection task pane

Alternatively, you can use the **Hide All** and **Show All** commands at the top of the **Selection** pane to hide or show floating objects en masse.

> **Nuance**
>
> The **Selection Pane** allows you to show or hide any object that floats above the worksheet, including but not limited to **PivotCharts**, Charts, Text Boxes, Slicers, Shapes and anything else that floats above the worksheet.

Since **Form Controls** float above the worksheet, it is easy to sometimes knock them out of alignment with each other, but you can group them together as follows:

1. Choose **Home | Find & Select | Select Objects** and then click on any form control.
2. Hold down the *Ctrl* key (⌘) and select as many additional **Form Controls** as you wish.
3. Right-click on any form control and choose **Group | Group**.

You can now move the controls around the worksheet en masse and preserve their alignment and spacing with each other. You will need to ungroup the controls if you want to edit any of them. To do so, right-click on any control in the group and choose **Group | Ungroup**. As you can see, **Form Controls** go beyond **Data Validation**. It is harder to keep track of the choices that a user makes with a form control since the form control floats above the worksheet, but setting cell link controls enables you to track the choices made.

Summary

In this chapter, you learned how to use **Data Validation** to limit users' responses within specific worksheet cells. The default rules you can establish include **Whole Number**, **Decimal**, **List**, **Date**, **Time**, and **Text length**. As you saw, you can also create custom rules to establish any sort of limit that you may need.

Data Validation is an imperfect feature that users can bypass by pasting data into cells that contain validation rules. Furthermore, any data that is already in cells that you apply **Data Validation** to is exempted from the rules. Fortunately, you can audit **Data Validation** entries by having Excel draw red circles around the invalid inputs.

Finally, you saw that **Form Controls** offer an alternative to **Data Validation** that creates restrictions that users cannot bypass by pasting data. In short, **Data Validation** and **Form Controls** are all about adding interactivity to spreadsheets.

In the following chapter, you'll see how you can use **What-If Analysis** tools in Excel to provide other forms of interactivity and automation in your spreadsheets.

6
What-If Analysis

Many users are unaware of the **What-If Analysis** features in Excel, which can be used to find answers to questions in an automated fashion. I'll start lead off by I'll start by showing you how to use the **Scenario Manager** feature to both you to back up key inputs and compare the results of different sets of inputs. I'll then use the **Goal Seek** feature to automate solving for a missing input within a calculation. After that I'll show you how the **Data Table** feature can streamline situations where, normally, the user would need to rewrite formulas to handle a variety of inputs, such as comparing what a mortgage payment would be at two different interest rates and loan terms. We'll use the **Forecast Sheet** feature to project amounts into the future, and then finish up with a brief look at Excel's **Solver** feature.

In this chapter, we will cover the following primary topics:

- PMT function
- CUMIMPT function
- CUMPRINC function
- **Scenario Manager** feature
- **Goal Seek** feature
- **Data Table** feature
- **Forecast Sheet** feature
- A brief introduction to the **Solver** feature

By the end of the chapter, you should have a much better understanding of how what-if features in Excel can eliminate guesswork and repetitive actions in your spreadsheets. In certain instances, the CUMIMPT and CUMPRINC functions might enable you to eliminate or verify amortization tables that you use in your spreadsheets. You'll see that **Goal Seek** works backward to provide a missing input, while **Solver** can work forward or backward. The **Data Table**, **Forecast Sheet**, and **Scenario Manager** features help you to look forward, too.

Technical requirements

Everything that I discuss in this chapter will work in any current version of Excel, except for the **Forecast Sheet** feature, which requires the Windows version of **Excel 2016** or later. This feature is not available in Excel for macOS or **Excel for the Web**. However, you can view **Forecast Sheets** that have been created in **Excel for Windows** in the macOS and online versions.

An example workbook that contains all of the formulas used in this chapter, along with work areas so that you can try the features I discuss, can be found on GitHub at https://github.com/PacktPublishing/Exploring-Microsoft-Excels-Hidden-Treasures/tree/main/Chapter6.

Let's lead with a look at a worksheet function that enables you to calculate loan payment amounts. I'll be using this function, and others, throughout this chapter as we work through various What-If Analysis scenarios.

The PMT function

The =-PMT(C3/12,C4*12,C5) formula in cell **C6** of the **PMT-CUMIPMT functions** worksheet, as shown in *Figure 6.1*, returns **$578.57** as the monthly payment for a $25,000 loan paid off over 4 years at 5.25% interest:

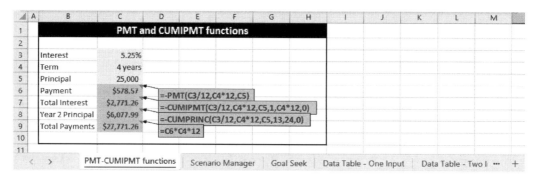

Figure 6.1 – The PMT, CUMIPMT, and CUMPRINC functions

Before I get to the PMT function, let me share a trick I used to display the word **years** in cell **C4**. Visually, you see **4 years** in the cell, but if you look in the formula bar, only the number **4** appears. This is because I used a custom number format to add the word **years**. This is a way of displaying text and numbers in the same cell while maintaining the cell as a numeric input. To do so, perform the following steps:

1. Select the cell(s) you wish to format, in this case, cell **C4**.
2. Choose **Format | Format Cells** or press *Ctrl + 1* (⌘ *+ 1* in Excel for macOS).

3. Choose **Custom** on the **Number** tab.
4. Enter `0" years"` in the **Type** field. In this case, 0 represents our numeric input, while anything in quotes will also visually appear in the cell but will not be part of the cell's contents.
5. Click on **OK** to close the **Format Cells** dialog box.

> Nuance
>
> The `PMT` function always assumes that loan payments are an outflow, so the result is always a negative amount. Often, I add a minus sign before `PMT` in the formula to return a positive amount instead.

The `PMT` function has three required arguments and two optional arguments:

- **Rate**: This required argument specifies the interest rate for the loan, which, in this case, is **5.25%** from cell **C3** divided by **12** since we are calculating a monthly loan payment.
- **Nper**: This required argument specifies the number of periods in the loan, which, in this case, is **4** from cell **C4** multiplied by **12** or **48** months.
- **Pv**: The name of this required argument is short for the present value, since money loses value over time, but is also known as the loan amount or principal from cell **C5**, which, in this case, is **$25,000**.
- **Fv**: The name of this optional argument is short for **future value**, and is for loans with a balloon payment at the end. In this case, **fv** is not provided since the loan is to be paid in full over four years.
- **Type**: This optional argument defaults to **0**, which signifies payments made at the end of a loan period, or you can specify **1** to signify payments made at the beginning of a loan period; in this case, payments are being made at the end of each loan period.

Now, let's calculate the interest paid over the entirety of the loan.

The CUMIPMT function

The `=-CUMIPMT(C3/12,C4,C5,1,C4,0)` formula in cell **C7** of *Figure 6.1* returns 2,771.26 as the interest due on a loan of $25,000 paid off over four years at an interest rate of 5.25%.

The `CUMIMPT` function has six required arguments:

- **Rate**: The interest rate for the loan, which, in this case, is **5.25%** from cell **C3** divided by **12** to create a monthly interest rate.
- **Nper**: The number of periods in the loan, which, in this case, is **4** years from cell **C4** multiplied by **12** or **48** months.

- **Pv**: This argument name is short for **present value**, since money loses value over time, but is also known as the loan amount or principal from cell **C5**, which, in this case, is $25,000.
- **Start_period**: The period number within the loan to start calculating the interest due—this is not a date, but a period number, for instance, `1` to represent the first period in the loan.
- **End_period**: The period number through which to calculate the interest amount, which, in this case, is **4** from cell **C4** multiplied by **12** or the **48th** month.
- **Type**: Unlike the `PMT` function, you *must* specify either `0` for payments made at the end of a loan period or `1` to signify payments made at the beginning; in this case, **0** signifies payments made at the end of each period. This argument is optional with `PMT`.

The `=-CUMPRINC(C3/12,C4*12,C5,13,24,0)` formula in cell **C8** of *Figure 6.1* calculates the principal paid in the second year of the loan, meaning months **13** through **24**. `CUMPRINC` requires the same six arguments as `CUMIPMT` but typically isn't used for the entirety of the loan if the goal is to repay the loan in full, as opposed to having a balloon payment after a certain number of months or years have elapsed.

> **Tip**
> You can add an amortization table to any workbook with just a couple of mouse clicks if you want to verify your work with the `PMT`, `CUMIMPT`, or `CUMPRINC` functions. In **Excel for Windows**, right-click on any worksheet tab and choose **Insert | Spreadsheet Solutions**. Double-click on **Loan Amortization**. In **Excel for macOS**, you can't insert the amortization table directly, but you can choose **File | New From Template**, and then use the **Search** field in the upper-right corner to search for `Amortization Schedule`. Double-click on the template of your choice, and then move the sheet into your existing workbook.

The `=C6*C4*12` formula in cell **C9** returns $27,771.26, which is the monthly payment multiplied by the number of years multiplied by **12**. In short, this formula verifies that the sum of all the payments matches the **$25,000** principal plus **$2,771.26** in interest.

Now that we have calculated a loan payment and total interest for a specific loan amount, let's work our way through the **What-if Analysis** features in Excel, starting with **Scenario Manager**.

Understanding the Scenario Manager feature

Scenario Manager can save you time as it eliminates the need to recreate portions of a worksheet to compare different sets of assumptions. Even better, Excel offers two reports that will compare the results of your sets of assumptions automatically.

Understanding the Scenario Manager feature

There are a couple of constraints to keep in mind:

- Scenarios are limited to a single worksheet, meaning all inputs in the scenario must be on the same worksheet.
- Each scenario is limited to **32** inputs. However, you can apply scenarios sequentially to go beyond the 32-item input.
- There is no limit to the number of scenarios that you can store on a given worksheet.

First, let's set up a calculation that serves as a vehicle for understanding scenarios. Following this, we'll create multiple scenarios that we'll swap through the calculation, and then use comparison reports to see the results of our scenarios side by side. Additionally, you'll see how to transfer scenarios between worksheets and between workbooks.

Setting the scene for a scenario

Let's say that you're contemplating purchasing two houses at two different price levels, and you want to compare **15-year** financing with **30-year** financing. For such a simple calculation, you'd probably set the calculations up in four columns. Instead, we'll use **Scenario Manager** to compare the results so that you can extrapolate how this can help streamline larger worksheets. The **Scenario Manager** worksheet in this chapter's example workbook has the inputs in place for our first scenario, as shown in *Figure 6.2*:

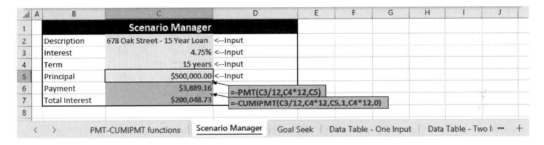

Figure 6.2 – The first of four scenarios

- Cell **C2** contains a **Description** input, which, in this case, is `678 Oak Street - 15 Year Loan`

> **Tip**
>
> If your scenario has fewer than 32 inputs, store a description of the scenario in a worksheet cell that you can include in the scenario. Doing so will help you stay aware of which scenario is presently applied to the worksheet. It's easy to lose track when swapping multiple scenarios into a worksheet.

- Cell **C3** contains the **Interest** input, which, in this case, is 4.75%
- Cell **C4** contains the **Term** input, which, in this case, is 15 for a 15-year loan
- Cell **C5** contains the **Principal** input, which, in this case, is **$500,000**

Cells **C2:C4** will comprise the scenario, while cells **C5:C6** contain calculations that each scenario will reference:

- Cell **C5** contains the =-PMT(C3/12,C4*12,C5) formula to calculate the monthly payment for the loan.
- Cell **C6** contains the =-CUMIPMT(C3/12,C4*12,C5,1,C4*12,0) formula to calculate the total interest that you would pay over the life of the loan.

> **Nuance**
>
> You only store text or numbers in a scenario—when you apply the scenario, Excel will warn you that any formulas will be converted into static values. Additionally, you cannot store **Data Type** cells in a scenario either. Data Types are a new type of input that is linked to online sources. Examples of Data Types include but are not limited to stocks and geography.

Now that we have the basis for calculating an established loan, let's create some scenarios.

Creating scenarios

Let's create our first scenario based on the inputs that are already in the worksheet:

1. Select cells **C2:C5**. If necessary, you can hold down the *Ctrl* (⌘) key to select any non-adjacent cells.
2. Choose **Data | What-If Analysis | Scenario Manager**.
3. Click on the **Add** button in the **Scenario Manager** dialog box (or click on the **plus sign** button in **Excel for macOS**).
4. Assign a name to the scenario, such as 678 Oak Street - 15 Year Loan, in the **Add Scenario** dialog box, as shown in *Figure 6.3*:

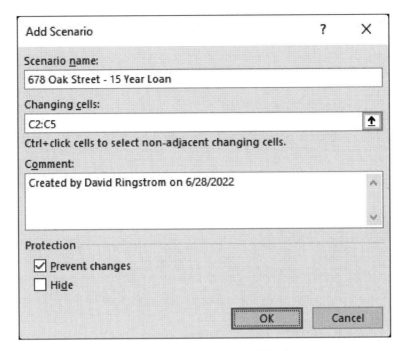

Figure 6.3 – The Add Scenario dialog box

5. Confirm the **Changing Cells** field encompasses the cells that you wish to include in your scenario.

> **Nuance**
>
> In this case, the **Changing Cells** field should be prefilled with the cells you wish to include in the scenario because we preselected them in *step 1*. If you forget to select the cells in advance, you can always use the **Changing Cells** field to choose the fields.

6. Optionally, choose **Prevent Changes** to prevent users from modifying the scenario if the worksheet is protected.

7. Optionally, choose **Hide** to prevent users from being able to apply the scenario if the worksheet is protected.

8. Click on **OK**.

9. Confirm the values to be captured in the **Scenario Values** dialog box, as shown in *Figure 6.4*. In **Excel for Windows**, you'll see a list of the cells and the values, whereas in **Excel for macOS**, you'll need to click on each cell reference to see the underlying values—although this will be the same information that you can see in the worksheet:

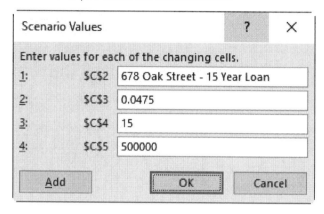

Figure 6.4 – The Scenario Values dialog box

10. At this point, you can click on **OK** to save the scenario or click on **Add** to create a new scenario. In this case, click on **Add**.
11. The **Add Scenario** dialog box reappears. Enter 678 Oak Street - 30 Year Loan in the **Scenario Name** field.
12. Optionally, click on **Prevent Changes** and/or **Hide**. Click on **OK**.
13. Change the value for cell **C2** to 678 Oak Street - 30 Year Loan.
14. Change the value for cell **C3** to 5.25%.
15. Change the value for cell **C4** to 30.
16. Click on **Add** to add another scenario.
17. Create two new scenarios for 345 Pine Street for the **15**-year and **30**-year loans, respectively. The **15-year loan** has an interest rate of 4.75%, the **30-year loan** has a rate of 5.25%, and the **Principal** amount is $450,000.
18. Click on **Close** to close the **Scenario Manager** dialog box.

Once you've created two or more scenarios, you can swap them in and out of your worksheet.

Showing scenarios

Now that we have four scenarios in place, let's apply one to our worksheet:

1. Choose **Data** | **What-If Analysis** | **Scenario Manager**.

2. Choose a scenario, such as `345 Pine Street - 30 Year Loan`, and click on **Show**.
3. As shown in *Figure 6.5*, cells **C2:C5** should reflect the inputs for your scenario:

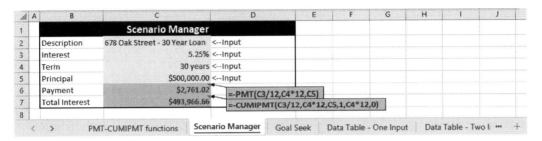

Figure 6.5 – The scenario applied to the worksheet

Clearly, being able to apply various scenarios to a worksheet can help improve spreadsheet integrity because you can reuse existing calculations in the worksheet. Also, **Scenario Manager** offers a means to back up sets of assumptions, particularly in situations where certain users might have a predisposition toward overwriting assumptions in a worksheet. However, one of the best aspects of **Scenario Manager** is the ability to run a scenario report that allows you to compare the inputs and outputs of your scenarios.

Scenario reports

Excel offers two different types of scenario reports:

- **Scenario Summary**: This provides comprehensive detail, including listing all the inputs used in the scenario and up to 32 result cells that are formulas that reference the inputs.

- **Scenario PivotTable**: This compares the results of the summaries in a **PivotTable** format but does not display the input values used in the scenario.

Each report appears on a new worksheet in your workbook every time you generate the report. Neither report contains any live formulas, so you'll need to recreate the scenario summaries any time you change the values in an existing scenario or add/delete scenarios.

The Scenario Summary report

The **Scenario Summary** report gives you the best comparison of your scenarios. The report shows the cell addresses for both inputs and outputs. In this context, an output is a formula that relies on one or more of the input cells. To create the **Scenario Summary** report, perform the following steps:

1. Choose **Data** | **What-If Analysis** | **Scenario Manager** | **Summary**.

2. If necessary, specify cells **C6:C7** in the **Result cells** field, as shown in *Figure 6.6*:

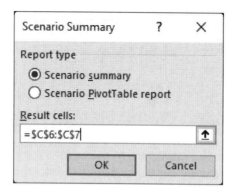

Figure 6.6 – Scenario Summary dialog box

3. Click on **OK** to accept the default choice of **Scenario Summary**.
4. A **Scenario Summary** report appears on a new worksheet, as shown in *Figure 6.7*:

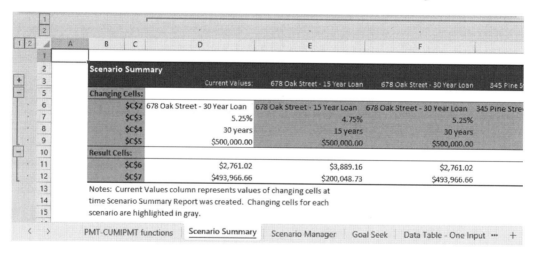

Figure 6.7 – The Scenario Summary report

Depending upon the complexity of your scenarios, it can become difficult to cross-reference the addresses in the **Changing Cells** column to your actual data. Fortunately, there's a simple fix:

1. Select cells **B2:C7** in the **Scenario Summary** worksheet.
2. Choose **Formulas | Create from Selection**.
3. Select **Left column**, and then deselect any other choices that were preselected, as shown in *Figure 6.8*:

Understanding the Scenario Manager feature

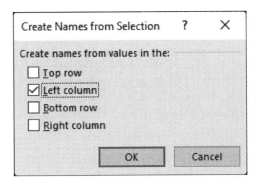

Figure 6.8 – Create Names from Selection dialog box

In this case, Excel will assign the words in column **B** to the inputs in column **C**. Now, let's create the **Scenario Summary** report again:

1. Active the **Scenario Summary** worksheet if needed.
2. Choose **Data | What-If Analysis | Scenario Manager | Summary**.
3. Click on **OK** to accept the default choice of **Scenario Summary**.
4. A second **Scenario Summary** report appears on a new worksheet, as shown in *Figure 6.9*:

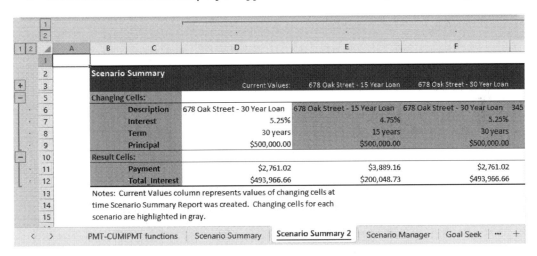

Figure 6.9 – Our second Scenario Summary report

Notice that range names appear in the **Changing Cells** column instead of cell addresses so that you can readily identify each input. Excel uses the **Outline** feature with the **Scenario Summary** report. This adds buttons adjacent to the worksheet frame that you can use to expand and collapse the report, which is a great way to manage information overload.

Now, let's contrast the **Scenario Summary** report with the **Scenario PivotTable** report.

The Scenario PivotTable report

The **Scenario PivotTable** report is generated in a similar fashion to the **Scenario Summary** report, but at first blush, it might seem that the report only provides the results and doesn't display the inputs. As you'll see in a moment, you can choose what the report includes. To create the **Scenario PivotTable** report, perform the following steps:

1. Choose **Data | What-If Analysis | Scenario Manager | Summary**.
2. Confirm that Excel has selected the result cells (sometimes, Excel will leave this field blank), which, in this case, are cells **C6:C7**.
3. Double-click on **Scenario PivotTable** (or click once on **Scenario PivotTable** and then click on **OK**).
4. A third new worksheet appears and displays the **Scenario PivotTable** report, as shown in *Figure 6.10*:

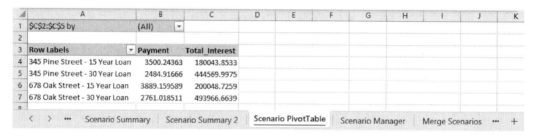

Figure 6.10 – The Scenario PivotTable report

Notice how any result fields in the **PivotTable** will have unformatted numbers. This is a default behavior in Excel, so you'll have to format the result fields any time you create a **Scenario PivotTable** report.

> **Nuance**
>
> By default, the **Scenario PivotTable** report option only displays the result cells, meaning the cells that contain formulas based upon the scenario inputs. If you change the **Result Cells** option to also include your input cells, which, in this case, are **C2:C7** instead of just **C6:C7**, then the **PivotTable** will display the inputs too, creating a much more helpful report. The one quirk is that any input cells you select that contain text will be represented by the number 1, which identifies how many times the text appears within that range of cells.

Although the **Scenario PivotTable** report looks like a regular **PivotTable**, it cannot be refreshed. Therefore, if you change any of the inputs in your scenario, you'll need to create the **Scenario PivotTable** report again. With that said, let's say that you discover something that you want to change about a scenario.

If you choose **Data | What-If Analysis | Scenario Manager** from a scenario report worksheet, **Scenario Manager** will report that no scenarios exist. This is true for the worksheet, but not the workbook. Remember, to change a scenario, you must return to the original worksheet where you first created the scenario. However, you can transfer scenarios from one worksheet to another worksheet or workbook.

Merging scenarios

You can move scenarios to any other worksheet in a workbook or from an external workbook by way of the **Merge** command. It's easy to misconstrue the word *merge* in this context because the scenarios don't really get merged—a more apt name for the command would be *transfer* or *copy*, as the scenarios get copied from one worksheet to another. Keep in mind that it will only make sense to merge scenarios between worksheets that are identically structured, at least in terms of the input cells; otherwise, you run the risk of unexpectedly overwriting data in your workbook. Here's how to merge scenarios:

1. Activate the **Merge Scenarios** worksheet.
2. Choose **Data | What-If Analysis | Scenario Manager**.
3. The **Scenario Manager** dialog box will report **No Scenarios defined** because, presently, no scenarios exist on this worksheet. Click on **Merge**.
4. As shown in *Figure 6.11*, the **Merge Scenarios** dialog box will show you a list of the worksheets in the current workbook. The number of scenarios available on the worksheet that you select from the **Sheet** list will appear below the list. The **OK** button will be disabled if no scenarios are available on a given worksheet. Select the **Scenario Manager** worksheet, and then click on **OK**.

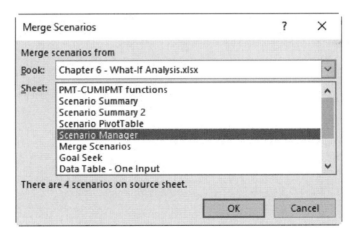

Figure 6.11 – The Merge Scenarios dialog box

5. The **Scenario Manager** dialog box reappears and displays the four scenarios that have been copied from the **Scenario Manager** worksheet. Choose a scenario and click on **OK**, or click on **Close** to dismiss the **Scenario Manager** dialog box.

> **Tip**
> The **Merge Scenarios** dialog box does not allow you to choose which scenarios get copied to your worksheet. It functions on an all-or-nothing basis, meaning you must copy *all* the scenarios from a worksheet. However, you can use the **Delete** button within the **Scenario Manager** dialog box to remove any extraneous scenarios.

As you can see, **Scenario Manager** is a powerful feature that can help you rein in your Excel workbooks by being able to swap sets of inputs through a single worksheet, rather than recreating calculations over and over. You do have to work within the 32-input constraint both for inputs and results. One workaround is that you can create related sets of scenarios that you can apply sequentially, such as `Scenario 1 (Set 1 of 2)` and `Scenario 1 (Set 2 of 2)`. You won't be able to create a **Scenario Summary** report that includes both sets of inputs, but you can apply the scenarios sequentially and then use this naming convention to create as many scenarios as you wish.

Now, let's look at the next command in the **What-If Analysis** menu, the **Goal Seek** feature.

The Goal Seek feature

Excel's **Goal Seek** feature is a means of automating guesswork in Excel. Let's say that you want to buy a car, and you know the interest rate, the term of the loan, and the payment that you're seeking, but you don't know how much you can borrow. Here are the steps:

1. Activate the **Goal Seek** worksheet.
2. Choose **Data** | **What-If Analysis** | **Goal Seek**.
3. Enter or select cell **C5** in the **Set cell** field of the **Goal Seek** dialog box, as shown in *Figure 6.12*:

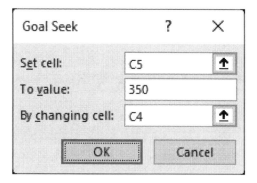

Figure 6.12 – The Goal Seek dialog box

4. Enter an amount, such as `350`, into the **To value** field.
5. Enter or select cell **C5** in the **By Changing Cell** field.

> **Nuance**
>
> Excel will show **$C$4** in the **Set cell** field and **$C$5** in the **By changing cell** field if you click on the worksheet with your mouse as opposed to typing the cell address into the field. The $ symbols indicate an absolute reference that is not required in this case because the **Goal Seek** feature will not remember the cells that you referenced if you later decide to solve for a different payment.

6. Click on **OK** to start the **Goal Seek** process.
7. As shown in *Figure 6.13*, the **Goal Seek Status** dialog box informs you if it finds an answer, and the missing input will appear in the **By changing cell** field that you specified.

As shown in *Figure 6.13*, the **Goal Seek** feature notifies you if it finds an answer or if it cannot find an answer. Most of the time, **Goal Seek** should return an answer depending upon the complexity of your underlying calculation:

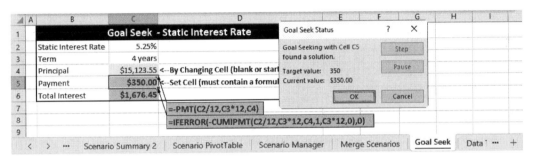

Figure 6.13 – The Goal Seek results

Let's look at a situation where it will be harder for **Goal Seek** to find a solution. Enter the formula =RANDBETWEEN(50,100)/1000 into cell **C11** of the **Goal Seek** worksheet to create a variable interest rate.

The RANDBETWEEN function has two arguments:

- **Bottom** – This is the smallest possible random number to be generated
- **Top** – This is the largest possible random number to be generated

In this case, dividing the result of RANDBETWEEN by **1,000** gives us a percentage between **5%** and **10%**. RANDBETWEEN is a volatile worksheet function, which means it recalculates every time a change is made anywhere in the workbook. Most worksheet functions in Excel are non-volatile, meaning that Excel only recalculates the formula when any cell that the formula references changes. In this case, we're creating a moving target that will be much harder for **Goal Seek** to hit as a way of emulating what you might experience in a complex workbook.

176 What-If Analysis

> **Nuance**
>
> RANDBETWEEN can only return integer values, which is why we must divide by `1,000`. If you're using **Microsoft 365** or **Excel 2021**, one alternative is to use RANDARRAY, which has five arguments: **rows**, **columns**, **min**, **max**, and **integer**. In cell **B1**, you'd enter `=RANDARRAY(1,1,.05,.10,FALSE)` to generate decimal values between `5%` and `10%`.

Now, let's try using the **Goal Seek** feature again:

1. Choose **Data | What-If Analysis | Goal Seek**.
2. Enter or select cell **C14** in the **Set cell** field.
3. Enter an amount, such as 350, into the **To value** field.
4. Enter or select cell **C13** in the **By changing cell** field.
5. Click on **OK** and note that **Goal Seek** will struggle to find an answer.
6. Click on **Pause** to temporarily halt the feature, as shown in *Figure 6.14*, **Cancel** to terminate the process, or wait until **Goal Seek** has worked through 100 iterations:

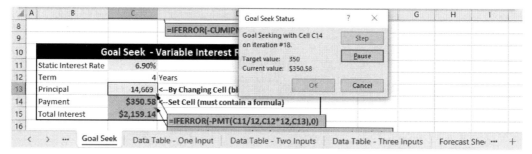

Figure 6.14 – Goal Seek Pause button

7. As you can see in *Figure 6.15*, sometimes, **Goal Seek** completely misses the mark and doesn't come close:

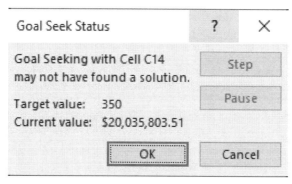

6.15 – Goal Seek ran amok

You can fine-tune **Goal Seek** by changing the level of precision used in the calculation. By default, Excel uses three decimal places of precision for calculations. You can change this level of precision by specifying a smaller tolerance, which prevents Excel from trying to reconcile immaterial amounts in the calculation:

1. Choose **File | Options | Formulas** (or **Excel | Preferences | Formulas** in **Excel for macOS**).
2. Set the **Maximum Change** field to `0.00000001` or a similarly small number.
3. Click on **OK** to close the **Options** dialog box, or close **Preferences**.

Now **Goal Seek** should perform faster as it won't be trying to find as precise of an answer. Later in the chapter, I'll compare **Goal Seek** to the **Solver** feature, but for now, let's look at the **Data Table** feature, which enables you to swap one or more inputs through a formula to create a table of comparative results.

The Data Table feature

Data Tables allow you to swap one or more inputs through a formula to return an array of results. I'm going to walk you through three different variations for calculating loan payments:

- Using one input with five interest rates
- Using two inputs, five interest rates, and five loan lengths
- Using three inputs with five interest rates, five loan lengths, and five loan amounts

The common factor between all three is that we'll start by calculating a loan payment in the fashion that I described in the `PMT` function. The `PMT` function will anchor all three of the **Data Tables** that we'll work through.

Creating a Data Table with one input

Cells **D2:D4** of the **Data Table-One Input** worksheet in this chapter's example workbook are the inputs used by the `=-PMT(D2/12,D3*12,D4)` formula in cell **D6**, which returns **$2,176.03** as the payment amount for a **30**-year loan of **$500,000** with a **3.25%** interest rate. Let's say that interest rates are climbing, and you want to see what the payment for that loan would be at other interest rates, too.

> **Nuance**
> Input cells related to a Data Table must reside on the same worksheet as the **Data Table** itself. If you copy a **Data Table** to a new worksheet, the table results that you paste will be converted into static values.

The formula in cell **D6** of *Figure 6.16* anchors the **Data Table**, while cells **C7:C11** provide the column input. In this context, the formula should always be in the first row and the second column of a two-column range:

	A	B	C	D	E	F	G	H	I	J	K	L	M	N
1			**Data Table - One Input**											
2			Interest	3.25%										
3			Term	30 years										
4			Principal	500,000										
5														
6				$2,176.03	=-PMT(D2/12,D3*12,D4)									
7		Column Input	3.25%	2,176.03	=TABLE(,D2)									
8			3.75%	2,315.58	=TABLE(,D2)									
9			4.25%	2,608.24	=TABLE(,D2)									
10			4.75%	3,078.59	=TABLE(,D2)									
11			5.25%	3,756.33	=TABLE(,D2)									
12														

Figure 6.16 – A single input Data Table

You can recreate the **Data Table** in the work area that starts on row **13**:

1. Select cells **C18:D23**.
2. Choose **Data | What If Analysis | Data Table**.
3. Specify cell **D14** as the **Column input** cell, and then click on **OK**.

Now, let's look at cells **D19:D23**. You'll notice that Excel did not copy the PMT formula to these cells, but used the TABLE function to create this formula in each cell: `{=TABLE(,D14)}`.

> **Nuance**
>
> You cannot use the **TABLE** function on your own to write a formula—it can only be used in conjunction with the **Data Table** feature. If you try, Excel will report *That function isn't valid.*.

The TABLE function has two unnamed inputs for row and column inputs, respectively. In this case, we don't have a row input, but our column input runs down cells **C7:C11**. In cell **D7**, the TABLE function replaces the reference to the **Column Input Cell**—in this case, **D14**—in the formula at the top of the **Data Table** with the corresponding inputs in column C. **Data Tables** run each input through the formula anchoring the table, which is where we specified cell **D14** as our **Column Input Cell**. The curly brackets around the outside of the formula signify that this is a formula, which performs multiple calculations on a single item. This is how the TABLE function can swap each interest rate through the PMT function simultaneously. This is an alternative to the `=-PMT(C30/12,D$27*12,D$28)` formula in cell **D30**, which I copied down through cell **D34**. Notice that, in this case, a $ sign is required in front of rows **27** and **28** in the formula to prevent Excel from changing the row numbers for those arguments.

The Data Table feature

> **Nuance**
>
> You cannot delete a row or column that intersects with an array formula. If you try to delete row **21**, Excel will return the *Can't change part of a data table* error. Although true, there is an easy workaround. Erase cells **D19:D23**, delete row **21**, and then repeat steps 1 through 3 above for cells **C18:D22**.

Now, let's create a **Data Table** that has two inputs.

Creating a Data Table with two inputs

The **Data Table** shown in *Figure 6.17* calculates loan payments based on five interest rates and five loan terms. I'm practically using the same inputs in cells **D2:D4** of the **Data Table – Two Inputs** worksheet as I did for the one-input example, but this time, the `=-PMT(D2/12,D3*12,D4)` formula is in cell **C7**:

	A	B	C	D	E	F	G	H	I	J	K
1				Data Table with Two Inputs							
2			Interest	3.25%							
3			Years	30 years							
4			Principal	500,000							
5	=-PMT(C3/12,C4*12,C5)										
6					Row Input (Loan Term in Years)						
7			$2,176.03	30	15	20	25	30			
8		Column Input Interest Rates	3.25%	$2,176.03	$3,513.34	$2,835.98	$2,436.58	$2,176.03			
9			3.75%	$2,315.58	$3,636.11	$2,964.44	$2,570.66	$2,315.58			
10			4.25%	$2,608.24	$3,889.16	$3,231.12	$2,850.59	$2,608.24			
11			4.75%	$3,078.59	$4,287.11	$3,654.64	$3,298.35	$3,078.59			
12			5.25%	$3,756.33	$4,850.70	$4,260.33	$3,942.25	$3,756.33	=TABLE(D3,D2)		
13											

Figure 6.17 – A Data Table with two inputs

Cells **D7:H7** contain five loan lengths, while cells **C8:C12** contain five interest rates. Cells **D8:H12** contain the `=TABLE(D3,D2)` formula. The `=-PMT($C33/12,D$32*12,$D$30)` formula in cell **D33** is a formula-based alternative. Notice, this time, additional $ signs are required to maintain the proper integrity of the arguments. The **Data Table** feature allows you to put a simpler formula in cell **C7** and know that the results will automatically use the correct inputs.

You can follow along in the work area of the **Data Table – Two Inputs** worksheet if you wish:

1. Select cells **C20:H25**.
2. Choose **Data | What If Analysis | Data Table**.
3. Enter `D16` in the **Row input cell** field.
4. Enter `D15` in the **Column input cell** field. Click on **OK**.

> **Nuance**
>
> Unlike typical Excel formulas, you can't type over the results in a **Data Table** because the results are provided by an array function. Results provided by array functions are banded together in a *one-for-all and all-for-one* fashion that protects the integrity of the results.

Now, let's see how we can create a **Data Table** that uses *three* inputs, even though the **Data Table** dialog box only allows space for two.

Creating a Data Table with three inputs

As you've seen the **Data Table** dialog box only offers two input fields, **Row Input Cell** and **Column Input Cell**, so how can we incorporate three or more inputs? This is possible by combining the term and principal inputs into a single cell separated by a slash, such as 120/375,000, as shown in *Figure 6.18*:

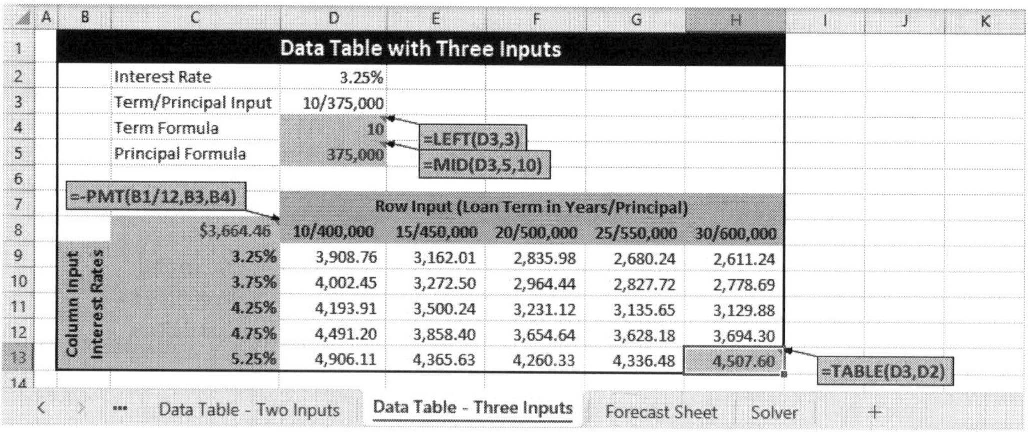

Figure 6.18 – A Data Table with three inputs

Then, we'll use the LEFT and MID functions to extract the inputs into separate cells that the PMT function will reference. The top row of the table will have the combined inputs for each scenario that we're trying to calculate. Everything is already established in cells **B1:H13**, but I'll walk you through entering the formulas in the work area, as shown in *Figure 6.19*:

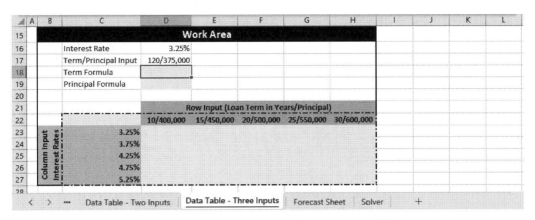

Figure 6.19 – The work area for a three-input Data Table

1. Enter =LEFT(D17,3) in cell **D18** to extract the first three digits from cell **D17**. The LEFT function has one required argument and one optional argument:

   - **Text**: This is a cell reference or string that you wish to extract characters from.
   - **Num_chars**: This is an optional number of characters that you want to extract, starting from the left-hand side, which defaults to **1** unless you specify otherwise.

2. Enter =MID(D17,5,10) in cell **D19** to extract the loan amount. The MID function has three required arguments:

   - **Text**: This is a cell reference or string that you wish to extract characters from.
   - **Start_num**: This is the position in the middle of the text where you want to start extracting characters.
   - **Num_chars**: This is the number of characters that you wish to extract. In this case, I entered 10 to pick a number larger than the number of characters that I plan to extract.

3. Enter =-PMT(D16/12,D18,D19) in cell **C22** to calculate the loan payment for the first scenario. The PMT function has three required arguments (see *The PMT function* section for a discussion of the two additional optional arguments:

   - **Rate**: This is the interest rate for the loan, which, in this case, is cell **D16**, divided by 12 to create a monthly rate.
   - **Nper**: This is the length of the loan. In this case, the formula references cell **D18** where we extracted the term from cell **D17** and then multiplied by **12** to convert the loan term into months.
   - **Pv**: This is the present value or principal amount. In this case, the formula references cell **D19** where we extracted the amount from cell **D17**.

4. Select cells **C22:H27**.
5. Choose **Data | What If Analysis | Data Table**.
6. Specify cell **D17** as the **Row Input Cell**. There's some nuance here as we want to pick the cell that has the combined inputs, not either of the cells where we separate the inputs.
7. Specify cell **D16** as the **Column Input Cell**.
8. Click on **OK** to create the **Data Table**.

You could calculate these amounts without using a **Data Table** if you broke out the term and loan amounts into two separate rows. Alternatively, you could incorporate `LEFT` and `MID` in the `PMT` function, such as `=-PMT($C23/12,LEFT(D$22,2)*12,MID(D$22,4,10))`. In this case, the **Data Table** both streamlines the calculation and ensures proper data integrity in each cell.

Depending on the size and complexity of your calculations, **Data Tables** can, sometimes, cause your worksheets to take longer than usual to recalculate. Fortunately, there's an easy solution if this situation arises.

Improving calculation performance

The array formula within a   can affect the calculation performance of your spreadsheet. Normally, Excel only recalculates formulas that are directly affected by a data entry change. On the other hand, **Array formulas** are recalculated every time you make a change anywhere in a workbook. If you find that this adversely slows down your spreadsheet, you can prevent **Data Tables** from constantly recalculating by choosing **Formulas | Calculation Options | Automatic except for data tables**.

You will now need to manually recalculate the Data Tables, as and when needed, by clicking on any cell that contains an array formula and then pressing *F9 (Fn+ F9)*, or you can click on the **Calculate Now** command in the **Formulas** tab. Choose **Formulas | Calculation Options | Automatic** to restore the default calculation method.

Now that you have a sense of the **Data Table** feature, let's see how you can use the **Forecast Sheet** feature to project time-based or date-based data into the future.

Projecting amounts with the Forecast Sheet feature

The **Forecast Sheet** feature is available in **Excel 2016** or later for Windows. You can use it with data that comprises dates/times and values, as shown in *Figure 6.20*. Let's assume that we want to protect this data through the end of 2024:

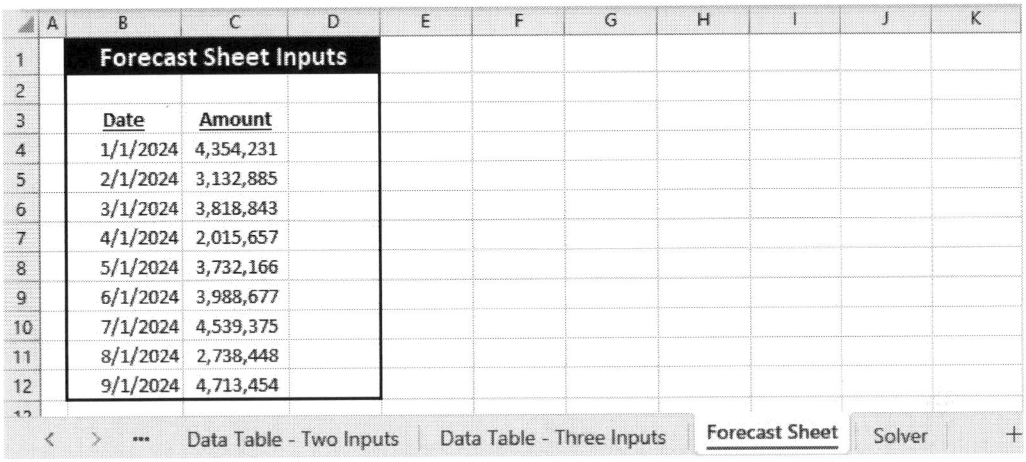

	A	B	C	D
1		**Forecast Sheet Inputs**		
2				
3		Date	Amount	
4		1/1/2024	4,354,231	
5		2/1/2024	3,132,885	
6		3/1/2024	3,818,843	
7		4/1/2024	2,015,657	
8		5/1/2024	3,732,166	
9		6/1/2024	3,988,677	
10		7/1/2024	4,539,375	
11		8/1/2024	2,738,448	
12		9/1/2024	4,713,454	

Figure 6.20 – The source data for a forecast

> **Nuance**
>
> The **Forecast Feature** adds a new worksheet to your workbook that uses the `FORECAST.ETS` and `FORECAST.ETS.CONFINT` worksheet functions to project your amounts. You can share a forecast with someone using **Excel 2013** or earlier for viewing. The catch is that any edits to the workbook could cause the forecast functions to recalculate. In that event, the forecasted amounts will return **#NAME?** because older versions of Excel cannot recognize those worksheet functions.

Now, let's give the **Forecast Sheet** feature a try:

1. Select any cell within your date-based or time-based data, such as cell **B4** on the **Forecast Sheet** worksheet of this chapter's example workbook.

2. Choose **Data | Forecast Sheet**.
3. Confirm the **Forecast End** date in the **Create Forecast Worksheet** dialog box, as shown in *Figure 6.21*:

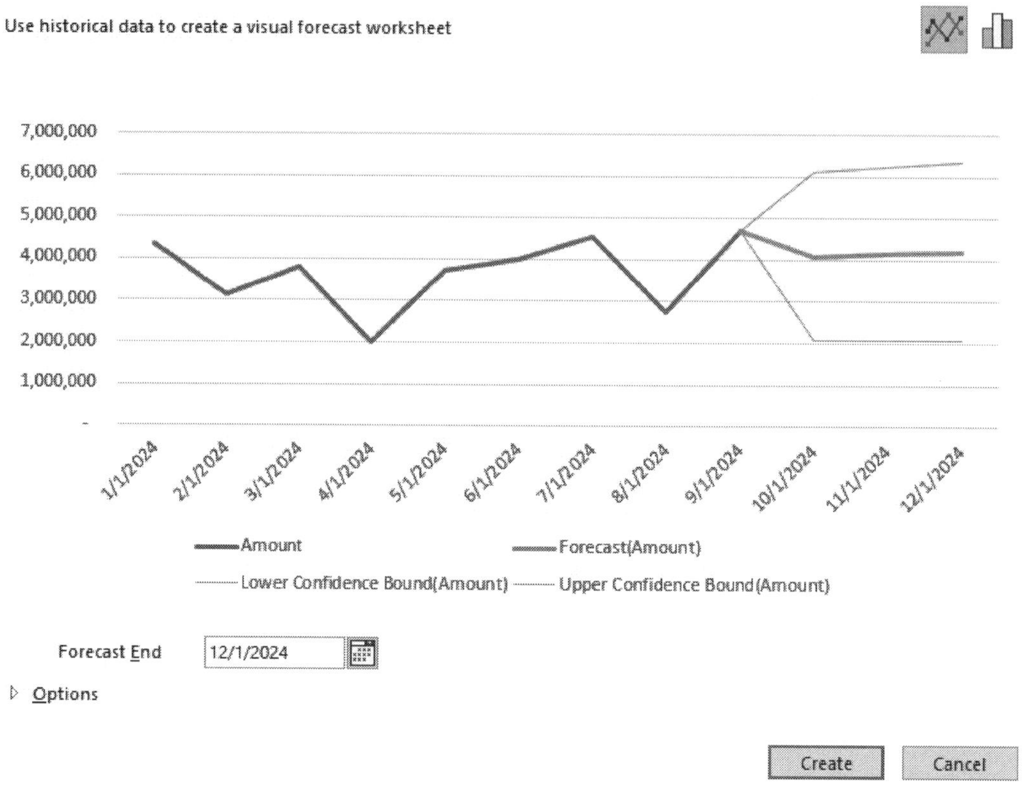

Figure 6.21 – Forecast Sheet dialog box

4. Optionally, expand the **Options** section to further fine-tune your forecast. You can also choose between a line chart and a column chart, although the line chart provides a more comprehensive forecast.
5. Click on **Create**.
6. As shown in *Figure 6.22*, Excel adds a **Forecast Sheet** to your workbook. By default, the chart will overlap the **Forecast Sheet** results, so plan on moving the chart to the side each time:

Introducing the Solver feature   185

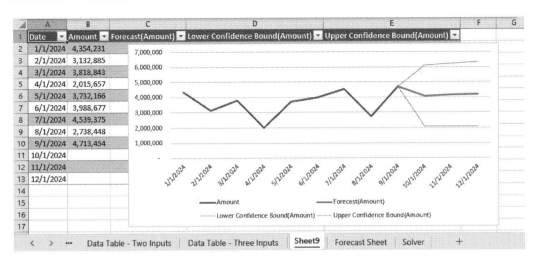

Figure 6.22 – The Forecast Sheet results

As you can see, the line chart created for the **Forecast Sheet** feature presents the best-case, most-likely, and worst-case scenarios based on the data present in your worksheet. The column chart version of the **Forecast Sheet** uses error bars to illustrate the best- and worst-case scenarios.

Now, let's finish out our tour of Excel's What-If Analysis features by unearthing the **Solver** feature, which only appears in Excel's ribbon upon request.

Introducing the Solver feature

I'm only going to lightly touch on Excel's **Solver** feature so that I can compare it to **Goal Seek**. Often, I describe **Solver** as **Goal Seek** on steroids. You can solve for multiple missing inputs, place constraints on the solve, and much more. With that said, if you like **Goal Seek**, you'll like **Solver** even more once you get past the busier user interface. The **Solver** feature is an Excel **add-in**, which enables additional functionality that is not available in the default installation of Excel. The first step to using **Solver** is to enable the **add-in**:

1. Choose **File** | **Options** | **Add-Ins** (or choose **Tools** | **Excel Add-Ins** in Excel for Mac).
2. Click on the **Go…** button in the **Manage: Excel Add-ins** section of the **Options** dialog box (skip this step in **Excel for Mac**).

3. Click on the **Solver Add-In** checkbox, as shown in *Figure 6.23*:

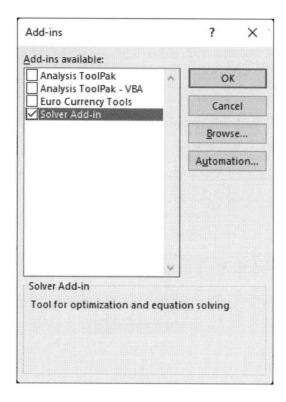

Figure 6.23 – Enabling the Solver Add-in checkbox

4. Click on **OK**.
5. Close the **Options** dialog box if needed.

At this point, a **Solver** command will appear on the **Data** tab of Excel's ribbon. Click on this button to display the **Solver** dialog box, as shown in *Figure 6.24*:

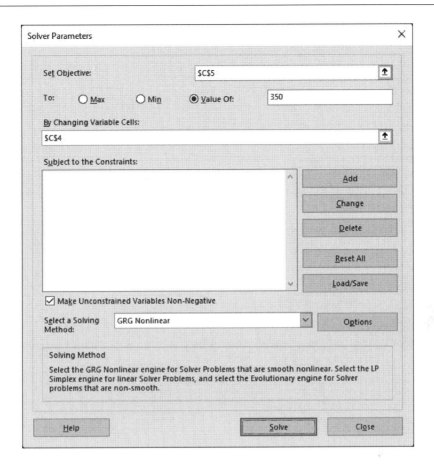

Figure 6.24 – The Solver Parameters dialog box

Let's say that you wanted to solve for a payment amount in the same fashion that we did for **Goal Seek**. You can use the same example that we used for **Goal Seek** if you change the interest rate back to 5.25% or any other static amount. Here are the steps for using **Solver** to determine the amount that you can borrow based on a particular interest rate, term, or payment:

1. Activate the **Solver** worksheet of this chapter's example workbook.
2. Choose **Data** | **Solver**.
3. Enter C4 in the **Set Objective** field of the **Solver Parameters** dialog box, as shown in *Figure 6.21*.
4. Choose **Value Of**.
5. Enter a payment amount in the field adjacent to **Value Of**, such as 350.
6. Set the **By Changing Variable Cells** field to C5.
7. Click on the **Solve** button.

8. Excel will display a **Solver Results** dialog box, as shown in *Figure 6.25*. Optionally, you can click on the **Return to Solver Parameters Dialog** checkbox if you want to change this payment amount or adjust any of the other variables that you might have included in a scenario that has more moving parts to it.

9. Click on **OK** to return to the worksheet or the **Solver Parameters** dialog box based upon your choice in the previous step:

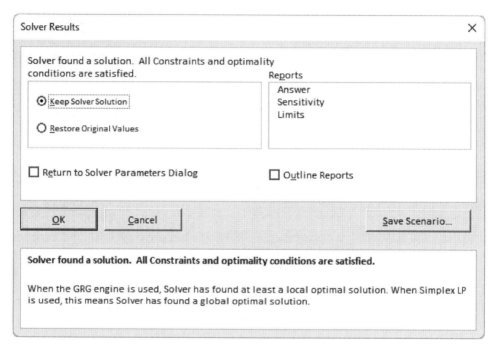

Figure 6.25 – The Solver Results dialog box

> **Nuance**
>
> One benefit of using **Solver** versus **Goal Seek** is that the **Solver** feature remembers the choices that you make, whereas the **Goal Seek** dialog box resets itself every time. You can prefill the **Set Cell** field in the **Goal Seek** dialog box if you click on the formula cell before initiating the **Goal Seek** command. In short, **Solver** is more efficient if you are carrying out repeated goal-seeking actions.

As you can see in *Figure 6.25*, you can also store **Solver** results in Excel's **Scenario Manager**, which I discussed in the *Understanding the Scenario Manager feature* section earlier.

Summary

Often, Excel's **What-If Analysis** features are overlooked as a means to automate repetitive tasks in Excel. In this chapter, you learned about the `PMT`, `CUMIPMT`, and `CUMPRINC` functions, which can be used to calculate loan payments and total interest for one or more periods in a loan. We used those functions as the basis for walking through the **What-If Analysis** features in Excel. For instance, the **Scenario Manager** feature enables you to swap different sets of inputs into a worksheet and compare the results by way of scenario reports. Alternatively, **Goal Seek** allows you to solve for a single missing input. This eliminates the manual guesswork that can otherwise be involved in trying to determine the missing amount.

Then, our trip through the Data | What-If Analysis menu took us to the **Data Table** feature. **Data Tables** can solve multiple equations at once based on swapping out one or more inputs. This gives your formulas better integrity because you don't have to try to link the inputs within the formula; you simply anchor the **Data Table** with a single formula and Excel swaps the inputs out.

If you want to project a series of numbers into the future, you can create a **Forecast Sheet** that will automate your projection. Such sheets cannot be created in **Excel for macOS** but can be accessed in that version. The chapter finished with an introduction to the hidden **Solver** feature that can be used to solve two or more missing inputs. I didn't have space to delve very far into **Solver,** but you saw how **Solver** can streamline tasks that you might normally carry out in **Goal Seek** because **Solver** remembers the most recent settings, whereas the **Goal Seek** dialog box resets itself each time you access it.

In *Chapter 7, Automating Tasks with the Table Feature*, you'll learn about numerous ways to automate Excel features by simply converting the underlying data into a Table. Additionally, I'll draw a distinction between the similarly named **Data Table**, **Table**, and **PivotTable** features.

7
Automating Tasks with the Table Feature

I consider the **Table** feature to be a superpower in Excel that unlocks tremendous automation capabilities with just a keyboard shortcut or a couple of mouse clicks. For instance, formulas and features that reference data in **Tables**, versus normal ranges of cells, automatically "see" any new data that you add to the **Table**. This eliminates having to rewrite formulas to expand the cell range and circle back to features such as **PivotTables** to expand the source data. **Slicers** eliminate the need to navigate drop-down menus when filtering, while enabling the **Total Row** option only tallies visible rows instead of the entire list. **Tables** allow **Charts** and **Sparklines** to be self-updating—the list truly goes on and on. In this chapter, I will cover the following main topics:

- Excel's unwritten rule
- What is a **Table**?
- **Table** enhancements
- **Table** automation opportunities
- Navigation and selection nuances
- Troubleshooting **Tables**

In short, this chapter is all about showing you how to simultaneously eliminate repetitive tasks and improve data integrity in one fell swoop. This chapter also supplements *Chapter 12, Power Query*, as data you extract from other sources by way of Power Query is typically returned to a **Table**.

Technical requirements

All the keyboard shortcuts in this chapter work in **Excel for Windows**, but only some of them will work in **Excel for macOS**. Unless otherwise noted, all features in this chapter will work the same way in **Excel for Windows** and **macOS**. A workbook with all the examples that I used in this chapter is available for download from GitHub at https://github.com/PacktPublishing/Exploring-Microsoft-Excels-Hidden-Treasures/tree/main/Chapter07.

Excel's unwritten rule

Over the years, I've observed an unwritten rule that I find many users unwittingly break: the first row of *any* list should be a *single* row of unique titles—or **Headers** in Excel vernacular. This applies to every list that you create in Excel, no matter if you're using the **Table** feature or not. **Headers** are so crucial that the **Table** feature adds placeholder **Headers** when needed. Both **Tables** and **PivotTables** require that each **Header** be unique and will append numbers to duplicate **Headers** to enforce compliance.

> **Tip**
> An addendum to the preceding rule is that lists should not have any blank rows or columns. Most Excel features act on the **Current Region**, which is the contiguous block of non-blank cells surrounding the active cell. Blank rows and columns truncate the **Current Region**, and they require you to manually select the entire list before sorting or filtering instead of being able to choose a cell within the list and then sort or filter.

When creating new spreadsheets, try to keep **Headers** to a single row and then use **Home | Wrap Text** if needed for multiline display. You can also press *Alt + Enter (Option + Enter)* at each point within a cell where you want a line break. If you want to keep multiline **Headers** in place, consider inserting a blank row just immediately above the last **Header Row** that you can then hide.

> **Tip**
> Additionally, you can use the `TEXTJOIN` function in **Excel 2019** and later to combine text from multiple cells into one. Once you copy and paste the results as values, you can then delete the original rows.

You might think *"I don't need to add titles, I know what's in each column."* That's a fair point, but Excel will treat the first row as **Headers** anyway, which, in turn, can result in side effects, such as not being able to create a **PivotTable** from a list, having a row of data omitted from a **PivotTable**, and more. Sometimes, you can get away with two rows of titles depending upon the feature that you're using. If you filter or sort the list in the **Excel's Unwritten Rule** worksheet of this chapter's example workbook, as shown in *Figure 7.1*, Excel will ignore row **1** and appropriately use row **2** as **Headers**. The **PivotTable** and **Recommended PivotTables** features will ignore the first row, too:

	A	B	C	D	E
1			Type of	Length	Length
2	Name	Country	Bridge	In Feet	In Meters
3	Danyang–Kunshan Grand Bridge	China	High-speed rail	540,700	164,800
4	Changhua–Kaohsiung Viaduct	Taiwan	High-speed rail	516,132	157,317
5	Kita-Yaita Viaduct Tohoku Shinkansen	Japan	High-speed rail	375,407	114,424
6	Tianjin Grand Bridge	China	High-speed rail	373,000	113,700
7	Cangde Grand Bridge	China	High-speed rail	380,200	115,900
8	Weinan Weihe Grand Bridge	China	High-speed rail	261,588	79,732
9	Bang Na Expressway	Thailand	Expressway	177,000	54,000
10	Beijing Grand Bridge	China	High-speed rail	157,982	48,153
11	Metro Manila Skyway System	Philippines	Expressway	128,600	39,200
12	Lake Pontchartrain Causeway	United States	Highway	126,122	38,442
13	Line 1, Wuhan Metro Bridge	China	Metro	123,976	37,788

Figure 7.1 – A dataset that breaks the unwritten rule

On the other hand, the **Table** feature *always* treats the first row of a list as **Headers**, which means, in this case, row **2** will become a **Body Row** and be treated as part of the dataset. Lists that have three or more rows of **Headers** are treated as having none by most Excel features.

One way around the unwritten rule is to select the last row of **Headers** along with the body of your list before making your data into a **Table** or using a feature that will get tripped up by multi-row **Headers**.

Now that we've covered the unwritten rule, let's distinguish the three Excel features that have the word "**Table**" in their name from each other.

What is a Table?

The **Feature Comparison** worksheet contrasts the **Table**, **PivotTable**, and **Data Table** features. Let's compare each feature:

- **Tables** – **Tables** transform static cell ranges into self-expanding lists, as shown in *Figure 7.2*, which, as you'll soon see, unlocks multiple layers of automation:

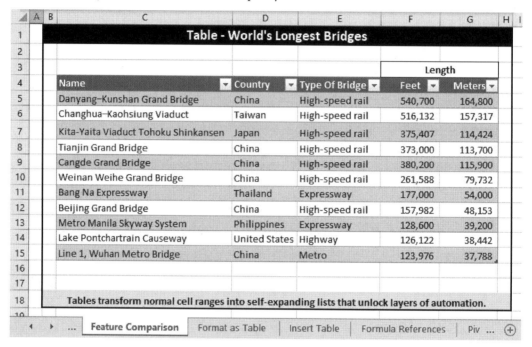

Figure 7.2 – Table

- **PivotTables** – **PivotTables** are a report-writing feature that summarizes lists of data inside cell ranges or **Tables** into concise formats, as shown in *Figure 7.3*:

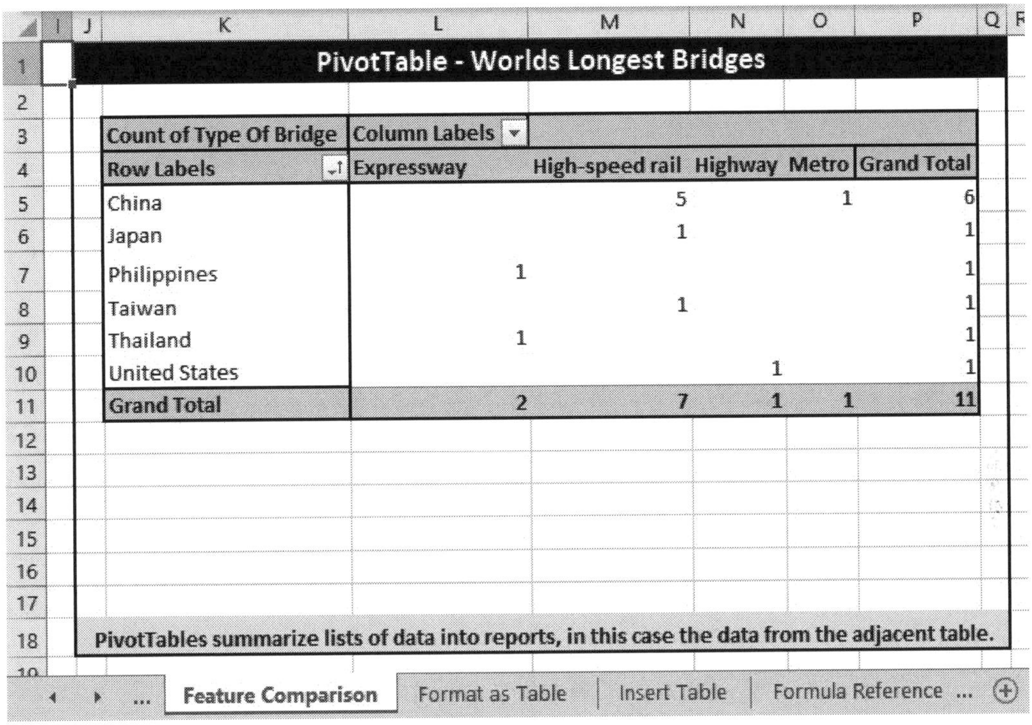

PivotTable - Worlds Longest Bridges

Count of Type Of Bridge	Column Labels				
Row Labels	Expressway	High-speed rail	Highway	Metro	Grand Total
China		5		1	6
Japan		1			1
Philippines	1				1
Taiwan		1			1
Thailand	1				1
United States			1		1
Grand Total	2	7	1	1	11

PivotTables summarize lists of data into reports, in this case the data from the adjacent table.

Figure 7.3 – PivotTable

> **Tip**
>
> I briefly explore **PivotTables** in this chapter and *Chapter 9, Excel Quirks and Nuances.*

- **Data Tables** – **Data Tables** enable you to swap one or more sets of inputs through a single anchor formula to compare multiple scenarios, as shown in *Figure 7.4*:

	T	U	V	W	X	Y	Z	AA	AB	AC	AD	AE	AF
1				Data Table - Compare Mortgage Payments									
2													
3				Interest	3.25%								
4				Years	10								
5				Principal	500,000								
6													
7							Years						
8				$4,885.95	10	15	20	25	30				
9			Interest	3.25%	4,885.95	3,513.34	2,436.58	1,862.71	1,579.48				
10				3.75%	1,747.31	1,712.73	1,662.80	1,618.16	1,588.34				
11				4.25%	1,989.98	1,987.69	1,984.46	1,981.76	1,980.17				
12				4.75%	2,604.29	2,604.26	2,604.21	2,604.19	2,604.17				
13													
14			=-PMT(W3/12,W4*12,W5)					=TABLE(D4,D3)					
15													
16													
17													
18			Data Tables create comparisons by swapping one or more inputs through a formula.										

Figure 7.4 – Data Table

> **Nuance**
>
> The TABLE worksheet function, as shown in *Figure 7.4*, is specific to the **Data Table** feature and is completely unrelated to the **Table** feature. I discussed **Data Tables** in detail in *Chapter 6, What-If Analysis*.

Now, let's see how to convert a normal range of cells into a **Table**.

The Format as Table command

As you'll see in the *Copying and pasting* **Tables** section, a potentially misleading way to identify **Tables** in an Excel workbook is based on the formatting. Excel offers 60 built-in **Table Styles** that you can choose from when converting a normal range of cells into a **Table** by way of the **Format as Table** command:

1. Select any cell from the list of the **Format as Table** worksheet.
2. Choose **Home | Format as Table**, and then choose the first **Table Style** option in the upper-left corner of the gallery, as shown in *Figure 7.5*, which is named **White, Table Style Light 1**:

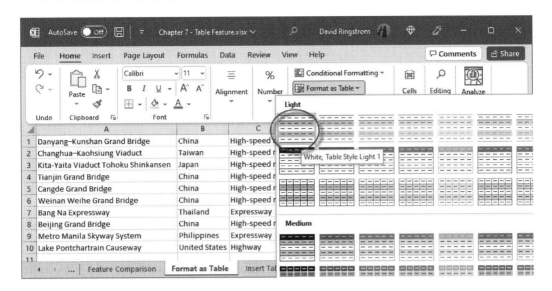

Figure 7.5 – The Format as Table command

3. The **Create Table** dialog box appears, as shown in *Figure 7.6*. In this case, Excel correctly determines that the first row of the list does not comprised **Headers** and deselects the **My Table has headers** checkbox. The **Where is the data for your Table?** field will display the cell coordinates for your entire list unless the list is interrupted by one or more blank rows and/or columns. Reselect the list if needed, and then click on **OK**:

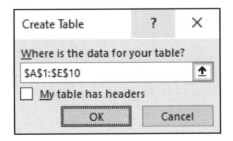

Figure 7.6 – The Create Table dialog box with My **Table** has **Headers** deselected

4. As shown in *Figure 7.7*, the list is transformed into a **Table** with placeholder titles in the **Header Row** that you can replace if desired:

	A	B	C	D	E
1	Column1	Column2	Column3	Column4	Column5
2	Danyang–Kunshan Grand Bridge	China	High-speed rail	540,700	164,800
3	Changhua–Kaohsiung Viaduct	Taiwan	High-speed rail	516,132	157,317
4	Kita-Yaita Viaduct Tohoku Shinkansen	Japan	High-speed rail	375,407	114,424
5	Tianjin Grand Bridge	China	High-speed rail	373,000	113,700
6	Cangde Grand Bridge	China	High-speed rail	380,200	115,900
7	Weinan Weihe Grand Bridge	China	High-speed rail	261,588	79,732
8	Bang Na Expressway	Thailand	Expressway	177,000	54,000
9	Beijing Grand Bridge	China	High-speed rail	157,982	48,153
10	Metro Manila Skyway System	Philippines	Expressway	128,600	39,200
11	Lake Pontchartrain Causeway	United States	Highway	126,122	38,442

Figure 7.7 – Placeholder titles in the Header Row

5. Type `WithoutHeaders` into the **Table Design** | **Name** field to distinguish this **Table** from other **Tables** that we'll create in this workbook.

If you'd rather not choose a style, the **Insert Table** command applies the default style for a given workbook, which I'll show you how to alter in the *Setting a default* **Table Style** section.

The Insert | Table command

Let's create a second **Table** and see how the default **Table Style** is automatically applied:

1. Select any cell from the list in the **Insert Table** worksheet, and then choose **Insert** | **Table**.

> **Tip**
> You can press *Ctrl* + *T* (⌘ +*T* in Excel for Mac) in lieu of choosing **Insert** | **Table**.

2. The **Create Table** dialog box appears, as shown in *Figure 7.8*. Excel correctly determines that the first row of the list comprises **Headers**, so **My Table has headers** is selected:

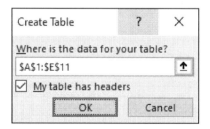

Figure 7.8 – The Create Table dialog box with My **Table** has **Headers** selected

What is a Table? 199

3. Click on **OK** to transform the list into a **Table**, which appears in *Figure 7.9*.
4. Type `WithHeaders` into the **Table Design | Name** field to replace the generic name that Excel assigns:

Name	Country	Type Of Bridge	Feet	Meters
Danyang–Kunshan Grand Bridge	China	High-speed rail	540,700	164,800
Changhua–Kaohsiung Viaduct	Taiwan	High-speed rail	516,132	157,317
Kita-Yaita Viaduct Tohoku Shinkansen	Japan	High-speed rail	375,407	114,424
Tianjin Grand Bridge	China	High-speed rail	373,000	113,700
Cangde Grand Bridge	China	High-speed rail	380,200	115,900
Weinan Weihe Grand Bridge	China	High-speed rail	261,588	79,732
Bang Na Expressway	Thailand	Expressway	177,000	54,000
Beijing Grand Bridge	China	High-speed rail	157,982	48,153
Metro Manila Skyway System	Philippines	Expressway	128,600	39,200
Lake Pontchartrain Causeway	United States	Highway	126,122	38,442

Figure 7.9 – The default **Table Style** for Insert | Table

Now that you know how to convert a normal range of cells into a **Table**, let's look at the automatic enhancements that appear, along with the optional settings that you can apply.

Table characteristics

A normal range of cells converted into a **Table** gains several other characteristics in addition to a **Table Style**. Let's discuss the characteristics that are automatically applied to a **Table**, and then we'll discuss the additional options.

Automatic changes

The following aspects of Excel or the list changes when you create a **Table** or when the active cell is within a **Table**:

- The **Table Design** tab appears in Excel's **Ribbon**, as shown in *Figure 7.10*:

Figure 7.10 – The Table Design menu

- **Filter buttons** appear in the **Header Row** of the worksheet, as shown in *Figure 7.9*, unless you scroll down the worksheet such that the Header Row is no longer visible.

Automating Tasks with the Table Feature

> **Tip**
>
> **Filter buttons** will always appear when you create a **Table**—there's no permanent way to disable this feature. You can turn off the buttons for an individual **Table** by clearing the **Filter Button** option in the **Table Design** menu.

- As shown in *Figure 7.11*, the **Headers** and **Filter Buttons** appear in the worksheet frame when the Header Row of a **Table** isn't visible on the screen. They both vanish when the active cell is located outside of a **Table**. You can use **Window | Freeze Panes | Freeze Top Row** to keep the **filter buttons** and **Headers Row** always visible on the screen when the active cell is not within the **Table**:

Name	Country	Type Of Bridge	Feet	Meters	F	G	H	I	J
Danyang–Kunshan Grand Bridge	China	High-speed rail	540,700	164,800					
Changhua–Kaohsiung Viaduct	Taiwan	High-speed rail	516,132	157,317					
Kita-Yaita Viaduct Tohoku Shinkansen	Japan	High-speed rail	375,407	114,424					
Tianjin Grand Bridge	China	High-speed rail	373,000	113,700					
Cangde Grand Bridge	China	High-speed rail	380,200	115,900					
Weinan Weihe Grand Bridge	China	High-speed rail	261,588	79,732					
Bang Na Expressway	Thailand	Expressway	177,000	54,000					
Beijing Grand Bridge	China	High-speed rail	157,982	48,153					
Metro Manila Skyway System	Philippines	Expressway	128,600	39,200					
Lake Pontchartrain Causeway	United States	Highway	126,122	38,442					

Figure 7.11 – The **Headers** and Filter Buttons in the worksheet frame

> **Tip**
>
> The **Header Row** will always appear when you create a **Table**—there's no permanent way to disable this feature either. You can hide the **Header Row** for an individual **Table** by clearing the **Header Row** option in the **Table Design** menu.

- **Tables** automatically expand to include new data that you add adjacent to the last row or column. Choose **Table Design | Resize Table** if the **Table** does not automatically incorporate the new data that you have added.

- Excel assigns a generic name of **Table1** to the first **Table** that you create in a workbook, **Table2** to the second **Table**, and so on. As with worksheets and Table headers, each **Table** must have a unique name. You can, and should, assign a more meaningful name to the **Table Name** field, as shown in *Figure 7.10*. Doing so will make it easier to navigate to a specific **Table**, as well as reference a specific **Table** when writing formulas that use structured references.

> **Tip**
>
> You can navigate to any **Table** in a workbook by clicking on the arrow in Excel's **Name Box** and then choosing a **Table Name** from the list. I discuss this technique in more detail in *Chapter 11, Names, LET, and LAMBDA*.

There are a few restrictions regarding naming a **Table**:

- The first character must be a letter or an underscore, and the name cannot contain spaces or punctuation other than periods.
- Numbers are permitted in the second position and beyond, but a **Table Name** cannot match a cell address. *Table 7.1* compares valid and invalid names:

Valid table names	Invalid table names
_2024_TAXES	2024_TAXES
_2024TAXES	2024TAXES
TAX_2024	TAX2024

Table 7.1 – Valid versus invalid **Table Names**

- No matter whether you change the **Table Name** or not, you can click on the arrow in the **Name Box** field and then select a **Table Name** to instantly navigate to the corresponding **Table**—if the worksheet that the **Table** appears on is not hidden.

> **Tip**
> I discuss names and the **Name Box** option in more detail in *Chapter 11, Names, LET, and LAMBDA*. If you assign a name to a worksheet cell, you cannot assign that name to a **Table** feature and vice versa.

- You can reference **Tables** by name in worksheet formulas instead of specifying or selecting the cell coordinates. Such formulas are referred to as structured references and can make formulas easier to write and audit. Whether you use structured references or normal cell references, typically, any formulas that reference a **Table** will automatically "see" any additional data that you add immediately below or to the right of the **Table**. I'll demonstrate this later in the chapter, and then point out two nuances that can cause formulas to not update in this fashion in the *Troubleshooting* **Tables** section.

> **Tip**
> The **Header Row** in **Tables** can only contain text. You cannot enter a formula in a **Header Row**, and any existing formulas in a **Header Row** will be converted into values when you convert a normal range of cells into a **Table**. Any dates or numbers that you type into a **Header Row** will be stored as text and not values.

Optional enhancements

As you saw in the previous section, you can turn *off* some automatic characteristics of a **Table** on a case-by-case basis. In this section, I'll show you additional enhancements that you can turn *on*, again on a case-by-case basis:

- **Total Row** – The **Total Row** option, as shown in *Figure 7.10*, automatically sums or counts the last column of your **Table**:

    I. Choose any cell in the **Table** on the **Feature Comparison** worksheet, and then choose **Table Design | Total Row**.

    II. As shown in *Figure 7.12*, sums is used in the **Meters** column because it comprises numbers. A count will appear instead when the last column comprises dates or other non-numeric values.

    III. Click on cell **F16** to display an arrow that will display several options for statistics that you can add to a given column, as shown in *Figure 7.12*. Choose **Sum** to add a total to the **Feet** column:

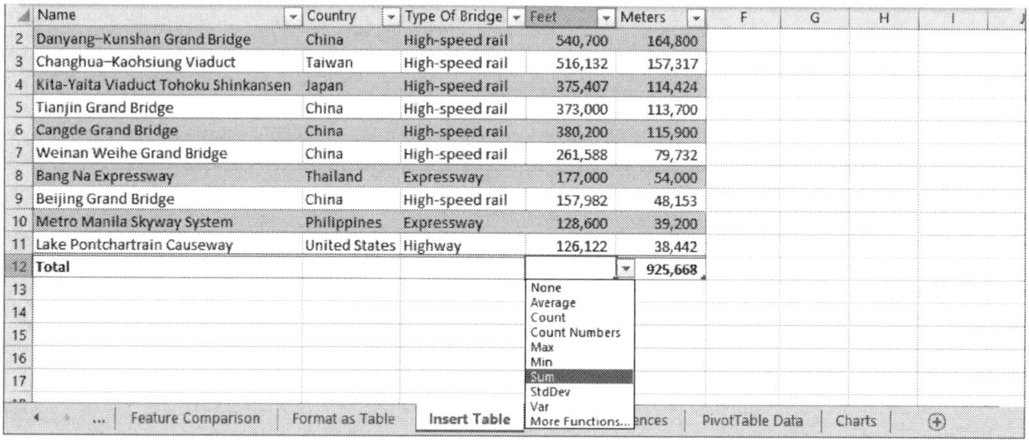

Figure 7.12 – Total Row

> Tip
> Turn the **Total Row** option off when you need to add more data, and then back on again to restore your settings. You can also press *Ctrl + Shift + Tab* (⌘ *+ Shift + T*) to enable or disable the **Total Row** option.

- **Banded Rows** – The default **Table Style** setting enables this option, as do some but not all choices in the **Table Styles** gallery. Clear the **Banded Rows** checkbox to override a style that shades every other row on your **Table**.

- **First Column** – None of the built-in styles in the **Table Style** gallery utilize this option. Enable the **First Column** setting if you want to apply **Bold** formatting to the first column of your **Table**. You can also enable this setting by creating a custom **Table Style**.

- **Last Column** – Similar to **First Column**, this option applies **Bold** formatting to the last column in your **Table**, and it is only enabled on demand or when you create a custom **Table Style**.

- **Banded Columns** – None of the built-in styles in the **Table Style** gallery utilize this option. Enable the **Banded Columns** setting if you want to shade every other column in your **Table**, or create a custom **Table Style** to apply this setting.
- **Table Styles** – The **Table Styles** (or **Quick Styles**) gallery appears on the right-hand side of the **Table Design** tab. Click on the arrow to display the gallery, position your mouse over any style to see a live preview, and then click on a style to apply it to your **Table**. As you'll see, any custom styles that you create will appear at the top of the gallery, above the built-in styles. Two commands appear at the bottom of the gallery, as follows:
  - **New Table Style** – This command enables you to create a new style from scratch.

> **Tip**
> The **New Table Style** and **Modify Table Style** dialog boxes offer a **Set as default Table Style for this document** option. Alternatively, you can right-click on any built-in style in the gallery, such as **None**, and choose **Set As Default** so that any additional **Tables** you create in the workbook will not have a style applied.

  - **Clear** – This command removes the **Table Style** from a **Table**, which makes it look like a normal range of cells. This command only removes shading and borders—no other functionality is affected. Additionally, you can choose **None** from the gallery as an alternative to the **Clear** command.

> **Nuance**
> Choosing **Clear** or **None** removes the formatting from a **Table** but does not reset the **Banded Rows**, **Banded Columns**, **First Row**, or **Last Row** settings in the **Table Design** tab. It can be confusing to see these options enabled but not applied within the **Table**. To avoid confusion, you should also clear these checkboxes when you remove the style from a **Table**.

I've lingered on the **Table Design** options because controlling formatting in a spreadsheet is often of paramount importance to Excel users. Don't worry, we're just one section away from getting into the good stuff, which is the automation aspects, right after we see how to convert a **Table** back into a normal range of cells.

Removing Tables

Typically, you'll want to keep **Tables** in place in your workbooks, but sometimes you might change your mind. Or you might find that the **Table** feature conflicts with another feature, such as **Custom Views** (see *Chapter 8, Custom Views*). Removing a **Table** can be as simple as choosing **Table Design | Convert to Range**; if you do so prematurely, you might solve one problem and create new ones. Here's what I recommend:

1. Select any cell within a **Table** and then activate the **Table Design** tab of Excel's **Ribbon**.
2. Choose **Clear** at the bottom of the **Table Styles** gallery.

> **Nuance**
>
> It's important to remove an existing **Table Style** *before* you convert a **Table** into a normal range of cells. Otherwise, you or another user might mistakenly rely on automation that isn't available in a normal range of cells masquerading as a **Table**. See the *Selecting a portion of a Table* section for more details.

3. Optionally, you can clear the **Total Row** option if enabled. Totals can remain at the bottom of the normal range of cells, but will then function like any other formula that you enter into a worksheet, meaning you'll no longer be able to access the drop-down list feature, as shown in *Figure 7.12*.
4. Choose **Table Design** | **Convert to Range**, and then click on **Yes**, as shown in *Figure 7.13*:

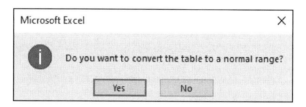

Figure 7.13 – A confirmation prompt for removing a Table from a worksheet

> **Tip**
>
> Choose the **Undo** command if you convert the wrong **Table** or change your mind.

Now that we've covered creating and removing **Tables**, let's see how you can automate aspects of your spreadsheets.

Table automation opportunities

Spreadsheets tend to involve lots of calculations, so first, we'll see how **Table** improve and sometimes alter formula behavior. Formulas that reference **Table**, either by residing within a **Table**, or referring to a **Table** will automatically reference additional data that you add to a **Table**. This eliminates the need to monitor and rewrite formulas that refer to normal ranges of cells. Then, I'll show you an easy technique for applying number formatting.

From there, I'll discuss the concept of **structured references** for formulas. Then, I'll look at filtering data within **Table** and automating certain filtering tasks with **Slicers**. We'll then see how **Table** eliminate a common data integrity issue with **PivotTables**, followed by enabling self-expanding charts.

Let's begin by seeing how to automate formula management within **Table**.

Calculated Columns

A **Calculated Column** within a **Table** consists entirely of formulas. As you'll see, whenever you change the formula in one cell of the column, your change is applied automatically applied to all other cells in that column:

1. Activate the **Insert Table** worksheet. If the list is not already formatted as a **Table**, click on any cell in the list, choose **Insert | Table**, and then click on **OK**.
2. Type Miles into cell **F1**, and press *Enter* to add a new column.
3. In cell **F2**, type in =D2/528 and then press *Enter* to create a **Calculated Column**—don't worry, I know this should be 5280, and we'll correct it in the next step. Double-click on any cell in the **Miles** column, add a zero, and then press *Enter* to see how all formulas in the column update at once.

> **Tip**
> See the *Troubleshooting* section at the end of this chapter if you encounter a situation where a **Calculated Column** does not update in this fashion.

4. Right-click on any cell in the **Miles** column, and then choose **Select | Entire Table Column** from the context menu.
5. Press *Ctrl + Shift + !* (⌘ + *Shift + !*) to apply the **Comma Style** number format or apply any number format of your choice.
6. Type Kilometers into cell **G1**, and press *Enter* to add a second column.
7. In cell **G2**, type in =, tap the left arrow to select cell E2, and then type in /1000.

8. Choose **Formulas** | **Show Formulas** to display the difference between the two columns. As shown in *Figure 7.14*, the formulas in the **Miles** column take the form of =D2/5280, while all cells in the **Kilometers** column contain the =[@Meters]/1000 formula, where =[@Meters] is a **structured reference** that refers to a **Header** instead of a cell reference:

	C	D	E	F	G	H
1	Type Of Bridge	Feet	Meters	Miles	Kilometers	
2	High-speed rail	540700	164800	=D2/5280	=[@Meters]/1000	
3	High-speed rail	516132	157317	=D3/5280	=[@Meters]/1000	
4	High-speed rail	375407	114424	=D4/5280	=[@Meters]/1000	
5	High-speed rail	373000	113700	=D5/5280	=[@Meters]/1000	
6	High-speed rail	380200	115900	=D6/5280	=[@Meters]/1000	
7	High-speed rail	261588	79732	=D7/5280	=[@Meters]/1000	
8	Expressway	177000	54000	=D8/5280	=[@Meters]/1000	
9	High-speed rail	157982	48153	=D9/5280	=[@Meters]/1000	
10	Expressway	128600	39200	=D10/5280	=[@Meters]/1000	
11	Highway	126122	38442	=D11/5280	=[@Meters]/1000	
12		=SUBTOTAL(109,[Feet])	=SUBTOTAL(109,[Meters])			

Figure 7.14 – Show Formulas mode

Here are a couple of things to keep in mind about structured references:

- The **Miles** column does not use structured references because we typed in the cell address as opposed to selecting the cell. Conversely, in the **Kilometers** column, we typed an = sign and then used the left arrow key or mouse to select cell **G2**. Excel creates structured references automatically when you click on or navigate to a cell within a **Table**.

- To disable automatic structured references, choose **File** | **Options** | **Formulas**, clear the **Use Table Names in formulas** option, and then click on **OK**.

- Structured references should return the same data as cell references, but sometimes they might return the value from the first **Body Row** of a **Table** in every cell. In such situations, I resolve the problem by replacing the **Header** with a cell reference instead.

- In this context, the @ symbol is known as the **This Row** operator and instructs the formula to refer to the cell on the same row as the formula, as opposed to the entire **Table** column.

9. Choose **Formulas** | **Show Formulas** to return them back to showing results instead of formulas.

> **Nuance**
>
> Microsoft's documentation states that the keyboard shortcut for **Show Formulas** is *Ctrl +* ` (grave accent) in Windows or Mac. The tilde (~) character resides on the same key, so users will often say press *Ctrl + ~* because many Excel users would be hard-pressed to identify the grave accent on a keyboard.

Now, let's see how to create self-resizing formulas that automatically include new data that is added to a **Table**.

Self-resizing formulas

The **Formula References** worksheet, as shown in *Figure 7.15*, contains a list in a normal range of cells in columns **C:D** and a **Table** in columns **L:M**:

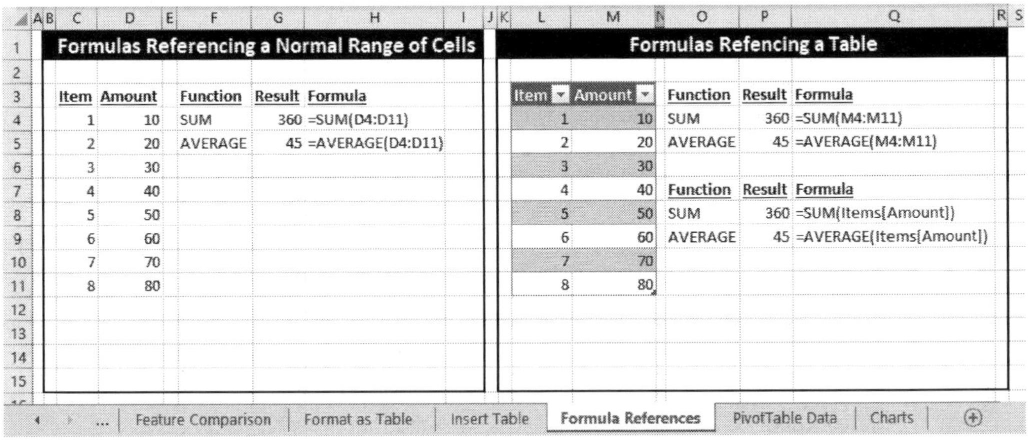
Formulas Referencing a Normal Range of Cells
Item Amount Function Result Formula
1 10 SUM 360 =SUM(D4:D11)
2 20 AVERAGE 45 =AVERAGE(D4:D11)
3 30
4 40
5 50
6 60
7 70
8 80
Formulas Refencing a Table
Item Amount Function Result Formula
1 10 SUM 360 =SUM(M4:M11)
2 20 AVERAGE 45 =AVERAGE(M4:M11)
3 30
4 40 Function Result Formula
5 50 SUM 360 =SUM(Items[Amount])
6 60 AVERAGE 45 =AVERAGE(Items[Amount])
7 70
8 80
Feature Comparison
Format as Table
Insert Table
Formula References
PivotTable Data
Charts

Figure 7.15 – Comparing formulas that refer to cell ranges versus **Tables**

Figure 7.15 also displays three types of formulas:

- **Cell reference to a normal range of cells** – Cells **G4:G5** are typical formulas in Excel.
- **Cell reference to a Table** – Cells **P4:B5** look like typical formulas in Excel but refer to a **Table**.
- **Structured reference** – Cells **P8:P9** contain structured reference formulas. Since the formulas are not within a **Table**, the **Table Name** precedes the column name that the formula references. These formulas do not include the **This Row** operator (@) because we want to reference the entire column.

Let's compare what happens when we increase the size of both datasets. There are three different types of formulas:

1. Select cells **C10:C11** and then drag **Fill Handle** down to cell **D13** to add two additional rows to the list.

> **Nuance**
>
> Cells **D4:D11** contain a formula that calculates an amount. Instead of dragging with your mouse, as described in *step 1*, you might be able to type `9` into cell **C12** and `10` into cell **C13** and observe that Excel fills cells **D12** and **D13** automatically, or at least it should. Sometimes, a range of normal cells will exhibit behavior similar to a **Calculated Column**.

2. Notice that the formulas in cells **G4:G5** do not reference the amounts in cells **D12:D13**, which means the formulas must be updated manually.

3. Type 9 into cell **L13** and 10 into cell **L14** and notice the following differences:

   - The **Amount** column is a **Calculated Column**, so cells **M12:M13** are filled automatically.
   - The formulas in cells **P4:P5** are updated automatically to include cells **M12:M13**, as shown in *Figure 7.16*:

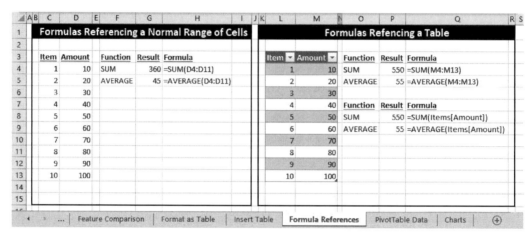

Figure 7.16 – Cells G4:G5 remain unchanged

Now, let's take structured references a step further by showing how to write formulas that reference data on another worksheet without switching worksheet tabs.

Using structured references to write formulas

The **Feature Comparison** worksheet contains a **Table Name**d Bridges that we'll reference in our next example by writing a formula in segments without needing to switch between worksheets:

1. Type =COUNTIF(Bridges[into cell **V4** of the **Formula References** worksheet.

2. Tap the down arrow three times to choose **Type of Bridge**, as shown in *Figure 7.17*, and then press the *Tab* key to add the field name to your formula. Then, type in] to close the field name:

Table automation opportunities   209

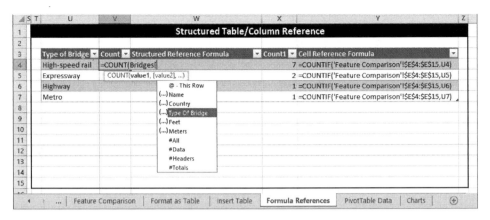

Figure 7.17 – Referencing a Table on the Feature Comparison worksheet without switching sheets

3. Type `,U4)` to finish the formula, and then press *Enter* to create a **Calculated Column**.

The **Cell Reference Formula** column in *Figure 7.17* shows what the formula looks like when cell references are used instead of structured references.

The COUNTIF function has two arguments:

- **Range** – A range of cells or a **Table** reference that you wish to search, in this case, `Bridges[Type of Bridge]` or `'Feature Comparison'!$E$4:$E$15`.

- **Criteria** – This argument is the data that you want to search the range field for, in this case, U4.

Here, again, the `=COUNTIF(Bridges[Type of Bridge])` formula does not include the **This Row** operator (@) because we are referencing the entire column. *Figure 7.18* shows an error prompt that you might encounter when you add an extraneous **This Row** operator (@) to a formula, such as one referencing an entire column. Although the error prompt makes no reference to it, the true error in this is the extraneous @ symbol, which, if removed, results in a formula that Excel will accept:

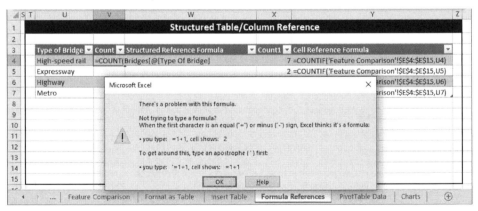

Figure 7.18 – An extraneous @ symbol creates a formula that Excel rejects

Now, let's move on from working with formulas and turn our attention to filtering data within **Tables** as a stepping-stone toward the automation that **Slicers** offer.

Filtering

The **Filter** feature enables you to focus on data that you wish to see by temporarily hiding rows that aren't relevant for a given search. For instance, let's say you only want to see bridges located in China:

1. Click on the **Filter button** option in cell **D4** of the **Feature Comparison** worksheet.
2. Clear **Select All**, choose **China**, and then click on **OK**.

> **Tip**
>
> A faster way to filter is to type one or more characters into the **Search** field and then press *Enter* when only the desired item(s) appear on the list.

3. Excel hides all rows in the **Table** except when China is in column **D**, as shown in *Figure 7.13*:

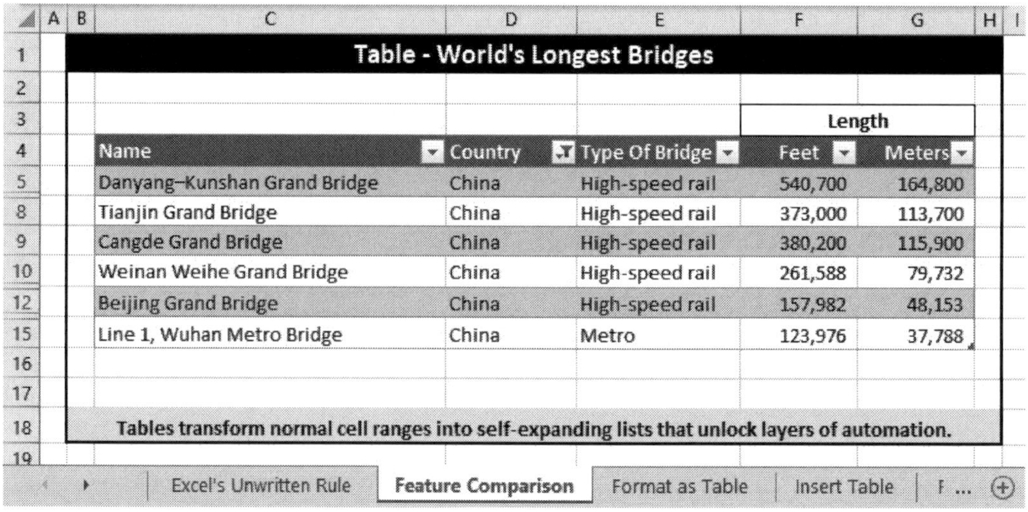

	Name	Country	Type Of Bridge	Length Feet	Meters
5	Danyang–Kunshan Grand Bridge	China	High-speed rail	540,700	164,800
8	Tianjin Grand Bridge	China	High-speed rail	373,000	113,700
9	Cangde Grand Bridge	China	High-speed rail	380,200	115,900
10	Weinan Weihe Grand Bridge	China	High-speed rail	261,588	79,732
12	Beijing Grand Bridge	China	High-speed rail	157,982	48,153
15	Line 1, Wuhan Metro Bridge	China	Metro	123,976	37,788

Tables transform normal cell ranges into self-expanding lists that unlock layers of automation.

Figure 7.19 – The filtered list

4. Choose **Data** | **Clear** (or **Home** | **Sort & Filter** | **Clear**) to display all rows in the **Table** again.

> **Tip**
>
> Also, you can choose **Clear** from the drop-down list in cell **D3**. Keyboard shortcut aficionados can press *Alt + Down* (*Option + Down*) in cell **D3**, use the down arrow to select the **Clear** command, and then press *Enter*. In a similar vein, the *spacebar* toggles checkboxes off or on within the drop-down menu.

As with a normal range of cells, you can filter a **Table** on as many columns as you want. Now, let's see how to automate filtering specific fields with **Slicers**.

Slicers

Slicers are objects that float on the worksheet and function as remote controls for the **Filter** drop-down menus. You can add one or more **Slicers** to a **Table** or **PivotTable**, but let's keep our focus on **Tables**:

1. Click on any cell in the **Table** on the **Feature Comparison** worksheet and then choose **Table Design | Insert Slicer**.

> **Tip**
> Additionally, you can click on any cell within a **Table** or **PivotTable** and choose **Insert | Slicer**.

2. Choose the field(s) that you wish to filter, such as **Country** and **Type of Bridge**, and then click on **OK**.

3. A **Slicer** appears for each field that you chose, as shown in *Figure 7.20*:

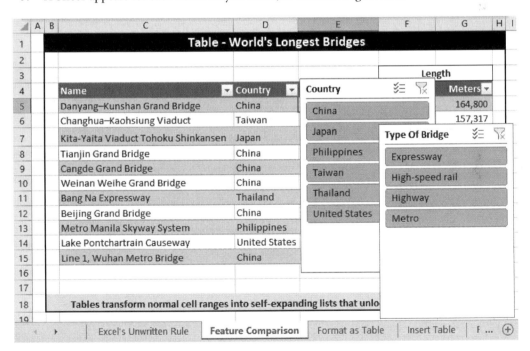

Figure 7.20 – **Slicers**

4. Choose **China** from the **Country Slicer** and **Metro** from the **Type of Bridge Slicer** to filter the list, as shown in *Figure 7.21*:

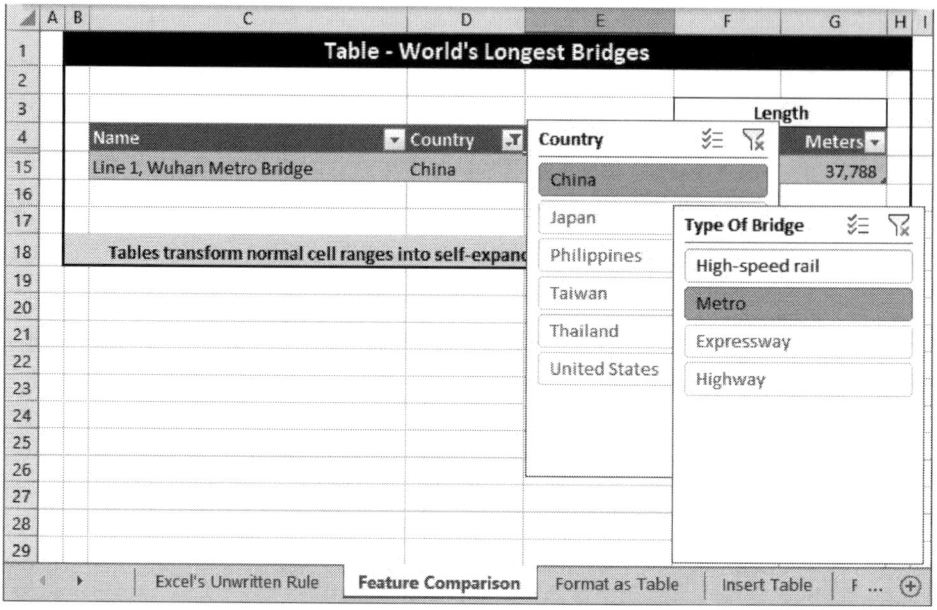

Figure 7.21 – A list filtered by Slicers

5. Click on the **Clear Filter** button in the upper-right corner of a **Slicer** to clear your selection and show all items again; alternatively, you can choose **Data | Clear**.

6. Notice how slicing enables you to collapse a list with a single click. Let's say that you wanted to see bridges located in China or the United States. To do so, simply hold down *Ctrl* (⌘) while you select the items you wish to see.

> **Tip**
> You can also select a group of items within a **Slicer** by holding down your left mouse button while you drag down the **Slicer**. Or you can click on the **Multi-Select** button in the **Slicer** and click on items you don't want to be visible in the **Table**.

To move a **Slicer** a short distance on screen, grab the margin of the object with your left mouse button and reposition as desired. To move a **Slicer** a longer distance, say from the bottom of a long list back to near the top, right-click on the **Slicer** and choose **Cut**. Then, paste the **Slicer** in the desired location. **Slicers** can be moved anywhere on a worksheet but cannot leave the worksheet.

A **Slicer** tab, as shown in *Figure 7.22*, appears in Excel's **Ribbon** when you have selected a **Slicer**, such as by clicking inside the margin of the object. The **Columns** field enables you to specify the number of columns that you wish a **Slicer** to have:

Table automation opportunities

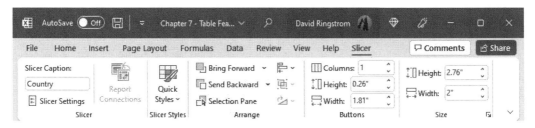

Figure 7.22 – The Slicer tab

The **Slicer | Slicer Settings** command displays the **Slicer Settings** dialog box, as shown in *Figure 7.23*, which you can use to control the caption, sorting, and filtering options:

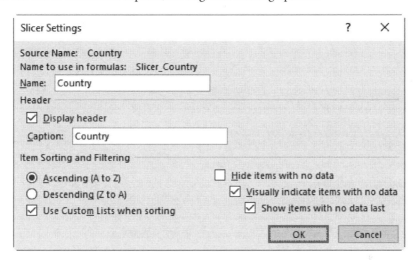

Figure 7.23 – The Slicer Settings dialog box

> **Tip**
>
> **Slicers** work with **PivotTables** in the same fashion as **Tables**. Choose **PivotTable Analyze | Insert Slicer** (or **Insert | Slicer**). To control two or more **PivotTables** at once, right-click on a **Slicer** and choose **Report Connections**, select the **PivotTables** to link, and then click on **OK**. This technique is only available for **PivotTables** that are based on the same data source.

You have a couple of options if you decide you no longer need a **Slicer**:

- Right-click on a **Slicer** and choose **Cut** (or **Remove**).
- Left-click on the edge of a **Slicer** and press *Delete*.
- Convert the **Table** back into a normal range of cells. **Slicers** can only be used with **Tables** and **PivotTables**, so Excel automatically removes any associated **Slicers** when a **Table** is converted into a normal range of cells.

> **Tip**
>
> To temporarily hide **Slicers**, choose **Home | Find & Select | Selection Pane**, and then click on the icon on the right-hand side of a **Slicer** in the list to hide the object. Click on the icon again to display the **Slicer** again.

Now, let's see how **Tables** can improve the integrity of **PivotTables**.

PivotTable integrity improvements

PivotTables are a report writing feature in Excel that allows you to instantly transform lists of data into meaningful reports. Let's begin with a brief overview of how to create a **PivotTable**, and then I will explain how the **Table** feature can improve the integrity of a **PivotTable**:

1. Click on any cell within the list that starts in cell **A3** of the **PivotTable Data** worksheet, and then choose **Insert | Recommended PivotTables**.
2. As shown in *Figure 7.24*, select **Sum of Feet by Country** and then click on **OK**:

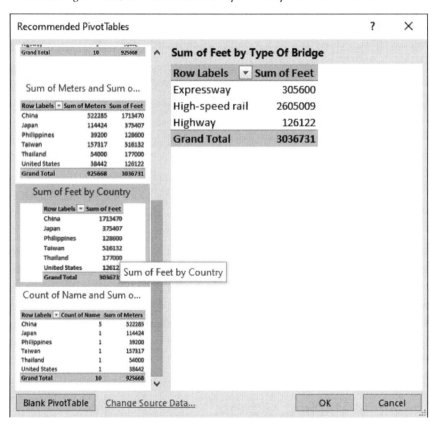

Figure 7.24 – The Recommended Pivot**Tables** dialog box

Table automation opportunities 215

> **Nuance**
>
> **Recommended PivotTables** in **Excel for macOS** unilaterally creates a **PivotTable** without giving you any choices.

3. As shown in *Figure 7.25*, a **PivotTable** appears on a new worksheet:

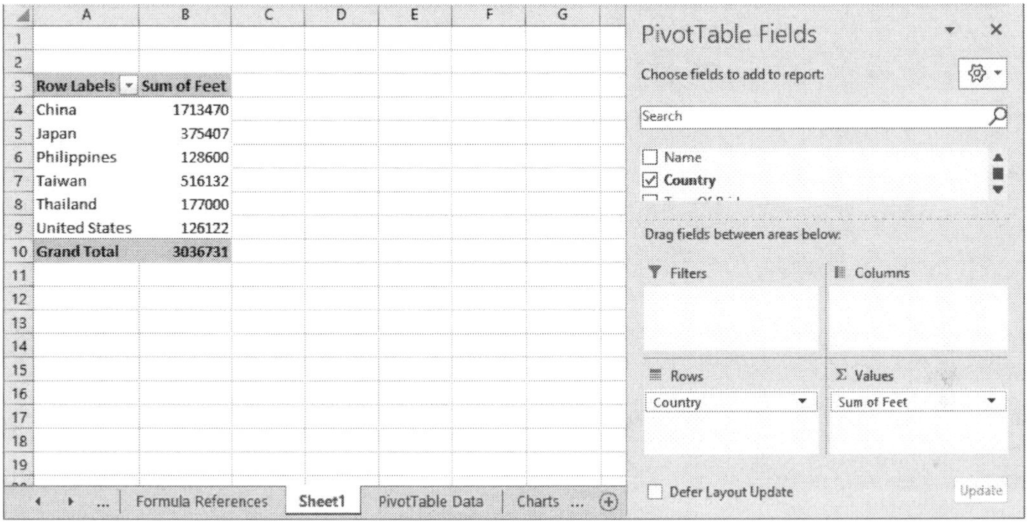

Figure 7.25 – The PivotTable report

4. Right-click on any cell within the **Sum of Feet** column, choose **Number Format**, choose a number format of your choice, and then click on **OK**.

5. Double-click on the new worksheet tab and assign the name **PivotTable Report**. Then, press *Enter*.

> **Tip**
>
> The **Number Format** command is only available when you right-click on a **PivotTable**. It allows you to format an entire column of a **PivotTable** without selecting any cells.

6. Select cells **G4:K13** on the **PivotTable Data** worksheet and press *Ctrl + C* (⌘ + C). Alternatively, you can choose **Home | Copy**.

7. Select cell **C14** and then press *Enter*, or choose **Home | Paste**.

8. Activate the **PivotTable Report** worksheet, and choose **PivotTable Analyze | Refresh**.

216 Automating Tasks with the Table Feature

> **Tip**
> You can also right-click on a **PivotTable** and choose **Refresh** or press *Alt + F5* in **Excel for Windows**.

9. Brunei Darussalam, Indonesia, Kuwait, and Peru do not appear because **PivotTables** based on a normal range of cells cannot automatically resize themselves. To manually resize a worksheet-based **PivotTable**, perform the following steps:

    I. Choose **PivotTable Analyze | Change Data Source**.

    II. Select cells **A3: E23**, as shown in *Figure 7.26*, and then click on **OK**, which will also refresh the **PivotTable** and cause the new countries to appear:

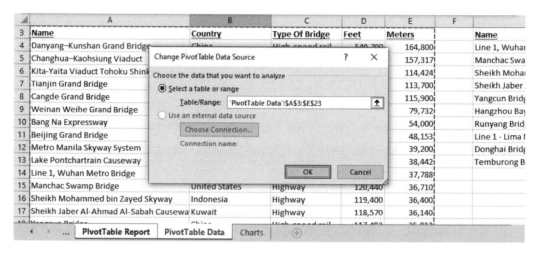

Figure 7.26 – The Change PivotTable Data Source dialog box

> **Nuance**
> The initial **PivotTable** alphabetized the country names; however, sometimes, resized **PivotTables** do not sort automatically. In this case, right-click on any country, choose **Sort**, and then **Sort A to Z** to alphabetize the list.

10. Now that you know how to manually resize a **PivotTable**, let's use the **Table** feature to eliminate the repetitive task:

    I. Activate the **PivotTable Data** worksheet.

    II. Select any cell within cells **A3:A23**, choose **Insert | Table**, and then click on **OK**.

    III. Copy the data from cells **M4:Q8**, and paste it into cell **A24**.

IV. Activate the **PivotTable Report** worksheet, click on any cell within the **PivotTable**, and then choose **PivotTable Analyze | Refresh**.

V. **India** should now appear on your **PivotTable**.

> **Tip**
>
> The **Table Design | Summarize with PivotTable** command makes it easy to create a **PivotTable** based on a list without needing to activate the **Insert** tab.

As you can see, **Tables** eliminate reselecting expanded datasets with the **Change Data Source** option, but you must still refresh your **PivotTables** any time you change the contents of a **Table** in any way—the same as with **PivotTables** that reference a normal range of cells.

Now, let's see how you can automate existing charts in a similar fashion.

Self-resizing charts

Charts are another feature that trap users in a repetitive cycle of resizing each time more data is added to a **Chart Range**. First, let's see how to manually resize a chart, and then we'll automate the process:

1. The **Charts** worksheet contains a chart that reflects `January` and `February`. Click on cell **E3** and type in `March` and then enter `300` in cell **E4**, and `600` in cell **E6**.

2. The chart will not reflect the `March` data until the chart has been resized. Click once on the chart and then use either of the following methods:

    - Drag the **Resize Handle** tool in cell **D5**, as shown in *Figure 7.27*, over to cell **E5**.

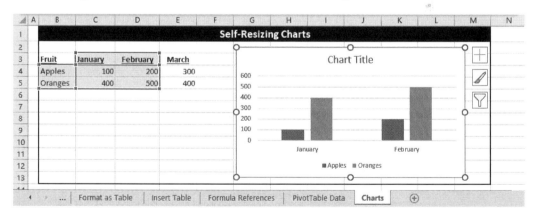

Figure 7.27 – Resize Handle

- Choose **Chart Design | Select Data**, select cells **B3:E5** in the **Chart data range** field, and then click on **OK**.

> **Nuance**
>
> Ensure your chart is referencing the entire source data range *before* you convert the range into a **Table**; otherwise, the chart will not automatically resize itself. If you skip *step 2* here, then your **Table** won't expand after you carry out *step 3* and *step 4*.

3. To automate the process, select any cell within **B3:E5**, choose **Insert | Table**, and then click on **OK**.
4. Type `April` into cell **F3**, `400` into cell **F4**, and `700` into cell **F5**. Your chart should look like *Figure 7.28*:

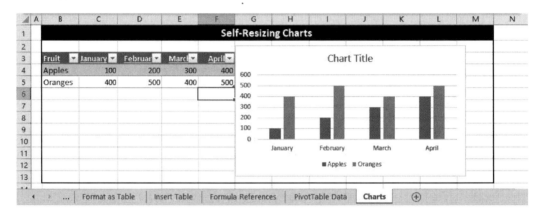

Figure 7.28 – A self-resizing chart

> **Tip**
>
> I will show how to use the **Table** feature to automate the **Sparklines** feature in *Chapter 9, Excel Quirks and Nuances*.

Now that you have a sense of the automation that's possible, let's look at some of the keyboard and mouse techniques that you can use to save time when working within **Tables**.

Other Table techniques

This section offers a grab bag of techniques related to **Tables**. First, I'll show you how to customize **Table Styles** and then how to transfer **Table Styles** that you have created between workbooks. After that, I'll show you how to copy data from a **Table** and then choose between pasting it as a **Table** or as normal range of cells. Finally, I'll compare how keyboard shortcuts that you might already use to navigate around worksheets can behave differently within **Tables**.

Customizing Table Styles

Ironically, the **Table** feature enables you to automate many repetitive tasks and yet will spawn new repetitive tasks for some users, meaning removing or changing **Table Styles**. There are only a couple of **Table**-related settings that you can manage on a global basis, which I'll discuss in the upcoming *Troubleshooting* **Tables** section. Otherwise, you must customize your **Table** settings on a workbook-by-workbook basis.

Setting a default Table Style

Let's start by seeing how to make **None** the default **Table Style** for a workbook:

1. Click any cell within a **Table** and choose **Table Design | Table Styles arrow** (**Quick Styles arrow**) to display the gallery.
2. Right-click on the first style in the top left, which is labeled **None**, and then choose **Set As Default**.

None is now the default style for this workbook, which means any new **Tables** that you create will have the same look as an unformatted normal range of cells. Now, let's go a bit further by customizing an existing style.

Customizing a built-in Table Style

You cannot edit any of the built-in **Table Styles**, but you can duplicate and then customize a built-in style:

1. Activate the **Format as Table** worksheet, click on any cell within the **Table**, and choose **Table Design | Table Styles arrow** (**Quick Styles arrow**). If the **Table Design** tab is not available, press *Ctrl + T* (⌘ *+ T*) and then press *Enter*.
2. Right-click on the first blue **Table Style** option in the **Medium** section of the gallery, and then choose **Duplicate**.

3. Assign a name, such as Three Row Style, to the **Modify Table Style** dialog box, as shown in *Figure 7.29*:

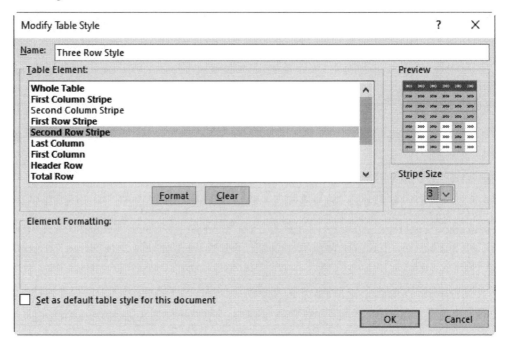

Figure 7.29 – The Modify Table Style dialog box

4. Choose **First Row Stripe**, and then choose **3** from the **Stripe Size** list.
5. Choose **Second Row Stripe**, and then choose **3** from the **Stripe Size** list.
6. Optionally, click on **Set as default Table Style for this document**.
7. Click on **OK** to create the **Table Style**.

> **Nuance**
> New styles you create will be added to a **Custom** section at the top of the **Table Styles** gallery but will not be applied to your **Table** until you choose from the gallery.

8. Choose **Table Design | Table Styles arrow** (**Quick Styles arrow**), and then choose the **Three Row Style** option from the **Custom** section to apply the style.

> **Tip**
> Hover your mouse over a style in the gallery to reveal its name.

Now, let's see how you can transfer custom **Table Styles** that you have created to other workbooks.

Transferring **Table Styles** to other workbooks

As you'll see, you can move custom **Table Styles** between workbooks by copying and pasting a **Table** from one workbook to another, or by moving a worksheet that contains one or more **Tables** between workbooks. The custom **Table Styles** then become a permanent part of the workbook if you remove the **Table** and/or worksheet that transferred the **Table Styles** over.

Copying and pasting **Tables** *to other workbooks*

Let's transfer a custom **Table Style** to a blank workbook:

1. Click on any cell in the **Header Row** on the **Format as Table** worksheet, press *Ctrl + A* (⌘ + A) to select the entire **Table**, and then press *Ctrl + C* (⌘ + C) or choose **Home | Copy**.

> **Tip**
> I discuss *Ctrl + A* (⌘ + A) and other **Table**-related keyboard shortcuts in the *Keyboard and mouse shortcuts* section later in this chapter.

2. Press *Ctrl + N* (⌘ + N) to create a new workbook (or choose **File | New | Blank Workbook**).
3. Press *Enter* to paste the **Table** you copied into the new workbook (or choose **Home | Paste**).
4. Choose **Table Design | Table Styles arrow** (**Quick Styles arrow**) and then notice that the **Three Row Style** option appears in the **Custom** section. Optionally, you can right-click on the style and choose **Set as Default** to make this style the default one for this workbook.
5. Optionally, choose **Home | Clear | Clear All** to erase the **Table**, and then choose **Home | Format as Table**. Observe that the custom style remains available in the workbook. Copying and pasting a **Table** that has a custom style applied makes the custom style a permanent addition to the workbook.

> **Nuance**
> I've found that, sometimes, Excel for macOS inexplicably changes the colors of a **Table** copied from one workbook to another. Normally, the **Home | Format Painter** command is my go-to to remedy situations like this, but it too causes the same color change.

Now, let's transfer custom **Table Styles** by copying or moving a worksheet between workbooks.

Copying or moving worksheets with **Tables** *to other workbooks*

Another way to transfer custom **Table Styles** between workbooks is to move or copy a worksheet:

1. Right-click on the **Format as Table** worksheet tab, and then choose **Move or Copy**. You can also choose **Home | Format | Move or Copy Sheet**).
2. Choose **(new book)** within the **To book** list to create a new workbook, or choose a workbook name from the list.
3. Optionally, select where the worksheet should appear by way of the **Before sheet** list if you chose an existing workbook from the **To book** list.
4. Click on **Create a copy** if you want to duplicate the worksheet, and then click on **OK** to move or copy the worksheet to the designated workbook.
5. Any custom **Table Styles** from the original workbook will appear when you choose **Home | Format as Table** or choose **Table Design | Table Styles arrow**. Additionally, you can set one of your custom styles as the default for the new workbook.

> Nuance
>
> In *Chapter 11, Names, LET and LAMBDA functions*, I will show you how to transfer custom worksheet functions between workbooks in the same fashion, which means you can create a centralized worksheet of LAMBDA functions and custom **Table Styles** that can be transferred together.

Now, let's see how to modify or remove Custom **Table Styles**.

Modifying or removing custom Table Styles

As you've seen, you can duplicate and then customize a built-in style. I haven't covered how to create a **Table Style** from scratch, but the only difference is that you choose **New Table Style** from the bottom of the gallery. First, let's see how to modify an existing **Table Style**:

1. Choose **Home | Format as Table**. Alternatively, you can choose **Table Design | Table Styles arrow** (**Quick Styles arrow**).
2. Right-click on the style you wish to change, and then choose **Modify**.
3. Make any changes you wish, and then click on **OK**.

> Nuance
>
> The **Modify** command is disabled when you right-click on a built-in style. In such case, choose **Duplicate** from the right-click menu instead of **Modify**.

Removing **Table Styles** works in a similar fashion. You cannot remove a built-in style, but you can remove any custom styles that you have created:

1. Choose **Home** | **Format as Table** or **Table Design** | **Table Styles arrow** (**Quick Styles arrow**).
2. Right-click on the style you wish to change, and then choose **Delete**.
3. Click on **OK** to confirm that you wish to delete the style.

Now, let's look at some of the nuances related to copying and pasting data from a **Table**.

Copying and pasting **Tables**

Copying and pasting **Tables** is like copying and pasting from a normal range of cells, but with the either/or choice of creating a new **Table** or pasting as a normal range of cells. Depending on the approach you take, existing column widths may get transferred to the area that you have pasted or may get left behind.

Selecting entire worksheet columns

As with a normal range of cells, column widths from the first **Table** get applied along with any data when you copy entire columns:

1. Copy columns **B:G** from the **Feature Comparison** worksheet.
2. Create a new workbook, and then paste the data into cell **A1**.
3. The **Table** is replicated with the same name as the original **Table**, and the column widths from the original worksheet are applied.

This is the most straightforward copy and paste technique if the columns outside of the **Table** are blank, or if you want to copy and paste that data, too.

Selecting the entire **Table**

Copying and pasting an entire **Table** creates a new **Table** in the location where you paste, but you'll have to carry out a couple of extra steps to apply the column widths, too:

1. Click on cell **C4** in the **Feature Comparison** worksheet and then press *Ctrl + A* (⌘ + *A*) to select the entire **Table**.

> **Nuance**
>
> In a normal range of cells, pressing *Ctrl + A* (⌘ + *A*) in cell **C4** would also select row **3** as part of the **Current Region** for cell **C4**. Since cell **C4** is within a **Table**, only the **Body Rows** are selected.

2. Create a new workbook and then paste the data into cell **A1**.

3. A new **Table** that has the same name as the original is created. To transfer the column widths, click on the **Paste Options** button and choose **Keep Source Column Widths** in the **Paste** section, as shown in *Figure 7.30*:

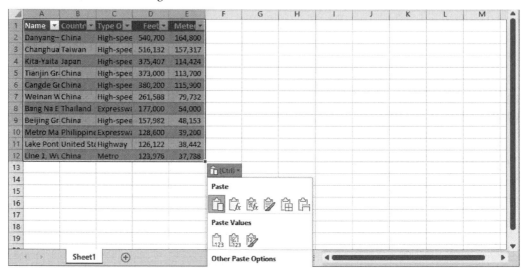

Figure 7.30 – The AutoFill Options command

> **Nuance**
>
> If you prefer to paste the data as a normal range of cells, choose **Paste Options | Values and Number Formatting** (the second command in the **Paste Values** section). However, you then cannot apply the column widths through the **Paste Options** button—doing so will convert the data back into a **Table**. Instead, copy the original **Table** again, select the first cell in the data you pasted, choose **Home | Paste | Paste Special | Column Widths**, and then click on **OK**.

Selecting a portion of a Table

If you copy a portion of a **Table**, you will paste a normal range of cells that masquerades as a **Table**:

1. Copy cells **B4:F14** in the **Feature Comparison** worksheet, such that you're copying everything except row **15**.
2. Create a new workbook, and after you paste the data, notice that the cells look like a **Table** but are a normal range of cells masquerading as a **Table**.

> **Tip**
>
> The presence or lack of the **Table Design** tab is categorical evidence as to whether a range of cells is an actual **Table** or imposter cells.

3. Click on the **Paste Options** button and choose **Formulas and Number Formatting** from the **Paste** section, or else choose **Values and Number Formatting** from the **Values** section.

> **Tip**
> You can also remove a **Table Style** from a normal range of cells by changing the **Fill Color** and **Borders** options to **None**. This will preserve any other formatting applied to the cells.

As you can see, different behaviors manifest depending upon how you copy and paste a **Table**, which also makes for a great segue to the different ways that keyboard and mouse shortcuts can shift.

Keyboard and mouse shortcuts

Keyboard and mouse tricks can help you navigate lists of any size with ease, as opposed to using the scrollbars to navigate. Let's look at a selection of keyboard shortcuts that you might find helpful within normal ranges of cells and **Tables**.

Selecting data within a worksheet or a Table

The following shortcuts enable you to select normal cell ranges and **Tables**:

- *Ctrl + A (⌘ + A)* – This selects the **Current Region** of a normal range of cells or an entire **Table** when the active cell is in a **Header** or **Total Row**; otherwise, only the **Body Rows** will be selected.
- *Shift + Spacebar* – This selects entire worksheet rows or **Table Rows** in **Excel for Windows** or macOS.
- *Ctrl + Spacebar* – This selects entire worksheet columns or **Table** columns in **Excel for Windows** only.

Inserting or deleting columns/rows

You can right-click within a **Table** to reveal **Insert** and **Delete** commands with submenus that are specific to **Tables**. The following keyboard shortcuts work in normal ranges of cells and **Tables**:

- In a normal range of cells, *Ctrl + Plus* displays the **Insert** dialog box or inserts rows/columns commensurate with the number of entire rows/columns currently selected. *Ctrl + Minus* displays the **Delete** dialog box or deletes entire rows/columns in the same fashion.
- When one or more cells in a **Body Row** of a **Table** are selected, *Ctrl + Plus* inserts a new **Body Row**, while *Ctrl + Minus* deletes the **current Body Row**.
- When two or more cells in a column in the body of a **Table** are selected, *Ctrl + Plus* inserts the number of columns that the current selection spans, while *Ctrl + Minus* deletes the number of columns that the selection spans.

> **Nuance**
>
> *Ctrl + Plus* or *Ctrl + Minus* do not function in a **Header Row** or **Total Row**.

Moving the cursor around within a worksheet or workbook

The following keyboard and mouse tricks are especially helpful when working in large **Tables**, but apply to normal ranges of cells, too:

- Hold down *Ctrl* (⌘) and tap an arrow key in a normal range of cells to move to the next blank or non-blank cell, depending upon the type of cell that you start from. However, if you're not careful, you might end up at the outer edges of a worksheet, meaning column **XFD** or row **1048576**. If this happens, press *Ctrl + Home* (*Fn + Ctrl + Left arrow*) to move the active cell to cell **A1**.

> **Nuance**
>
> Double-clicking on the border of a non-blank cell moves the active cell in the same fashion. Your mouse will display a four-pointed arrow when properly positioned for this technique.

- Within a **Table**, *Ctrl + Any arrow key* (⌘ + *Any arrow key*) will move you to the corresponding edge of the **Table**.

> **Nuance**
>
> The cursor stops at the last row of a **Table** when you press *Ctrl + Down* (⌘ + *Down*) in a blank column, as opposed to moving you down to row **1048576** if you are in a normal range of cells.

Now, let's see how you can reorganize a **Table** by moving columns.

Moving columns

You can move columns within a **Table** with your mouse:

1. Position your mouse at the bottom edge of any cell in the **Header Row**.
2. When a four-pointed arrow appears, drag the column to the left or right within the **Table** and then release your mouse button to reposition the column. Be sure to keep your mouse within the **Header Row**; otherwise, you will encounter the prompt shown in *Figure 7.31*, or else misalign a column within the **Table**:

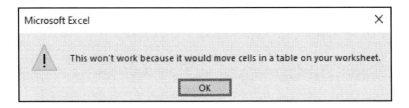

Figure 7.31 – Your cursor must remain in the Header Row to move columns

> **Nuance**
> You can use two different mouse tricks to move columns within worksheets. First, select one or more columns, and then hold down the *Shift* key while you drag either the left or right edge of the selection to a new position. Then, release your mouse and the *Shift* key. Alternatively, drag the selection into a new position with your right mouse button. When you release the mouse, a context menu will appear that will allow you to move or copy the column. If you get either of these techniques wrong, Excel will assume that you want to overwrite the existing data and will display a confirmation prompt.

Once you become accustomed to using **Tables**, it can be frustrating when the automation doesn't work as expected. In the next section, I'll show you what to look out for.

Troubleshooting Tables

Tables *should* always expand to incorporate new data that you add immediately to the right or below the **Table**. However, as you'll see, it's relatively easy to accidentally turn off the **Include new rows and columns in Table** option. Turning this setting back on requires a bit of persistence. You can inadvertently turn off the **Fill formulas in Tables to create calculated columns** option in a similar fashion. Even when both options are enabled, another scenario can cause **Tables** and **Calculated Columns** to not work as expected.

The Include new rows and columns in **Table** option

First, let's purposefully prevent a single **Table** from expanding to incorporate a new row of data:

1. Activate the **Formula References** worksheet and then type a number in the next available row of the **Item** column, such as 11 in cell **L14**.

2. Click on the **AutoCorrect Options** button, and then choose **Undo Table AutoExpansion**, as shown in *Figure 7.32*:

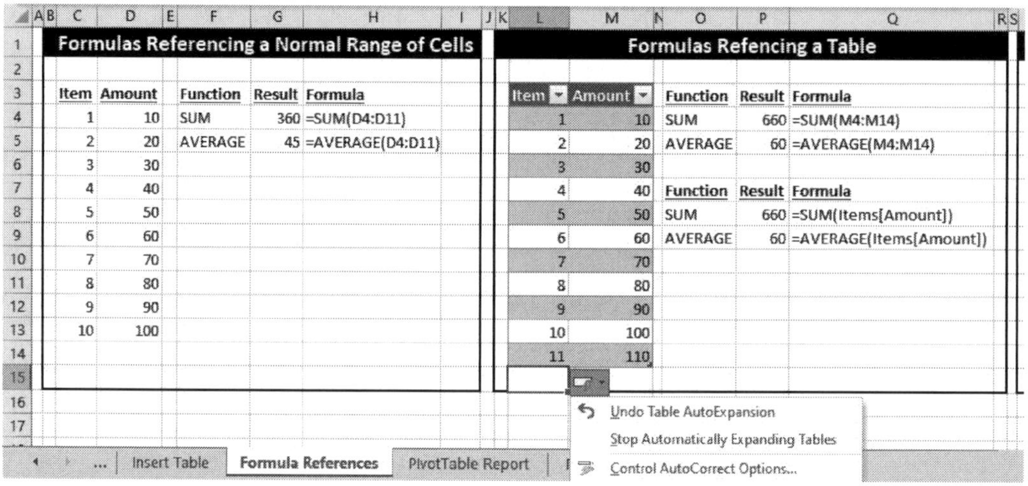

Figure 7.32 – AutoCorrect Options

3. The **Table** returns to its previous size and removes the formula that was added to the **Amount** column. The last number in the **Item** column is no longer part of the **Table**.

> **Tip**
>
> You can also press *Ctrl + Z* (⌘ + Z) to undo a **Table** expansion. If you change your mind, press *Ctrl + Y* (⌘ + Y) to restore the expansion.

If you choose **Stop Automatically Expanding Tables** from the menu, you'll prevent all **Tables** from expanding to incorporate new data that you add below or to the right of the **Table**.

> **Nuance**
>
> The **Control AutoCorrect Options** command is a shortcut to the setting that will enable auto-expansion for **Tables** again, but you won't be able to get there from here. The **AutoCorrect Options** button ceases to appear on the screen after you choose **Stop Automatically Expanding Tables**.

Here's the gauntlet you'll need to run in order to restore the auto-expansion of **Tables**:

1. Choose **File | Options | Proofing | AutoCorrect Options | AutoFormat As You Type**.
2. Click on the **Include new rows and columns in Table** checkbox, as shown in *Figure 7.33*, and then click on **OK** twice:

Troubleshooting Tables

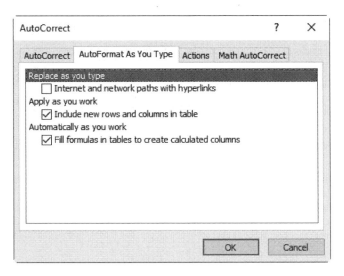

Figure 7.33 – The AutoCorrect Options dialog box

Fill formulas in Tables to create Calculated Columns

The **AutoCorrect** button provides slightly different settings within a **Calculated Column**:

1. Double-click on cell **M4** in the **Formula References** worksheet, add a zero so that `10` becomes `100`, and then press *Enter*.

2. Click on the **AutoCorrect Options** button, and then choose **Undo Calculated Column**, as shown in *Figure 7.34*:

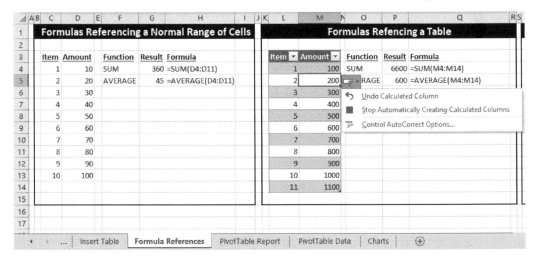

Figure 7.34 – Undo Calculated Column

3. The formulas in all other cells revert to the previous formula, while only the cell that you edited contains the new formula.

4. Going forward, this column now functions like a normal range of cells, where changes to one cell do not affect the other cells. There are a couple of ways that you can restore the **Calculated Column**:

   - Manually copy the same formula to all cells in the column.
   - If you see an error alert button with an exclamation mark, click on the drop-down menu and choose **Restore to Calculated Column Formula**.
   - If you overwrite another formula in the column, the **AutoCorrect Options** button will offer an **Overwrite all cells in this column with this formula** option.

If you choose **Stop Automatically Creating Calculated Columns**, you'll no longer have **Calculated Columns** in any of your **Tables** until you restore the setting. You can do so by using the steps in the previous section to access the **Fill formulas in Tables to create calculated columns** setting.

Now, let's look at a subtle way that data can be omitted from a **Table**, which can affect **Calculated Columns**, too.

Deleting rows prevents Table expansion

Generally, **Tables** automatically expand when you enter new data below or to the right of a **Table**. An exception to this rule is when you try to expand a **Table** by deleting rows or columns to merge two datasets together:

1. Copy cells **G4:K13** from the **PivotTable Data** worksheet and then paste them into cell **A13** of the **Format as Table** worksheet. In this case, do not paste the data into cell **A12**—for now, leave a one- or two-row gap.

2. If cell **A1** of the **Format as Table** worksheet contains Danyang-Kunshan Grand Bridge, then convert cells **A1:A10** into a **Table**.

3. Delete the blank row(s) to merge the two datasets. As shown in *Figure 7.35*, the **Table** does not automatically incorporate the new data:

	Column1	Column2	Column3	Column4	Column5
2	Danyang–Kunshan Grand Bridge	China	High-speed rail	540,700	164,800
3	Changhua–Kaohsiung Viaduct	Taiwan	High-speed rail	516,132	157,317
4	Kita-Yaita Viaduct Tohoku Shinkansen	Japan	High-speed rail	375,407	114,424
5	Tianjin Grand Bridge	China	High-speed rail	373,000	113,700
6	Cangde Grand Bridge	China	High-speed rail	380,200	115,900
7	Weinan Weihe Grand Bridge	China	High-speed rail	261,588	79,732
8	Bang Na Expressway	Thailand	Expressway	177,000	54,000
9	Beijing Grand Bridge	China	High-speed rail	157,982	48,153
10	Metro Manila Skyway System	Philippines	Expressway	128,600	39,200
11	Lake Pontchartrain Causeway	United States	Highway	126,122	38,442
12	Line 1, Wuhan Metro Bridge	China	Metro	123,976	37,788
13	Manchac Swamp Bridge	United States	Highway	120,440	36,710
14	Sheikh Mohammed bin Zayed Skyway	Indonesia	Highway	119,400	36,400
15	Sheikh Jaber Al-Ahmad Al-Sabah Cause	Kuwait	Highway	118,570	36,140
16	Yangcun Bridge	China	High-speed rail	117,493	35,812
17	Hangzhou Bay Bridge	China	Expressway	117,037	35,673

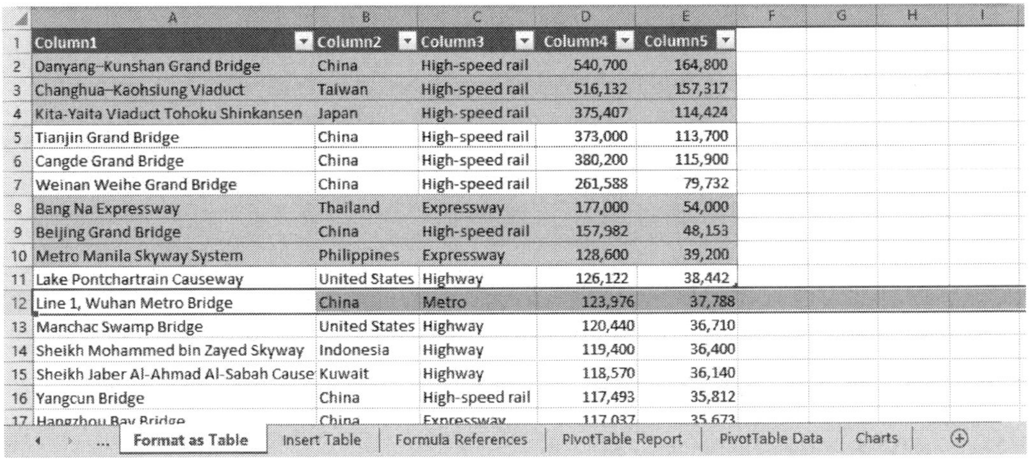

Figure 7.35 – **Tables** do not expand when merging data sets by deleting columns or rows

4. You can resize the **Table** in two ways:

   - Pull the **Resize Handle** tool in cell **E11** down through cell **E21**.
   - Choose **Table Design | Resize Table**, select cells **A1:E21**, and then click on **OK**, as shown in *Figure 7.36*:

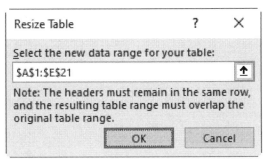

Figure 7.36 – The Resize Table dialog box

Alrighty, let's take a moment to recap what you've learned in this chapter.

Summary

This chapter began with a discussion of Excel's unwritten rule, which is about ensuring that the first row of any lists in your spreadsheet comprises a single row of unique titles. We then compared **Tables**, **PivotTables**, and data **Tables**, followed by a discussion of two approaches for converting a normal range of cells into a **Table**. The **Table** feature adds automatic enhancements, some of which you can disable or supplement with additional characteristics. Remember to be mindful when converting **Tables** into a normal range of cells to prevent anyone from mistakenly relying on non-existent automation in a normal range of cells that is masquerading as a **Table**.

Tables particularly enhance formulas in Excel, both by way of **Calculated Columns** within **Tables** and self-resizing formulas outside of **Tables**. Structured references make it easier to write and audit formulas that reference data within **Tables**. We went from formulas to filtering, and then you saw how **Slicers** can kick a **Table's** automation up another notch. **Tables** pair particularly well with **PivotTables** and charts by eliminating repetitive resizing and uncertainty about whether a report or chart includes all the data that it should.

Excel offers 60 built-in **Table Styles**, but you can also roll your own, or make the **None** style the default on a workbook-by-workbook basis. You can create custom styles from scratch or use an existing style as a starting point, and then migrate custom **Table Styles** to other workbooks by copying and pasting **Tables** or transferring a worksheet that contains one or more **Tables**.

Speaking of copying and pasting **Tables**, you learned it's not always just a straightforward copy/paste, especially if you want to convert the **Table** into a normal range of cells and keep the column widths of the **Table** as well. Keyboard and mouse shortcuts aren't necessarily straightforward either, which is why books like this one are written. We wrapped up the chapter with some troubleshooting tips on how to restore buried settings that, when tripped, will disable critical automation aspects related to **Tables**. Apart from that, even the most routine task of deleting rows to bring two datasets together can have unintended consequences as well.

In the next chapter, we will explore the **Custom Views** feature, which also offers a prominent level of automation of day-to-day tasks in Excel, such as hiding and unhiding worksheets, applying filters, creating multipurpose worksheets, applying two or more sets of print settings to a worksheet, and much more.

8
Custom Views

In this chapter, you'll learn about a powerful automation tool that can instantly transform workbooks. The overlooked **Custom Views** feature can vastly improve the accessibility of spreadsheets. Among other things, **Custom Views** can hide and unhide rows, columns, and worksheets. The **Custom Views** feature can also apply print settings, apply filter settings, adjust the positions of windows in Excel, and more. The **Table** and, sometimes, **Power Query** features disable the **Custom Views** feature, so I'll show you how to identify when that situation has arisen.

We will cover the following main topics in this chapter:

- Introducing **Custom Views**
- Multipurpose worksheets
- Creating a **Custom Views Quick Access Toolbar** dropdown
- Hiding and unhiding worksheets
- Automating filtering
- **Custom Views** conflicts

By the end of this chapter, you'll be able to automate repetitive tasks for yourself and others. You may be able to minimize ongoing spreadsheet maintenance in certain cases, and you'll have a clear sense of when you can and cannot use the **Custom Views** feature in a workbook.

Technical requirements

The **Custom Views** feature is available in all versions of Excel. The workbook that I used in this chapter can be downloaded from GitHub at `https://github.com/PacktPublishing/Exploring-Microsoft-Excels-Hidden-Treasures/tree/main/Chapter08`.

Introducing Custom Views

Custom Views captures and applies visual aspects of Excel workbooks and worksheets. To be clear, **Custom Views** does not change the contents of worksheets cells. In that regard, I discussed Excel's **Scenario Manager** feature in *Chapter 6, What-If Analysis*, which does enable you to swap out different sets of inputs. **Custom Views** enables you to manage the following aspects of an Excel workbook:

- Worksheet and feature settings:
  - Hidden or visible status of worksheets
  - Hidden or visible status of rows and columns
  - Freeze panes settings
  - Cell selection and cursor positioning
  - **Filter Buttons and settings**
  - Page Setup settings, including print ranges and page orientation
  - Displaying page breaks
  - Displaying worksheet columns from right to left (instead of left to right)
- Visual settings:
  - Display modes, including **Normal**, **Page Break Preview**, and **Page Layout**
  - Window sizes and positions
  - Worksheet zoom settings
  - Row and column headings
  - Displaying formulas instead of calculated results
  - Displaying a zero in cells that have a zero value
  - Displaying outline symbols if an outline is applied
  - Displaying gridlines
  - Gridline colors

In short, you can capture and then later reapply different combinations of these settings on demand by way of the **Custom Views** feature. However, you cannot change the status of objects in a workbook with **Custom Views**. This means that you cannot do the following:

- Change the filter settings in a **PivotTable**, **PivotChart**, or chart
- Hide or unhide any object such as a chart, shape, or slicer

- Make certain changes within protected worksheets
- Hide or unhide worksheets in a protected workbook

Despite the limitations, **Custom Views** still offers several ways to streamline working in Excel spreadsheets. Let's begin by creating a multipurpose worksheet.

Creating multipurpose worksheets

You've likely reached the tipping point in an Excel worksheet where so much data accumulates that you think, *Wow, I should create a summary of this information*. And away you go, adding another worksheet to your workbook. This, in turn, raises the bar on spreadsheet maintenance, as adding more information to the detailed worksheet can then require making continuous changes to keep the summary worksheet up to date. Instead of adding more worksheets, you may be able to use the **Custom Views** feature to have both detail and summary views on a single worksheet.

The *Figure 8.1* shows a hypothetical financial report that we'll use as the basis for our **Custom Views**. We'll be able to toggle the worksheet between views to see details for the entire year and activity by quarter, as well as a third executive summary view, all from a single worksheet:

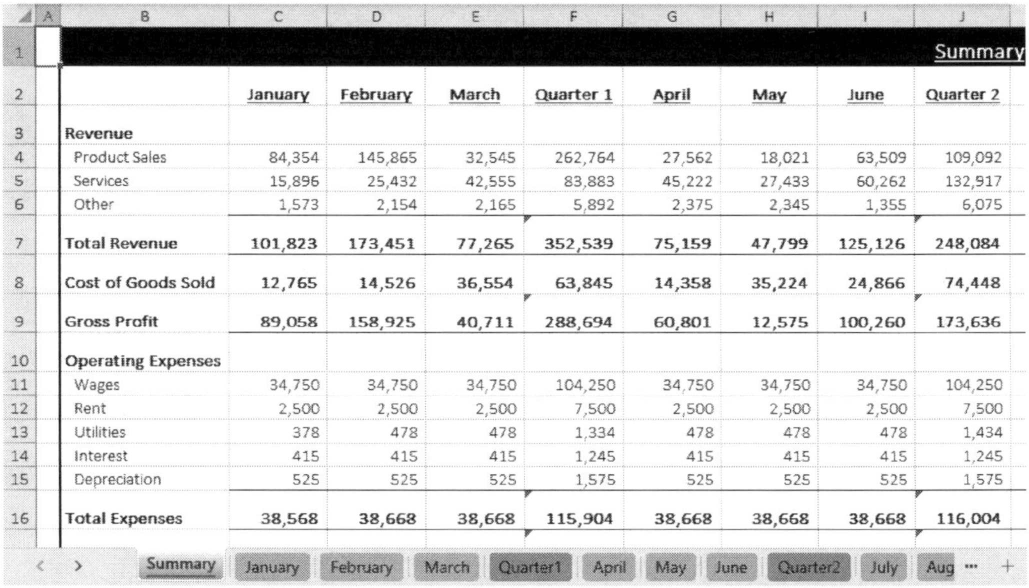

		January	February	March	Quarter 1	April	May	June	Quarter 2
									Summary
	Revenue								
	Product Sales	84,354	145,865	32,545	262,764	27,562	18,021	63,509	109,092
	Services	15,896	25,432	42,555	83,883	45,222	27,433	60,262	132,917
	Other	1,573	2,154	2,165	5,892	2,375	2,345	1,355	6,075
	Total Revenue	101,823	173,451	77,265	352,539	75,159	47,799	125,126	248,084
	Cost of Goods Sold	12,765	14,526	36,554	63,845	14,358	35,224	24,866	74,448
	Gross Profit	89,058	158,925	40,711	288,694	60,801	12,575	100,260	173,636
	Operating Expenses								
	Wages	34,750	34,750	34,750	104,250	34,750	34,750	34,750	104,250
	Rent	2,500	2,500	2,500	7,500	2,500	2,500	2,500	7,500
	Utilities	378	478	478	1,334	478	478	478	1,434
	Interest	415	415	415	1,245	415	415	415	1,245
	Depreciation	525	525	525	1,575	525	525	525	1,575
	Total Expenses	38,568	38,668	38,668	115,904	38,668	38,668	38,668	116,004

Figure 8.1 – Example data for creating a Custom View

Creating a base view

First, I will create what I call a *base view*, meaning a view that doesn't have any hidden rows or columns:

1. Open the example workbook for this chapter and then activate the **Summary** worksheet.
2. As shown in *Figure 8.2*, click the top left-hand corner of the worksheet to select all the rows and columns. Right-click on any column, such as column **B** in this case, and choose **Unhide**:

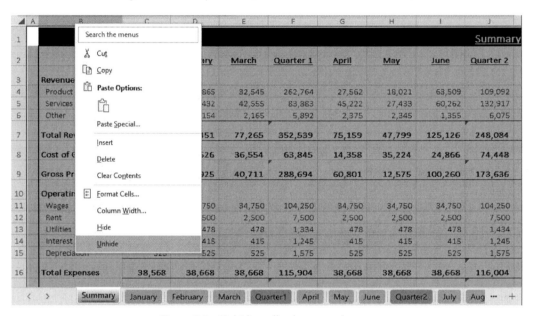

Figure 8-2 – Unhiding all columns and rows

3. Right-click any row, such as row **2**, and choose **Unhide**.
4. Select cell **C3** and choose **View | Freeze Panes | Freeze Panes** to freeze rows **1** and **2** at the top of the screen and columns **A** and **B** on the left-hand side of the screen. This action will select a single cell versus the entire worksheet. This also sets the location for the cursor to return to when you reapply the view.

> **Tip**
> **Custom Views** captures your cursor position as well as the selection status of any cells on the worksheet when you create a view. This means you can create a view to automatically preselect cells that you frequently copy and paste to eliminate the repetitive task of selecting the cells by hand.

5. Choose **View | Custom Views** and then click **Add**, as shown in *Figure 8.3*:

Creating multipurpose worksheets   237

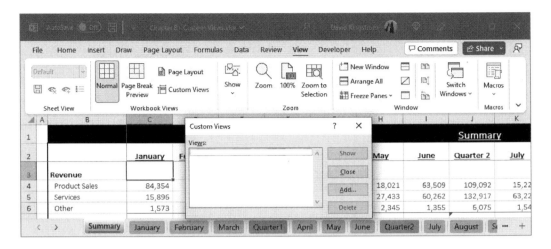

Figure 8.3 – The Custom Views dialog box

6. Type Entire Worksheet in the **Name** field of the **Add View** dialog box, shown in *Figure 8.4*, and then click **OK**:

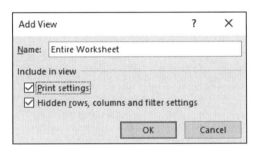

Figure 8.4 – The Add View dialog box

> **Tip**
> The **Custom View** we created to display all columns and rows on the **Summary** worksheet is capturing the settings of all other worksheets in the workbook as well. **Custom Views** are always applied at a workbook level, even when your focus is on a single worksheet.

Now, let's test the view:

1. Select one or more columns, such as **C:R**.
2. Right-click on any column in the selection and choose **Hide** (or choose **Home** | **Format** | **Hide & Unhide** | **Hide Columns**).
3. Choose **View** | **Custom Views** and then click **OK** since we only have a single view.

The **C:R** columns should now be visible again. A single **Custom View** can be a great way to reset a worksheet, but bigger benefits accrue when you can toggle a worksheet between two or more views. So, let's add a second view.

Creating a Quarters Only view

Now that we have a base view in place that unhides all columns and rows, let's make our workbook more interactive by creating additional **Custom Views**:

1. Select the **C:E** column on the **Summary** worksheet and then press *Ctrl + 0 (zero)* (⌘ + 0 in **Excel for macOS**) to hide them. As you saw in the previous section, you can also right-click the selection and choose **Hide** (or choose **Home | Format | Hide & Unhide | Hide Columns**).
2. Hide the **G:I**, **K:M**, and **O:Q** columns.
3. Click on any visible cell, such as cell **B3**, that you want your cursor to return to when you apply the view.
4. Choose **View | Custom Views | Add**, type `Quarters Only` in the **Name** field, and then click **OK**.

You now have two views that you can switch between:

1. Choose **View | Custom Views**, select **Entire Worksheet**, and then click **Show** to show all columns.

> **Tip**
> In Excel for Windows, you can skip the **Show** button by double-clicking on the name of any **Custom View**. Similarly, you can skip the **OK** button in most dialog boxes by double-clicking on list items or option buttons. You cannot double-click checkbox-based options as doing so will only toggle the checkbox on or off.

2. Choose **View | Custom Views**, select **Quarters Only**, and then click **Show** to hide the month columns.

Now that we can hide and unhide columns with our **Quarters Only** and **Entire Worksheet** views, respectively, let's take things a step further by creating a view that will also hide rows and increase the zoom size of the worksheet.

Creating an Executive Summary view

Now, let's create an **Executive Summary** view that will hide columns and rows, as well as change the zoom level of the worksheet:

1. Hide the **C:R** columns on the **Summary** worksheet.

2. Select rows **3:6** and then press *Ctrl + 9* (⌘ + 9). You can also right-click the selection and choose **Hide** (or choose **Home** | **Format** | **Hide & Unhide** | **Hide Rows**).

3. Hide rows **10:15**.

4. Select cell **S7** as the position for your cursor to be placed when **Custom Views** is applied.

5. As shown in *Figure 8.5*, choose **View** | **Zoom**, select **200%**, and then click **OK**:

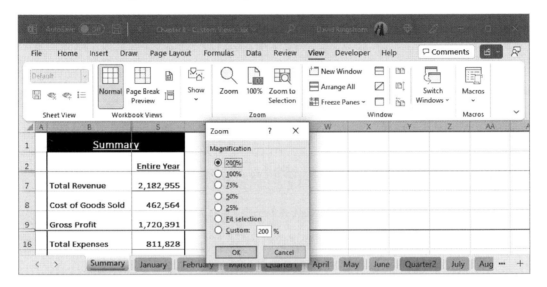

Figure 8.5 – The Zoom dialog box

6. Choose **View** | **Custom Views** | **Add**, type `Executive Summary` in the **Name** field of the **Add View** dialog box, and then click **OK**.

You now have three views you can toggle between. The worksheet will be displayed at the **100%** zoom level when you choose the **Entire Worksheet** or **Quarters Only** views, or at the **200%** zoom level when you choose the **Executive Summary** view. **Custom Views** are available to all users of a workbook, which means you can't create views that only certain users can choose. Anyone opening the workbook will have unfettered Custom Views access unless you protect the workbook, which I discuss in the **Custom Views** conflicts section.

Page Layout view conflict

The **View** | **Page Layout** command enables you to switch your workbook to **Page Layout** view, which enables you to easily add headers and footers to pages, as well as see how the data will lay out on the printed page. A downside to the **Page Layout** view is illustrated by the prompt shown in *Figure 8.6*, which shows that the **Freeze Panes** and **Page Layout** features are incompatible with each other.

Custom Views offers a way around this situation so that you don't have to repetitively re-establish frozen panes on worksheets where you need to go back and forth between the **Normal** view and the **Page Layout** view.

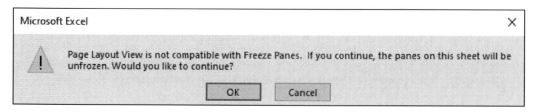

Figure 8.6 – Freeze Panes and Page Layout are incompatible

The key is to create a **Custom View** in advance where the worksheet panes are frozen, as we did in the *Creating a base view* section earlier in this chapter. Doing so enables you to automatically restore any frozen panes that **Page Layout** has unfrozen. Keep in mind that you can also create a **Custom View** that switches to **Page Break Preview** or **Page Layout**, although typically it's just as easy to choose either command on the **View** menu.

Now, let's learn how to make it easier for users to realize that **Custom Views** are available for use within a given workbook.

Creating a Custom Views Quick Access Toolbar shortcut

It's easy to forget or be unaware that **Custom Views** have been created in a workbook. Adding a **Custom Views** drop-down list to the **Quick Access Toolbar** for specific workbooks provides instant access and eliminates the need to train users on how to switch views.

> Tip
> See *Chapter 3, Quick Access Toolbar Treasures*, if your **Quick Access Toolbar** isn't visible in **Microsoft 365**.

Here's how to add the **Custom Views** drop-down list to your **Quick Access Toolbar**:

1. Carry out the steps in the *Creating multipurpose worksheets* section of this chapter if you haven't done so to create at least two **Custom Views**.

2. Choose **File | Options | Quick Access Toolbar** to display the **Quick Access Toolbar** section of the **Excel Options** dialog box.

3. As shown in *Figure 8.7*, choose the name of your workbook, such as **Chapter 8 – Custom Views**, from the **Customize Quick Access Toolbar** list at the top-right of the **Excel Options** dialog box:

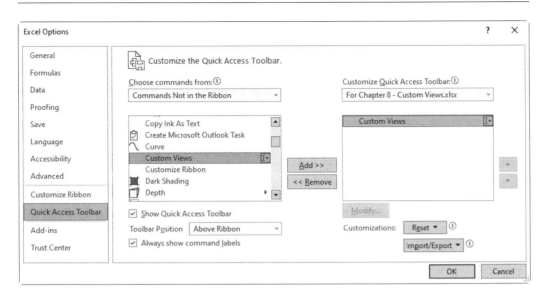

Figure 8.7 – The Quick Access Toolbar section of the Excel Options dialog box

4. Choose **Commands Not in the Ribbon** from the **Choose commands from** list.
5. Scroll down the list on the left, select **Custom Views**, and then click **Add**.
6. Click **OK** to close the **Excel Options** dialog box.
7. As shown in *Figure 8.8*, a **Custom Views** drop-down list has appeared in the **Quick Access Toolbar** area. You can now apply views by making a choice from the list instead of choosing **View | Custom Views**. A quirk of this list is that the views are listed in the order you created them in, as opposed to alphabetically:

Figure 8.8 – The Custom Views drop-down in the Quick Access Toolbar area

> **Nuance**
>
> Notice that I said to choose a specific workbook in *step 3*. If you skip this step, you'll add **Custom Views** to the default **Quick Access Toolbar** that appears in Excel, which means that 99% of the time, the list will be blank, as you may only situationally use **Custom Views**. Conversely, commands that you add to a specific workbook will be available in the **Quick Access Toolbar** area for anyone that opens the workbook. This greatly improves the accessibility of the **Custom Views** feature and ensures that you can benefit from your handiwork by having a visual reminder that the views are available.

If your **Quick Access Toolbar** is shown below the **Ribbon**, you may see the **Custom Views** command label appear adjacent to the list. Command labels such as this are not available in older versions of Excel. You can show or hide the command labels by way of the **Customize Quick Access Toolbar** menu.

Now, let's see how the **Custom Views** drop-down list appears and disappears when moving between workbooks:

1. Press *Ctrl + N* (⌘ + N) to create a new workbook or choose **File | New | Blank Workbook**.
2. Notice how the **Custom Views** drop-down list vanishes from the **Quick Access Toolbar** area.
3. Choose **View | Switch Windows** and then choose the **Chapter 8 – Custom Views** workbook.
4. The **Custom Views** drop-down list will reappear.

Now, let's learn how to use **Custom Views** to hide and unhide worksheets in a workbook.

Hiding and unhiding worksheets

As I mentioned previously, the **Custom Views** feature captures views for the entire workbook, including the hidden or visible status of each worksheet. First, let's learn how to manually hide and unhide worksheets, which we'll then automate with a **Custom View**.

You can easily hide any number of worksheets:

1. Open the example workbook for this chapter.
2. Select the **January** worksheet, hold down the *Shift* key, and click on the **Table Feature** worksheet.
3. Right-click any worksheet tab and then choose **Hide** (or choose **Home | Format | Hide & Unhide | Hide Sheet**).

At this point, only the **Summary** worksheet should be visible. Excel requires that you have at least one visible worksheet in each workbook.

> **Tip**
> If you want to hide an entire workbook but still keep it open in Excel, choose **View** | **Hide**. You can then choose **View** | **Unhide** to redisplay the workbook.

Historically, unhiding worksheets in Excel has been a tedious endeavor. In **Excel 2019** and earlier, you can only unhide one worksheet at a time:

1. Right-click any sheet tab and then choose **Unhide** (or choose **Home** | **Format** | **Hide & Unhide** | **Unhide Sheet**).

> **Tip**
> The **Unhide** or **Unhide Sheet** commands are disabled when a workbook does not contain any worksheets that have been hidden with the **Hide** or **Hide Sheet** commands.

2. Choose any worksheet to unhide, and then click **OK**.
3. Repeat *steps 1* and *2* until you've unhidden all worksheets that you wish to make visible in the workbook.

Conversely, in **Microsoft 365** and **Excel 2021**, you can unhide all hidden worksheets at once:

1. Right-click on any sheet tab and choose **Unhide** (or choose **Home** | **Format** | **Hide & Unhide** | **Unhide Sheet**).
2. Select the first worksheet in the **Unhide one or more sheets** list.
3. Scroll to the bottom of the list of sheets and hold down the *Shift* key and select the last worksheet. Or, hold down the ⌘ key if you only want to choose individual worksheets to unhide.
4. Click **OK** to unhide the selected worksheets.

No matter what version of Excel you're using, you can condense unhiding all worksheets in a workbook down to a single keystroke by creating a macro in Excel, as you'll see in the next section.

Unhiding worksheets with a macro

Macros are programming code that can be embedded within Excel workbooks. The procedure I'm going to show you works in any version of Excel, and if you store the macro in **Personal Macro Workbook**, it will be available for use in any open Excel workbook.

Let's use Excel's **Macro Recorder** to initiate the macro in the proper location. Then, we'll add the programming code that will unhide all worksheets:

1. Choose **View** | **Macros drop-down** | **Record Macro**.

2. Type UnhideAllSheets in the **Macro Name** field, as shown in *Figure 8.9*. Spaces and punctuation are not permitted in macro names in Excel:

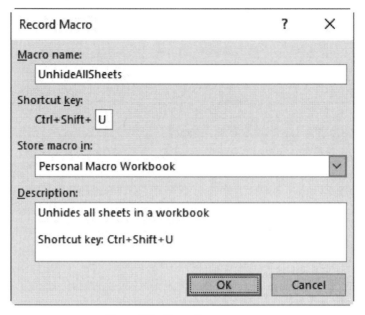

Figure 8.9 – Recording a macro

3. Optional: Assign a shortcut key, such as *Ctrl + Shift + U*. Type a capital letter in the **Shortcut Key** field to incorporate the *Shift* key into the shortcut.

> **Nuance**
> Be careful when assigning shortcut keys to Excel macros as you can easily supersede built-in functionality. Let's say that you entered a lowercase letter *u* in the **Shortcut Key** field. Your macro would then have a shortcut key of *Ctrl + U*. Your macro's shortcut would then override the normal behavior of *Ctrl + U*, which is to toggle the underline format on or off.

4. Choose **Personal Macro Workbook** from the **Store macro in** list.
5. Optional: Enter a description of the macro. If you assigned a keyboard shortcut in *step 4*, I strongly encourage you to document the shortcut in the **Description** field so that you can easily see the shortcut in the **Macro** dialog box when you click on the macro's name.
6. Click **OK** to start **Macro Recorder**.
7. Click the **Stop Recording** button, which is represented by a little square on Excel's **Status Bar**, or choose **View | Macros drop-down | Stop Recording**. The steps that we want to automate with code cannot be recorded, but **Macro Recorder** has created the macro so that we can manually add the programming code we need.

8. Choose **View** | **Unhide** and then click **OK** to close the **Unhide** window and unhide **Personal Macro Workbook**. This step is necessary due to a quirk in Excel that prevents you from using the **Edit** button in the **Macro** dialog box to access macros in hidden workbooks. An alternative is to edit the macro directly in **Visual Basic Editor**, but that can be daunting if you're unfamiliar with macros in Excel.

9. Choose **View** | **Macros** (meaning the top half of the **Macros** command) or press *Alt + F8* (on some keyboards, you may have to use *Alt + Fn + F8*).

10. As shown in *Figure 8.10*, click once on the macro you created – in my case, **UnhideAllSheets** – and then click the **Edit** button to display Excel's **Visual Basic Editor**:

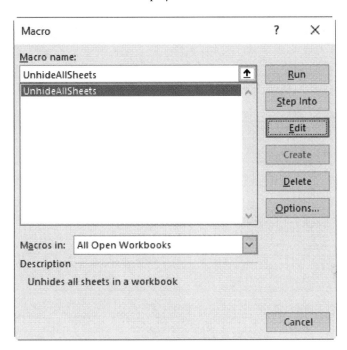

Figure 8.10 – Editing an existing macro

11. Before you edit the macro, switch back to Excel, make sure that the **Personal** workbook is active, and choose **View** | **Hide** to hide the personal macro workbook again.

> **Nuance**
>
> You must only unhide **Personal Macro Workbook** for long enough to get to the macro. It's important to keep **Personal Macro Workbook** hidden so that it remains open in the background. If it remains visible, the chances of you closing it accidentally or intentionally increase exponentially, which will then prevent you from being able to use the macros within the workbook if it is closed.

12. Return to **Visual Basic Editor** and enter the following line of code shown in *Figure 8.11*:

    ```
    For Each s In Sheets: s.Visible = True: Next
    ```

    This macro loops through each worksheet in the workbook and sets the **Visible** property to **True**. This is three lines of programming code condensed down to one, thanks to the colons. The word `Sheets` represents the `Sheets` object, which is a collection of all worksheets in the workbook. `s` is a variable that keeps track of which worksheet to process. `Visible` is a property that can be set to `True`, `False`, or `xlSheetVeryHidden` if you want to hide a worksheet in such a fashion that it can only be unhidden via **Visual Basic Editor** and not through Excel's user interface. The word `Next` instructs Excel to loop through to the next worksheet until all worksheets have been processed.

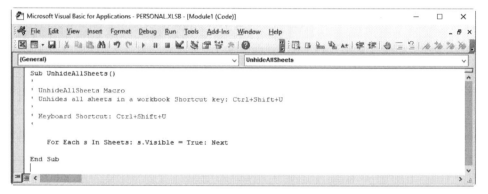

Figure 8.11 – Visual Basic Editor

13. Click **File | Save** in **Visual Basic Editor** to save the changes.
14. Choose **File | Close and Return to Microsoft Excel**.

To run your macro, you can use the keyboard shortcut you assigned, which in my case is *Ctrl + Shift + U*, or you can choose **View | Macros**, click once on the macro name in the **Macros** dialog box, and then click **Run**.

Hiding and unhiding worksheets with Custom Views

Now, let's see how **Custom Views** can streamline the process of hiding and unhiding worksheets:

1. If you haven't done so already, use one of the procedures highlighted previously to unhide all worksheets in the example workbook for this chapter.
2. Choose **View | Custom Views | Add**, type `All Sheets` in the **Name** field of the **Add View** dialog box, and then click **OK**.

This gives you a view that will unhide all worksheets with a couple of mouse clicks in any version of Excel. Next, we'll create a view that hides all worksheets in a workbook except for one.

Creating a Summary Only view

Now, let's create a view that hides all monthly and quarterly worksheets:

1. Activate the **January** worksheet in the example workbook for this chapter.
2. Hold down the *Shift* key and select the **Quarter 4** worksheet.
3. Right-click any worksheet tab and then choose **Hide** (or choose **Home** | **Format** | **Hide & Unhide** | **Hide Sheet**).
4. Activate the **Summary** worksheet and, optionally, click a cell near the top-left corner of the worksheet.
5. Choose **View** | **Custom Views** | **Add**, type `Summary Only` in the **Name** field of the **Add View** dialog box, and then click **OK**.

Now, you can toggle between the two views:

- Choose **View** | **Custom Views**, select **All Sheets**, and then click **Show** to display all worksheets.
- Choose **View** | **Custom Views**, select **Summary Only**, and then click **Show** to hide all the monthly and quarterly worksheets.

You can use **Custom Views** to hide or display varying combinations of worksheets. This is a huge time saver with large workbooks as you can create views for related worksheets so that you can spend much less time slogging through the workbook.

> **Nuance**
>
> You'll need to update any existing **Custom Views**, as described in the *Updating a Custom View* section, later in this chapter, if you add new worksheets to the workbook.

Now, let's see how to apply filters automatically with **Custom Views**.

Automating filtering

The **Custom Views** feature can apply one or more filters at once, rather than you having to do so individually. First, we'll briefly look at the **Filter** command. Many Excel users are familiar with the **Sort** command, which physically rearranges data within a list. Conversely, the **Filter** feature displays a subset of information in a list, thus hiding rows with data that doesn't match the filter.

Let's filter the list shown in *Figure 8.12* for beaches greater than `100 kilometers` in length:

1. Activate the **Filtering** worksheet of this chapter's example workbook and select any cell within the list.

> **Tip**
> There are only a few instances in Excel where it's necessary to select an entire list before filtering, such as when a list contains blank rows or blank columns. Another instance that comes to mind is when a list contains three or more header rows. In that case, you'll want to select from the last header row down through the bottom of the list to position the **Filter Buttons** properly. Otherwise, Excel will place the buttons correctly when your cursor is anywhere within the list.

2. Use any of these approaches to enable the **Filter Buttons** at the top of each column:

   - Choose **Data** | **Filter**
   - Choose **Home** | **Sort & Filter** | **Filter**
   - Press *Ctrl + Shift + L* in Excel for Windows:

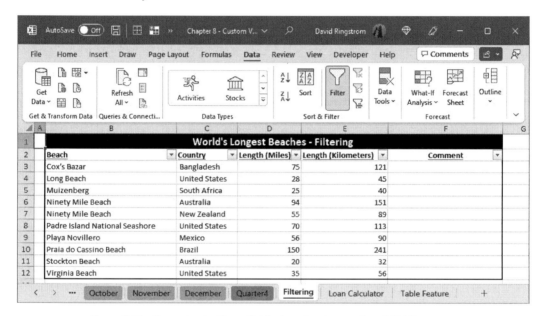

Figure 8.12 – Preparing to filter a list for beaches longer than 100 kilometers

3. Click the **Filter** arrow at the top of the **Length (kilometers)** column. Then, choose **Number Filters** and then **Greater Than**, as shown in *Figure 8.13*:

Automating filtering

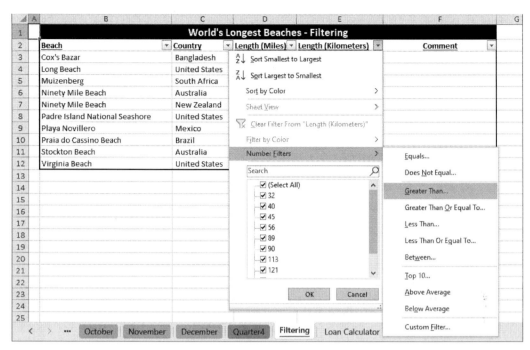

Figure 8.13 – The Greater Than filter

4. Enter `100` as shown in *Figure 8.14* and then click **OK**:

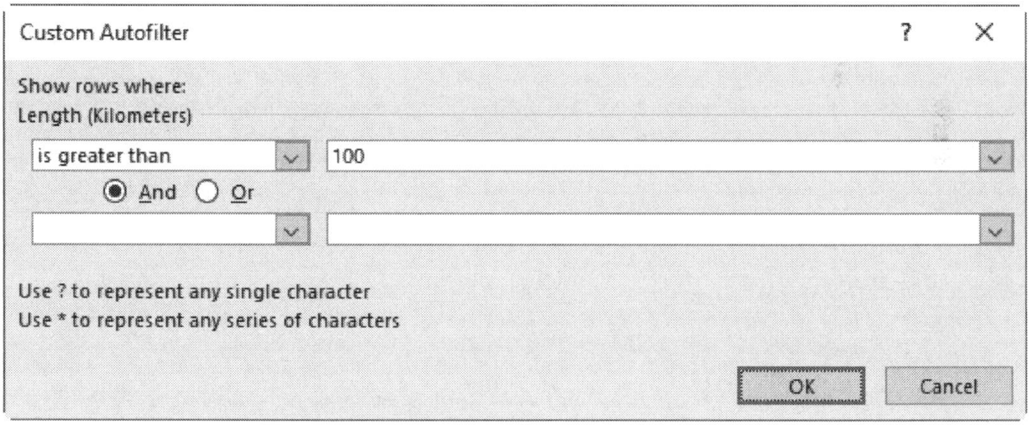

Figure 8.14 – Setting the Greater Than number filter

As shown in *Figure 8.15*, Excel hides the rows that don't match your filter criteria. You can filter on as many columns as you wish:

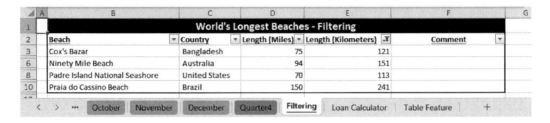

Figure 8.15 – A filtered list

> **Tip**
> Any changes you make to filtered data only affect the visible cells. For instance, if you delete rows **3:6** in *Figure 8.15*, rows **4:5** will not be affected.

Now, let's take our filtering a step further by automating it with a **Custom View**:

1. Choose **View** | **Custom Views** | **Add**.
2. Assign a name to the view, such as Beaches Longer than 100 Kilometers, and then click **OK**.

To test your **Custom View**, follow these steps:

1. Although not necessary, choose **Data** | **Filter** (or **Home** | **Sort & Filter** | **Filter**, or press *Ctrl + Shift + L*) to turn off the **Filter** feature so that you can see how **Custom Views** will turn the feature back on.
2. Choose **View** | **Custom Views**, select **Beaches Longer than 100 Kilometers**, and then click **Show**.

The **Filter Buttons** will reappear and only beaches longer than 100 kilometers will be shown. You can create as many **Custom Views** as you wish to easily toggle between various criteria within a list.

> **Tip**
> **Custom Views** are specific to the workbooks and worksheets where you create the view, so, unfortunately, this isn't a global solution for filtering lists that appear in multiple workbooks. In that case, you'd have to either apply the filters manually or create new **Custom Views**. Unfortunately, you also cannot transfer **Custom Views** between workbooks.

Applying print settings on demand

By default, **Custom Views** captures the print settings currently in place for each worksheet included in the view, unless you clear the **Print Settings** checkbox when creating a view. Let's create an audit view of a worksheet that will illustrate some additional settings that you can manage by way of the **Custom Views** feature:

1. Open the example workbook for this chapter and activate the **Loan Calculator** worksheet.
2. Maximize the worksheet window if necessary so that you can see how **Custom Views** can resize windows:

    - **Excel for Windows**: Click the **Maximize** button, which looks like a square in the top right-hand corner of the title bar.

    > **Tip**
    > If you see two overlapping squares in the top right-hand corner of the title bar – which represent the **Restore Down** button – then your window is already maximized.

    - **Excel for macOS**: Click the green **Enter Full Screen** button in the title bar of the window.

3. Choose **View** | **Custom Views** | **Add** and type `Loan Calculator - Normal` in the **Name** field of the **Add View** dialog box. Then, click **OK**.
4. Now, let's configure the settings for a second view. To begin, choose **Page Layout** | **Orientation** | **Landscape**.
5. Click the **Print** checkboxes for both **Gridlines** and **Headings** in the **Sheet Options** section of the **Page Layout** tab of the **Ribbon**.
6. Choose **Formulas** | **Show Formulas** to display all the formulas on the worksheet.
7. Reduce the size of the Excel window so that is no longer full screen:

    - **Excel for Windows**: Click the **Restore Down** button on the top right-hand side of the title bar, which looks like two stacked squares
    - **Excel for macOS**: Click the green **Exit Full Screen** button to reduce the size of the window

8. Click the button in the top left-hand corner of the worksheet frame to select all cells on the worksheet, to illustrate how **Custom Views** captures and then reapplies the selection status of worksheet cells.
9. Choose **File** | **Print** to display the print preview shown in *Figure 8.16*. Notice how the printout will include the worksheet frame and gridlines, as well as display all formulas. Then, press *Escape* to close the print preview:

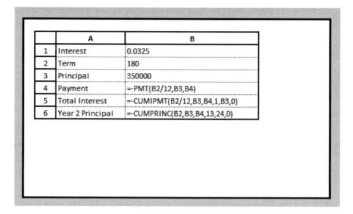

Figure 8.16 – A print preview of the Loan Calculator – Audit view

10. Choose **View | Custom Views | Add** and then type Loan Calculator - Audit in the **Name** field of the **Add View** dialog box.

11. Choose **View | Custom Views**, select **Loan Calculator – Normal**, and click **Show**. Notice how Excel maximizes the window and only one cell is selected.

12. Choose **File | Print** to display the print preview shown in *Figure 8.17*. The printout is in portrait orientation and looks like a normal Excel worksheet:

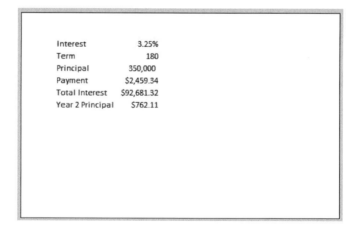

Figure 8.17 – A print preview of the Loan Calculator – Normal view

13. Choose **View | Custom Views**, select **Loan Calculator – Audit**, and then click **Show**. Notice how the Excel window resizes and that all cells are selected. If you choose **File | Print Preview**, you'll see that the print settings have changed as well.

I hope that at this point, you have a better sense of how many settings can be captured and applied with Excel's **Custom Views** feature. So far, we've focused on creating new Custom Views. Now, let's learn how to update views that have already been created.

Updating a Custom View

You cannot edit existing Custom Views that you've created, but you can replace a view using either of these approaches:

- Delete and recreate the view:

    I. Choose **View | Custom Views** and then click once on the view that you wish to update.

    II. Click the *Delete* button and then click **Yes** to confirm that you wish to delete the view.

    III. Create a new version of the view.

- Replace an existing view:

    I. Choose **View | Custom Views | Add**, enter the exact name of an existing **Custom View** in the **Name** field of the **Add View** dialog box, and then click **OK**.

    II. Click **Yes** on the prompt that informs you that the view already exists and asks if you would like to delete it and continue.

Removing all Custom Views from a workbook

Sometimes, you may encounter a workbook that has numerous **Custom Views**. For instance, the **Review | Share Workbook** command creates a **Custom View** for each user that accesses the workbook. Over time, this can result in an overwhelming number of **Custom Views** in a workbook.

Before you embark on clearing the views from a workbook, make sure that you apply any view that will unhide worksheets and columns, as well as undo filtering; otherwise, you'll have some manual effort to redisplay and unfilter since deleting the view will also delete the automation.

> **Tip**
> **Review | Share Workbook** no longer appears in the **Ribbon** area, but it can be added to the **Quick Access Toolbar** area, as discussed in *Chapter 3, Quick Analysis Toolbar Treasures*.

You can use a single line of programming code to remove all **Custom Views** from a workbook in one fell swoop:

1. Press *Alt + F11 (Option + F11)* (on some keyboards, this may be *Alt + Fn + F11*; alternatively, choose **Developer | Visual Basic**).

> **Tip**
>
> I discussed how to enable the **Developer** tab in Excel's **Ribbon** area in *Chapter 5, Data Validation and Form Controls*.

2. In **Visual Basic Editor**, choose **View | Immediate Window** or press *Ctrl + G* (*Ctrl + ⌘ + G*).

3. As shown in *Figure 8.18*, the **Immediate** window is a space where you can execute a single line of code without creating a formal macro. Type the following line of code into the **Immediate** window and then press *Enter*:

   ```
   For each v in ActiveWorkbook.CustomViews: v.Delete: Next
   ```

Just like the macro for unhiding sheets, which we covered earlier in this chapter, this is a three-line macro condensed to a single line. `ActiveWorkBook.CustomViews` represents a collection of all **Custom Views** in the current workbook. `v` is a variable that stores the name of the **Custom View** currently being processed. `Delete` is a method that removes the view:

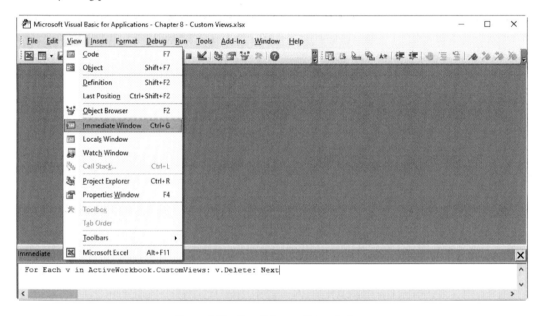

Figure 8.18 – Excel's Immediate window

If you find that you need to use this code regularly, you can formalize it into a macro by using the same techniques that I showed in the *Unhiding worksheets with a macro* section earlier in this chapter.

> **Warning**
> Keep in mind that you cannot undo actions carried out via programming code in Excel, so think through the implications to ensure that you don't solve one problem and create new ones by running macros like this. It's always a good idea to create a backup copy of a workbook before running a macro if you're not certain of the outcome.

So far, we've focused on creating **Custom Views** that affect a single worksheet. Now, let's learn how to create **Custom Views** that can help you manage the hidden or visible status of individual worksheets in a workbook.

Custom Views conflicts

After singing the praises of **Custom Views** all through this chapter, I now have some sad news to deliver. The **Custom Views** feature is unavailable any time that you use the **Table** feature, which I sang the praises of in *Chapter 7, Automating Tasks with the Table Feature*. A conflict can sometimes arise with the **Power Query** feature, which I will discuss in *Chapter 12, Power Query*. Older versions of **Excel for macOS** permitted users to use **Custom Views** and the **Table** feature together in the same workbook, but the Windows version never has. This means you will sometimes have to choose between which feature (**Custom Views**, **Table**, or **Power Query**) will offer the biggest most effective automation and data integrity in each a given workbook. In addition, the **Review | Protect Sheet** and **Review | Protect Workbook** commands can also sometimes pose conflicts with **Custom Views**.

> **Nuance**
> **Power Query** only disables **Custom Views** when results are returned to a **Table**. This means that you can use **Custom Views** and **Power Query** in the same workbook if you return the **Power Query** results to a **PivotTable** or **PivotChart** instead of a **Table**. Doing so enables you to display the **Power Query** results in a workbook but still be able to use the **Custom Views** feature.

Let's see specifically how the **Table** feature makes the **Custom View** feature unavailable for use.

Table feature conflicts

Let's create and then resolve the conflict so that you won't be caught by surprise in the future:

1. Open the example workbook for this chapter and then activate the **Table Feature** worksheet.
2. Click any cell within **A1:D11**.
3. Choose **Insert | Table** and then click **OK** to convert the list into a **Table**.

4. The **View | Custom Views** command appears dimmed, as shown in *Figure 8.19*:

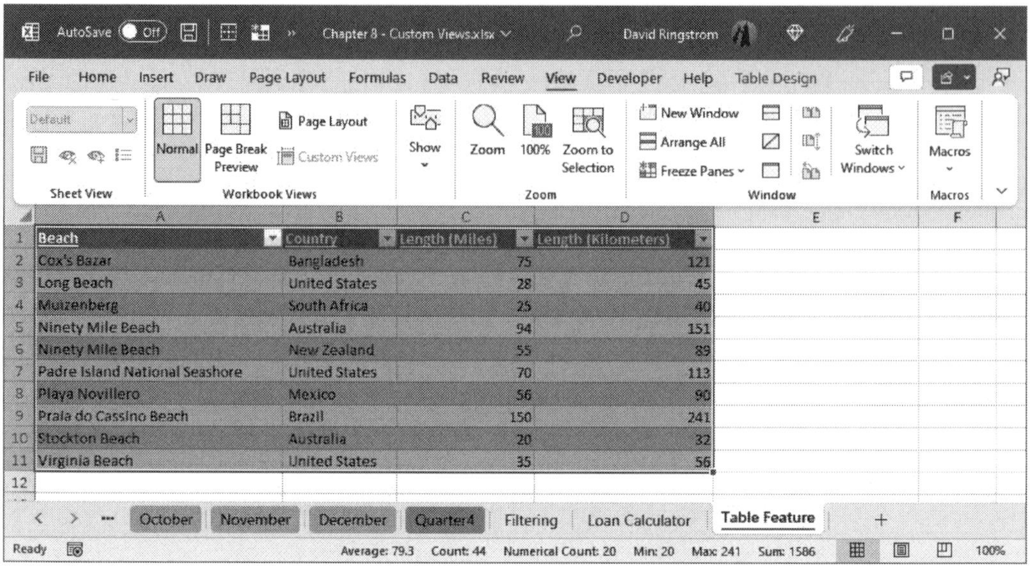

Figure 8.19 – Tables disable the Custom Views command

> **Nuance**
>
> Any views that you created before implementing the **Table** are still in the workbook but are unavailable until all **Tables** are removed from the workbook.

Removing all **Tables** from the workbook will make **View | Custom Views** available again:

1. Select any cell within the **Table**.
2. Choose **Table Design | Table Styles drop-down | Clear** to remove the shading from the **Table**.
3. Choose **Table Design | Convert to Range** and then click **Yes** to turn the **Table** feature off for this list.
4. Notice how **View | Custom Views** is enabled, and that any existing views can be shown again.

> **Tip**
>
> You can choose **Formulas | Name Manager** to identify the location of **Tables** anywhere in a workbook. Click the **Filter** button and then choose **Table Names** to see a list of **Tables** in your workbook. You cannot delete **Tables** by way of **Name Manager**, but you can identify the cell addresses where **Tables** reside.

Custom Views conflicts 257

It's one thing when **View | Custom Views** is disabled by the **Table** feature, and completely another when the feature mysteriously malfunctions as a side effect of protected worksheets or workbooks.

Worksheet protection conflicts

In this section, I'll show you how the **Review | Protect Sheet** command can sometimes create one or more conflicts with the **Custom Views** feature. Although the **Locked** status is automatically enabled for every cell in a worksheet, this has no impact until you protect the worksheet. If you plan to use **Review | Protect Sheet** you must first unlock any cells that you want users to be able to carry out actions in such as editing, filtering, and so on. Here's how to unlock cells within a worksheet:

1. Activate the **Filtering** worksheet of this chapter's example workbook.
2. Choose **Data | Clear** (or **Home | Sort & Filter | Clear**) if one or more rows have been filtered.
3. Select cells **F3:F12**.
4. Choose **Home | Format | Format Cells** or press *Ctrl + 1* (⌘ + 1) to display the **Format Cells** dialog box.

> **Tip**
> You can also click the **Font Settings**, **Alignment Settings**, or **Number Format** buttons in the respective corners of the **Home** tab of the **Ribbon** to display the **Format Cells** dialog box.

5. Activate the **Protection** tab of the **Format Cells** dialog box, clear the **Locked** checkbox, as shown in *Figure 8.20*, and then click **OK**.

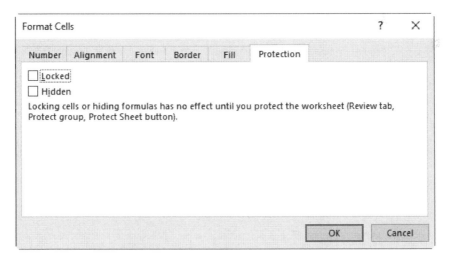

Figure 8.20 – Unprotecting worksheet cells

258 | Custom Views

> **Nuance**
>
> Alternatively, you could select cells **F3:F12**, and then choose **Home** | **Format** | **Lock Cell**. I tend not to use this approach because it's harder to tell if I just locked or unlocked cells since the menu vanishes when you click on **Lock Cell**. In *Chapter 3, Quick Access Toolbar Treasures*, I use this command to create a way to monitor and toggle the **Locked** status of cells on or off with a single mouse click or keyboard shortcut.

Changing the Locked status of a cell has no impact on a worksheet until you turn **Review** | **Protect Sheet** feature on. I'm going to give you a two-for-one in this section, meaning that I'm going to explain nuances related to both filtering on protected worksheets and using **Custom Views**. Let's first enable the **Protect Sheet** feature:

1. Follow the steps in the *Automating filtering* section earlier in this chapter, if you haven't done so already, to create a **Custom View** that you can apply when a worksheet is protected.
2. Activate the **Filter** worksheet in this chapter's example workbook.
3. Choose **Review** | **Protect Sheet**.
4. Click the **Format Columns** and **Use AutoFilter** checkboxes, as shown in *Figure 8.21*, and then click **OK**. Leave the **Password to unprotect sheet field** empty since we're going to use the **Review** | **Unprotect Sheet** command in a moment:

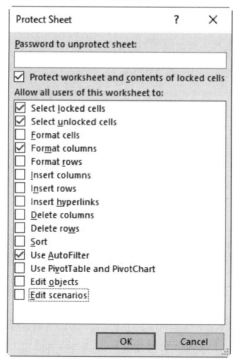

Figure 8.21 – Protecting a worksheet

5. Even though you turned on the **Use AutoFilter** setting, the **Data | Filter** and **Home | Sort & Filter | Filter** commands are unavailable because the worksheet is protected, and yet you can still use the **Filter Buttons** on the worksheet.

> **Nuance**
>
> The **Review | Protect Sheet** command always causes the **Data | Filter** and **Home | Sort & Filter | Filter** commands to be unavailable until you unprotect the worksheet by choosing **Review | Unprotect Sheet**. Any **Filter Buttons** on a protected worksheet will be unusable unless you turn the **Use AutoFilter** setting on within the **Protect Sheet** dialog box. Users cannot change the status of disabled **Filter Buttons** within protected worksheets.

6. Choose **View | Zoom**, choose **75%**, and then click **OK**.
7. Choose **Page Layout | Orientation | Landscape**.
8. Click on cell **F1** and press *Ctrl + 0 (zero)* (⌘ + 0), or right-click on the F column and choose **Hide** (or choose **Home | Format | Hide & Unhide | Hide Columns**).
9. Choose **View | Custom Views**, select **Beaches Longer than 100 Kilometers**, and then click **Show**.
10. Click **OK** on the **Some view settings could not be applied** prompt, as shown in *Figure 8.22*:

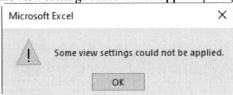

Figure 8.22 – Warning prompt related to the Custom Views feature and protected worksheets

Even though the worksheet is protected, the **Custom Views** feature can carry out the following steps:

- Restore the zoom level of the worksheet back to **100**% from **75**%
- Change the print orientation to **Portrait** from **Landscape**

However, **Custom Views** *can't* do the following:

- Apply **Filter** settings even when **Use AutoFilter** is enabled. You can use any **Filter Button** with your mouse or *Alt + Down (Option + Down)*. Navigate by keyboard with *Tab*, *Up*, or *Down*. Use *Space* to toggle options on or off, and press *Enter (Esc)* to close the list.
- Unhide column F, even though **Format Columns** is enabled. On the other hand, you can manually select columns **E:G**, right-click on any column in the selection, and then choose **Unhide** (or choose **Home | Format | Hide & Unhide | Hide Columns** or press ⌘ + *Shift* +*0 (zero)* in **Excel for macOS**).

> **Nuance**
>
> You can unhide columns with *Ctrl + Shift + 0 (zero)* in **Excel for Windows** once more if you disable a **Windows** setting. Click the **Windows Start button** and then choose **Settings**. Enter Language in the **Find a Setting** field and then choose **Language Settings | Keyboard**. Click **Language bar options | Advanced Key Settings | Between input languages**. Click the **Change Key Sequence** button, choose **Not Assigned** in the **Switch Keyboard Layout** section, click **OK** twice, and then close the **Settings** dialog box.

It's quirky that you can carry out certain tasks by hand on a protected sheet, such as hiding columns or unhiding columns, which the **Custom Views** feature cannot do unless you unprotect the worksheet:

1. Choose **Review | Unprotect Worksheet**.

> **Tip**
>
> In **Excel for Windows**, you can also choose **File | Info** and then click **Unprotect** to the right of any worksheet names in the **Protect Workbook** section. If you do not see any worksheet names listed, then no worksheets within the workbook are currently protected.

2. Choose **View | Custom Views**, select **Beaches Longer than 100 Kilometers**, and then click **Show** to observe that the **Custom View** feature works properly now.

In the next section, we'll cover an even bigger quirk when you try to apply a **Custom View** that hides or unhides worksheets in a protected workbook.

Workbook protection

Worksheet protection affects individual worksheets, whereas *workbook protection* affects the workbook as a whole. Protecting a workbook prevents users from carrying out the following actions:

- Hiding worksheets
- Unhiding worksheets
- Moving worksheets
- Inserting worksheets
- Deleting worksheets
- Renaming worksheets

The **Custom Views** feature can only carry out the first two items on the list and, as you'll see, only in *unprotected* workbooks:

1. Open the example workbook for this chapter and then activate the **Summary** worksheet.

2. Choose **View** | **Custom Views** | **Add**, type `Display Summary Worksheet` in the **Name** field of the **Add View** dialog box, and then click **OK**.

> **Tip**
> If **View** | **Custom Views** is disabled, you must remove any Tables you created in the example workbook by using the technique discussed in the *Table feature conflicts* section earlier in this chapter.

3. Right-click on the **Summary** worksheet tab and choose **Hide** (or choose **Format** | **Hide & Unhide** | **Hide Sheets**) to hide the **Summary** worksheet.
4. Choose **Review** | **Protect Workbook** and then click **OK** as shown in *Figure 8.23*:

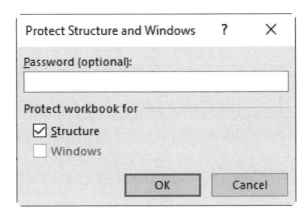

Figure 8.23 – Protecting a workbook

5. Choose **View** | **Custom Views**, select **Display Summary Worksheet**, and then click **OK**.

Remember, applying a **Custom View** to a *protected worksheet* will at least trigger the vague prompt shown in *Figure 8.22*. Conversely, you will not receive any feedback when you apply a **Custom View** that hides or unhides worksheets in a *protected workbook*. Further, no worksheets will be unhidden or hidden until you turn off the workbook protection:

1. Choose **Review** | **Protect Workbook** (notice the command has a shaded background when workbook protection is enabled).
2. Choose **View** | **Custom Views**, select **Display Summary Worksheet**, and then click **OK**.

The **Summary** worksheet will now appear without issue. Now, let's review what you've learned in this chapter.

Summary

In this chapter, you saw the range of features that can be controlled by way of Excel's **Custom Views** feature. Instead of creating supplemental worksheets that offer summarized views of detailed worksheets that you must maintain when the detailed worksheets change, you may instead be able to use the **Custom Views** feature to create multipurpose worksheets.

It's easy to overlook **Custom Views** that you or others have created. You can make this feature more accessible by adding the **Custom Views** drop-down menu to the **Quick Access Toolbar** of any workbook that utilizes the **Custom Views** feature. Remember, you cannot edit a **Custom View**, but you can save over an existing view. You can also delete an view and then create a replacement.

You can also spend less time navigating within large workbooks by hiding sheets that aren't relevant to your current task, and then easily unhide all sheets again with a couple of mouse clicks. You can also assign multiple print ranges and print settings to individual worksheets rather than replicating data on additional worksheets simply to accommodate printing requirements. As you saw, **Custom Views** can also automate repetitive filtering tasks.

It's hard to find an Excel feature without rough edges, and **Custom Views** is no exception. The **Custom View** feature is unavailable in workbooks that contain one or more **Tables**, including those that contain results from **Power Query**. **Custom Views** also can go haywire when applied to protected worksheets or workbooks. Excel will at least offer a vague prompt when a **Custom View** cannot be fully implemented on one or more protected worksheets. Conversely, Excel surreptitiously refuses to apply **Custom Views** in protected workbooks.

I consider the eccentricities I shared in this chapter to be an appetizer, if you will, for the buffet of peculiarities that I'm going to share in Chapter 9, Excel Quirks and Nuances.

9

Excel Quirks and Nuances

We've all had experiences where something goes awry in a spreadsheet. Software bugs can are not unheard of in Excel, but much of the time there is a disconnect between what we tell Excel to do versus what we intend for Excel to do. I wrote this book to broaden awareness of what's possible in Excel, with a specific hope that going forward you won't experience such instances nearly as often. And yet, sometimes things are just flat out weird in Excel. In this chapter I've assembled an array of features and techniques that can and do catch unsuspecting users by surprise, along with a powerful spreadsheet auditing feature that Microsoft has deigned only certain users can access.

Along the way you will learn about the following topics:

- **Compatibility Checker** feature
- Mouse tricks for navigating within worksheets
- **Enter** mode versus **Edit** mode
- Excluding weekend dates from charts
- **Sparklines**
- Circular references
- **Inquire** add-in

By the end of this chapter, you'll be able to identify compatibility issues between newer and older versions of Excel, since not every user has any say with regard to the version of the software that they're using. You'll be able to gracefully avoid a couple of stumbling blocks that lurk within in certain dialog fields. You'll also understand categorically what a circular reference is and how to track those pesky formulas down.

Technical requirements

Some but not all features will work in **Excel for macOS**, while most will work in all versions of **Excel for Windows**. The **Inquire** add-in requires a **Microsoft 365 Apps for enterprise** subscription. An example workbook is available on GitHub at https://github.com/PacktPublishing/Exploring-Microsoft-Excels-Hidden-Treasures/tree/main/Chapter09.

Compatibility Checker feature

If you share spreadsheets with others, both inside and outside of your organization, there's a decent chance that the recipient is using an older version of Excel, meaning **Excel 2016** or earlier. **Microsoft 365** brings us a steady stream of new functionality, such as the dynamic array functions that I discuss in *Chapter 10*, *Lookup and Dynamic Array Functions*, and the somewhat new LET function as well as the newer LAMBDA function that I discuss in *Chapter 11*, *Names, LET, and LAMBDA*. It's invigorating to have new tools to bear in Excel, until the user you shared a workbook with asks "Why am I seeing #NAME? everywhere in this workbook?". It's hard to keep tabs on what new functionality works where. For instance, you can use LET but not LAMBDA in **Excel 2021**. You can't use either in **Excel 2019** and earlier. I regret to inform any **Excel for macOS** users that the **Compatibility Checker** is not available to you, but it is available to all **Excel for Windows** users. Here's how to use it:

1. Open the Chapter 9 - Quirks and Nuances.xlsx example workbook for this chapter.
2. As shown in *Figure 9.1*, the **Compatibility Checker** worksheet contains worksheet functions that are incompatible with as far back as **Excel 2007**:

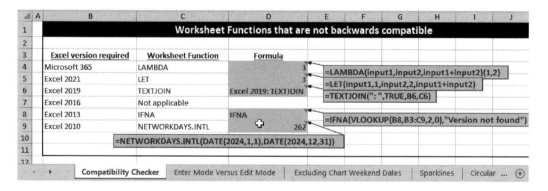

Figure 9.1 – Worksheet functions that will trigger Compatibility Checker

3. Depending upon your version of Excel, one or more of the formulas in column **D** may return #NAME? as soon as you open the workbook, or you may see the amounts shown in *Figure 9.1*. Seeing a valid value in a worksheet cell doesn't mean that the worksheet function is compatible with an older version, though. If you double-click on cell **D4** or **D5** in **Excel 2019** or earlier and then press *Enter*, the corresponding cells that you edited will return #NAME? because

Excel will recalculate the formula and realize that it does not recognize the LAMBDA or LET functions. Regardless, choose **File | Info | Check for Issues | Check Compatibility** to display the dialog box shown *Figure 9.2*:

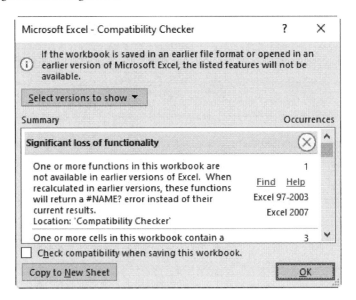

Figure 9.2 – Compatibility Checker

4. The **Compatibility Checker** dialog box may report one or more scenarios, with some examples provided here:

   • **Significant loss of functionality**: Click the **Find** link adjacent to each issue to navigate to the cell or cells that utilize worksheet functions or features that are not backwards compatible with one or more versions of Excel. Incompatible functions may initially return valid results when the spreadsheet is opened, but then such worksheet functions will return #NAME? when any change is made that triggers Excel to recalculate the worksheet.

> **Nuance**
>
> The **Select versions to show** drop-down list shown in *Figure 9.2* allows you to determine which prior version of Excel you want to ensure compatibility with so that you can minimize false alarms. Keep in mind that this list only appears when one or more **Significant loss of functionality** issues appear. If you care about compatibility with, say, **Excel 2019** or later, you can select that version from the list so that you won't be alerted to incompatibilities in **Excel 2016** and earlier. Enable **Check compatibility when saving this workbook** if you want Excel to automatically run **Compatibility Checker** each time you save your file, or you can manually run **Compatibility Checker** from time to time. This is not a global setting in Excel, meaning you'll have to configure **Compatibility Checker** on a workbook-by-workbook basis.

- **Minor loss of functionality**: This typically signifies that you have used a font or fill color that is incompatible with **Excel 97-2003**. Back in the day, Excel had a color palette of 256 colors, but starting with **Excel 2007**, you can access 4.3 billion colors, meaning almost any color you choose won't be one of the original 256. In such cases, old versions of Excel simply choose a color that is as close to a match as possible. Most of us can safely remove **Excel 97-2003** from the **Select versions to show** list so that we aren't needlessly presented with this warning. **Compatibility Checker** does not offer a **Find** link for identifying affected cells because it's a benign issue.

- **No compatibility issues were found**: **Compatibility Checker** determined that you didn't use any features or worksheet functions that are incompatible with the previous versions of Excel that are enabled on the **Select versions to show** list.

> **Tip**
>
> The **Standard Color** options within the **Fill Color** and **Font Color** commands on Excel's **Home** tab are a subset of the original 256 colors. Any other colors that you specify will trigger a **Compatibility Checker** warning when the feature is set to include **Excel 97-2003**.

Although **Compatibility Checker** will help you ensure compatibility with older versions of Excel, it does leave a huge blind spot for **Microsoft 365** users when Microsoft rolls out new features. **Microsoft 365** users generally fall into one of three different update channels: **Current**, **Monthly Enterprise**, and **Semi-Annual Enterprise**. The **Current** and **Monthly Enterprise** channels usually receive program updates on a monthly basis, which can include new features. **Semi-Annual Enterprise** users only receive program updates in January and July, which means that there can be a lag of six months or more before new features that **Microsoft 365** users in the **Current** and **Monthly Enterprise** channels are using become available. This means that if you share your workbooks with others outside of your organization, you should tread carefully when using new or fairly new features such as the LAMBDA function. Your best defense is to check the build number on your computer and on computers that you wish to share a spreadsheet with by choosing **File | Account**. If the **Version** and **Build** numbers next to the **About Excel** button are the same as yours or higher, it will be safe to jump in and implement those new capabilities in your spreadsheets. You can also identify which channel your computer has been assigned via this screen as well.

Let's now contrast **Compatibility Checker** with **Compatibility Mode**.

Compatibility Mode

The tricky part of compatibility in modern versions of Excel is that you will not know whether you have used a feature that is not backward compatible unless you happen to know which features and functions work with which versions of Excel, or you run **Compatibility Checker**. The exception to this rule is when you open a workbook that uses the **Excel 97-2003 Workbook (.XLS)** format. In such cases, Excel launches **Compatibility Mode**, as shown in *Figure 9.3*:

Compatibility Checker feature

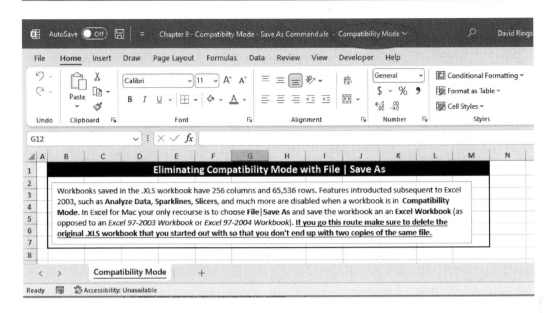

Figure 9.3 – Compatibility Mode

Compatibility Mode protectively disables any modern features that you cannot save to the .XLS file format. If you're not aware of the nuance, then you may be baffled as to why certain features are disabled. To be clear, not every disabled feature in Excel's **Ribbon** is attributable to **Compatibility Mode**. Although not shown in *Figure 9.3*, the **Redo** command is often disabled if the **Undo** stack has been cleared or you haven't yet started editing a workbook. Conversely, **Compatibility Mode** purposefully disables the **Analyze Data** feature on the **Home** tab because the **PivotTables** and **PivotCharts** that you create with this feature cannot be saved to **Excel 97-2003** workbooks.

> Nuance
>
> **Compatibility Checker** runs automatically when you save .XLS workbooks unless you clear the **Check compatibility when saving this workbook** checkbox in a given workbook.

The best way to eliminate **Compatibility Mode** confusion is to convert .XLS workbooks to the modern file format, but if you're not careful, you might solve one problem and create a new one.

Save As versus Convert command

Not that you would, but you could resave .XLS workbooks in the modern .XLSX format in this fashion:

1. Open the `Chapter 9 - Compatibility Mode - Save As.xls` workbook.
2. Choose **File** | **Save As** | **Browse**.

3. Change the workbook type to **Excel Workbook**.
4. Click **Save**.

At this point, you would now have *two* copies of the same workbook. The odds of someone—including you—opening the wrong file and making changes there are staggeringly high if you don't immediately delete the `.XLS` file. Granted, this is your only option to convert an `.XLS` workbook in **Excel for macOS**, but there's a better way in **Excel for Windows**, as detailed in the following steps:

1. Open the `Chapter 9 - Compatibility - Convert command.xls` example workbook for this chapter.
2. Choose **File | Info | Convert**, as shown in *Figure 9.4*:

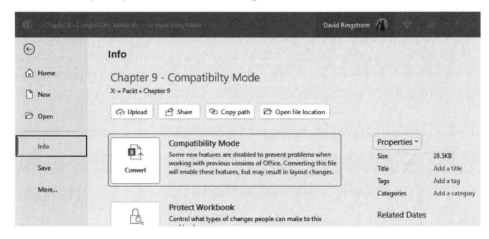

Figure 9.4 – Convert command

> **Nuance**
> The **Convert** command only appears when a workbook is in **Compatibility Mode**, so you won't usually see it in the **Info** section of **Backstage View** in **Excel for Windows**.

3. If needed, click the **Do not ask me again about converting workbooks** checkbox in the first dialog box that appears to permanently suppress the informational prompt about converting workbooks, and then click **OK**.

> **Nuance**
> You will see a **Save As** dialog box in place of the informational prompt if an `.XLSX` workbook with the same name as the `.XLS` workbook exists in the current folder.

4. Always click **Yes** when asked whether you want to close and reopen a workbook, as shown in *Figure 9.5*:

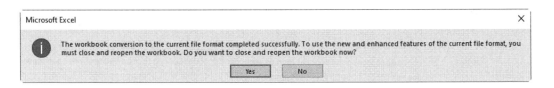

Figure 9.5 – Always click Yes on this prompt

> **Nuance**
>
> Eliminating the prompt shown in *Figure 9.5* is high on my wish list for Excel because the correct answer is always **Yes**. If you click **No** on this prompt, your workbook converts to the .XLSX file format, but your Excel workbook remains stuck in **Compatibility Mode** until you close and reopen the workbook.

Double-click trick for navigating within worksheets

Let's say that you want to edit the contents of a worksheet cell. Many of us reflexively double-click on the cell in question and get to work. Folks that are into keyboard shortcuts often press *F2* (*Fn + F2* on certain keyboards) instead of double-clicking. Or you might select a cell and then click into the **Formula Bar**. All three are valid, but a slight variation on the first approach may make you think Excel is possessed. Allow me walk you through a scenario:

1. Activate the **Double-Click Navigation** worksheet, as shown in *Figure 9.6*:

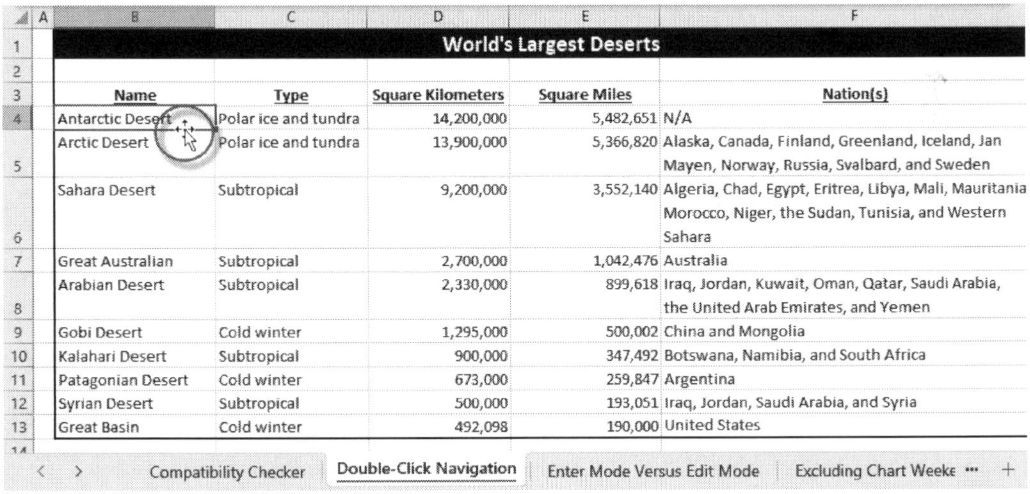

	A	B	C	D	E	F
1				World's Largest Deserts		
2						
3		Name	Type	Square Kilometers	Square Miles	Nation(s)
4		Antarctic Desert	Polar ice and tundra	14,200,000	5,482,651	N/A
5		Arctic Desert	Polar ice and tundra	13,900,000	5,366,820	Alaska, Canada, Finland, Greenland, Iceland, Jan Mayen, Norway, Russia, Svalbard, and Sweden
6		Sahara Desert	Subtropical	9,200,000	3,552,140	Algeria, Chad, Egypt, Eritrea, Libya, Mali, Mauritania Morocco, Niger, the Sudan, Tunisia, and Western Sahara
7		Great Australian	Subtropical	2,700,000	1,042,476	Australia
8		Arabian Desert	Subtropical	2,330,000	899,618	Iraq, Jordan, Kuwait, Oman, Qatar, Saudi Arabia, the United Arab Emirates, and Yemen
9		Gobi Desert	Cold winter	1,295,000	500,002	China and Mongolia
10		Kalahari Desert	Subtropical	900,000	347,492	Botswana, Namibia, and South Africa
11		Patagonian Desert	Cold winter	673,000	259,847	Argentina
12		Syrian Desert	Subtropical	500,000	193,051	Iraq, Jordan, Saudi Arabia, and Syria
13		Great Basin	Cold winter	492,098	190,000	United States

Figure 9.6 – A four-pointed arrow indicates the navigation mode

2. Position your mouse over the middle of cell **B4** and notice how your cursor presents as a white cross, and then click once to select cell **B4**.

3. Position your mouse over the bottom border of cell **B4** and notice how your cursor changes to a four-pointed arrow, as shown in *Figure 9.6*. Now, here's the nuance: double-click on the bottom border of cell **B4** and notice how your cursor moves down to cell **B13**, which is the last filled cell in this area of the worksheet.

This is a hidden double-click trick in Excel that can make you feel like Excel is running amok if you're not aware of the technique. You can also use keyboard shortcuts to navigate in a similar fashion, as outlined here:

- *Ctrl + down arrow* key moves the cursor down to the next empty or filled cell—depending upon where you're starting from—or the bottom of the worksheet. This means row **1048576** if you carry this out in a cell outside of the area of the worksheet where your data resides. The mouse equivalent is to double-click the bottom edge of a cell.

- *Ctrl + up arrow* key moves the cursor up the column to the next empty or filled cell, again depending upon where you're starting from. The mouse equivalent is to double-click the top edge of a cell.

- *Ctrl + right arrow* key moves your cursor across the current row to the next empty or filled cell, again depending upon the type of cell that you start from. If you're working to the right of your data, pressing *Ctrl + right arrow* key will take you to column **XFD**, which is the last column to the right. The mouse equivalent is to double-click the right-hand border of a cell.

- *Ctrl + left arrow* key moves your cursor left across the current row to the next empty or filled cell. The mouse equivalent is to double-click on the left-hand border of a cell.

> **Nuance**
>
> *Ctrl + arrow* keyboard shortcuts work everywhere in Excel, meaning that if your cursor is in cell **B13** and you press *Ctrl + down*, you'll end up at cell **B1048576**, meaning the very last row of the spreadsheet. Conversely, the mouse double-click trick only works when navigating within or to filled areas of the spreadsheet. If you click on cell **B16** and then double-click on the bottom border, nothing will happen. However, if you double-click on the top border of cell **B16**, your cursor will move to cell **B14**, which is the empty cell adjacent to your data. This means you can double-click within or toward your data, but you can't inadvertently double-click your way to a far edge of the worksheet the way that *Ctrl + arrow* shortcuts can.

There isn't a mouse equivalent for pressing the *Home* key (*Fn + left arrow* in Excel for Mac) to move your cursor to column **A** of the current row that you're on or pressing *Ctrl + Home* (*Fn + ⌘ + left arrow* in Excel for Mac).

Let's now explore an even trickier nuance in Excel, which is the difference between **Enter** and **Edit** modes.

Enter Mode Versus Edit Mode

Often, users add data to a chart and then must manually resize the chart to include the new data. I show how to eliminate this repetitive task in *Chapter 7, Automating Tasks with the Table Feature*, but I want to compare two manual approaches here. Let's jump in:

1. Activate the **Enter Mode Versus Edit Mode** worksheet in the example workbook for this chapter.
2. Notice that the chart does not reflect the **March** values. The first way to resolve this is to do the following:

    I. Click once on the chart.

    II. Drag the **Selection Handle** shown in cell **D5** in *Figure 9.7* across to cell **E5**:

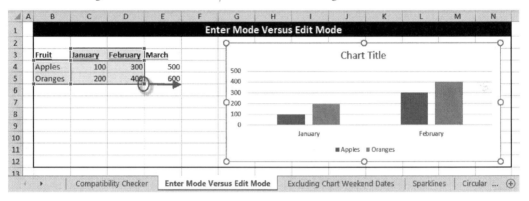

Figure 9.7 – Using the Selection Handle to resize charts

    III. At this point, your chart should reflect the month of **March**.

> **Nuance**
>
> If you don't see the **Selection Handle** in *Figure 9.7*, choose **File | Options | Advanced**, and then turn on the **Enable fill handle and cell drag-and-drop** setting.

3. Now, let's add **April** and resize the chart using a second approach so that I can show you the difference between **Enter** mode and **Edit** mode. To begin, enter these values:

    - Cell **F3**: `April`
    - Cell **E4**: `700`
    - Cell **E5**: `800`

4. Once again, **April** does not appear on the chart, so click once on the chart and then this time choose **Chart Design | Select Data**.

5. Here's where the nuances come in. Fields such as **Chart data range** (shown in *Figure 9.8*) are **RefEdit** fields, short for **Reference Edit**, that enable you to select or specify a range of cells or sometimes enter data. **RefEdit** fields have three different modes, as outlined here:

   - **Point**: As shown in *Figure 9.8*, the word **Point** initially appears in Excel's **Status Bar** when you open a dialog box that contains a **RefEdit** field, and a marquee border appears around the cells being referenced:

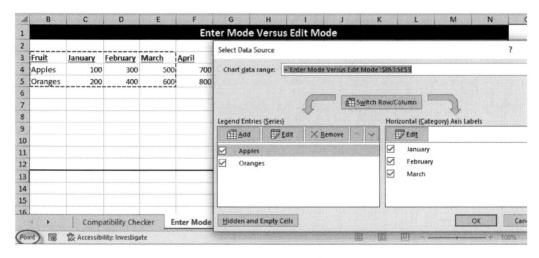

Figure 9.8 – Point mode

   - **Enter**: When you click on a **RefEdit** field in **Excel for Windows**, the word **Enter** appears in Excel's Status Bar, in place of **Point**, as shown in *Figure 9.9*:

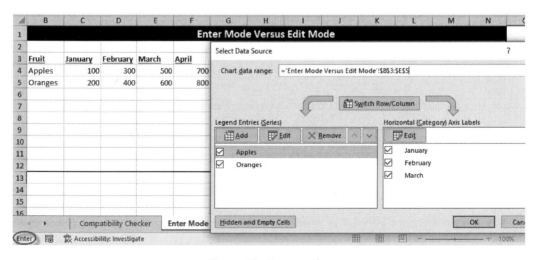

Figure 9.9 – Enter mode

Depending upon which action you choose next, tricky things may happen, as detailed here:

- You can resize the range of cells by holding down the *Shift* key and using the arrow keys on your keyboard, which switches the field to **Point** mode. This is actually your only viable keyboard-based action in **Enter** mode unless you first clear the contents of the **RefEdit** field. If you don't get the steps right though, you'll end up inadvertently carrying out the technique presented next.

- If you click on the worksheet with your mouse, you will append one or more cells to the **RefEdit** field contents, which typically results in an invalid cell reference such as =' Enter Mode Versus Edit Mode'!$C$4:$E$5+'Enter Mode Versus Edit Mode'!$F$4:$F$5.

- Similarly, pressing the left or right arrow keys on your keyboard will also append an additional cell reference in the same fashion as using your mouse. However, you can select the field with your mouse and then press *Delete* to clear the field, and then reselect the cells with your mouse.

> **Nuance**
>
> Excel for Mac does not use **Enter** mode, so you can only toggle between **Point** and **Edit** modes on that platform, which means that **Point** mode on the Mac functions the same as **Enter** mode in Windows.

- **Edit**: As shown in the following screenshot, **Edit** appears in the status bar when you press *F2* after clicking into a **RefEdit** field, enabling the use of your keyboard to navigate within the field or for editing the field contents:

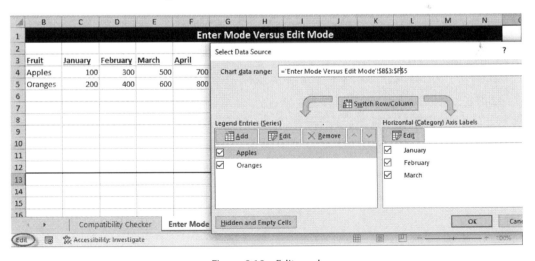

Figure 9.10 – Edit mode

You can use these keyboard shortcuts in **Edit** mode in **Excel for Windows**:

- Press *left arrow* or *right arrow* to navigate one character at a time in the field
- Press *Ctrl + left arrow* or *Ctrl + right arrow* to navigate one word or cell reference at a time
- Press *Home* or *End* to jump to the beginning or end of a field
- Press *Shift + Home* or *Shift + End* to select from the location of the cursor in the field to either end of the field

> **Nuance**
>
> Sometimes, Excel's **Formula Bar** drops into **Enter** mode, which you can toggle back to **Edit** mode by pressing *F2* (*Fn + F2*). You can also press *F2* to edit the contents of a worksheet cell or to edit a column heading in **Power Query**.

6. Use **Edit** mode to navigate to the column **E** reference in =' Enter Mode Versus Edit Mode'!$B$3:$E$5 and change it to column **F**.

> **Nuance**
>
> I'm going to drop an unrelated chart tip here: the **Hidden and Empty Cells** button shown in *Figure 9.10* allows you to instruct Excel whether to treat empty cells as gaps or as zeros, to treat #N/A as an empty cell, and to show data in hidden rows and columns or not.

Now that you know the difference between **Enter** and **Edit** modes, you'll hopefully be less inclined to want to throw your keyboard or mouse out the window when you encounter a **RefEdit** field. Let's switch gears slightly by looking at another chart-related situation that might also put your mouse in peril.

Excluding weekend dates from charts

Sometimes, Excel becomes overly helpful, leaving us having to figure out how to undo the unwanted help. For instance, as shown in *Figure 9.11*, the **Excluding Chart Weekend Dates** worksheet in the example workbook includes data for two Monday to Friday periods, and yet Excel insists on creating a gap for the weekend:

Excluding weekend dates from charts

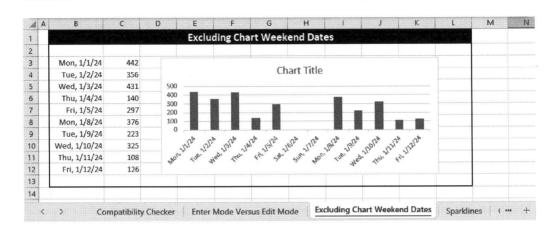

Figure 9.11 – Phantom dates inserted into a chart

Fortunately, there's an easy fix, although many of us would be hard-pressed to figure it out on our own. Check this out:

1. Right-click on the **Horizontal (Category)** axis and then choose **Format Axis**.
2. Choose **Axis Options** | **Axis Type** | **Text axis** to close the gap. The settings are illustrated in *Figure 9.12*:

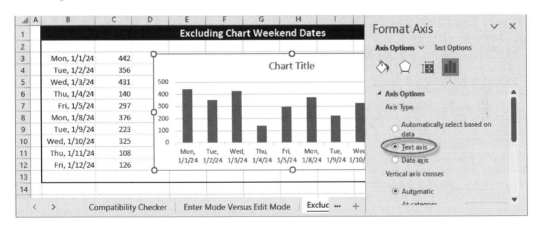

Figure 9.12 – Choosing Text axis to remove phantom dates from charts

As you can see, when the **Chart Axis** options are set to **Automatically select based on data** or **Date axis**, Excel interpolates any missing dates to display every day of the week. Choosing **Text axis** instructs Excel to only display dates that are present in the underlying chart data. The good news is this is an easy fix, but the bad news is it can mean yet another repetitive task in Excel—unless you create a chart template that has this setting in place.

Tip

The first step in creating a chart template is to right-click on a chart that has all of the settings you want to use going forward, and then choose **Save as Template**. Assign a name for your template, and then click on **Save**. To utilize your template, click on a dataset that you wish to chart, and then choose **Insert | Recommended Charts | All Charts | Templates**. Double-click on your template of choice to skip the **OK** button.

Let's continue our exploration of charts in Excel by walking through a quirk related to the **Sparklines** feature.

Sparklines

Traditional charts in Excel may to take up a lot of space on the screen or printed page, but are not the only game in town. **Sparklines** are tiny charts that appear within worksheet cells, as shown in cells **B4:B8** in *Figure 9.13*:

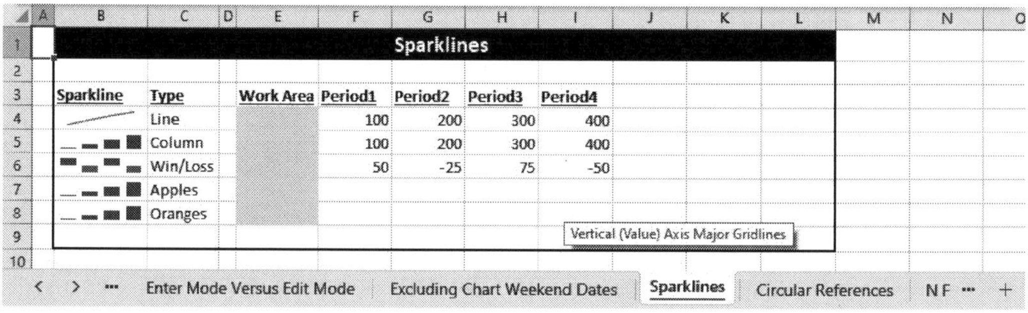

Figure 9.13 – Sparklines

For instance, you might use **Sparklines** as part of a dashboard, which is a spreadsheet that communicates a large amount of information in compact form. Let's first walk through the process of creating each type of **Sparkline** and then I'll show you an odd quirk. Follow the next steps:

1. Activate the **Sparklines** worksheet in the example workbook for this chapter.

2. Select cells **F4:I4** and then **Insert | Line** within the **Sparklines** group to display the **Create Sparklines** dialog box.

3. As shown in *Figure 9.14*, the **Data Range** setting is prefilled with the range of cells you selected:

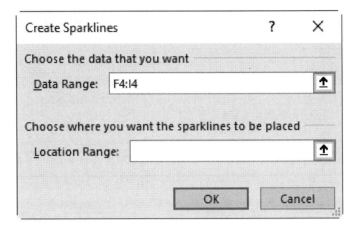

Figure 9.14 – Create Sparklines dialog box

> **Nuance**
> Often in Excel, we select the data that we want to work with before initiating a command, as described previously. Although you *can* do that with **Sparklines**, it's best to do the opposite, and *first* select the cell or cells where you want **Sparklines** to appear, as you'll see later in this chapter.

4. Click in the **Location Range** field, then click on cell **E4** or type E4, and then click **OK** to make a **Line Sparkline** appear in cell **E4**.

> **Tip**
> The size of a **Sparkline** chart correlates with the height and width of a cell. Increase the row height and/or column width of the underlying cell if you wish to make **Sparklines** larger.

5. Select cell **E5**, and then choose **Insert | Column** from within the **Sparklines** group.
6. The **Location Range** setting is set to **E5**, so specify cells **F5:I5** for the **Data Range** field, and then click **OK** to create a **Column Sparkline**.
7. Select cell **E6**, and then choose **Insert | Win/Loss**.
8. **Location Range** is set to **E6**, so specify **F6:I6** for the **Data Range** field, and then click **OK** to create a **Win/Loss Sparkline**.

> **Tip**
> **Line** and **Column Sparklines** offer a sense of scale, while a **Win/Loss Sparkline** simply gives an indication of which amounts are positive and which are negative.

9. Now that you've created one of each type of **Sparkline**, let's get into the quirk. Activate the **Enter Mode Versus Edit Mode** worksheet.
10. Select cells **C4:F5** and then **Insert | Column**.
11. Click in the **Location Range** field, and then try to click on the **Sparklines** worksheet. Inexplicably, you can only select cells on the active worksheet from the **Location Range** field. Click **Cancel** to close the **Create Sparklines** dialog box.
12. Select cells **E7:E8** on the **Sparklines** worksheet, and then choose **Insert | Column**.
13. Specify cells **C4:F5** on the **Enter Mode Versus Edit Mode** worksheet in the **Data Range** field, and then click **OK**. Notice that now you *can* add **Sparklines** to multiple cells if you wish.

> **Tip**
>
> You can create self-expanding sparklines by turning the source data into a Table. I discuss Tables in more detail in *Chapter 7, Automating Tasks with the Table Feature*. In this case, click on cell **B3** of the **Enter Mode Versus Edit Mode** worksheet, choose **Insert | Table**, and then click **OK**. New periods that you add to column **F** and beyond will now automatically appear in the **Sparklines** in cells **E7:E8** of the **Sparklines** worksheet.

Notice that a **Sparkline** tab appears in Excel's **Ribbon** when you click on a cell that contains a **Sparkline**. This tab enables you to do the following:

   I. Edit the data range that a **Sparkline** refers to, including controlling the settings for hidden and empty cells in a similar fashion to what I described with charts in the previous section.
   II. Toggle to a different type of **Sparkline**.
   III. Identify various points within **Sparkline**—for instance, the minimum and maximum values.
   IV. Change the style and color of **Sparklines**.
   V. Control axis settings.
   VI. Clear **Sparklines** from one or more cells.

> **Nuance**
>
> You should choose **Sparkline | Clear** or **Home | Clear | Clear All** to remove **Sparklines**. Pressing the *Delete* key in a cell that contains a **Sparkline** will erase the cell contents (if any) but will leave the **Sparkline** intact, which means you can type other information in a cell that contains a **sparkline** if you wish. The **Clear All** command will erase not only the **Sparkline** but any other cell formatting or contents as well.

Let's move on from working with charts and see how to resolve circular references that can arise within your spreadsheets.

Circular references

Circular references are formulas that refer to themselves, like a snake trying to eat its own tail. Let's say that you entered the formula =SUM(B3:B5) in cell **B5** of the **Circular References** worksheet, as shown in *Figure 9.15*. Typically, circular references are created accidentally. Excel alerts you with the prompt shown in *Figure 9.15*.

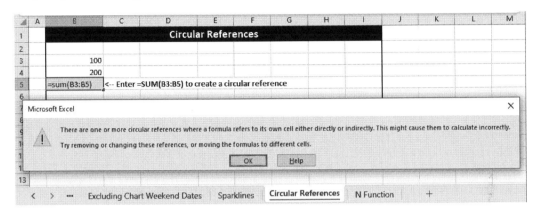

Figure 9.15 – Circular reference

If you click **OK** on this prompt, the formula may return an amount, or it may return zero. Excel displays a **Circular References** message on the **Status Bar** informing you of the cell that contains a circular reference, as shown in *Figure 9.16*:

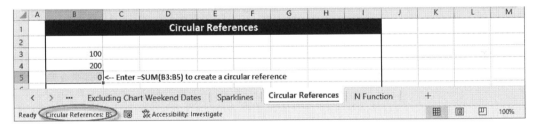

Figure 9.16 – Circular reference Status Bar message

Conversely, if a circular reference exists on another worksheet or even another open workbook, no cell reference will appear, and the status bar will simply report **Circular References**. Fortunately, there's a hidden menu command that you can use to navigate directly to circular references by following these steps:

1. Choose the **Formulas** | **Error Checking** dropdown | **Circular References**, and then choose a cell reference, as shown in *Figure 9.17*:

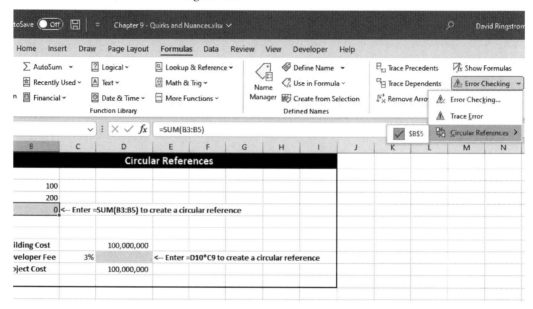

Figure 9.17 – Circular References menu command

> **Nuance**
>
> The **Circular References** command is unavailable when no open workbooks contain circular references, or if the **Enable iterative calculation** option discussed in the next section is enabled.

2. Excel activates the worksheet cell that you selected.
3. Edit the formula to eliminate the circular reference, meaning adjust the cell reference so that it does not include the cell that the formula is in.
4. Repeat *steps 1* through *3* as needed until you eliminate all circular references.

Although most circular references are accidental, let's see what to do when you purposefully want to create a circular reference.

Enable iterative calculation option

You might occasionally run across a situation where you purposefully need to use a circular reference in a spreadsheet. Let's say that a real-estate developer has been tasked with constructing a new building that costs 100 million **United States dollars** (**USD**), for which the developer will earn a 3% development fee. If the developer agrees to the fee being 3% of the *building cost*, they will earn $3 million.

As you're about to see, it behooves the developer to negotiate their fee as 3% of the *project cost* instead. Here's what you can do:

1. Enter =D10*C9 in cell **D9** of the **Circular References** worksheet of this chapter's example workbook.
2. Click **OK** to dismiss the circular reference warning.
3. Choose **File | Options | Formulas** and then click **Enable iterative calculation**, as shown in *Figure 9.18*, and then click **OK**:

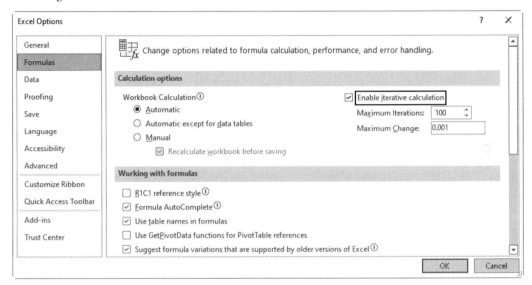

Figure 9.18 – Enable iterative calculation setting

> **Nuance**
>
> The **Maximum Iterations** field controls the number of times that Excel will attempt to resolve the circular reference before giving up. **Maximum Change** represents the threshold that Excel looks at to determine when to stop trying to resolve the circular reference. In rare instances, I have needed to change this field to 0.01, but usually, the default of 0.001 is acceptable.

4. The word **Calculate** appears in the status bar in place of the **Circular Reference** prompt. This is an indication that one or more open workbooks have purposeful circular references.

> **Nuance**
>
> **Calculate** can also appear in the status bar when a workbook has been set to **Manual Calculation** mode, which Excel sometimes does of its own accord. If you see the word **Calculate** in the status bar, choose **Formulas | Calculation Options**, and then choose **Automatic** if needed. If a workbook is set to **Automatic** and you still see the word **Calculate**, then you'll know that an open workbook has at least one circular reference and that **Enable iterative calculation** is enabled.

5. When calculated as 3% of the project cost, the developer fee comes to $3,092,784, or $92,784 more than the non-circular calculation.

> **Nuance**
>
> You must set **Enable iterative calculation** on a workbook-by-workbook basis when needed.

As you can see, there is sometimes a place for purposeful circular references, but that is very much the exception rather than the rule in Excel. I struggled with tracking down circular references for far longer than I should have until, one day, I ran across the **Circular References** command buried in the **Error Checking** drop-down menu. In any case, I'm about to show you a feature that is buried even deeper, and only available to certain Excel users.

Inquire add-in

Most Excel features are baked into the software, but sometimes Microsoft provides features through a type of software known as add-ins. I discuss the **Solver** add-in for **Excel for Windows** in *Chapter 6, What-If Analysis*. Since you cannot enable add-ins within **Excel for macOS** the Solver feature is built into the Data tab of the **Ribbon**. Let's turn our attention to the **Inquire** add-in, which is available in **Microsoft 365 Apps for enterprise**. I'm going to cross my fingers and hope you can access this great feature:

1. Choose **File | Account**.
2. As shown in *Figure 9.19*, the **Account** screen may display **Microsoft 365 Apps for enterprise**, or it may simply reference **Microsoft 365**.

If you don't see the words **Apps for enterprise** as shown in *Figure 9.19*, then this section will be a dead end for you; otherwise, read on to see how to enable the **Inquire** add-in:

Inquire add-in 283

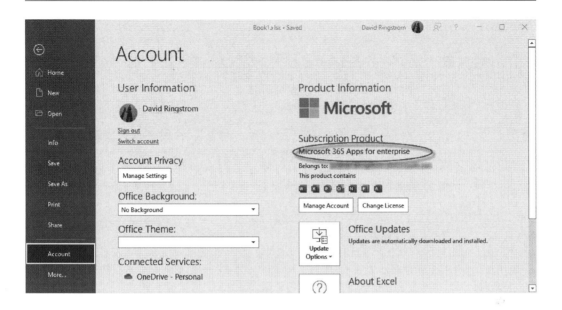

Figure 9.19 – Account page of Excel's Backstage view

Here's how to enable the **Inquire** add-in if it is available in your version of Excel:

1. Choose **File | Options | Add-ins**.
2. Choose **COM Add-ins** from the **Manage Excel Add-Ins** drop-down menu and then click **Go**.
3. Choose **Inquire**, as shown in *Figure 9.20*, and then click **OK**:

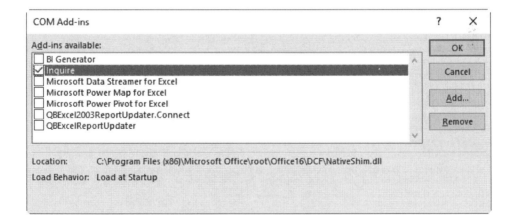

Figure 9.20 – COM Add-ins dialog box

4. An **Inquire** tab appears on Excel's **Ribbon**, as shown in *Figure 9.21*:

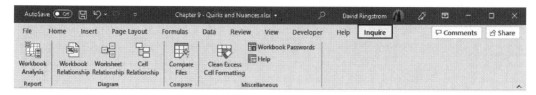

Figure 9.21 – Inquire Ribbon tab

You now have access to a suite of auditing tools in Excel that you can use to create extensive documentation of any workbook, including relationship flow charts. You can also compare two different versions of the same workbook and improve the integrity of workbooks by removing excess formatting. The **Inquire** add-in offers the following commands:

- **Workbook Analysis**: This command can generate exhaustive documentation of an Excel workbook. To use this feature, do the following:

    I. Save your workbook.

    II. Choose **Inquire | Workbook Analysis**.

    III. Click **Items**, as shown in *Figure 9.22*, to create a full analytical report, or else make individual selections:

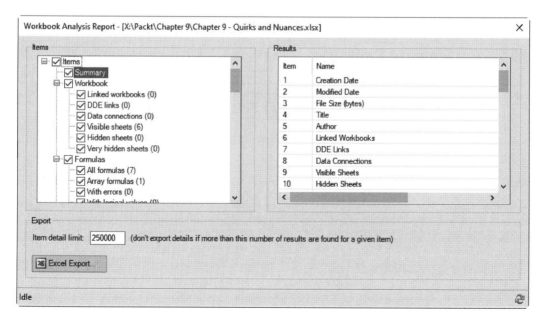

Figure 9.22 – Workbook Analysis feature

IV. Click **Excel Export** to export the findings to a new Excel workbook.

V. Click **Load Export File** to open a workbook with up to 47 worksheets that document almost every aspect imaginable of an Excel workbook.

- **Workbook Relationship**: Creates a graphical illustration of how the current workbook links to other workbooks via formulas or features such as **Power Query**.

> **Nuance**
> If the current workbook does not have any formulas that link to other workbooks, then only the workbook name will appear in the **Workbook Relationship Diagram** dialog box. If you use **Power Query** to link to other workbooks, as we will discuss in *Chapter 12, Power Query*, then a generic `$Workbook$` placeholder will appear instead of a workbook name.

- **Worksheet Relationship**: Creates a graphical illustration of how worksheets within the current workbook reference each other via formulas.
- **Cell Relationship**: Creates a graphical illustration of how a formula in the current cell links directly or indirectly to cells on other worksheets and—optionally—other workbooks.
- **Compare Files**: This feature enables you to compare two versions of an Excel workbook.
- **Clean Excess Cell Formatting**: Users often unwittingly apply formatting to entire columns instead of only specific cells, which, over time, results in bloated Excel workbooks that are subject to data corruption. **Clean Excess Cell Formatting** removes formatting such as fonts, borders, and fill colors from cells that do not contain data.
- **Workbook Passwords**: This feature allows you to store workbook passwords for password-protected workbooks that you plan to in conjunction with the **Inquire** add-in.

It's unfortunate that Microsoft limits the use of the **Inquire** add-in to **Microsoft 365 Apps for enterprise** users only, as the tools contained within it can be a benefit to all Excel users. Granted, the **Formulas** menu does offer commands such as **Trace Precedents** and **Trace Dependents**, but there's no comparison when it comes to the extensive documentation that you can create instantly with the **Inquire** add-in. Third-party auditing add-ins are available for Excel for those that want to go beyond the **Inquire** add-in, or in place of the add-in.

Summary

In this chapter, you learned how to ensure that your spreadsheets are backwards compatible with Excel 2021 and earlier. The rolling release of new features across three channels presents a special challenge for Microsoft 365 users looking to take advantage of the rapid pace of improvements. You can determine if other users have the same functionality as you --or better --by comparing the build and version numbers between your copy of Excel and theirs.

You also learned about one of the biggest nuances in Excel, the difference between **Enter** mode and **Edit** mode, so that you can now spend less time fighting with Excel when you need to make changes to formulas and cell references. We also looked at an odd quirk of the **Sparklines** feature where the order in which you carry out steps will predicate whether you can complete a task or not. Fortunately, this is an outlier in Excel—I don't know of any other feature that has this curious restriction.

If circular references have caused you gnash your teeth, you're now empowered to trace such formulas anywhere, any time. And should you purposefully need to create a circular reference, you can do that as well. Finally, I hope that you have access to the **Inquire** add-in, or that Microsoft makes it more widely available. It is a tremendous resource for documenting spreadsheets, identifying certain types of errors, and removing the excess formatting that can culminate in damaged workbooks if left unchecked. In *Chapter 10, Lookup Functions and Dynamic Arrays*, I will share worksheet functions that can retrieve data from **Tables** and lists of data in any version of Excel. I will also show you how to leverage dynamic array functions in **Microsoft 365**, **Excel 2021**, **Excel for the Web**, and **Excel Mobile**. Think of these as super-functions that can spill results into as many worksheet cells as needed.

Part 3: Data Analysis

According to Microsoft, VLOOKUP is the third most frequently used worksheet function, falling behind the SUM and AVERAGE functions. Despite its popularity, VLOOKUP hasn't aged well, and so modern times call for a modern lookup function known as XLOOKUP. The XLOOKUP function is part of a new class of worksheet functions known as dynamic arrays that can spill results into as many adjacent cells as needed. Even better, almost every worksheet function in Excel now has the ability to take on dynamic characteristics. This part will then delve into two other recent additions to Excel, the LET and LAMBDA functions, that can greatly simplify complex formulas. This part closes out with a discussion of Power Query. The Power Query feature isn't new, but most Excel users are unaware of this code-free solution for connecting to data sources. Power Query enables you to easily transform results into refreshable connections that protect data from being overwritten.

The following chapters are included in this part:

- *Chapter 10, Lookup and Dynamic Array Functions*
- *Chapter 11, Names, LET and LAMBDA*
- *Chapter 12, Power Query*

10
Lookup and Dynamic Array Functions

In this chapter, we'll discuss two types of worksheet functions that will literally transform your workbooks. **Lookup functions** have long allowed us to create formulas that can retrieve data from elsewhere in a spreadsheet without requiring us to connect directly to the individual cells. **Dynamic array functions** are a quantum leap forward, enabling us to create single formulas that can return results to multiple cells. The new SORT, FILTER, and UNIQUE functions enable us to automate tasks that, previously, always had to be carried out by hand. The new XLOOKUP function is both a lookup function and a dynamic array function that is a modern replacement for both VLOOKUP and MATCH/INDEX. As you'll discover, dynamic array functions can vastly improve spreadsheet integrity by creating self-resizing schedules, such as a dynamic amortization schedule. Amortization schedules are used to document the interest, principal, and running balance over the life of a loan. You'll see how to create a schedule that simply adds or removes rows as you adjust the term of the loan. Additionally, you'll see how the new **Spilled Range Operator** (#) can be used to make even long standing worksheet functions in Excel take on dynamic array capabilities.

In this chapter, you'll learn about lookup functions and dynamic array functions, and how many of Excel's traditional worksheet functions can function dynamically, too. I'll be covering the following concepts:

- VLOOKUP, INDEX, and MATCH functions as traditional ways of looking up data from a list
- XLOOKUP function for looking up data from a list
- XMATCH function for finding the position of a piece of data in a range of cells
- UNIQUE function for removing duplicates from a list
- SORT and SORTBY functions for sorting data
- FILTER function for filtering data
- Spilled Range Operator (#)

- The dynamic amortization table
- The #SPILL! and #CALC! errors
- The RANDARRAY function and alternatives for generating random numbers

By the end of the chapter, you'll have a clear understanding of the differences between VLOOKUP, INDEX/MATCH, and XLOOKUP, along with several ways that XLOOKUP allows you to look up information in ways that simply weren't possible in earlier versions of Excel. You'll be able to manipulate data with worksheet functions instead of having to carry out tasks such as sorting, filtering, and removing duplicates with menu commands. Also, you will be able to create resizable formulas that expand to encompass more rows or fewer rows, depending upon the inputs that you supply, which eliminates the need to manually expand or contract rows of formulas.

Technical requirements

Dynamic array functions are available in **Microsoft 365, Excel 2021, Excel for Web, Excel for iPad, Excel for iPhone**, and **Excel for Android**. These functions return #NAME? in **Excel 2019** and earlier, the use of the Spilled Range Operator (#) could result in other errors too, such as #VALUE.

An example workbook that contains all of the formulas used in this chapter can be found on GitHub at https://github.com/PacktPublishing/Exploring-Microsoft-Excels-Hidden-Treasures/tree/main/Chapter10.

Now that we've taken a look at the prerequisites for this chapter, let's begin with the VLOOKUP and INDEX/MATCH functions, which are often used to look up information in spreadsheets, and see how XLOOKUP enables you to do so much more than you might have previously imagined.

The VLOOKUP function

Lookup functions in Excel enable you to retrieve data from a list. The =VLOOKUP(G3,B3:E12,3,FALSE) formula in cell **H3** of the *VLOOKUP and IFNA* worksheet of this chapter's example workbook returns **94** as the length of **Ninety Mile Beach** in miles, as shown in *Figure 10.1*. Later in this section, I'll discuss why VLOOKUP only returns a single match:

The VLOOKUP function

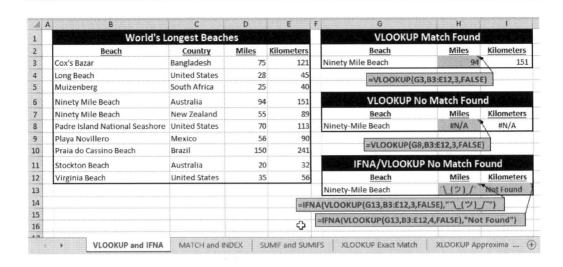

Figure 10.1 – The VLOOKUP and IFNA functions

VLOOKUP has four arguments:

- **Lookup_value** – This is the value that you're searching for within a list, which, in this case, is G3. VLOOKUP looks down the first column of the *table array* for this value.

- **Table_array** – This refers to the cell coordinates of the list that you wish to search; in this case, they are B3:E12.

- **Col_index_num** – This is the column position within table_array that you wish to return data from; in this case, 3 represents the *third* column so that we can look up the length in miles.

- **Range_lookup** – FALSE instructs VLOOKUP to find an *exact* match, while TRUE allows an *approximate* match.

> **Tip**
> You can use 0 (zero) to indicate an exact match or 1 for an approximate match in lieu of FALSE and TRUE within VLOOKUP.

VLOOKUP is widely used in Excel but has some frustrating constraints:

- VLOOKUP can only return data from the right-hand side of a list, meaning you cannot look up data from the left-hand side of a lookup column.

- VLOOKUP requires you to specify a column position within the list. Many users will enter a static number here that can result in a #REF! error if one or more columns are removed from the list or else return data from the wrong column if new columns are added.

- VLOOKUP defaults to an approximate match, which means if you don't declare that you want an exact match, an incorrect match could be made.

- VLOOKUP can only return a single match. So, as shown in cell **H3** of *Figure 10.1*, the formula matches with the first instance of **Ninety Mile Beach** in cell **B6** but ignores any other instances, such as the second instance in cell **B7**. Later in this chapter, you'll see how you can use the FILTER function to return multiple values from a list such as this. It is curious that Australia's Ninety Mile Beach is **94** miles long, while New Zealand's Ninety Mile Beach is only **55** miles long. But to be clear, these are not typos.

- The =VLOOKUP(G8,B3:E12,3,FALSE) formula in cell **H8** of *Figure 10.1* returns #N/A because cell **G8** contains the hyphenated **Ninety-Mile Beach** version, which does not match any of the values in cells **B3:B12**. Any formulas that reference a cell that contains #N/A will return #N/A too, sometimes causing a ripple effect throughout a spreadsheet.

Inconsistent data such as this can be the bane of your existence in Excel. Fortunately, we can resolve the #N/A issue by wrapping the IFNA function around VLOOKUP.

The IFNA function

The =IFNA(VLOOKUP(G13,B3:E12,3,FALSE),"¯_(ツ)_/¯") formula in cell **H13** returns a whimsical emoji shrug, ¯_(ツ)_/¯, in place of the #N/A error. In comparison, the =IFNA(VLOOKUP(G13,B3:E12,4,FALSE),"Not Found") formula in cell **I14** returns a more practical message of **Not Found** when VLOOKUP returns #N/A.

> **Nuance**
> Sometimes, users inadvertently bump the spacebar when entering data in Excel, which can result in trailing spaces that are tricky to track down. Inconsistencies such as this cause users to assume Excel is broken or that they simply don't understand lookup functions. When you double-click on a cell, check to see whether the cursor is positioned immediately adjacent to the last character in the cell. If not, press *backspace* as needed to eliminate the extra spaces, or use the TRIM function.

IFNA has two arguments:

- **Value** – This is a calculation that could return #N/A, such as VLOOKUP(G13,B3:E12,3,FALSE).

- **Value_if_na** – This is what to display instead of the #N/A error, which can include numbers, text, or another formula, such as "Not found".

Some users rely on the IFERROR function, which has a value_if_error argument in place of value_if_na. IFERROR is useful if you need to mask errors other than #N/A, such as #DIV/0!, or if you need compatibility with Excel 2010 and earlier. IFNA works in Excel 2013 and later and will only mask #N/A errors so that you can easily see whether other errors such as #REF! or #VALUE arise. In short, IFERROR masks *all* errors, which can complicate lookup formula troubleshooting efforts. Now that we've explored VLOOKUP and how to handle any errors that can arise, let's see how the MATCH function can make VLOOKUP more versatile or be used to eliminate VLOOKUP entirely.

The MATCH function

The =MATCH(G3,B3:B12,0) formula in cell **H3** of the *MATCH and INDEX* worksheet in *Figure 10.2* returns **2** because it found **Long Beach** in the second row of the B3:B12 range:

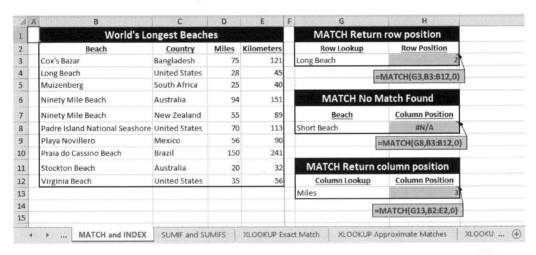

Figure 10.2 – The MATCH function

The MATCH function has three arguments:

- **Lookup_value** – What to look for, which, in the case of cell **H3**, is the contents of cell G3.
- **Lookup_array** – This can be a row, column, or array to search; in the case of cell **H3**, it is the B3:B12 range.
- **Match_type** – This optional argument offers three choices:
  - -1 – Find the closest match that is equal to or less than lookup_value.
  - 0 – Find an exact match with lookup_value, which I specified in cell **H3**.
  - 1 – Find the closest match that is equal to or greater than lookup_value. This is the default value for MATCH if you don't specify the third argument.

The =MATCH(G8,B3:B12,0) formula in cell **H8** of *Figure 10.2* returns #N/A because **Short Beach** does not appear in cells B3:B12. Conversely, the =MATCH(G13,B2:E2,0) formula in cell **H13** of *Figure 10.2* returns 3 because Miles appears in the third column of cells **B2:E2**.

Cell **K3** of *Figure 10.3* contains the =VLOOKUP($J3,$B$2:$E$12,3,FALSE) formula, while cell **L3** contains the =VLOOKUP($J3,$B$2:$E$12,4,FALSE) formula. The only difference between the two formulas is that, in cell **K3**, I specified a col_index_num argument of 3 for miles, and I specified 4 for kilometers in cell **L3**. Having to manually change the col_index_num argument is another frustrating constraint of VLOOKUP:

	A	B	C	D	E	I	J	K	L
1		\multicolumn{4}{l}{World's Longest Beaches}			VLOOKUP Return Miles/Kilometers		
2		Beach	Country	Miles	Kilometers		Beach	Miles	Kilometers
3		Cox's Bazar	Bangladesh	75	121		Stockton Beach	20	32
4		Long Beach	United States	28	45		=VLOOKUP($J3,$B$2:$E$12,3,FALSE)		
5		Muizenberg	South Africa	25	40		=VLOOKUP($J3,$B$2:$E$12,4,FALSE)		
6		Ninety Mile Beach	Australia	94	151				
7		Ninety Mile Beach	New Zealand	55	89		VLOOKUP/MATCH Return Miles/Kilometers		
8		Padre Island National Seashore	United States	70	113		Beach	Miles	Kilometers
9		Playa Novillero	Mexico	56	90		Stockton Beach	20	32
10		Praia do Cassino Beach	Brazil	150	241		=VLOOKUP($J3,$B$2:$E$12,MATCH(K2,$B$2:$E$2,0),FALSE)		
11		Stockton Beach	Australia	20	32		=VLOOKUP($J3,$B$2:$E$12,MATCH(L2,$B$2:$E$2,0),FALSE)		
12		Virginia Beach	United States	35	56				

Figure 10.3 – The VLOOKUP and VLOOKUP/MATCH functions

> **Nuance**
>
> The $ sign in $J3 represents a **mixed reference**, which instructs Excel not to change the reference from column **J** to column **K** and beyond when copying the formula to the right, but the row number will change to **4** and beyond when copying down the column. The $ signs in $B$2:$E$12 represent absolute references, where Excel will not change the column or row numbers. A cell reference with no $ sign, such as B2, is a relative reference, meaning that Excel will change the column letter or row number when you copy the formula across a row or down a column.

The =VLOOKUP($J9,$B$2:$E$12,MATCH(K8,$B$2:$E$2,0),FALSE) formula in cell **K9** of *Figure 10.3* shows you how to use the MATCH function inside VLOOKUP to create a double lookup. VLOOKUP will look down the first column of table_array, and MATCH can look across a row to determine which column you want VLOOKUP to return information from. Although this improves the integrity of VLOOKUP, you're still bound by the other constraints unless you use the INDEX function instead. The =INDEX(D3:D12,MATCH($N3,$B3:$B12,0)) formula in cell **O8** of *Figure 10.4* shows you how to use the MATCH function inside the INDEX function to return the length, in miles, of **Stockton Beach** in a similar fashion to VLOOKUP:

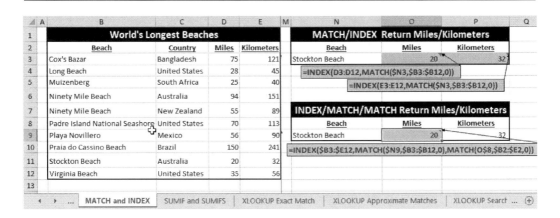

Figure 10.4 – The INDEX/MATCH functions

The INDEX function has three arguments:

- **Array** – A range of cells in a row or column, or an array of data; in this case, it is D3:D12.
- **Row_num** – The row number or the range of cells to return data from, which can be provided by the MATCH function; in this case, it is MATCH($N3,$B3:$B12,0).
- **Column_num** – Optionally, you can specify a column position within the array, which I omitted in this case.

The INDEX/MATCH function eliminates a lot of frustration that VLOOKUP causes because the combination can return information from the left-hand side or the right-hand side of the **Lookup** column, or even perform a two-way lookup that looks down a row and across a column to search for information based upon two criteria. The =INDEX($B3:$E12,MATCH($N9,$B3:$B12,0),MATCH(O$8,$B2:$E2,0)) formula in cell **O9** of *Figure 10.4* shows you how to perform a double match. The first MATCH function identifies which row **Stockton Beach** appears in, and the second MATCH function returns the column that the word **Miles** appears in. As written, this formula can be copied to cell **P9** to look up the length in kilometers, too.

A limitation of both VLOOKUP and INDEX/MATCH is that they can only match a single piece of data. SUMIF enables you to search for one or more instances of criteria and then add up the corresponding values.

The SUMIF function

The =SUMIF($B3:$B12,$G3,D3:D12) formula in cell **H3** of *Figure 10.5* returns **149** as the sum of the miles for both instances of **Ninety Mile Beach**:

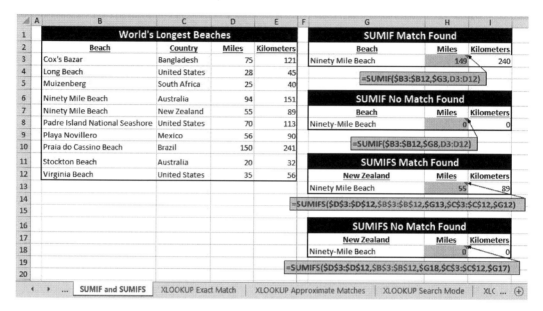

Figure 10.5 – The SUMIF function

The SUMIF function has three required arguments:

- **Range** – This refers to a row or column that you wish to search, which, in this case, is $B3:$B12.
- **Criteria** – This refers to a value to search for, which, in this case, is $G3.
- **Sum_range** – This refers to a row or column that you wish to add up values from, which, in this case, is D3:D12.

As shown in cell **H8** of *Figure 10.5*, the =SUMIF($B3:$B12,$G8,D3:D12) formula returns 0 because the hyphenated **Ninety-Mile Beach** version does not appear in cells **B3:B12**. As we saw previously, in such situations, VLOOKUP and MATCH would return #N/A. Typically, you would not want to add both Ninety Mile Beaches together but would instead want to look up the length of one beach or the other, which you can do with the **SUMIFS** function.

The SUMIFS function

The =SUMIFS(D3:D12,$B$3:$B$12,$G13,$C$3:$C$12,$G12) formula in cell **H13** of *Figure 10.5* returns **55** as the distance of **Ninety Mile Beach** in **New Zealand**.

The SUMIFS function can sum data based on up to 127 criteria:

- **Sum_range** – This refers to a row or column that you wish to add up values from, which, in this case, is D3:D12.
- **Criteria_range1** – This refers to a row or column that you wish to search, which, in this case, is $B$3:$B$12.
- **Criteria** – This refers to a value to search for, which, in this case, is $G13 for **Ninety Mile Beach**.
- **Criteria_range2** – This refers to a row or column that you wish to search, which, in this case, is $C$3:$C$12.
- **Criteria2** – This refers to a value to search for, which, in this case, is $G12 for **New Zealand**.

SUMIFS returns zero if a match cannot be found, as shown in cell **H18** of *Figure 10.5*. Keep adding additional criteria ranges and criteria as needed when you need to add more specifications to your formula. Now that we have reviewed the lookup functions most widely used in Excel, let's look at the relatively new XLOOKUP function.

The XLOOKUP function

As you will see, XLOOKUP not only eliminates the frustrations I mentioned for VLOOKUP, it enables you to create a simpler formula than INDEX/MATCH and adds much more functionality. The =XLOOKUP($G3,$B3:$B12,D3:D12) formula in cell **H3** of the XLOOKUP Exact Match worksheet in *Figure 10.6* returns **94** as the length of **Ninety Mile Beach** in miles. As with VLOOKUP, XLOOKUP stops looking after it finds an initial match:

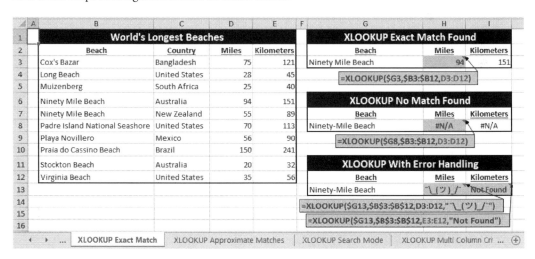

Figure 10.6 – The XLOOKUP function

Lookup and Dynamic Array Functions

> **Tip**
> XLOOKUP eliminates most, but not all, of the previous uses for INDEX/MATCH. XLOOKUP doesn't allow you to simultaneously search down a column and across a row like INDEX with two MATCH functions allows, so it's good to have both approaches in your repertoire.

XLOOKUP has a total of six arguments, but often, you'll only need to enter the three required arguments:

- **Lookup_value** – A value that you're searching for, such as the contents of cell $G3
- **Lookup_array** – A column or row that you wish to search, such as $B3:$B12
- **Return_array** – A column or row that you wish to return data from, such as D3:D12

As shown in cell **H8** of *Figure 10.6*, XLOOKUP returns #N/A if a match cannot be found, which is the same as VLOOKUP and MATCH. The difference is that XLOOKUP has a fourth argument that allows us to indicate what should be displayed in lieu of #N/A, which generally obviates the need to wrap IFNA or IFERROR around XLOOKUP.

The if_not_found argument

The =XLOOKUP($G13,$B$3:$B$12,D3:D12,"¯\_(ツ)_/¯") formula in cell **H13** returns a whimsical emoji shrug, ¯\_(ツ)_/¯, in place of the #N/A error, while the =XLOOKUP($G13, $B$3:$B$12,E3:E12,"Not Found") formula in cell **I13** returns a more practical message of **Not Found** when XLOOKUP cannot find a match.

The initial matches we've made have been based upon exact matches with the lookup value, but sometimes, you might need to return results based upon an approximate match instead.

The match_mode argument

The =XLOOKUP(G3,D3:D12,B3:B12,,-1) formula in cell **H3** of the XLOOKUP Approximate Matches worksheet in *Figure 10.7* returns **Playa Novillero** as the beach that is closest to **60** miles long without going over:

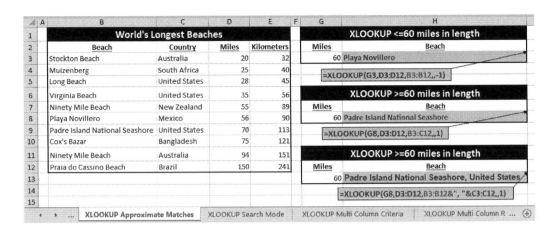

Figure 10.7 – Approximate matches

In this case, I omitted the `if_not_found` argument because XLOOKUP should always find a match in this context, but I did add a fifth argument:

- **Match_mode** – The four options include the following:

  - `0` – Exact match, or return #N/A, which is the default response unless you specify otherwise.
  - `-1` – Exact match, or return the next smaller item, as shown in cell **H3** of *Figure 10.7*.
  - `1` – Exact match, or return the next larger item, as shown in cell **H8** of *Figure 10.7*.
  - `2` – A wildcard match using *, ?, or ~ for performing partial text matches.

> **Nuance**
> Be mindful of the sort order of your data if you're performing an approximate match on numbers. XLOOKUP will match with the first value it finds and then stops looking. It's a good practice to sort text-based lists if you're performing an approximate match, but it isn't necessarily required.

The `=XLOOKUP(G8,D3:D12,B3:C12,,1)` formula in cell **H8** of *Figure 10.7* returns **Padre Island National Seashore** as the beach that is closest to but greater than **60** miles in length. Again, I omitted the `if_not_found` argument and specified `1` for the `match_mode` argument to have XLOOKUP find the next highest value greater than or equal to **60**. Conversely, VLOOKUP can only return the next lowest value.

Now, let's explore the `search_mode` argument for XLOOKUP.

Combining results into a single column

The =XLOOKUP(G8,D3:D12,B3:B12&", "&C3:C12,,1) formula in cell **H13** of *Figure 10.7* shows you how to concatenate, or combine together, values from two or more columns by using ampersands (&) along with a comma and a space inside double quotes between the two column references. This causes XLOOKUP to return the beach and country in a single cell.

Concatenation is by no means unique to XLOOKUP. You can join two or more pieces of text together by using the CONCAT function in **Excel 2019** and later, the CONCATENATE function in any version of Excel, or as I've done, simply use the ampersand in any version of Excel. Any text that isn't in a worksheet cell must be enclosed in double quotes as shown.

Now, let's look at the sixth and final argument for XLOOKUP.

The search_mode argument and returning results to multiple columns

The =XLOOKUP(G3,B3:B12,C3:E12,"Not found",1,1) formula in cell **H3** of *Figure 10.8* returns the *first* instance of **Ninety Mile Beach**, while the =XLOOKUP(G3,B3:B12,C3:E12,"Not found",1,-1) formula in cell **H8** returns the *last* instance. The only difference is the sixth argument, search_mode:

	A	B	C	D	E	F	G	H	I	J
1		World's Longest Beaches					XLOOKUP Top Down Search			
2		Beach	Country	Miles	Kilometers		Beach	Country	Miles	Kilometers
3		Cox's Bazar	Bangladesh	75	121		Ninety Mile Beach	Australia	94	151
4		Long Beach	United States	28	45		=XLOOKUP(G3,B3:B12,C3:E12,"Not found",1,1)			
5		Muizenberg	South Africa	25	40					
6		Ninety Mile Beach	Australia	94	151		XLOOKUP Bottom Up Search			
7		Ninety Mile Beach	New Zealand	55	89		Beach	Country	Miles	Kilometers
8		Padre Island National Seashore	United States	70	113		Ninety Mile Beach	New Zealand	55	89
9		Playa Novillero	Mexico	56	90		=XLOOKUP(G3,B3:B12,C3:E12,"Not found",1,-1)			
10		Praia do Cassino Beach	Brazil	150	241					
11		Stockton Beach	Australia	20	32					
12		Virginia Beach	United States	35	56					

Figure 10.8 – The top-down and bottom-up lookups

The search_mode argument offers four options:

- 1 – This default value, which I used in cell **H3** of *Figure 10.8*, instructs XLOOKUP to search from the top of the list to the bottom, just the same as VLOOKUP. The data does not necessarily need to be sorted to perform this type of search.

- -1 – This value, which I used in cell **H8** of *Figure 10.8*, instructs XLOOKUP to search from the bottom of the list up, which is a new functionality for any worksheet function in Excel. Again, the data doesn't necessarily need to be sorted.

- 2 – This value instructs XLOOKUP to perform a binary search from top to bottom. If you do not sort the list in ascending order, invalid results might be returned.

- -2 – This value instructs XLOOKUP to perform a binary search from bottom to top. Once again, if you do not sort the list in descending order, invalid results might be returned.

Binary searches offer faster performance, whereas non-binary searches are more forgiving of users who don't take the time to sort their lists or aren't aware of the need to sort. Also, note that **return_array** in both formulas is C3:E12, which means XLOOKUP returns *three* columns of data instead of just one. I'll share more examples of this capability in the next two sections. Now, let's see how to perform a match based upon criteria from two or more columns.

Matching on multiple column criteria

The =VLOOKUP($H3&" "&$I3,$B3:$F12,4,FALSE) formula in cell **J3** of *Figure 10.9* shows you how to use VLOOKUP to find a match on two or more criteria. lookup_value of $H3&" "&$I3 combines the beach and country together, but a *helper* column is required for this to work:

	A	B	C	D	E	F	G	H	I	J	K
1		**World's Longest Beaches**						**VLOOKUP Match on Beach/Country**			
2		Helper Column	Beach	Country	Miles	Kilometers		Beach	Country	Miles	Kilometers
3		Cox's Bazar Bangladesh	Cox's Bazar	Bangladesh	75	121		Muizenberg	South Africa	25	40
4		Long Beach United States	Long Beach	United States	28	45			=VLOOKUP($H3&" "&$I3,$B3:$F12,4,FALSE)		
5		Muizenberg South Africa	Muizenberg	South Africa	25	40					
6		Ninety Mile Beach Australia	Ninety Mile Beach	Australia	94	151		**XLOOKUP Match on Beach/Country**			
7		Ninety Mile Beach New Zealand	Ninety Mile Beach	New Zealand	55	89		Beach	Country	Miles	Kilometers
8		Padre Island National Seashore Uni	Padre Island Nation	United States	70	113		Muizenberg	South Africa	25	40
9		Playa Novillero Mexico	Playa Novillero	Mexico	56	90			=XLOOKUP(H8&I8,C3:C12&D3:D12,E3:F12)		
10		Praia do Cassino Beach Brazil	Praia do Cassino Be	Brazil	150	241					
11		Stockton Beach Australia	Stockton Beach	Australia	20	32					
12		Virginia Beach United States	Virginia Beach	United States	35	56					
13		=C3&" "&D3									

Figure 10.9 – Multiple column lookups

The =C3&" "&D3 formula in cell **B3** of *Figure 10.9* is an example of a helper column that is required with VLOOKUP if you wish to match on multiple criteria. The formula, which I copied down to cell **B12**, combines the beach and country together so that VLOOKUP has a single column that it can match. Fortunately, you do not need to create helper columns when you use XLOOKUP.

The =XLOOKUP(H8&I8,C3:C12&D3:D12,E3:F12) formula in cell **J8** of *Figure 10.9* shows you how XLOOKUP can match multiple criteria *without a helper column*. The formula can be broken down as follows:

- **Lookup_value** – H8&I8 combines the beach and country together into a single input.
- **Lookup_array** – C3:C12&D3:D12 instructs XLOOKUP to combine columns C and D into a single list.

- **Return_array** – E3:F12 instructs XLOOKUP to return both miles and kilometers, which is another example of XLOOKUP returning results to two or more columns.

Returning results from multiple cells

The =XLOOKUP(B11,B3:B7,C3:N7) formula in cell **C11** of *Figure 10.10* returns results for the **Blue** team for **January** through **December**. Historically, you would have needed to enter a formula using VLOOKUP or SUMIF in cell **C11** and then copy the formula across to column **N**. XLOOKUP accomplishes this same task with a single formula:

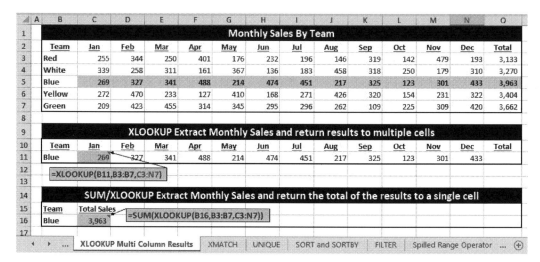

Figure 10.10 – XLOOKUP returns results and addresses of results

> **Dynamic Array Function Compatibility**
>
> Dynamic array formulas return a set of data, known as an **array**, and can spill the data into adjacent cells. This functionality is only available in Microsoft 365, Excel 2021, Excel Mobile, and Excel for the Web. Dynamic array formulas will return an error such as #NAME? or #VALUE! in older versions of Excel. As you'll see later in this chapter, dynamic array functionality is not limited to modern functions such as XLOOKUP but can be used with almost any worksheet function when you employ the Spilled Range Operator (#).

Further, XLOOKUP returns both the results shown *and* the addresses of the result cells.

The =SUM(XLOOKUP(B16,B3:B7,C3:N7)) formula in cell **C16** of *Figure 10.10* sums multiple lookup results because, in this context, the SUM function is using the cell addresses of the matches returned by XLOOKUP versus the values themselves. No function in Excel has been capable of the feats that XLOOKUP does handily.

> **Nuance**
>
> XLOOKUP can only return results from a single row but it can return results from multiple columns. Conversely, SUMIF and SUMIFS can return results from multiple rows, but only for a single column. If you specify multiple sum_range columns, SUMIF only returns results from the first column, while SUMIFS returns #VALUE!.

Now, let's compare XLOOKUP with XMATCH.

The XMATCH function

The =XMATCH(G3,B3:B12) formula in cell **H3** of *Figure 10.11* returns **9** because it found Stockton Beach in the ninth row of the B3:B12 range. The =XMATCH(G8,B3:B12) formula in cell **H8** returns #N/A because Short Beach does not appear within cells B3:B12. Finally, the =XMATCH(G13,B2:E2) formula in cell **H13** of *Figure 10.11* returns **3** because it found Miles in the third column of the B2:E2 range. As you can see, XMATCH can look down rows or across columns, just like the MATCH function:

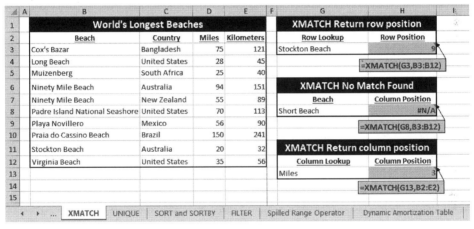

Figure 10.11 – The XMATCH function

The XMATCH function has four arguments:

- **Lookup_value** – What to look for.
- **Lookup_array** – A row, column, or array to search.
- **Match_type** – This optional argument offers the same four choices as XLOOKUP:
    - 0 – Exact match, or return #N/A
    - -1 – Exact match, or return the next smaller item
    - 1 – Exact match, or return the next larger item
    - 2 – Wildcard match using *, ?, or ~

- **search_mode** – The argument has the same options as XLOOKUP:

  - **1** – This default value instructs XMATCH to search from the top of the list to the bottom. The data does not necessarily need to be sorted to perform this type of search.

  - **-1** – This value instructs XMATCH to search from the bottom of the list up, which, like XLOOKUP, is a new functionality for any worksheet function in Excel. Again, the data doesn't necessarily need to be sorted.

  - **2** – This value instructs XMATCH to perform a binary search from top to bottom. If you do not sort the list in ascending order, invalid results might be returned.

  - **-2** – This value instructs XMATCH to perform a binary search from bottom to top. Once again, if you do not sort the list in descending order, invalid results might be returned.

Just as XLOOKUP enables you to go far beyond what VLOOKUP offers, XMATCH expands the previous limitations of the MATCH function. Now, let's look at other functions that have been recently added to Excel, such as the UNIQUE function.

The UNIQUE function

The **UNIQUE** function gives you a self-updating means of removing duplicates from another list. The =UNIQUE(C3:C12) formula in cell **G3** of *Figure 10.12* returns one of each country's names from the list in cells C3:C12, spilling the results into cell **G4** and beyond as needed:

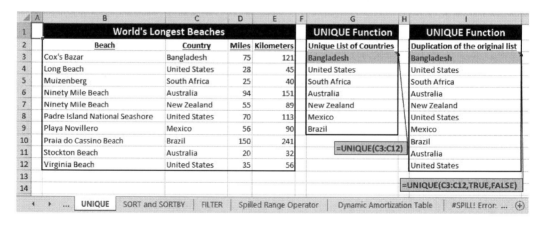

Figure 10.12 – The UNIQUE function

The UNIQUE function has three arguments:

- **Array** – The range of cells that you wish to remove duplicates from, which, in this case, is cells C3:C12.

- **by_col** – An optional argument that defaults to TRUE, which instructs Excel to remove duplicates from columns. Use FALSE if you wish to instead remove duplicates across rows. In this case, I omitted the argument.

- **exactly_once** – An optional argument that defaults to TRUE to remove duplicates. Use FALSE if you wish to display every item from the original range. In this case, I omitted the argument.

The =UNIQUE(C3:C12,TRUE,FALSE) formula in cell I3 of *Figure 10.12* returns every item from the original list. This is useful if you want to replicate the original list in a new location. Doing so enables you to use the Spilled Range Operator (#) in formulas, as I'll discuss in *The Spilled Range Operator* section of this chapter.

> **Nuance**
>
> Sometimes, you can omit arguments within Excel formulas by placing commas in lieu of the argument itself, such as =UNIQUE(C3:C12,,FALSE). The default by_col value is TRUE, but in this case, Excel assumes FALSE instead, which duplicates the entire list in the same fashion as the formula in cell I3 instead of removing duplicates. Watch out for unintended consequences if you omit function arguments in this fashion.

Next, let's look at how to dynamically sort data based on a formula.

The SORT function

In *Figure 10.13*, I clicked on cell **D3** and then clicked on **Sort Largest to Smallest** on the **Data** tab of Excel's ribbon. The =SORT(B3:E12) formula in cell **G3** shows the list sorted back into alphabetical order again. In this case, the SORT function is spilling results into columns H:J and rows 4:12:

A	B	C	D	E	F	G	H	I	J
1	World's Longest Beaches					SORT Function (Alphabetical by Beach)			
2	Beach	Country	Miles	Kilometers		Beach	Country	Miles	Kilometers
3	Praia do Cassino Beach	Brazil	150	241		Cox's Bazar	Bangladesh	75	121
4	Ninety Mile Beach	Australia	94	151		Long Beach	United States	28	45
5	Cox's Bazar	Bangladesh	75	121		Muizenberg	South Africa	25	40
6	Padre Island National Seashore	United States	70	113		Ninety Mile Beach	Australia	94	151
7	Playa Novillero	Mexico	56	90		Ninety Mile Beach	New Zealand	55	89
8	Ninety Mile Beach	New Zealand	55	89		Padre Island National Seashore	United States	70	113
9	Virginia Beach	United States	35	56		Playa Novillero	Mexico	56	90
10	Long Beach	United States	28	45		Praia do Cassino Beach	Brazil	150	241
11	Muizenberg	South Africa	25	40		Stockton Beach	Australia	20	32
12	Stockton Beach	Australia	20	32		Virginia Beach	United States	35	56
13						=SORT(B3:E12)			

Figure 10.13 – The SORT function

The SORT function has the following arguments:

- **Array** – The range of cells that you wish to sort, which, in this case, is cells **B3:E12**.

> **Tip**
> Make sure that you don't include your heading row in the array; otherwise, you'll most likely sort the column headings into the body of your list.

- **Sort_index** – An optional column position that you wish to sort on. In this case, I omitted this argument, but I'll show you an example later.
- **Sort_order** – This optional argument defaults to 1, which indicates you want to sort in ascending order, or you can enter -1 to instruct Excel to sort in descending order. In this case, I omitted sort_order.
- **By_col** – Optionally, enter FALSE to confirm the default sort order of sorting by rows, or enter TRUE if you wish to sort sideways by columns, which, again, I omitted in this case.

> **Tip**
> You can wrap the SORT function around the UNIQUE function to sort a dynamic list of unique items, as discussed in the previous section.

The =SORT(B3:E12,3) formula in cell **L3** of *Figure 10.14* sorts the list in ascending order based on miles:

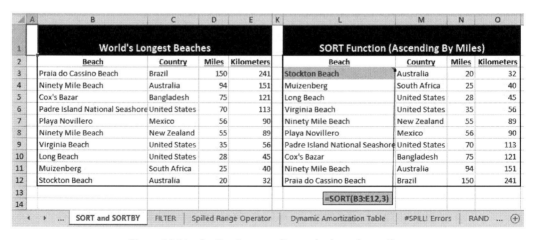

Figure 10.14 – Sorting in ascending order based on miles

In this case, 3 indicates that we want to sort based on the third column of the `array`.

The `=SORT(SORT(B3:E12,3,-1),2)` formula in cell **Q3** of *Figure 10.15* shows you how to sort alphabetically by country and then in descending order by miles:

	B	C	D	E		Q	R	S	T
1	World's Longest Beaches					Two SORT Functions (Alphabetically By Country, Descending By Miles)			
2	Beach	Country	Miles	Kilometers		Beach	Country	Miles	Kilometers
3	Praia do Cassino Beach	Brazil	150	241		Ninety Mile Beach	Australia	94	151
4	Ninety Mile Beach	Australia	94	151		Stockton Beach	Australia	20	32
5	Cox's Bazar	Bangladesh	75	121		Cox's Bazar	Bangladesh	75	121
6	Padre Island National Seashore	United States	70	113		Praia do Cassino Beach	Brazil	150	241
7	Playa Novillero	Mexico	56	90		Playa Novillero	Mexico	56	90
8	Ninety Mile Beach	New Zealand	55	89		Ninety Mile Beach	New Zealand	55	89
9	Virginia Beach	United States	35	56		Muizenberg	South Africa	25	40
10	Long Beach	United States	28	45		Padre Island National Seashore	United States	70	113
11	Muizenberg	South Africa	25	40		Virginia Beach	United States	35	56
12	Stockton Beach	Australia	20	32		Long Beach	United States	28	45
13									
14						=SORT(SORT(B3:E12,3,-1),2)			

Figure 10.15 – The nested SORT functions

In this case, the first sort, meaning the inside `SORT` function, sorts the list in descending order based on miles. The outside `SORT` function arranges the list in alphabetical order by country since I specified the second column as `sort_index`. The nuance is that the `SORT` functions must be nested in the proper order to achieve the desired result.

> **Nuance**
>
> You can use the `SORT` function to sort data from another workbook. Excel's online help states that dynamic arrays between workbooks only work when both workbooks are open at the same time. However, my experience is that dynamic arrays do indeed still return results whether the other workbook is open or not.

Conversely, the alternative =SORTBY(B3:E12,C3:C12,1,D3:D12,-1) formula, as shown in cell **V3** of *Figure 10.16*, achieves the same outcome:

	A	B	C	D	E	U	V	W	X	Y
1		\multicolumn{4}{c}{World's Longest Beaches}			\multicolumn{4}{c}{SORTBY Function (Alphabetically By Country, Descending By Miles)}			
2		Beach	Country	Miles	Kilometers		Beach	Country	Miles	Kilometers
3		Praia do Cassino Beach	Brazil	150	241		Ninety Mile Beach	Australia	94	151
4		Ninety Mile Beach	Australia	94	151		Stockton Beach	Australia	20	32
5		Cox's Bazar	Bangladesh	75	121		Cox's Bazar	Bangladesh	75	121
6		Padre Island National Seashore	United States	70	113		Praia do Cassino Beach	Brazil	150	241
7		Playa Novillero	Mexico	56	90		Playa Novillero	Mexico	56	90
8		Ninety Mile Beach	New Zealand	55	89		Ninety Mile Beach	New Zealand	55	89
9		Virginia Beach	United States	35	56		Muizenberg	South Africa	25	40
10		Long Beach	United States	28	45		Padre Island National Seashore	United States	70	113
11		Muizenberg	South Africa	25	40		Virginia Beach	United States	35	56
12		Stockton Beach	Australia	20	32		Long Beach	United States	28	45
13										
14							=SORTBY(B3:E12,C3:C12,1,D3:D12,-1)			

Figure 10.16 – The SORTBY function

The SORTBY function allows you to sort based upon up to 126 columns and has the following arguments:

- **Array** – The range of cells that you wish to sort, which, in this case, is **B3:E12**.

- **By_array1** – The cell coordinates of the first column that you wish to sort on, such as **C3:C12**.

- **Sort_order1** – Enter 1 to confirm the default sort order of ascending, or enter -1 to sort in descending order. I chose 1 for ascending.

- **By_array2** – The cell coordinates of the second column that you wish to sort on, such as **D3:D12**.

- **Sort_order2** – All sort_order arguments default to 1 for ascending or -1 for descending. In this case, I specified -1 for descending.

> **Nuance**
>
> You can only sort rows with the SORTBY function. If you wish to sort two or more columns sideways, you'll need to nest two or more SORT functions, as described earlier.

Now that you can dynamically sort data with a formula, let's up our game by seeing how to filter a list by using the FILTER function.

The FILTER function

The =FILTER(B3:E12,B3:B12=H2) formula in cell **G6** of *Figure 10.17* displays all the beaches for the name entered in cell **H2**, in this case, Ninety Mile Beach. Earlier in the chapter, you saw that functions such as VLOOKUP, MATCH, and XLOOKUP stop looking after finding an initial match. The FILTER function gives you a way to return multiple values from a list:

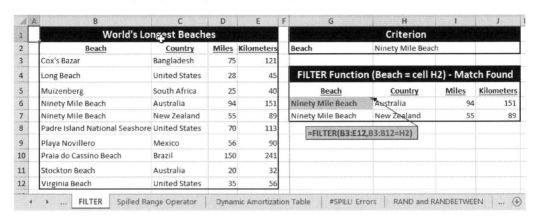

Figure 10.17 – The FILTER function

> **Tip**
> It's best not to embed criteria within the formula itself. Using input cells such as cell **H2** enables you or other users to change the criteria without having to edit the formula.

The **FILTER** function has two required arguments and one optional argument:

- **Array** – This required argument is a list composed of one or more columns that you wish to filter, which, in this case, is B3:E12.

- **Include** – This required argument is the cell coordinates of the column that you wish to filter on and the criteria itself, which, in this case, is B3:B12=H2. You can only provide one criterion per column, but you can filter on multiple columns.

- **If_empty** – An alternate message to display, which I omitted in this case but will be illustrated later.

The =FILTER(B3:E12,B3:B12=M2) formula in cell **L6** of *Figure 10.18* shows that if you omit the if_empty argument, the FILTER function returns #CALC! if no matches are found. In this case, cell **M2** contains the hyphenated Ninety-Nine Mile Beach version, which does not appear in cells **B3:B12**:

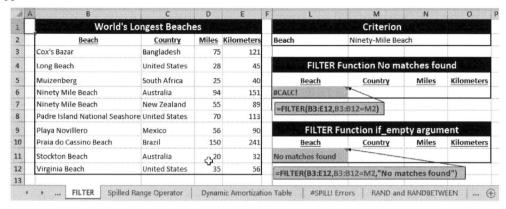

Figure 10.18 – The #CALC! error and the if_empty argument

The =FILTER(B3:E12,B3:B12=M2,"No matches found") formula in cell **L11** of *Figure 10.18* indicates that you can display an alternate message instead of #CALC! if no match is found. Additionally, if you wish, you could nest the FILTER function in this argument with other criteria that might match.

The =FILTER(B3:E12,C3:C12=R2,"No matches found") formula in cell **Q6** of *Figure 10.19* displays records where the country matches the value in cell **R2**, which, in this case, is United States. By default, the FILTER function presents results in the same order that the items appear in the specified array, but you can use the SORT function to change the sequencing:

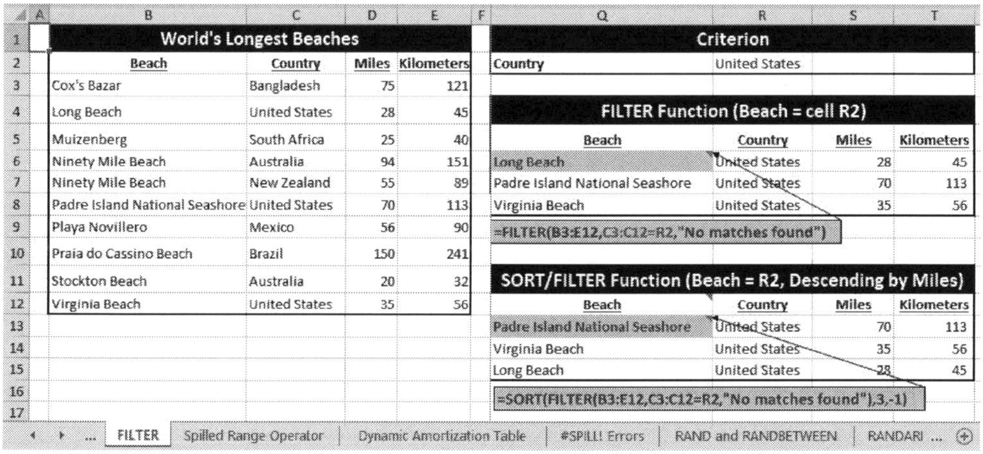

Figure 10.19 – Records being shown in default order and sorted order

The =SORT(FILTER(B3:E12,C3:C12=R2,"No matches found"),3,-1) formula in cell **Q13** of *Figure 10.19* sorts those same records in descending order. The **3** value means the sort is based on the third column, and **-1** corresponds with the descending order.

The =FILTER(B3:E12,(C3:C12=W2)*(D3:D12>=W3)) formula in cell **V7** of *Figure 10.20* shows that you can filter on two or more columns:

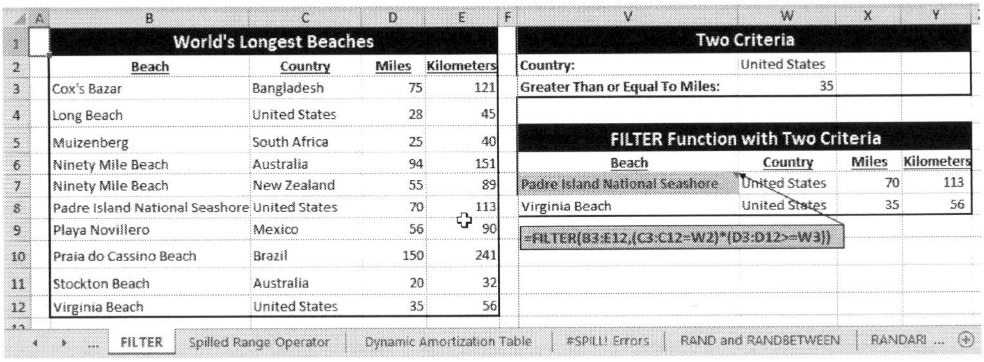

Figure 10.20 – FILTER allows one criterion per column

However, you can only provide a single criterion for each column. Each `include` statement must be enclosed in parentheses and connected with an asterisk. The formula looks at cells **C3:C12** for the words **United States**, which appear in cell **W2**, and simultaneously looks at cells **D3:D12** for amounts that are greater than or equal to 35 miles, which is listed in cell **W3**. Let's look at one more example, which will illustrate how to omit columns from the results that FILTER returns.

The =FILTER(B3:B12&": "&D3:D12&" miles",C3:C12=AA3) formula in cell **AA6** of *Figure 10.21* concatenates the beach name and length in miles together. Instead of the array being **B3:E12**, in this case, the array is **B3:B12** and **D3:D12**, with a colon inserted after the results from column **B** and the word `miles` after the results from column **D**. The concatenation causes the results to be returned to a single column instead of multiple columns as before:

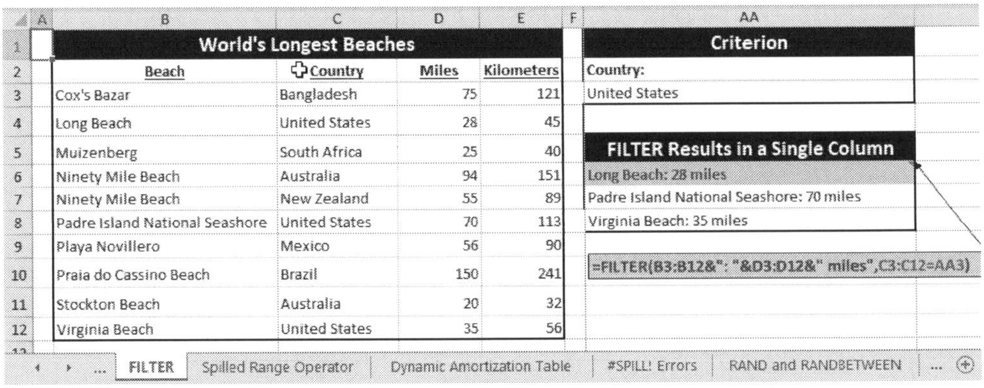

Figure 10.21 – Omitting columns from the FILTER results

Now we'll look at the Spilled Range Operator, which you can use to enable many Excel worksheet functions to take on dynamic characteristics.

The Spilled Range Operator

The average spreadsheet user spends a lot of time managing formulas in spreadsheets, particularly when new data is added to a list. The **Table** feature, which I discuss in *Chapter 7, Automating Tasks with the Table Feature*, offers one approach for eliminating this manual task. A second approach involves using the **Spilled Range Operator** (#) to create formulas that expand into more rows or contract into fewer rows based on changes in your data.

> **Nuance**
>
> You can only use the Spilled Range Operator in conjunction with formulas that reference results generated by a dynamic array function. This means the Spilled Range Operator is not available in Excel 2019 and earlier. If you use the Spilled Range Operator to reference data that is not in a dynamic array, the formula might return zero or a #VALUE! error.

The =SORT(UNIQUE(FILTER(C3:C12,D3:D12>H2))) formula in **G6** of *Figure 10.22* combines several concepts from this chapter to generate an alphabetical list of countries that have beaches greater than or equal to the number of miles in cell **H2**:

	A	B	C	D	E	F	G	H	I
1		World's Longest Beaches					Criterion		
2		Beach	Country	Miles	Kilometers	>=Miles:		25	
3		Cox's Bazar	Bangladesh	75	121				
4		Long Beach	United States	28	45		Spilled Range Operator (#)		
5		Muizenberg	South Africa	25	40		Country	Beaches	
6		Ninety Mile Beach	Australia	94	151		Australia	1	
7		Ninety Mile Beach	New Zealand	55	89		Bangladesh	1	
8		Padre Island National Seashore	United States	70	113		Brazil	1	
9		Playa Novillero	Mexico	56	90		Mexico	1	
10		Praia do Cassino Beach	Brazil	150	241		New Zealand	1	
11		Stockton Beach	Australia	20	32		United States	3	
12		Virginia Beach	United States	35	56				
13									
14							=SORT(UNIQUE(FILTER(C3:C12,D3:D12>H2)))		
15							=COUNTIFS(C3:C12,G6#,D3:D12,">="&H2)		

Figure 10.22 – The SORT/UNIQUE functions and the Spilled Range Operator (#)

In this case, the FILTER function in cell **G6** is filtering the list of countries that have beaches greater than the number listed in cell **H2**, which, in this case, is 25. The UNIQUE function then removes duplicates from the resulting list of countries, and the SORT function sorts the list in alphabetical order.

The `=COUNTIFS(C3:C12,G6#,D3:D12,">="&H2)` formula in cell **H6** of *Figure 10.22* utilizes the Spilled Range Operator (#).

The `COUNTIFS` function allows you to count instances of items based on up to 127 criteria pairs. Its arguments take the following form:

- **Criteria_range1** – The first range of cells to search, which, in this case, is **C3:C12**.
- **Criteria1** – The value to search for, which, in this case, is the country name in cell **G6**. I'll explain how the Spilled Range Operator (#) works later.
- **Criteria_range2** – The second range of cells to search, which, in this case, is **D3:D12**.
- **Criteria2** – The value to search for, which, in this case, is the lengths in miles that are greater than or equal to the number in cell **H2**.

Using G6# as the input for **criteria1** causes the `COUNTIFS` function in cell **H6** to become dynamic. To test this, change the value in cell **H2** to 60. When cell **H2** was set to 25, the formula in cell **G6** displayed six countries but should now only show four countries. Accordingly, the `COUNTIFS` function shrank its results to only four rows. If you change cell H2 to 0, then all seven countries will be listed in column **G** and the corresponding beach counts will appear in column **H**.

This brings us to one of my favorite ways to demonstrate the Spilled Range Operator: a dynamic amortization table.

The dynamic amortization table

An amortization table details how loan payments are allocated on a period-by-period basis, such as monthly. Additionally, an amortization table shows how the amount of the loan declines over time, typically down to zero or to an agreed-upon balloon payment to be made at the end. You might have encountered an amortization table in the paperwork provided along with the purchase of a car or a house. Historically, amortization tables generally required manual adjustments to accommodate different loan lengths. For instance, an amortization table for a 48-month car loan would need to have 12 more rows added if you opted for a 60-month loan instead. Dynamic array functions now enable us to create dynamic amortization tables that do not require much maintenance but instead expand or contract automatically to match the length of the loan.

Prior to the advent of dynamic array functions, you could create a macro to resize an amortization table on demand, or you could use the `IF` function to craft formulas that make cells appear blank in rows that are greater than the length of the loan. The **Conditional Formatting** feature, which I discuss in *Chapter 4, Conditional Formatting*, can be used to hide formulas, too. Fortunately, we no longer need to rely on workarounds.

> **Tip**
>
> Columns **G:K** of the `Dynamic Amortization Table` worksheet of this chapter's example workbook contains a work area where you can follow along with the text by entering dynamic array formulas in cells **G9:K9**.

As shown in *Figure 10.23*, when you change the number of years in cell **B4**, the detail rows in the amortization table will expand or contract accordingly. The amortization table is based upon the following inputs:

- **Start Date**: Cell **B2** in *Figure 10.23* specifies `1/1/2024` as the starting date of the loan:

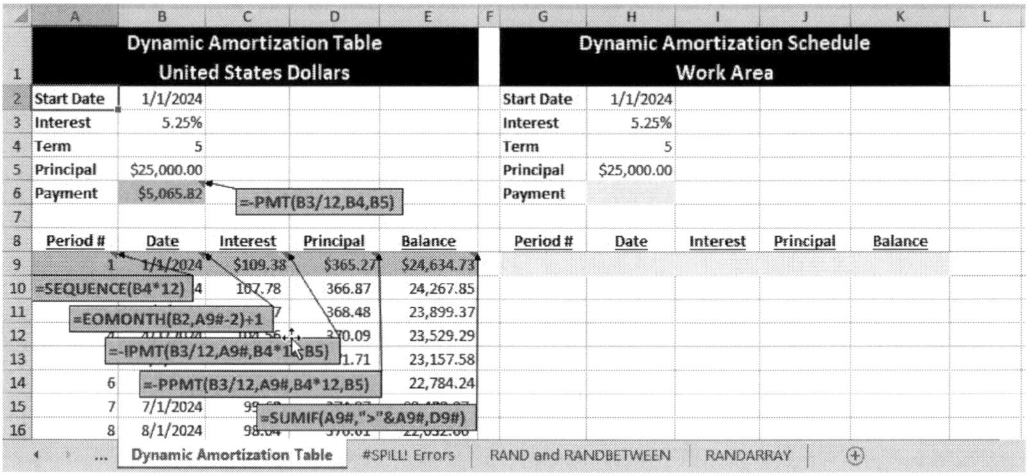

Figure 10.23 – The initial setup of our dynamic amortization table

- **Interest**: Cell **B3** in *Figure 10.23* specifies `5.25%` as the interest rate for the loan.

> **Nuance**
>
> The words interest rate and annual percentage rate are often used interchangeably for loans. Typically, although we think of interest rates in annual terms, the `PMT`, `IPMT`, and `PPMT` functions that we're going to use expect a monthly interest rate, which is easy to accomplish by simply dividing the annual interest rate by 12 within the worksheet functions.

- **Term** – Cell **B4** in *Figure 10.23* specifies the length of the loan in years, which, in this case, is 5.

> **Nuance**
>
> The `PMT`, `IPMT`, and `PPMT` functions all expect the term to be expressed in months, so I'll multiply the term by `12` to convert the input from years into months.

- **Principal** – Cell **B5** in *Figure 10.23* specifies the value of the loan, which, in this case, is $25,000.

The =-PMT(B3/12,B4*12,B5) formula in cell **B6** of *Figure 10.23* will not be referenced in the amortization table itself but does show the monthly payment amount. The PMT function has five arguments, but here, we only need the first three:

- **Rate** – B3/12 returns a monthly interest rate. If you forget to divide by 12, your annual interest rate will be applied monthly instead of annually. In this case, that would mean an interest rate of 5.25% per month and 63% per year.
- **Nper** – B4*12 represents the number of monthly periods. In this case, we have a 5-year loan, so 5 x 12 = 60 months.
- **Pv** – Cell **B5** contains the loan amount, which is often referred to as the **present value** (**pv**) because money loses value over time.

By default, the PMT function returns a negative number. I entered a minus sign after the equal sign in cell B6 so that the payment will be shown as a positive number instead, but this is an optional personal preference. This number won't be referenced in the body of our amortization table, as we'll use the IPMT and PPMT functions to calculate the monthly interest and principal portions of the loan payments, respectively, instead.

Enter =-PMT(H3/12,H4*12,H5) in cell **H6** of the work area of the Dynamic Amortization Table worksheet of this chapter's example workbook if you'd like to follow along in Excel.

Now that we have the amortization table inputs in place and the columns laid out, we'll use the **SEQUENCE** function to dynamically create the period numbers.

The SEQUENCE function

The =SEQUENCE(B4*12) formula in cell **A9** of *Figure 10.23* creates a range of numbers from **1** to **60**. The SEQUENCE function has the following arguments:

- **Rows** – The number of rows where you wish to display a series of numbers, which, in this case, is B4*12 to reference the term of the loan in months. If cells **B4** or **H4** contained 60, you wouldn't multiply by 12 and would simply refer to cell **B4** or **H4**, respectively.
- **Columns** – The number of columns where you wish to add a series of numbers, which I omitted in this case.
- **Start** – The starting value of the series of numbers; in cell **A9**, this defaults to **1** because I omitted the argument, but you can enter any number you wish.
- **Step** – The increment to increase each number; in cell **A9**, this defaults to **1** because I omitted the argument, but you can enter any number you wish.

This initial column anchors our amortization table and will allow us to use the Spilled Range Operator (#) to make the other worksheet functions behave dynamically, too. Now we'll add a series of dates to our table. Enter =SEQUENCE(H4*12) in cell **G9** if you're following along in Excel. In this context, you'll see that SEQUENCE creates a series of numbers from **1** to **60**.

The EOMONTH function

The =EOMONTH(B2,A9#-2)+1 formula in cell B9 of *Figure 10.23* creates a series of dates. EOMONTH is short for *End of Month* and has two arguments:

- Start_date – A date to use as a starting point, which, in this case, is the value in cell **B2**.
- Months – The number of months in the past or future that you wish to calculate a new date for; in this case, A9#-2 resolves to -1, which means EOMONTH returns the last day of the previous month, or 12/31/2023.

Adding +1 after EOMONTH rolls the date one day forward to 1/1/2024. The Spilled Range Operator (#) instructs EOMONTH to return a series of dates through 6/1/2024, which corresponds with the number of periods listed in column **A**.

Enter =EOMONTH(H2,G9#-2)+1 in cell **H9** if you're following along in the work area. The formula will return a series of date serial numbers that you can convert into dates by selecting cells **H9:H68**, and then choose **Short Date** from the **Number Format** menu in the **Number** group of the **Home** tab in Excel's ribbon or type the letter s and press *Enter* in the **Number Format** menu field.

Now, let's calculate the monthly interest due on the loan.

> **Tip**
> Date serial numbers in Excel represent the number of days elapsed since 12/31/1899.

The IPMT function

The =-IPMT(B3/12,A9#,B4*12,B5) formula in cell **C9** of *Figure 10.23* calculates the interest portion of each loan payment. IPMT has six arguments:

- **Rate** – The interest rate per period for the loan, which, in this case, is B3/12 to return a monthly interest rate.
- **Per** – The period number for which you want to calculate the interest amount; in this case, A9# utilizes the Spilled Range Operator (#) to create a dynamic cell reference to the period numbers in column **A**.
- **Nper** – The term of the loan, which, in this case, is the value in cell **B4**. If cell **B4** specified years instead of months, you would use B4*12, as we have done.

- **Pv** – The present value of the loan, which, in this case, is the amount in cell B5.
- **Fv** – This is optional and refers to the future value of a loan, which defaults to **0** (zero) unless you indicate otherwise.
- **Type** – This is optional. IPMT defaults to **0** (zero) for payments made at the end of a loan period, but you can enter 1 to indicate payments made at the beginning of a loan period. I accepted the default of payments made at the end of the period by omitting the argument.

By default, IPMT returns a negative amount, which you can change to a positive amount by adding a minus sign after the equals sign.

Enter =-IPMT(H3/12,G9#,H4*12,H5) in cell **I9** if you're following along in the work area. The next formula will calculate the amount that the loan will be paid down by each month.

The PPMT function

The =-PPMT(B3/12,A9#,B4*12,B5) formula in cell **D9** of *Figure 10.23* calculates the principal portion of each loan payment. The formula arguments are identical to IPMT, so I won't spell them out again. If you're following along in the work area, you can click on cell **I9**, select the formula in the formula bar, press *Ctrl* + *C* (or ⌘ + *C* in **Excel for macOS**) or right-click and choose **Copy**, and then paste the formula into cell **J9**. All you'd then need to do is change the letter I in IPMT to P for PPMT. Alternatively, you can enter =-PPMT(H3/12,G9#,H4*12,H5) in cell **J9**. Now, we'll finish our dynamic amortization table by using the Spilled Range Operator (#) in conjunction with the SUMIF function to calculate the running balance of the loan.

The SUMIF function

The =SUMIF(A9#,">"&A9#,D9#) formula in cell **E9** of *Figure 10.23* calculates the ending balance for each loan period. SUMIF has three arguments:

- **Range** – A row or column that you wish to search; in this case, A9# uses the Spilled Range Operator (#) to create a range that extends down to the last period listed in column **A**.
- **Criteria** – A value to search for; in this case, ">"&A9# uses the Spilled Range Operator (#) to instruct Excel to include the period numbers that are greater than the current period. In this context, the greater than operator must be enclosed in double quotes and concatenated with the cell reference.

> **Nuance**
> If you omit the Spilled Range Operator, then SUMIF will only return a single value in cell **E9**.

- **Sum_range** – A row or column that you wish to add up values from; in this case, D9# uses the spilled range operator to create a range that extends down to the last cell in column **A**.

In effect, the SUMIF function returns the ending balance by adding the remaining principal payments for each period of the loan. If you're following along in the work area, enter =SUMIF(G9#,">"&G9#,J9#) in cell **K9**. The dynamic amortization table illustrates the transformative capabilities of dynamic array functions. Of course, every feature in Excel has one or more rough edges, so let's look at two errors that are specific to dynamic array functions.

The #SPILL! errors

As you might expect, new functionality in Excel such as dynamic array functions can result in new types of error prompts, too. In *The Filter function* section, I discussed the #CALC! error. In this section, I'll discuss the #SPILL! error. The first error that we'll look at arises when other data resides in the immediate area that a dynamic array function needs to display its results. This error can also arise when a user overwrites data that has been returned by a dynamic array function.

The **#SPILL!** error can appear under two different conditions:

- Cell **G7** in *Figure 10.24* contains the words Obstruction blocking UNIQUE. If you subsequently enter the =UNIQUE(C3:C12) formula into cell **G3**, Excel will return #SPILL! instead of the list of countries you're expecting. That's because the contents of cell **G7** fall within the range that UNIQUE needs to display its results. As shown, when you click on a cell that contains #SPILL!, such as **G3**, Excel draws a border around the area that needs to be cleared in order for the formula to return its results. Clear cell **G7**'s contents or move its contents to eliminate the #SPILL! error. Alternatively, click on the exclamation mark to display menu options related to understanding and resolving such errors:

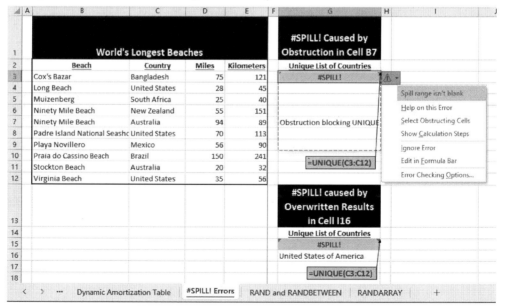

Figure 10.24 – The #SPILL! error

The =UNIQUE(C3:C12) formula in cell **G15** of *Figure 10.24* returns #SPILL! because I replaced **United States**, which the function returned in cell **G16**, with United States of America. If a user types over any result returned by a dynamic array function, the formula will return #SPILL! until any overwritten cells are cleared. In short, the #SPILL! and #CALC! errors are designed to give you immediate feedback when dynamic array functions cannot return any result due to the conditions within your spreadsheet.

Now, let's see how to generate random numbers in Excel spreadsheets.

The RANDARRAY function

Excel has three different functions that enable you to generate random numbers. Let's look at the two longstanding options, and then we'll look at RANDARRAY. The =RAND() formula in cell **B2** of *Figure 10.25* generates a random number between 0 and 1:

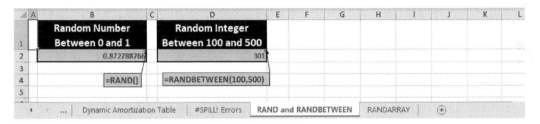

Figure 10.25 – The RAND and RANDBETWEEN functions

The =RANDBETWEEN(100,500) formula in cell **D2** of *Figure 10.25* allows you to generate random integers between 100 and 500. RANDBETWEEN has two arguments:

- **Bottom** – The lowest possible integer you want to return, which, in this case, is 100
- **Top** – The highest possible integer you want to return, which, in this case, is 500

> **Nuance**
>
> All random number functions in Excel are volatile, meaning that, unlike most formulas, they recalculate every time you change any cell anywhere in the workbook. Normally, Excel only recalculates formulas when you change a value that the formula directly or indirectly references.

320   Lookup and Dynamic Array Functions

The =RANDARRAY(3) formula in cell **F2** of *Figure 10.26* returns three random numbers between **0** and **1**:

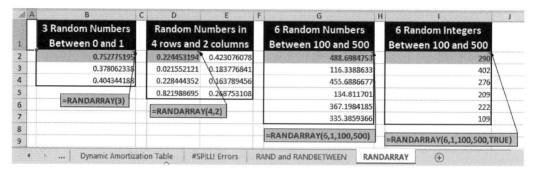

Figure 10.26 – The RANDARRAY function

The RANDARRAY function has five arguments:

- **Rows** – This is an optional argument that allows you to specify the number of rows you want to display random numbers within. The argument defaults to 1; in this case, I entered 3.

- **Columns** – This is an optional argument that allows you to specify the number of columns that you wish to display random numbers within. The argument defaults to 1.

- **Min** – This is an optional argument for the smallest number you would like to display, which I omitted in this case.

- **Max** – This is an optional argument for the largest number you would like to display, which I omitted in this case.

- **Integer** – This is an optional argument, which I omitted in this case, that allows you to specify the following:

    - TRUE to display whole numbers.
    - FALSE to display decimal numbers; this is the default argument.

The =RANDARRAY(4,2) formula in cell **D2** of *Figure 10.26* shows you how to return random numbers across four rows and two columns. The =RANDARRAY(6,1,100,500) formula in cell **G2** of *Figure 10.26* uses four arguments to return random numbers with decimal places across **6** rows and **1** column that are between **100** and **500**. Finally, the =RANDARRAY(6,1,100,500,TRUE) formula in cell **I2** of *Figure 10.26* adds the fifth argument with a value of TRUE, which instructs RANDARRAY to return integers, also known as whole numbers. Often, random numbers are used with statistical sampling in Microsoft Excel but have many other uses, too.

Summary

In this chapter, you learned about the concept of dynamic array functionality in Excel. Some functions, such as UNIQUE, SORT, SORTBY, FILTER, RANDARRAY, and SEQUENCE, were written from the ground up as dynamic array functions. The XLOOKUP function is a hybrid that can work as a replacement for the VLOOKUP function. Alternatively, it can work as a modern dynamic array function returning multiple results to a block of cells or summarized within another function, such as the SUM or AVERAGE functions.

Additionally, by way of the spreadsheet that we put together in the *Dynamic amortization schedule* section, we saw that longstanding functions in Excel such as EOMONTH, IPMT, PPMT, and SUMIF can all take on dynamic characteristics. We used the **spilled range operator** (#) in conjunction with referencing a set of data returned by a dynamic array function.

Dynamic array functions empower you to streamline your formulas, as a single formula can return results to hundreds or even thousands of rows at once. The risk of users typing over one or more values in a list of formulas is eliminated, as doing so will raise a #SPILL! error in the worksheet. Dynamic array functions set the modern versions of Excel completely apart from all previous versions of Excel, meaning **Excel 2019** and earlier.

In the next chapter, I'll walk you through the LET and LAMBDA functions, which offer even more potential for improvements in spreadsheet integrity than ever possible before. Both functions streamline complex formulas and can make complex formulas more accessible.

11
Names, LET, and LAMBDA

If you've ever thought, *"Oh, I wish Excel had a way to automate calculating x,"* your day has arrived. There will be some nuances and increasing complexity along the way, which is why I've chosen a straightforward path for us to follow. We'll start with simple multiplication to calculate the volume of a box, and then riff on that calculation several ways as we make our way to the LET and LAMBDA functions. I'll introduce the concept of **Names**, which are sometimes referred to as range **Names**. **Names** can streamline formula writing and make it easier to determine what a formula references and is calculating. The LET and LAMBDA functions share some characteristics with **Names**. For the benefit of anyone using an older version of Excel, I'll also briefly discuss creating custom worksheet functions with Visual Basic for Applications programming code.

In this chapter, I will cover the following topics:

- PRODUCT, IF, CHOOSE, SWITCH, IFERROR, and ISERROR functions
- Assigning Names worksheet and inputs
- Introducing the LET function
- Introducing the LAMBDA function
- Going deeper with LAMBDA functions
- Custom VBA worksheet functions

By the end of this chapter, you'll be empowered to create custom worksheet functions in Excel. Along the way, you'll be able to compare the pros and cons of each approach, and hopefully expand your Excel toolbox as well.

Technical requirements

The IF, CHOOSE, and PRODUCT functions, as well as **Names**, work in any version of Excel. The SWITCH function requires **Excel 2019** or later, while the LET function requires **Excel 2021** or **Microsoft 365**. The LAMBDA function works in **Microsoft 365** and **Excel for the web**. There are two example workbooks for this chapter: the Chapter 11 - Names, LET, and LAMBDA.xlsx workbook can be opened in any version of Excel, although `SWITCH`, `LET`, and `LAMBDA` will return `#NAME?` in unsupported versions of Excel. The `Chapter 11 - BOX_VOLUME and XBOX_VOLUME.xlsm` workbook contains programming code used to create custom worksheet functions and may be blocked by your network or **Microsoft Windows**. I'll show you how to resolve a **Windows** block when we get to that part of this chapter. Both workbooks can be downloaded from GitHub at `https://github.com/PacktPublishing/Exploring-Microsoft-Excels-Hidden-Treasures/tree/main/Chapter11`.

Simple volume calculations in Excel

Throughout this chapter, we will be computing the volume of a rectangular shape, such as a shipping box by multiplying its length by its width and height. Having a consistent calculation to follow this chapter will make it easier to focus on the Excel features and functions that I'll be covering along the way. Let's open the `Chapter 11 - Names, LET, and LAMBDA.xlsx` example workbook for this chapter and get started.

Multiplication

Anyone new to Microsoft Excel typically starts out with basic computations such as addition, subtraction, multiplication, and division, so let's begin there. Rest assured, we won't linger long here; we're mostly establishing a framework that we can build onto:

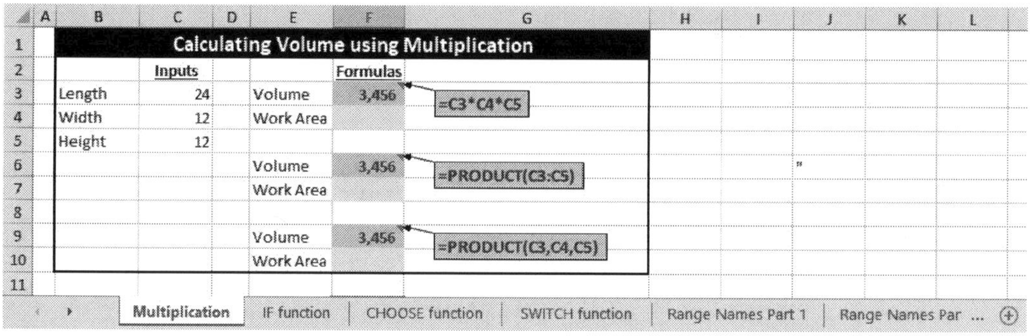

Figure 11.1 – Contrasting simple multiplication with the PRODUCT function

Cells **C3:C5** of the `Multiplication` worksheet in *Figure 11.1* contain the length, width, and height of a hypothetical box in the measurement of your choice. Cell **F3** contains the `=C3*C4*C5` formula and returns `3,456` as the cubic volume of our container. Cell **F4** represents a work area where you can follow along if you want to recreate the formula. You'll see similar work areas throughout the example workbook.

Now, let's use the `PRODUCT` function to multiply cells together.

PRODUCT function

Cell **F6** of the `Multiplication` worksheet, shown in *Figure 11.1*, contains the `=PRODUCT(C3:C5)` formula and returns 3,456. The `PRODUCT` function multiplies all values together and returns the result, so the formula in **F6** is equivalent to `=C3*C4*C5`.

The `PRODUCT` function has the following arguments:

> `number1, number2…`: A number, cell reference, or range of cells that you wish to multiply; up to 255 arguments

Cell **F9** contains the `=PRODUCT(C3,C4,C5)` formula and returns 3,456 to illustrate that you can reference individual cells as well. Now, let's move on to some worksheet functions that you can use to perform decision-making in Excel.

Decision-making functions

I'm going to set aside our volume calculation track for a moment so that I can introduce some decision-making worksheet functions that I feel will help pave the way toward both the `LET` and `LAMBDA` functions. We'll start with the `IF` function, which I will then contrast to the `CHOOSE` function, followed by the `SWITCH` function.

IF function

Cell **D3** of the `IF function` worksheet, shown in *Figure 11.2*, contains the `=IF(C3>=70,"Pass","Fail")` formula and returns `Fail` because cell **C3** contains 61, which is less than 70. Conversely, cell **D4** contains the `=IF(C4>=70,"Pass","Fail")` formula, which returns `Pass` because **C4** contains a number that is greater than or equal to 70:

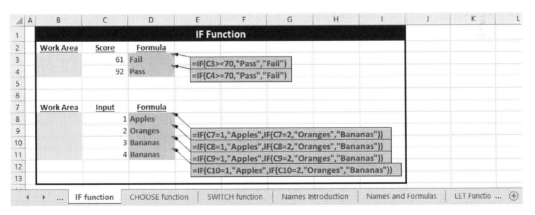

Figure 11.2 – IF function

The `IF` function has three arguments:

- `logical_test`: A calculation that evaluates to either TRUE or FALSE. In cell **D3**, we're checking to see if **C3** is greater than or equal to **70**.

- `value_if_true`: A numeric value, text, or formula to return or calculate if `logical_test` evaluates to **TRUE**. In this case, we want to return the word `Pass` for scores greater than or equal to 70. As you can see, text-based values within Excel formulas must be enclosed within double quotes.

- `value_if_false`: A numeric value, text, or formula to return or calculate if `logical_test` evaluates to FALSE. In this case, we'll return the word `Fail`.

You can nest up to 64 `IF` functions together, so you can place additional `IF` functions within the `value_if_true` or `value_if_false` arguments as needed. Honestly, I was perfectly content back with **Excel 2003**, which limited us to up to eight `IF` functions within a single formula. Time and again I've found that whenever I find myself trying to nest more than two or three levels of `IF` functions, there is almost always a better function to use instead or a better way to structure the data. Let's look at an example of how nesting `IF` functions can cause in spreadsheet errors.

Cell **D8** contains the `=IF(C8=1,"Apples",IF(C8=2,"Oranges","Bananas"))` formula, as shown *Figure 11.2*. In this case, I've nested two levels of `IF` functions together. If **C8** is equal to 1, I want to display the word `Apples`; otherwise, I'll perform a second `IF` calculation. If **C8** is equal to 2, I'll display the word `Oranges`; otherwise, I'll display `Bananas`. This same formula appears in cells **D9:D11**. Notice how cell **C11** contains 4 yet the `IF` function in **D11** returns `Bananas`. The formula did not contemplate a fourth option being available, so it returned the final option, which is `Bananas`. It's easy for users, especially those not well versed in Excel, to assume that if a formula returns a result, then the result must be correct. The more `IF` functions that you string together, the harder it becomes to test every outcome.

For situations such as this, the `CHOOSE` function can a better alternative.

CHOOSE function

Cell **D3** of the `CHOOSE function` worksheet, shown in *Figure 11.3*, contains the `=CHOOSE(C3,"Apples","Oranges","Bananas")` formula, which displays the first item from a list – in this case, `Apples` – because cell **C3** contains the number 1:

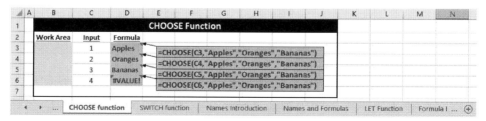

Figure 11.3 – CHOOSE function

The CHOOSE function has the following arguments:

- `index_num`: This argument must contain a number, formula, or cell reference that evaluates to a number between 1 and 254.
- `value1, value2…`: A number, text, or formula that you wish to return that corresponds to `index_num` provided. Your list can contain up to 254 values, but each value must be listed within the function. This means you can't reference a list that resides in a range of cells.

As shown in cell **D6**, CHOOSE returns #VALUE if `index_num` does not have a corresponding *value*. In this case, we've asked CHOOSE to return a fourth value, but we only specified three in the formula. Unlike IF, CHOOSE offers a safety net if you pass an unexpected input through to the formula.

The CHOOSE function is helpful when inputs are numbers between 1 and, say, 5. I don't want to contemplate writing out a CHOOSE function that has many options beyond that. This brings us to the SWITCH function, which lets us return a result based upon matching numbers or text, and we don't have to start at 1.

SWITCH function

Cell **D3** of the SWITCH function worksheet, shown in *Figure 11.4*, contains the =SWITCH(C3,10,"Apples",20,"Oranges",30,"Bananas","Unknown") formula, which returns Apples because cell **C3** contains 10:

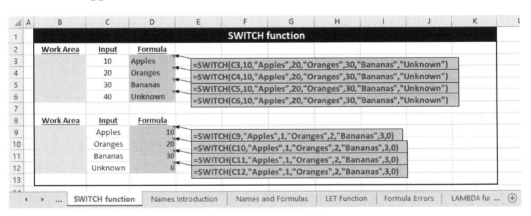

Figure 11.4 – SWITCH function

The SWITCH function has the following arguments:

- `expression`: This argument must contain a number, text, or a formula that returns a number or text. In this case, this is 10 in cell **C3**.
- `value1 …`: This argument contains a number or a formula that returns a number or piece of text that you wish to match on – in this case, 10.

- `result1` ...: This argument is what you want to return if the value matches – in this case, `Apples`.

- `default_or_value2`: You can provide up to 126 result/value pairs, while the final argument should be a default number, text, or formula that you want to return if none of the value arguments match. So, in this case, 20 is switched for `Oranges`, 30 is switched for `Bananas`, and any other value will be switched for `Unknown`.

Cell **D9** contains the `=SWITCH(C9,"Apples",10,"Oranges",20,"Bananas",30,0)` formula, which shows that, unlike CHOOSE, you can match on numbers or text. The formula returns `10` because cell **C9** contains `Apples`. Later in this chapter, you'll see that LET and LAMBDA offer another level of swapping functionality, but first, let's look at assigning **Names** to worksheet cells.

Naming worksheet cells

Naming worksheet cells allows you to reference a cell or block of cells by way of a **Name** that you assign instead of a cell reference. You can use **Names** and cell references interchangeably in your spreadsheets. Excel offers four ways to assign **Names** to cells: **Name Box**, **Create from Selection**, **Define Name**, and **Name Manager**. There are a couple of rules to keep in mind:

- **Names** must begin with a letter, underscore (_), or backslash (\), so `2024TAX` is not a valid Name.

- **Names** can be as short as a single letter, but you cannot assign the letters *C* or *R* as a name. This is because you when type `C` in the **Name Box** and press *Enter* Excel will select the current column, while `R` and *Enter* selects the current row.

- **Names** cannot be the same as any cell reference, such as `TAX2024`. The last column in an Excel worksheet is **XFD**, so combining a word with one to three letters and a number together will constitute an invalid name.

- **Names** cannot contain spaces, so `TAX 2024` is not a valid name, but `TAX_2024` is.

Now, let's use **Name Box** to assign **Names** and see how doing so can transform your Excel formulas.

Name Box

As shown in *Figure 11.5*, **Name Box** appears just above the top left-hand corner of every worksheet and typically shows the address of the active cell or the address of the first cell in a range of cells that you have selected. In this case, I've selected cell **C3** of the `Names Introduction` worksheet, so **Name Box** displays **C3** as well. If this were a longer book, I'd show you over two dozen activities that can be carried out in this one innocuous field. Regardless, I want to stay focused on our journey toward LET and LAMBDA, so I'll restrain myself and only show you a few:

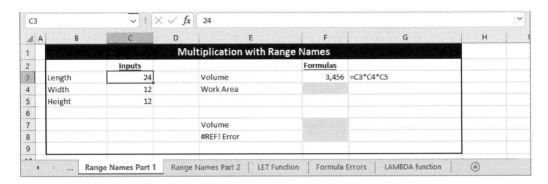

Figure 11.5 – Name Box displaying a cell address

Let's use **Name Box** to assign **Names** to three cells:

1. Select cell **C3** on the `Names Introduction` worksheet, type the letter L into the **Name Box** area, and then press *Enter*.

2. As shown in *Figure 11.6*, the letter L now appears in the **Name Box** area instead of the cell address when you click on cell **C3**, which indicates the **Name** that has been assigned to the cell:

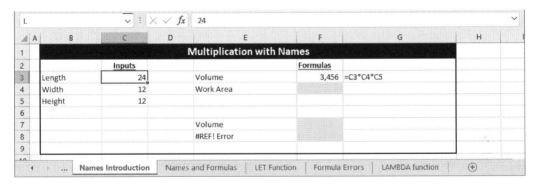

Figure 11.6 – Name Box displaying a Name

> **Tip**
> Press *Ctrl + Z* (⌘+ *Z* in **Excel for macOS**) or click the **Undo** command to undo the action if you inadvertently name the wrong cell.

3. Select cell **C4**, type the letter W into the **Name Box** area, and press *Enter*.

4. With cell **C5** selected, type the letter H into the **Name Box** area, and press *Enter*.

5. Cell **F3** contains the =C3*C4*C5 formula, which we'll replicate in cell **F4** by entering =L*W*H. Your formula should return 3,456, though it will return #NAME? if you missed assigning any of the **Names**.

> **Tip**
> Cells **G3** and **G4** use the `IFNA` and `FORMULATEXT` functions together so that you can compare cell referenced-based formulas to name-based formulas. Cell **G3** contains the `=IFNA(FORMULATEXT(F3),"")` formula, which either displays the formula entered in cell **F3** or makes cell **G3** appear to be blank if cell **F3** does not contain a formula.

6. Select cell **F3:F4** and press *Ctrl + C* (⌘ + C) (or choose **Home | Copy**).
7. Select cell **F7** and press *Enter* (or choose **Home | Paste**).

> **Tip**
> You can press the *Enter* key instead of pressing *Ctrl + V* (⌘+ V) or choosing **Home | Paste** when pasting cells that you've copied. Keep in mind that Excel does erase the clipboard after you press *Enter*, so only use this shortcut for data that you're pasting once. This technique does not work for data that you copy from the **Formula Bar** area, within a cell, or for any objects that float above the worksheet.

In this case, copying the formulas from cell **F3:F4** to **F7** accomplishes two things:

- Notice how the formula in cell **F7** refers to cells **C7**, **C8**, and **C9** because the formula in cell **F3** did not contain a dollar sign ($) before the row numbers. Due to this, Excel changed the row numbers commensurate to the number of rows down that we pasted.

- The formula in cell **F8** correctly returns 3,456 because named cells that you reference in formulas have absolute references. Conversely, if the formula in cell **F3** were =C$3*C$4*C$5 or =$C$3*$C$4*$C5, then you could copy it to cell **C7** without issue.

- We'll refer to the formula in cell **F8** later in this chapter as an error that can arise when named cells are deleted from a worksheet.

As you can see, the **Name Box** area allows you to assign one **Name** at a time to a cell or block of cells, and to navigate to any location in a workbook. Keep in mind that you cannot edit **Names** by way of **Name Box**; any attempts to do so will simply assign an additional name to the range in question. Later in this chapter, you'll learn how to use **Name Manager** to edit or delete **Names** that you have created.

> **Tip**
> You can use **Name Box** as a navigation aid: select cell **A1** in a worksheet, type C4 in **Name Box**, and press *Enter* to move your cursor to cell **C4**. Type a reference such as `Multiplication!A1` or `'CHOOSE Function'!A1` to move your cursor to another worksheet (remember to enclose worksheet **Names** with spaces with single quotes). To navigate by name, click the arrow in the **Name Box** area and select from the list. Press the *F5 (Fn + F5 on some keyboards)* key (or choose **Home | Find & Select | Go To**) and then press *Enter* to return to the previous cell.

Now, let's see how the **Formulas | Create from Selection** command enables you to assign individual **Names** within a block of cells.

Create from Selection

It can be tedious to use the **Name Box** area to name multiple cells, which brings us to the **Create from Selection** command. As shown in *Figure 11.7*, cells **B3:B5** of the **Names and Formulas** worksheet contains text that we'll assign as **Names** to cells **C3:C5**:

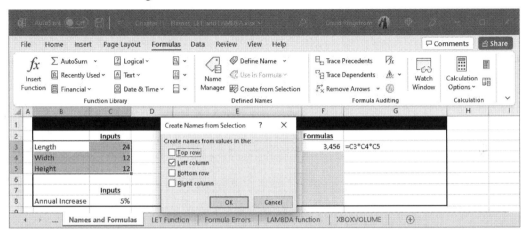

Figure 11.7 – Create **Names** from Selection dialog box

Let's create multiple **Names** at once:

1. Select cells **B8:C10** and choose **Formulas | Create from Selection** or press *Ctrl + Shift + F3* to display the **Create Names from Selection** dialog box.

> **Tip**
> The **Create from Selection** command requires you to select two columns or two rows. You can only name individual cells when using this command. The **Top row** option **Names** the cells in the second row of the selection, while the **Bottom row** option **Names** cells in the first row. **Right-column** assigns **Names** to the first column in the selection. Spaces and punctuation within the text to be used as **Names** are replaced with underscores, and an underscore is added to the start of any **Names** where the first character of the text is a number. This means `Annual Increase` would become `Annual_Increase`, while `2024 Taxes` would become `_2024_Taxes`.

2. Accept the default selection of **Left column** and then click **OK**. Here, Excel has correctly assumed that we wish to assign the values from the left column of our two-column selection to the cells in the right column. Although not applicable here, you can clear extraneous checkboxes that Excel selects.

3. Click on cells **C3**, **C4**, and **C5** and notice how the **Length**, **Width**, and **Height** for the name have been assigned, respectively.

4. Type =L in cell **F4** and notice how the **AutoComplete** menu in **Excel for Windows**, shown in *Figure 11.8*, displays a list of **Names** and worksheet functions, along with any **Table Names** that match the characters that you've typed. Now, type ENG and notice that the list only displays LENGTH. Press the *Tab* key to choose **Length**. Type * and then choose **Width**. Type * again, choose **Height**, and then press *Enter*. We'll refer to this formula later in this chapter when we discuss deleting **Names**:

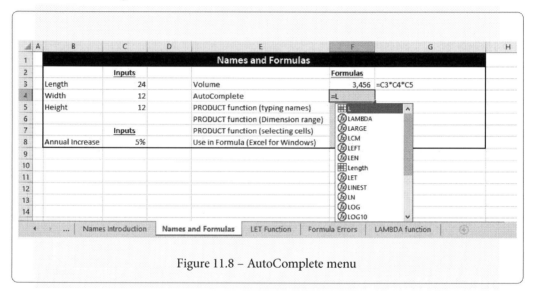

Figure 11.8 – AutoComplete menu

Now, let's look at a third way of naming cells, which will also come into play when using LAMBDA to create custom worksheet functions.

Define Name

The **Formulas | Define Name** command offers a bit more control over creating **Names** in your workbooks. First, you can create a name that can be recognized by all worksheets in a workbook, or only by the worksheet that contains the named range. Second, you can associate a description of up to 255 characters with the name. Apart from that, the process is like using **Name Box**:

1. Choose cell **C8** of the Names and Formulas worksheet.

2. Choose **Formulas | Define Name** to display the **New Name** dialog box, shown in *Figure 11.9*:

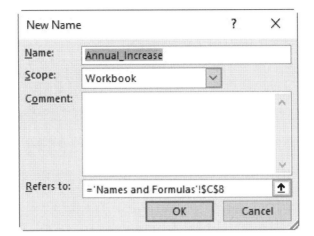

Figure 11.9 – New Name dialog box

3. `Annual_Increase` appears in the **Name** field because Excel assumes you want to use the text in the adjacent cell as the name for cell **C8**. You can update the **Name** field as needed. An alternative name you could use is `AnnualIncrease`, as capitalizing letters within a compound word is another way around not using spaces but keeping **Names** easy to read.

4. You'll usually accept the default of **Workbook** from the **Scope** list but choosing **Worksheet** here will limit the scope of a name to a single worksheet if you need to do so. This means that using the name on any other worksheet will result in a #NAME? error.

> **Nuance**
>
> Note that the second instance of a name in a workbook will have a scope of **Worksheet**. You cannot create a name a second time in the **Name Box** area, as typing in a duplicate name moves your cursor to the existing name. If you try doing this in the **Define Names** dialog box, you will be informed that **Names** must be unique. The loophole is that you can use **Create Names from Selection** to duplicate an existing name. You will not be warned or notified, and any duplicate **Names** will have a **Worksheet** scope. In turn, errors can arise as you may unwittingly reference the wrong cell.

5. Optional: Enter a description, such as `Annual increase amount`, in the **Comment** field to create a `ScreenTip` that will appear when typing the name into a formula. Comments can also be viewed in the **Name Manager** dialog box.

6. Accept the default cell reference of ='Names and Formulas'!$C$8 in the **Refers To** field unless you wish to assign the name to a different cell. You do not need to add an equals sign (=) or a dollar sign ($) as Excel will do so automatically when you click **OK**.

7. Click **OK** to create the name.

8. Type =Annual in any cell and notice how the **AutoComplete** menu displays the full name, along with the comment that you entered. Then, press *Escape* to discard the entry.

> **Nuance**
>
> You can also enter numbers, text, or formulas in the **Refers To** field. Text must be enclosed in double quotes, and formulas must begin with an equals sign (=). This approach offers a way to make it harder for others to alter key inputs in your workbook because the information won't appear in a worksheet cell, but can be referenced by its name as if it were. The data associated with such **Names** can be edited in the **Name Manager**. Formulas that you enter in the **Refers to** field should have dollar signs ($) before the column and row; otherwise, you may find your name referring to random cells as you move your cursor from cell to cell.

Now that we've created **Names** in three different ways, let's use **Name Manager** to edit or delete them.

Name Manager

Every name that's created within an Excel workbook will appear in the **Name Manager**, along with any **Tables** in the workbook. The Name Manager allows you to do the following task:

- Add or remove comments for **Names** or **Tables**
- Change **Names** and **Table Names**
- Change the **Refers to** field for **Names**, and **Delete Names**.

> **Tip**
>
> In *Chapter 7, Automating Tasks with the Table Feature*, I showed you how to edit and rename **Tables**, as well as how to convert a **Tables** back into a normal range of cells.

Let's walk through the **Name Manager**:

1. Choose **Formulas | Name Manager** to display the dialog box shown in *Figure 11.10*:

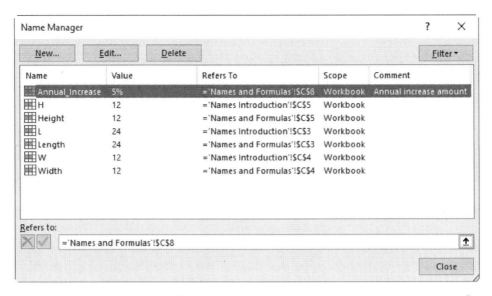

Figure 11.10 – Name Manager

2. Click **New** to display the **New Name** dialog box, which is an alternative to choosing **Formulas | Define Name**. Press *Escape* or click **Cancel** to close the **New Name** dialog box.

3. Choose any name on the list and then click **Edit** to display the **Edit Name** dialog box, as shown in *Figure 11.11*, which is identical to the **New Name** dialog box. You can edit any field except for **Scope** for **Names** – you can only edit the **Name** and **Comment** fields for **Tables**. Press *Escape* (or click **Cancel**) to close the **Edit Name** dialog box without making any changes; otherwise, press *Enter* (or click **OK**). You must delete and then recreate a name to change its scope:

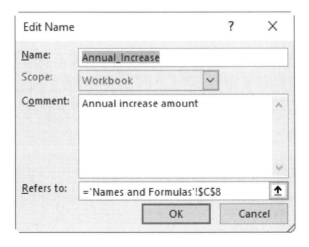

Figure 11.11 – Edit Name dialog box

> **Nuance**
>
> Fields such as **Refers to** default to **Enter** mode, which means that touching the left or right arrow keys will insert an often-unwanted cell reference instead of moving your cursor left or right. Press the *F2 (Fn + F2)* key to switch to **Edit** mode to enable navigation within the field. I discuss this concept in more detail in *Chapter 9, Excel Quirks and Nuances*.

4. Choose **Height** from the list, click the *Delete* button, and then click **Close**.
5. Notice how the formula in cell **F4** of the `Names and Formulas` worksheet returns #NAME?. This error arose because we deleted the **Height** range, which the formula still refers to. If you didn't enter a formula in cell **F4** yet, type =Height and press *Enter*, which will also return #NAME?.

> **Tip**
>
> **Names** referred to within formulas do not revert to cell references when the name is deleted. To resolve a #NAME? error that arises from deleted **Names**, you must either manually update any formulas to use cell references instead or recreate the **Names**. Note that the #NAME? error can also arise when you misspell a name or worksheet function name, or when you refer to a non-existent name or worksheet function.

6. Click on cell **C5**, type Height in the **Name Box** area, and then press *Enter*. Notice how the formula in cell **F4** now returns a proper result.

> **Tip**
>
> Any of the methods we've used to create **Names** can also be used to recreate deleted **Names**.

Now, let's return to the `Names Introduction` worksheet and see what happens when named cells are deleted:

1. Double-click cell **F3**, press *Ctrl + A* (⌘ + A) to select the entire formula, press *Ctrl + C* (⌘ + C) to copy the formula, and then press *Escape* so that you don't accidentally modify the formula.
2. Click on cell **F7** and then press *Ctrl + V* (⌘ + V) or choose **Home | Paste** to paste the formula, which should return 3,456.

> **Nuance**
>
> Copying formulas from the **Formula Bar** area, as opposed to from the cell, prevents Excel from changing the column letters and/or row numbers. Pressing *Ctrl + A* (⌘+ A) in the **Formula Bar** area is an easy way to select an entire formula.

3. Enter the =L*W*H formula in cell **F8** if needed. This formula should also return 3,456.

4. Select rows **2:5** on the `Names Introduction` worksheet and choose **Home | Delete** (or right-click on the selection and choose **Delete**).

5. The formulas that were in **F7:F8** are now in cells **F4:F5** and return #REF! because the underlying cells being referenced were deleted.

6. Choose **Formulas | Name Manager** and notice how the **Refers to** column now returns #REF! for the **L**, **H**, and **W Names**, as shown in Figure 11.12:

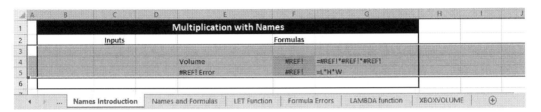

Figure 11.12 – Deleted cells cause Names to return #REF!

7. Deleting the rows removed the cells, but not the **Names**. To resolve a #REF! error related to a named cell, you can do the following:

   - Use the **Undo** command to restore the deleted cells.
   - Recreate the **Names** in a new location.
   - Delete the **Names** by way of **Name Manager**:
     - Click on a name and then click **Delete**.
     - Click the **Value** heading to group the deleted **Names**, click on the first name that you wish to remove, hold down the *Shift* key while you click on the last name, and then click **Delete**.
     - Hold down *Ctrl* (⌘), select two or more **Names**, and then click **Delete**

8. While we're here, let's finish up our tour of **Name Manager**: click the **Name** column if you have sorted on another column and wish to arrange the **Names** back into alphabetical order. You can sort **Names** based on any column heading.

9. Click the **Filter** button to filter **Names** based on their scope, error status, and type of name. Choose **Clear** from the top of this list at any point to redisplay all **Names**.

10. The **Refers to** field at the bottom of **Name Manager** enables you to edit the cell reference or data associated with a name without displaying the **Edit Name** dialog box. Click the **checkmark** button if you make any changes or click the **X** button to discard any edits that you have embarked on and then wish to discard.

11. Press *Escape* (or click **Close**) to dismiss the **Name Manager** dialog box.

> **Tip**
> If you are assiduous about naming inputs in your workbooks, **Name Manager** gives you the ability to audit the inputs from a different perspective. Many times, we get so used to seeing inputs in cells that we get tunnel vision, so being able to view the inputs from a different angle, such as an alphabetical listing, can help you find issues you may otherwise overlook.

Now, let's take another look at using **Names** within formulas.

Using **Names** within formulas

Naming cells can make formulas easier to write, as you don't necessarily have to navigate to cells to use them in formulas; you can just type the **Names** instead. Let's look at a few examples of utilizing **Names** in formulas:

1. Enter =PRODUCT(Length:Height) into cell **F5** of the Names and Formulas worksheet. This illustrates that you can specify **Names** for cells that bookend a range that you wish to refer to. The formula will return 3,456 if you enter it correctly.

2. Select cells **C3:C5**, type Dimensions into the **Name Box** area, and then press *Enter*. Now, a total of four **Names** have been assigned to cells **C3:C5**: **Length**, **Width**, **Height**, and **Dimension**.

3. In cell **F6**, type =PRODUCT(Dimensions) and press *Enter*. This illustrates that you can refer to a named range of two or more cells within a formula. This formula should also return 3,456.

4. In cell **F7**, type =PRODUCT(and then click on cell **C3**, type :, click on cell **C5**, and then type)) and press *Enter* – the resulting formula should be =PRODUCT(Length:Height), which shows how Excel automatically incorporates **Names** into formulas from cells that you select. Choosing or typing Names in cells eliminates switching between worksheets. The formula should return 3,456.

5. If you're using **Excel for Windows**, select cell **F8**, and then choose **Formulas | Use in Formula** and select **Height**, type *, choose **Use in Formula** and select **Length**, type *, choose **Use in Formula** and select **Width**, and then press *Enter*. The formula should return 3,456.

> **Tip**
> The **Use in Formula** command is unavailable when a workbook does not contain any **Names**. You cannot choose **Table Names** from the **Use in Formula** menu, but you can type **Table Names** in formulas.

As we discussed, you can create **Names** that are scoped to an entire workbook or a single worksheet. The LET function goes further by enabling us to create **Names** that are scoped to a single cell.

Introducing the LET function

The LET function requires at least one **Name**, which is known as a **Variable**. Such **Names** only work within the context of a single cell. This means that you can reuse **Variables** as much as you like, although it is best to assign **Names** to input cells that you reference repeatedly. As we have discussed, you can use the **New Name** dialog box to store a formula in a **Name**. However, such formulas are often difficult at best to use within formulas that reside in worksheet cells. Conversely, **Variables** within the LET function can contain text, numbers, or calculations that can then be referenced by **Name** in the **calculation** argument. As you'll see, this can eliminate repetitive calculations in formulas.

Cell **G3** of the LET function worksheet contains the =LET(length,C3,width,C4,height,C5,length*width*height) formula and returns 1,000. As shown in *Figure 11.13*, this is like using **Names**, but you don't have to create the **Variables** in advance – you simply add them to your formula as you write it:

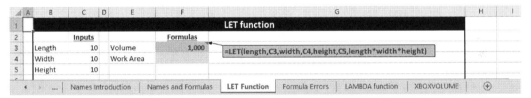

Figure 11.13 – The LET function

The LET function has the following arguments:

- Name1: This required argument **Names** a **Variable** that you will use within the formula – in this case, len. You can specify up to 126 **Names**.

> **Nuance**
>
> Excel's LEN function calculates the number of characters in a worksheet cell or string of text, but within LET, using len (or LEN) in a name argument would create a Variable that supersedes the LEN worksheet function. LET also ignores **Names** that already exist.

- name_value1: This required argument is a value or calculation to store in the Name1 **Variable** – in this case, cell **C3**. name_value arguments can be cell references, numbers, text that is enclosed in double quotes, or calculations. You can specify up to 126 name_value arguments, each of which must be paired with a **Name**.
- calculation_or_Name2: After you specify name1 and name_value1, you can either add additional name/name_value pairs or enter a calculation. So, in this context, we'll create a **Variable** named width.
- name_value2: Each **Name** must have a corresponding name_value, so in this case, we'll reference cell **C4**.

- `calculation_or_Name3`: Our third **Variable** is named `height`.
- `name_value3`: **C5** is assigned as the value of the `height` **Variable**.
- `calculation_or_Name4`: Now that all of the inputs have been named, we can specify our calculation; that is, `length*width*height`.

You may recall that we used the `=Length*Width*Height` formula in cell **F4** of the `Names and Formulas` worksheet. If you haven't changed the original inputs, that cell returns `3,456`. Conversely, the LET function returns `1,000` because the **Variables** refer to cells **C3:C5** on the `LET function` worksheet as opposed to the named cells on the `Names and Formulas` worksheet.

In a moment, we'll learn how to use LET to eliminate duplicate calculations in a formula but first, I want to compare the IFERROR and ISERROR worksheet functions.

Handling formula errors

IFERROR and ISERROR both test calculations for errors. If the calculation does not evaluate to an error, IFERROR displays the calculation result. Conversely, if the calculation evaluates to an error such as `#DIV/0!`, `#N/A`, and so on, IFERROR returns an alternate value that you specify, which can be a number, text, or calculation.

ISERROR returns TRUE if a calculation returns an error or FALSE if it does not return an error. Cell **D3** of the `Formula Errors` worksheet, as shown in *Figure 11.14*, contains the `=(C3-D3)/D3` formula. This formula returns `11%` because both cells **C3** and **D3** contain non-zero values. In cell **D4**, the `=(C4-D4)/D4` formula returns `#DIV0!` because Excel does not allow division by zero. Cell **E3** contains the `=D4` formula, which also returns `#DIV/0!` because of the cascade effects that # errors cause in Excel. The IFERROR function is a modern approach to managing such errors:

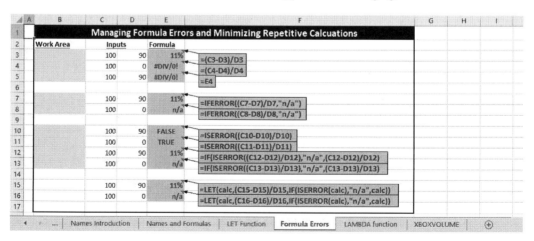

Figure 11.14 – Formula error handling

Now, let's delve further into `IFERROR`.

The IFERROR function

Cell **D7** of the `Formula Errors` worksheet, as shown in *Figure 11.14*, contains the =IFERROR((C7-D7)/D7,"n/a") formula and returns 11%. Conversely, cell **D8** contains the =IFERROR((C7-D7)/D7,"n/a") formula and returns n/a because cell **D8** contains a zero.

The `IFERROR` function has two arguments:

- `value`: This is a calculation that could return any sort of # sign error in Excel, such as #DIV/0!, #NAME?, #CALC!, and so on. In cell **E7**, `IFERROR` returns 11% because (C7-D7)/D7 does not evaluate to an error.
- `value_if_error`: This is an alternate value or calculation to return when the `value` argument returns an error. Cell **D8** displays n/a because (C8-D8)/D8 does evaluate to an error.

> **Tip**
> A downside of `IFERROR` is that it masks all errors, which can muddy the waters when unexpected errors arise. In **Excel 2013** and later, `IFNA` only masks #N/A errors but displays all other errors, such as #REF!, which arises when you delete a cell that a formula refers to.

If you've been using Excel for 15 years or more, you may recall a time when the `IFERROR` function did not exist. Back then, error handling often involved using the `IF` and `ISERROR` functions together.

The ISERROR function

Cell **E10** of the `Formula Errors` worksheet contains the =ISERROR((C10-D10)/D10) formula and returns **FALSE** because (C10-D10)/D10 does not evaluate to an error. Conversely, cell **E11** contains the =ISERROR((C11-D11)/D11) formula and returns **TRUE** because (C11-D11)/D11 does evaluate to an error.

> **Nuance**
> The `ISERR` function is like `ISERROR` with one exception: it does not consider #N/A to be an error. Always make sure that you use `ISERROR` instead of `ISERR` if there's any chance that an #N/A error can arise in a calculation that you're testing.

Cell **E12** contains the =IF(ISERROR((C12-D12)/D12),"n/a",(C12-D12)/D12) formula and returns 11%. Cell **E13** contains the =IF(ISERROR((C13-D13)/D13),"n/a",(C13-D13)/D13) formula and returns n/a.

I offer this as a simple example of how repetitive calculations such as (C13-D13)/D13, which appears twice in cell **E13**, can creep into our formulas. IFERROR was added to Excel to eliminate repetitive calculations when handling formula errors, but there are countless ways that we can find ourselves repeating a chunk of a formula more than once. It's always tricky trying to make the same edit in multiple places in a formula, if you miss just *one* spot, then you can have an error in your formula that could affect other cells as well. This brings us back to the LET function.

Eliminating repetitive calculations

Cell **E15** of the Formula Errors worksheet contains the =LET(calc,(C15-D15)/D15,IF(ISERROR(calc),"n/a",calc)) formula and returns 11% because (C15-D15)/D15 does not evaluate to an error. Let's break the formula down:

- Name1: This argument establishes a calc Variable that we can use later in the formula.

- name_value1: This argument contains the repetitive part of our calculation, (C15-D15)/D15, which we will be able to refer to by the calc **Variable** rather than repeating the calculation twice.

- Name2_or_calculation: Since we only need one **Variable**, the third argument contains the IF(ISERROR(calc),"n/a",calc) calculation. Now, (C15-D15)/D15 only appears once in the formula but is used twice. This means that if we need to edit the formula, we only need to do so in one place.

If you're following along in column **B**, you can copy the formula you entered in cell **B15** down to cell **B16** without making any edits.

> **Tip**
> The LET function will return #NAME? in **Excel 2019** and earlier. In *Chapter 9, Excel Quirks and Nuances*, I explained how you can use **Compatibility Checker** to determine if a worksheet utilizes any worksheet functions or features that are not backward compatible with older versions of Excel.

Now, let's create a third calculation using LET so that I can elaborate further on how **Variables** work.

Variables restrictions

Let's return to the LET function worksheet, as shown *Figure 11.15*, so that I can show you how to establish **Variables** in the LET function without using them in your calculation:

Introducing the LET function

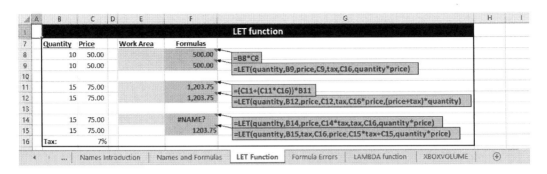

Figure 11.15 – The LET function's calculations

Cell **F8** contains the =B8*C8 formula, which multiplies the quantity in cell **B8** by the price in **C8** to give you a frame of reference. Cell **F9** of the LET function worksheet contains the =LET(quantity,B8,price,C8,tax,B15,quantity*price) formula. In this case, the tax **Variable** is created but not referenced in the *calculation* argument. **Variables** can make formulas easier to audit since each input can be labeled, but does not have to be, as you can incorporate as many unnamed cell references as you wish.

Let's walk through the remaining formulas on the LET function worksheet:

- Cell **F11** contains the =(C11+(C11*C16))*B11 formula, which returns 1,203.75. Cell **C11** contains the price, which the formula references individually and then a second time so that the price is multiplied by the tax rate, all of which is then multiplied by the quantity in cell **B11**.

- Cell **F12** contains the =LET(quantity,B9,price,C9,tax,B15*price, (price+tax)*quantity) formula, which also returns 1,203.75. This illustrates that one **Variable** can reference another when working from left to right. In this case, the quantity **Variable** refers to cell **B12**, price refers to **C12**, and tax multiplies cell **C16** by the price **Variable**. The *calculation* argument adds price and tax together and then multiplies the result by quantity.

> **Tip**
> I am fond of selecting all or part of a formula inside a cell or the formula bar and then pressing *F9 (Fn + F9)* to display the underlying value. For this to work you must select an entire cell reference or a calculation within the formula. Be sure to press *Escape* or *Ctrl + Z (⌘ + Z)* to undo your changes so that you don't embed a hard-coded value into your formula. You can undo up to 100 actions in an Excel worksheet, but only *one* action in the **Formula Bar**. Also, the LET function does not support this technique: Excel will return #NAME? instead of the calculation result if you select (price+tax)*quantity in cell **F12** and then press *F9 (Fn + F9)*. You can, however, use **Formulas | Evaluate Formula** to debug LET functions that return an unexpected result.

- Cell **F14** contains the `=LET(quantity,B14,price,C14*tax+C14,tax,C16,quantity*price)` formula, which returns #NAME? because I referred to the `tax` **Variable** before it was established, which broke the left-to-right convention. In this case, `quantity` refers to cell **B14**, `price` refers to cell **C14** multiplied by `tax` plus **C14**, and then `tax` refers to cell **C16**. The *calculation* argument multiplies `quantity` by `price`. The #NAME? error is caused by `price` referring to `tax` *before* an amount was assigned to the `tax` **Variable**.
- Cell **F15** contains the `=LET(quantity,B15,tax,C16,price,C15*tax+C15,quantity*price)` formula, which returns `1,203.75`. Notice that simply changing the order of the **Variables**, meaning creating the `tax` **Variable** before the `price` **Variable**, resolves the #NAME? error that arose in cell **F14**.

As you can see, things can get tricky with LET, which is why I've stuck with simple calculations. LET opens many possibilities for documenting formulas and improving spreadsheet integrity by eliminating repetitive calculations. Now, let's see how we can use the LAMBDA function to create custom worksheet formulas that are based on mashups of built-in worksheet functions—without using any programming code.

Introducing the LAMBDA function

Before the advent of LAMBDA, creating custom worksheet functions in Excel required writing programming code, such as with Visual Basic for Applications in Excel or by using other languages to create add-ins for Excel. You'll be relieved, and perhaps even amazed, to know that, you don't need any programming experience to use LAMBDA. The ability to write formulas in Excel and an understanding of defining **Names** are all that you need to create custom worksheet functions with LAMBDA.

> **Tip**
> JavaScript-based worksheet functions can be created in **Microsoft 365**, **Excel 2021**, and **Excel for Web**.

LAMBDA functions can get wildly complex as you can create recursive formulas where a LAMBDA function refers to itself more than once, akin to a circular reference, as discussed in *Chapter 9, Excel Quirks and Nuances*. I do not have space to dive deep into LAMBDA, which means I won't create any recursive formulas, but I can give you a running start with creating custom worksheet functions.

Developing a LAMBDA formula

The LAMBDA function has **Parameters** that are like the **Variables** we used in LET, along with a **calculation** argument. The difference is **Parameters** are not embedded inside the function like they were with LET. Instead, **Parameters** function like the arguments in most Excel functions, where you enter cell references or inputs in a prescribed order into the function. You are not required to have any

Parameters, although generally, you will want to have at least one. As you'll see later in this chapter, you can create optional **Parameters** that the user can opt to omit when using the LAMDBA function.

There are four stages to creating a worksheet function with LAMBDA:

- Use the LAMBDA function to name the **Parameters** and define the calculation
- Evaluate the LAMBDA function by making a function call that provides the specified inputs
- Formalize the LAMBDA function by assigning a **Name**
- Use the LAMBDA function in the same fashion as you would any built-in worksheet function

Let's work through the first stage.

Naming Parameters and defining the calculation

Cell **F3** of the LAMBDA Function worksheet, as shown in *Figure 11.16*, contains the =LAMBDA(length,width,height,length*height*width) formula and returns #CALC! because no inputs have been provided, meaning I didn't add a function call yet:

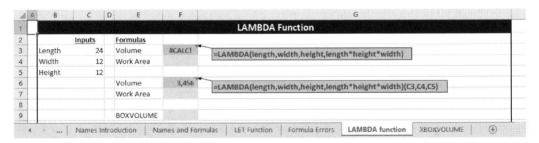

Figure 11.16 – The LAMBDA function

The LAMBDA function can have as little as one argument, but will generally have two or more:

- parameter: This optional argument contains information that you want to pass to the function, such as a cell reference, number, or text. The formula in cell **F3** has three **Parameters**: length, width, and height. You can enter up to 253 **Parameters**.
- calculation: This required argument must always be the last one in the formula and represents a formula that you want to calculate. As with LET, you may think of this as a formula within a formula. If you don't provide a **Parameter**, then calculation will be the first argument.

> **Tip**
> You can designate **Parameters** as optional by enclosing the **Name** in square brackets, such as [parameter]. Then, you can use the ISOMITTED function in the calculation argument to determine whether the **Parameter** was provided or not.

As with the LET function, having **Names** that overlap with our **Parameters** does not pose a conflict. The fourth argument, `length*height*width`, represents the calculation that we want the LAMBDA function to perform.

The second stage of writing a LAMBDA function involves passing inputs to the formula.

Evaluating a LAMBDA function

Cell **F6** on the `LAMBDA function` worksheet contains the `=LAMBDA(length, width,height,length*height*width)(C3,C4,C5)` formula and returns `3,456`. In this case, the `(C3,C4,C5)` portion of the formula is a **function call** that enables us to evaluate our formula by passing values from cells **C3**, **C4**, and **C5** to the LAMBDA function for evaluation:

- **C3** corresponds to the `length` **Parameter**
- **C4** corresponds to the `width` **Parameter**
- **C5** corresponds to the `height` **Parameter**

> **Tip**
> As with all Excel's built-in worksheet functions, you must pass the **Parameters** through in the prescribed order, which you designate in the first stage of creating the LAMBDA function.

Since the **Parameters** are all filled, the LAMBDA function can return a result. If you omit a **Parameter**, the LAMBDA function will return #VALUE! unless you mark the **Parameter** as optional.

Now that we have a functional LAMBDA formula, the next step is to make the formula reusable.

Creating reusable LAMBDA functions

We will now use the **Define Name** command to create a range name associated with our LAMBDA function. However, instead of referencing a specific cell, the **Name** will become a new worksheet function in Excel named BOXVOLUME:

1. Double-click on cell **F3** and press *Ctrl + A* (⌘ + A) to select the entire formula. Then, press *Ctrl + C* (⌘ + C) (or right-click on the selection and choose **Copy**).

> **Tip**
> Make sure that you do not include function calls such as `(C3,C4,C5)` in cell **G6** when copying the LAMBDA function to the clipboard. Function calls allow you to test the formula before formalizing it with a **Name**. Also, you cannot copy a cell that contains LAMBDA; however, you edit the formula by double-clicking on the cell or clicking into the **Formula Bar** area and then copying the formula.

2. Choose **Insert | Define Name** (or **Formulas | Name Manager | New**).
3. Enter BOXVOLUME in the **Name** field, as shown in *Figure 11.17*:

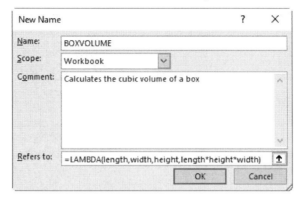

Figure 11.17 – Formalizing LAMBDA into a custom worksheet function

> **Nuance**
>
> I recommend using all caps to name your function for consistency with Excel's built-in functions, but you can use title case or mixed case, such as BoxVolume or even bOxVoLuMe.

4. *Important:* Make sure that the **Scope** field is set to **Workbook**.
5. Enter Calculates the cubic volume of a box in the **Comment** field. Any information you put in the **Comment** field will appear as a **ScreenTip** when you type enough characters of the function's **Name** in a worksheet cell for **AutoComplete** to match the **Name**.
6. Erase the contents of the **Refers to** field and paste in the formula that you copied in *step 1*.
7. Click **OK** to create your new custom worksheet function.
8. Type =BOX in cell **F9** and notice how the function name appears, along with a **ScreenTip** if you filled in the **Comment** field in *step 5*, as shown in *Figure 11.18*:

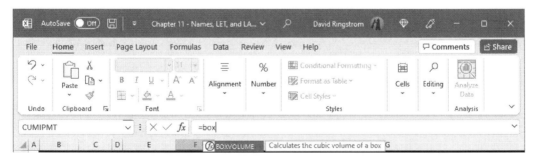

Figure 11.18 – Formula documentation ScreenTip

9. Press the *Tab* key to fill out the rest of the function name. Notice that the **Parameters** appear in a new **ScreenTip**, as shown in *Figure 11.19*:

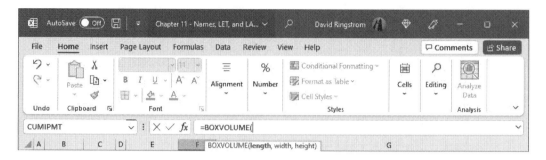

Figure 11.19 – Parameter ScreenTip

10. Enter C3,C4,C5 along with closing parenthesis, and then press *Enter*. The formula should return 3,456.

You can now use the BOXVOLUME function anywhere in the workbook where you created the LAMBDA function, plus you can transfer it to other workbooks.

Moving LAMBDA functions between workbooks

You can transfer LAMBDA functions to other workbooks by copying cells or copying worksheets. Let's begin by copying a cell that uses our BOXVOLUME function:

1. Copy cell **F9** of the LAMBDA function worksheet, which should contain a functional BOXVOLUME formula.

2. Press *Ctrl + N* (⌘ + N) and choose **File | New | Blank Workbook** to create a new workbook or open an existing workbook.

3. Press *Enter* (or choose **Home | Paste**) to paste the BOXVOLUME formula into any worksheet cell, which, depending on where you paste, will return 0 or #REF!.

4. Choose **Formulas | Name Manager** to confirm that BOXVOLUME appears, as shown in *Figure 11.20*:

Figure 11.20 – BOXVOLUME transferred to another workbook

> **Nuance**
> Any comment that you enter in the **New Name** or **Edit Name** dialog box does not transfer to the new workbook when you copy and paste the formula in this fashion. #VALUE! appears in the **Value** column of **Name Manager** because the function does not have any **Parameter** values passed through in this context. This error is to be expected and does not signify that your LAMBDA function is broken or damaged. That determination gets made in a worksheet cell.

A second way to transfer LAMBDA functions is to copy a worksheet that utilizes one or more LAMBDA functions to another workbook:

1. Right-click on the LAMBDA function worksheet and then choose **Move or Copy** (or activate the LAMBDA function worksheet and choose **Home | Format | Move or Copy Sheet**).

2. Choose **(new book)** from the **To book** list or choose workbook from the list.

3. Click the **Create a copy** checkbox so that you don't inadvertently move the worksheet, and then click **OK**.

4. Choose **Formulas | Name Manager** to confirm that your LAMBDA functions are available in the workbook, as shown in *Figure 11.21*:

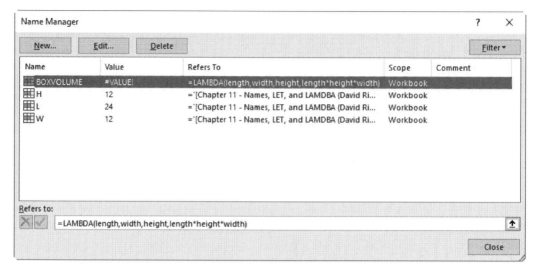

Figure 11.21 – Copying sheets to other workbooks can inadvertently copy Names

5. Optional: Delete any **Names** that have been assigned to worksheet cells that were carried over to the new workbook, as shown in *Figure 11.21*. Otherwise, you will encounter the dreaded **This workbook contains links** prompt every time you open the workbook that you copied the worksheets to. Note that the H, L, and W **Names** were assigned to a different worksheet than what we copied, and yet Excel arbitrarily copied the **Names** over anyway.

> **Tip**
> You can keep the worksheet you copied in the new workbook or delete the sheet. The LAMBDA functions will remain available either way.

Now that you have seen how to create LAMBDA functions, let's dig further into some of the details.

Going deeper with LAMBDA functions

At this point, I've only covered the tip of the iceberg with LAMBDA, but I do have space to delve a bit further. First, we'll look at incorporating optional arguments into LAMBDA functions. After that, I'll detail some of the errors and conflicts that can arise when creating and using LAMBDA functions. Then, I'll introduce the free **Advanced Formula Environment**, which offers a programming interface for creating complex LAMBDA functions. We'll also create an XBOXVOLUME custom worksheet function that allows you to pass a two-column, three-row block of cells to the LAMBDA function, which will convert any measurements in feet into inches before computing the cubic volume of a box.

Optional LAMBDA Parameters

Cell **F11** of the LAMBDA function worksheet, as shown in *Figure 11.22*, contains the =LAMBDA(quantity,price,[tax],(price+IF(ISOMITTED(tax),0,price*tax))*quantity) formula, which has an optional [tax] **Parameter**, as indicated by the square brackets:

	A	B	C	D	E	F	G
1						**LAMBDA Function**	
2			Inputs		Formulas		
3		Length	24		Volume	#CALC!	=LAMBDA(length,width,height,length*height*width)
4		Width	12		Work Area		
5		Height	12				
6					Volume	3,456	=LAMBDA(length,width,height,length*height*width)(C3,C4,C5)
7					Work Area		
8							
9					BOXVOLUME	3,456	=BOXVOLUME(C3,C4,C5)
10		Quantity	Price				
11		10	100.00		PRICE	#CALC!	=LAMBDA(quantity,price,[tax],(price+IF(ISOMITTED(tax),0,price*tax))*quantity)
12		10	100.00		PRICE	1,000	=LAMBDA(quantity,price,[tax],(price+IF(ISOMITTED(tax),0,price*tax))*quantity)(B12,C12)
13		10	100.00		PRICE	1,070	=LAMBDA(quantity,price,[tax],(price+IF(ISOMITTED(tax),0,price*tax))*quantity)(B13,C13,C14)
14		Tax	7%				

Figure 11.22 – Optional [tax] Parameter and ISOMITTED

The formula also uses the ISOMITTED function, which returns TRUE if the **Parameter** being tested was not provided, or FALSE if the **Parameter** is specified. This calculation is like what we carried out with the LET function. The calculation argument for the LAMBDA function takes the price **Parameter** and determines if tax should be calculated or not. If no tax **Parameter** is provided, the IF function returns 0; otherwise, it multiplies price by tax. The result that IF returns is added to price multiplied by quantity.

Cell **F12** adds a function call of (B12,C12) that passes B12 to quantity and C12 to price, but omits tax, so the formula returns 1,000.

Cell **F13** adds a function call of (B13, C13,C14) that passes **B13**, **C13**, and **C14** to quantity, price, and tax, respectively, so the formula adds tax and returns 1,070.

The IF function in these formulas illustrates how to incorporate existing Excel worksheet functions into LAMBDA. Simply create a **Parameter** for every argument that an existing worksheet function requires, plus any other inputs that you want to include.

Now, let's see what happens if you assign the **Name** of an existing worksheet function to a LAMBDA function.

LAMDBA conflicts and errors

The LAMBDA function opens an endless array of possibilities in Excel, but only for users with **Microsoft 365**. If someone opens a workbook that uses one or more LAMBDA functions in **Excel 2021** or earlier, the formulas will return #NAME? because other Excel versions cannot recognize your LAMBDA as a valid function.

> **Tip**
> LAMBDA does work in **Excel for the web** (http://www.office.com), which only requires a free Microsoft account for access. At the time of writing, the **Define Name** and **Name Manager** commands are not offered in **Excel for the web**, so you cannot use that platform to create LAMBDA functions. However, you can use existing functions.

Let's formalize the LAMBDA function in cell **F11** into a worksheet function named PRICE to see if a conflict arises with the built-in PRICE function in Excel, which is used to calculate prices for securities:

1. Double-click on cell **F11** and press *Ctrl + A* (⌘ + *A*) to select the entire formula. Then, press *Ctrl + C* (⌘ + *C*) (or right-click on the selection and choose **Copy**).
2. Choose **Insert | Define Name** (or **Formulas | Name Manager | New**).
3. Enter PRICE in the **Name** field, as shown in *Figure 11.23*:

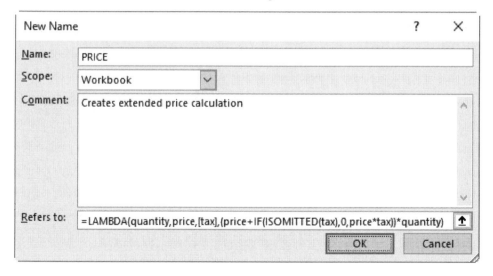

Figure 11.23 – Creating a LAMBDA function named PRICE

4. Important: Make sure that the **Scope** field is set to **Workbook**.
5. Enter `Creates extended price calculation` in the **Comment** field.
6. Erase the contents of the **Refers to** field and paste in the formula that you copied in *step 1*.

7. Click **OK** to create the custom worksheet function.
8. Type =PRICE in cell **F14** and notice how the **AutoComplete** menu displays the PRICE function twice. No matter which one you choose, Excel will default to the built-in PRICE function. You cannot override built-in Excel functions as it would wreak havoc in spreadsheets if you could. Press *Escape* to discard your edits to cell **F14**.
9. Choose **Formulas | Name Manager**, select **PRICE**, and then click **Edit**.
10. Erase the **Name** field, enter EXTEND, click **OK**, and then **Close**.
11. Now, you can use the EXTEND function to calculate extended prices.

> **Tip**
> To avoid conflicts such as this, type =PROPOSEDNAME in a blank worksheet cell, where PROPOSEDNAME is the **Name** that you're considering for your LAMBDA function. If no matches appear in the **AutoComplete** menu, your LAMBDA name is fair game.

Here's an overview of other errors that can arise:

- As you saw in *Figure 11.16*, LAMBDA returns #CALC! if you enter the function into a worksheet cell without including a function call.
- LAMBDA functions will return #NAME? if you misspell a **Parameter** name within the calculation argument or refer to a **Parameter** that does not exist.
- LAMBDA functions will also return #NAME? if you select the calculation argument in the **Formula Bar** area and then press *F9*, as discussed in the *Variables restrictions* section earlier in this chapter. You can use **Formulas | Evaluate formula** to debug LAMBDA functions that include function calls.
- LAMBDA functions return #VALUE! if you pass an incorrect number of **Parameters**.
- Circular references within a LAMBDA, as opposed to recursive, will return #NUM!.
- Although you can use periods in range **Names**, you cannot use periods in LAMBDA function **Parameter**.

Removing a LAMBDA function from a workbook is as simple as deleting a **Name**:

1. Choose **Formulas | Name Manager**.
2. Click on the **Name** of the LAMBDA function and then click **Delete**.
3. Press *Escape* (or click **Close**) to dismiss the **Name Manager** dialog box.

Any formulas in the workbook that use a LAMBDA function that has been deleted will return #NAME?. If you get frustrated using the **New Name** and **Edit Name** dialog boxes to create and edit LAMBDA functions, I have a solution for you.

The Advanced Formula Environment add-in

Advanced Formula Environment is a free add-in that Microsoft developed that gives you a much better environment for viewing and editing LAMBDA functions. Here's how to add it to your version of Excel:

1. Click **Insert** which unlike add-ins such as **Inquire** that I discuss in Chapter 9, Excel Quirks and Nuances, is available in **Excel for macOS**.
2. Type **Advanced** in the **Search** field and then press *Enter*.
3. Click the **Add** button next to **Advanced Formula Environment** shown in the *figure 11.24*:

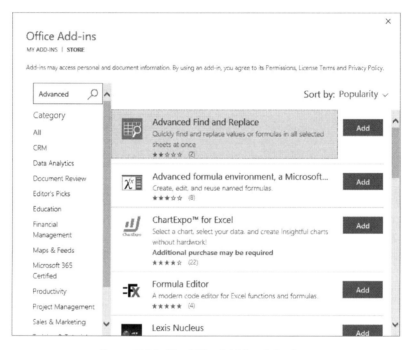

Figure 11.24 – The Office Add-ins dialog box

> **Nuance**
> Add-ins that you add in this fashion are associated with your Microsoft account. If you use Excel on two or more computers, then on your second computer, you can choose **Get Add-ins** and click **MY ADD-INS** in the top left-hand corner. You may need to click **Refresh** in the top right-hand corner to see the add-ins that you've added from your other computers.

Going deeper with LAMBDA functions 355

4. Click **Continue** on the confirmation prompt that appears.
5. Click **Got it** to confirm that the **Advanced Formula Environment** command appears on the **Home** tab of Excel's ribbon.
6. Choose **Home | Advanced Formula Environment** to display a task pane that has **Manager** and **Editor** views. As shown in *Figure 11.25*, the **Manager** view displays a card for each LAMBDA and named range in the active workbook:

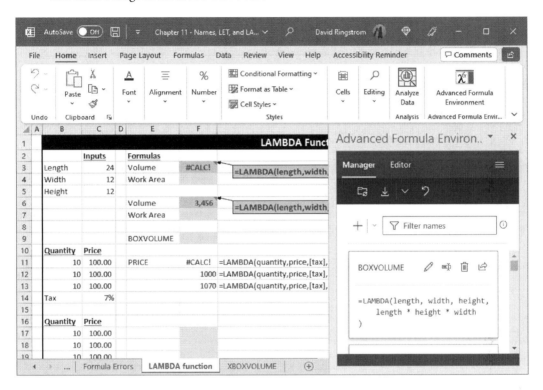

Figure 11.25 – The Advanced Formula Environment Manager view

The **Editor** tab includes a programming interface through which you can spread your LAMBDA out over multiple rows, as shown in *Figure 11.26*. Comments can be enclosed between /* and */, as shown, and you can press *Enter* as needed to spread the formula out for easier comprehension:

Names, LET, and LAMBDA

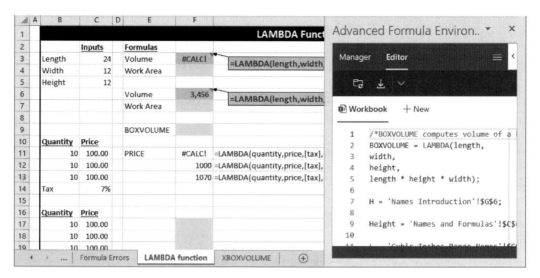

Figure 11.26 – The Advanced Formula Editor view

> **Tip**
> If you don't find **Advanced Formula Environment** helpful, you can remove it by choosing **Insert | My Add-ins**, clicking the three-dot menu for **Advanced formula environment**, and then choosing **Remove**.

Now, let's see how to create a LAMBDA by way of **Advanced Formula Environment Manager**.

The XBOXVOLUME function

Cell **G3** of the XBOXVOLUME worksheet contains the formula =LAMBDA(range, INDEX(range, 1,1)*IF(INDEX(range,1,2)="feet",12,1)*INDEX(range,2,1)*IF(INDEX(range,2,2)="feet",12,1)*INDEX(range,3,1)*IF(INDEX(range,3,2)="feet",12,1))(C3:D5). This formula can calculate the volume of a box based on feet or inches when you specify a six-cell range that is two columns wide and three rows tall.

Let's use **Advanced Formula Environment** to add a new LAMBDA to our workbook based upon this formula:

1. Copy the formula from cell **G3** of the XBOXVOLUME worksheet, except for the (C3:D5) function call at the end and the equals sign (=) at the beginning.

> **Nuance**
>
> When using the **Define Name** command to create a LAMBDA function, you must include the equals (=) sign at the start of the formula. When using **Advanced Formula Environment**, you must *omit* the equal sign (=). In both cases, you'll also omit any **Parameters** that you have included in parentheses at the end of the formula.

2. Click the plus sign (+) button on the **Manager** view of **Advanced Formula Environment**.

> **Nuance**
>
> You can click the plus (+) sign on the **Editor** view of **Advanced Formula Environment** as well. The screen will prompt you to enter a **Name** for your function and then click **Add**. After that, you can paste your LAMBDA function into one or more rows in the editor.

3. Enter a **Name**, such as XBOXVOLUME, in the **Formula name** field, as shown in the following screenshot:

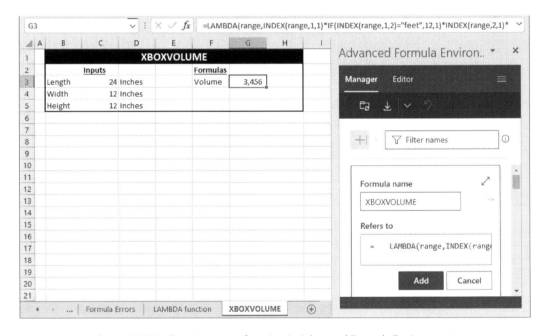

Figure 11.27 – Creating a new function in Advanced Formula Environment

4. Paste the formula from *step 1* into the **Refers to** field.
5. Click **Add** to create the new function.
6. Click the **Sync** button, which is represented by two arrows or a folder icon, on the toolbar of **Advanced Formula Environment**.

> **Nuance**
>
> New functions that you create in **Advanced Formula Environment** are not available for use in Excel until you click the **Sync** button to synchronize the **Names** with Excel's **Name Manager**. After you click the **Sync** button for the first time, the icon will change from two arced arrows into a folder with two smaller arced arrows. Similarly, if you delete a LAMBDA function by way of **Advanced Formula Environment**, the custom function will remain available in your workbook's **Name Manager** until you click the **Sync** button.

LAMBDA represents the future of custom worksheet functions in Excel, which I think you will appreciate further when you see one of the previous leading methods was used to create custom worksheet functions prior to the LAMBDA function.

Custom VBA worksheet functions

VBA is short for **Visual Basic for Applications**, which is the programming language that you can use in **Excel for Windows** and **Excel for macOS** to create macros and custom worksheet functions known as **user-defined functions**. Over the years, I've made a few half-hearted attempts to learn other programming languages, but I never got any traction because I find the ability to program in Excel to be practically limitless, at least for my purposes. With that said, I do write much less code these days, thanks to **Power Query**, which I will discuss in the next chapter.

> **Tip**
>
> **Excel for the web** does not support Visual Basic for Applications, which means you cannot even *open* workbooks that contain macros on that platform.

The Chapter 11 - BOX_VOLUME and XBOX_VOLUME.xlsm workbook already has the programming code installed for two user-defined worksheet functions. You may encounter the security warning shown in *Figure 11.28*, which means you won't be able to access the macros in this workbook in **Excel for Windows** until you unblock the file:

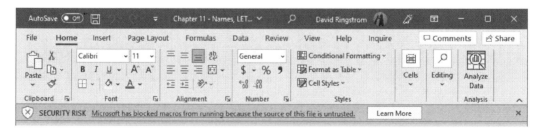

Figure 11.28 – Blocked macros security warning

Here's how to unblock the file:

1. Close the `Chapter 11 - BOX_VOLUME and XBOX_VOLUME.xlsm` workbook.
2. Use **File Explorer** to navigate to the folder where you saved the workbook.
3. Right-click on the file and choose **Properties**.
4. As shown in *Figure 11.29*, click **Unblock** and then click **OK**:

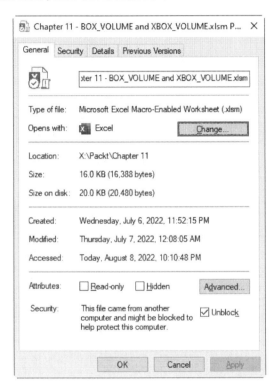

Figure 11.29 – The Microsoft Windows File Properties dialog box

5. Open the workbook and then click **Enable Content** when prompted if you want to be able to try the custom worksheet functions.

Here's how to test the functions:

1. Enter `=BOX_VOLUME(C3,C4,C5)` in cell **G3** of the `User-Defined Functions` worksheet. The formula should return `3,456`.

> **Nuance**
> Custom worksheet functions written in VBA do not offer the **ScreenTip** functionality offered by `LAMBDA`, so you'll have to remember which arguments to enter, and in what order.

2. Enter =XBOX_VOLUME(C8:D10) in cell **G8** of the User-Defined Functions worksheet. The formula should return 3,456.

You should find that both functions work in the same fashion as the LAMBDA functions. Both functions have an underscore in their name to distinguish them from the LAMBDA functions.

Now, let's learn how to create the BOX_VOLUME function in VBA, which, unlike the LAMBDA function, will work in any version of **Excel for Windows** or **Excel for macOS**. The function name includes an underscore to distinguish it from the LAMBDA-based function we created in the previous section. Here are the steps:

1. Erase cells **G3** and **G8**.
2. Choose **Home | Format | Move or Copy Sheet** (or right-click on the **Worksheet** tab and then choose **Move or Copy**).
3. Choose **(new book)** from the **To book** list.
4. Click the **Create a copy** checkbox so that you don't inadvertently move the worksheet.
5. Click **OK** to move a copy of the worksheet to a new workbook.
6. Press *Alt + F11 (Option + F11)* to display Excel's **Visual Basic Editor** or choose **Developer | Visual Basic** if you have enabled the **Developer** tab in Excel's ribbon.
7. Choose **Insert | Module** within **Visual Basic Editor**.
8. Enter the following programming code into the module sheet:

   ```
   Function BOX_VOLUME(length, height, width)
   BOX_VOLUME = length * height * width
   End Function
   ```

9. Activate the User-Defined Functions worksheet in your new workbook.
10. Enter =BOX_VOLUME(C3,C4,C5) in cell **G3**.

If cells **C3**, **C4**, and **C5** contain valid amounts, and you specify all three arguments, the BOX_VOLUME function will compute the amounts; otherwise, it will return #VALUE!. In this case, length, height, and width are **Variables** that are used to store data used by the function. The words Function and End Function inform Excel that this segment of code is a calculation as opposed to a subroutine that would carry out a task. Subroutines can carry out calculations as well, but only when the macro is triggered, whereas functions recalculate automatically.

Granted, this is a simplistic worksheet function that is on par with using LET. VBA opens a whole world of possibilities, such as a worksheet function that you can pass a range of cells to, as we did with LAMBDA.

> **Nuance**
>
> Workbooks that contain user-defined functions must be saved as **macro-enabled workbooks** (.XLSM files); otherwise, the programming code that you added for the custom function will be discarded. This also means that you'll need to enable macros each time you open the workbook. I discussed how to suppress this prompt in *Chapter 2, Disaster Recovery and File-Related Prompts*.

The `Chapter 11 - BOX_VOLUME and XBOX_VOLUME.xlsm` workbook also contains the programming code for the `XBOX_VOLUME` function. The following steps will enable you to see the programming code for that function. You can use these steps whenever you want to edit a function that you have created:

1. Press *Alt + F11 (Option + F11)* to display Excel's **Visual Basic Editor** or choose **Developer | Visual Basic**.
2. Choose **View | Project Explorer** or press *Ctrl + R (Ctrl + ⌘ + R)*.
3. Expand the corresponding **VBAProject** for `Chapter 11 - BOX_VOLUME and XBOX_VOLUME.xlsm`, and then expand the `Modules` folder within.
4. Double-click on the `modBOX_VOLUME` module sheet to display the programming code. You can edit the function if you wish.

> **Tip**
>
> To remove a custom worksheet function written in VBA, select the programming code starting from the word `Function` down through `End Function` and then press **Delete**. Another approach is to choose **File | Save As** and save the workbook as an **Excel Workbook**, as opposed to a **Macro-Enabled Workbook**. Keep in mind that doing so will remove *all* Visual Basic programming code from the workbook, not just custom functions.

In this chapter, I was only able to give you a small nudge in the direction of using LAMBDA and VBA functions but hopefully, you can see the immense power that custom functions can bring. LAMBDA functions have the potential to make complex calculations in Excel far more accessible for countless spreadsheet users without them requiring any knowledge of programming code. Furthermore, LAMBDA functions can empower more users to harness Excel's power because performing complex calculations can become as simple as passing a few **Parameters** to a pre-written LAMBDA function.

Summary

This chapter led you down a path that started with computing the cubic volume of a box with simple multiplication. Then, we layered on more and more complexity as we made our way to the LET and LAMBDA functions. The phrase *game-changing* often feels trite, but if you write complex formulas in Excel, both LET and LAMBDA empower you to write formulas today that you won't cringe at when you see them again in the future. I've thought *"what planet was I on that day?"* more than a few times throughout my career when revisiting formulas that span multiple rows in the **Formula Bar** area.

We made several stops, including visiting functions such as PRODUCT, IF, CHOOSE, and SWITCH. I included these because of similarities in how you can pass information to the functions, or swap information around as stepping-stones toward LET and LAMBDA. From there, we embarked on creating **Names**, partly to correlate the similarities between the LET and LAMBDA functions, but also because **Names** are how we formalize LAMBDA into custom worksheet functions. Apart from that, **Names** create built-in navigation aids and streamline formula writing and auditing.

One of the biggest benefits of LET and LAMBDA is the ability to eliminate repetitive segments in formulas. I feel like LET offers the easiest approach, which is to store the repetitive calculation in a **Variable** that you then reference in the *calculation* argument as needed. LAMBDA functions do require you to spell out repetitive calculations each time you need them in the calculation, but you only need to think about it when creating the LAMBDA function. Once you formalize the LAMBDA function with a **Name**, the repetitive calculations occur in the background without being seen, so you can simply focus on passing the correct inputs through to the custom worksheet function. I didn't have enough pages to explore it, but you can use LET within a LAMBDA function and then have the best of both worlds.

Now that we have LAMBDA at our disposal, the final section in this chapter feels more like a "*not that would, but you could*" kind of thing. If you don't have any programming experience, creating custom worksheet functions with VBA can feel like walking into the water at a beach and suddenly finding yourself in deep water. I included that section partly as an homage to Excel's past, but primarily to draw a sharp contrast with how empowering LAMBDA feels for modern Excel users.

In the next chapter, we will explore **Power Query**, which enables you to connect your Excel workbooks to a variety of data sources, including Excel workbooks, text files, PDF files, databases, and more.

12
Power Query

In a book about nuances and quirks in Excel, I have saved what I consider to be the most nuanced and quirky feature for last: **Power Query**. I can attest that I picked up and sat down with **Power Query** multiple times over a series of months before it finally *clicked* for me. This feature has been around for 10 years, yet most Excel users are unaware of its immense potential.

In this chapter, my goal is to help you use **Power Query** to automate repetitive processes without writing any programming code. I only have room to share a few examples with you, but along the way, I'll point out a variety of obstacles and timesavers that will jumpstart your effectiveness. If you find this chapter whets your appetite, **Power Query** *Cookbook*, by Andrea Janicijevic, is a comprehensive resource that goes far beyond what I had space to share here.

In this chapter, we will cover the following topics:

- Introducing **Power Query**
- Creating a list of worksheets
- Automatic report cleanup
- Extracting data from PDF files
- Unpivoting data
- Appending and merging data from multiple sources
- Connecting to databases and installing ODBC drivers

Technical requirements

You will have the best experience in **Power Query** if you're using **Microsoft 365** or **Excel 2021**, but most of what I will share can be conducted in **Excel 2010** and later. At the time of writing, **Power Query** is in beta testing for **Microsoft 365** users of **Excel for macOS**. Anyone using **Excel 2010** or **Excel 2013** will need to download and install the free **Power Query** add-in. You can access **Power Query** in Excel 2016 by way of **Data** | **New Query** instead of **Data** | **Get Data**, which you must do in **Excel 2019** and later. **Microsoft 365** or **Excel 2021** is required to extract data from PDF files. The workbooks, PDF file, and text files that I used in this chapter can be downloaded from GitHub at `https://github.com/PacktPublishing/Exploring-Microsoft-Excels-Hidden-Treasures/tree/main/Chapter12`.

Introducing Power Query

Each time you use **Power Query**, you will work through a series of at least three, and sometimes as many as five, phases:

- **Connecting**: **Power Query** enables you to connect to a variety of data sources, including worksheet ranges, workbooks, text files, PDF files, and databases.

> **Nuance**
> Any worksheet ranges that you connect to within an Excel workbook will automatically be converted into **Tables**.

- **Transforming**: The **Power Query Editor** enables you to shape your data, much like a potter shapes a lump of clay, but in this case, you can opt to remove unnecessary rows and columns, add columns, separate data from a single column into two or more columns, and much more.

- **Combining**: The optional combining phase enables you to stack different datasets together, such as combining individual worksheets from a workbook into a single list or merging data, which is akin to using lookup formulas in Excel to match related data from a second list into list, which I discuss in detail in *Chapter 10, Lookup Functions and Dynamic Arrays*.

- **Loading**: This phase returns the data to your Excel workbook and maintains a refreshable connection. Data is typically returned to Excel as a **Table**, so make sure that you read *Chapter 7, Automating Common Excel Tasks with the* **Table** *Feature*, to see how you can take your **Power Query** results further.

- **Refreshing**: Refreshing a **Power Query** connection means replacing the existing data in your workbook with a fresh copy from the data source. If you only have a one-time need to access a dataset, then you may not need to worry about refreshing. More often, though, the purpose of **Power Query** is to establish updatable, persistent connections to data sources. As you'll see, you can refresh connections either manually or automatically.

Typically, you must only work through the steps in the first four phases once, as opposed to the unending work involved in manually cleaning up reports. You can, of course, edit the steps at any point. Another unique aspect of **Power Query** is that you will be able to walk back and forth through the steps of your transformations to see how the data looked both before and after you add another step to the process.

Let's begin with a simple exercise that will generate a clickable index that you can use to navigate to any worksheet in a workbook. This will kick off our exploration of **Power Query**.

Creating a list of worksheets

I can visualize situations where an auto-generated list of worksheets would be a helpful addition to many workbooks. A couple of ideas include tracking the progress of a workbook audit, eyeballing a simple list of all worksheets in a workbook, or maybe taking things up a level by building a clickable worksheet index. Such an index may feel redundant. After all, when right-click on the navigation arrows in the bottom left-hand corner of Excel you can navigate by double-clicking on any worksheet **Name** the Activate dialog box. On the other hand, this index will be a self-updating listing that includes the **Names** of hidden worksheets and can be sorted alphabetically if desired. Let's jump in::

1. Open the `Chapter 12 - Workbook Index.xlsx` example workbook for this chapter, which contains 17 worksheets.
2. Activate the **Summary** tab so that your index will appear as the first sheet in the workbook.

> **Tip**
> When you load data from **Power Query** into a workbook, a new worksheet will be created to the left of the active worksheet.

3. Choose **Data | Get Data | From File | From Excel Workbook** in **Excel 2019** or later. Choose Data | New Query | From File | From Excel Workbook in Excel 2016. In **Excel 2013** and 2010 you must download and install the free **Power Query** add-in before you can choose **Power Query** | From File | From Workbook in **Excel 2013** and 2010.
4. Navigate to and select the `Chapter 12 - Workbook Index.xlsx` workbook again and then click **Import**. As you will see, a **Power Query** connection can refer to the workbook that you're working in. This may feel like you're creating a circular reference, but we're simply using the current workbook as our data source.
5. Choose `Chapter 12 - Periodic Income Statement.xlsx` from the list in the **Navigator** dialog box and click the Transform Data button shown in *Figure 12.1*. The **Load** button loads data that you've connected directly to Excel worksheets, while **Transform Data** launches the **Power Query Editor** so that you can make changes before returning the data to the workbook. The area that reads **No data selected for preview** gives you a glance at the data you've selected if you choose a **Table** or worksheet, but in this case, we've chosen the workbook itself.

> **Nuance**
> You cannot work in Excel when the the **Power Query** Editor is open. As you'll see, you can return data to Excel at any time from **Power Query** and then circle back and continue editing in **Power Query** later.

> **Tip**
> Depending on the type of data source you're connecting to, you may see **Tables**, worksheets, or pages from PDF files in the list along the left. You can connect to any item in the list and, optionally, click **Select multiple items** to create two or more connections.
>
>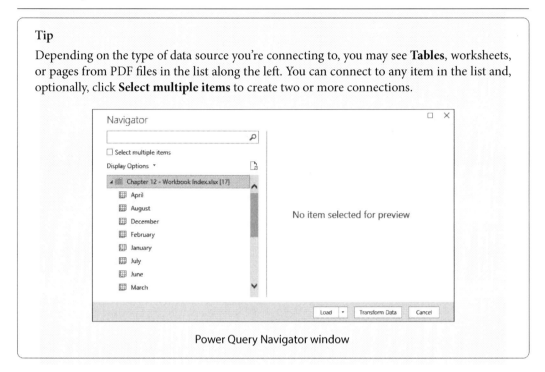
>
> Power Query Navigator window

6. The **Power Query Editor** will open, as shown in *Figure 12.2*:

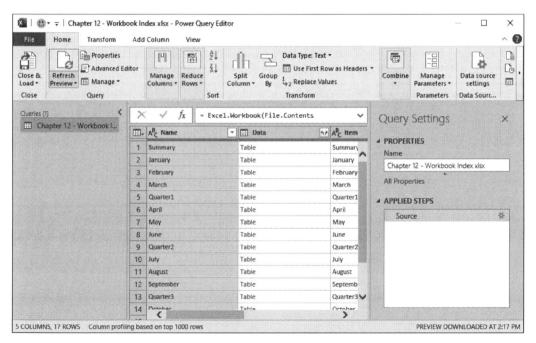

Figure 12.1 – The Power Query Editor

As shown in *Figure 12.2*. The **Power Query Editor** has the following aspects:

- **Ribbon interface**: Power Query uses a **Ribbon** concept similar to Microsoft Excel.
- **Query listing**: The task pane that appears along the left-hand side that lists all the connections that are present in the current workbook.
- **Data preview**: This is a grid that offers a preview of what your data will look like once you load it into an Excel worksheet.
- **Query Settings task pane**: The panel that appears along the right-hand side of the screen. It records each step that occurs in the data transformation.

7. Enter a new **Name** for the query, such as Index, in the **Name** field of the **Query Settings** task pane.
8. Right-click on the **Name** column and choose **Delete Other Columns**. This will leave a list of the worksheet **Names** in the **Data Preview** window, as shown here:

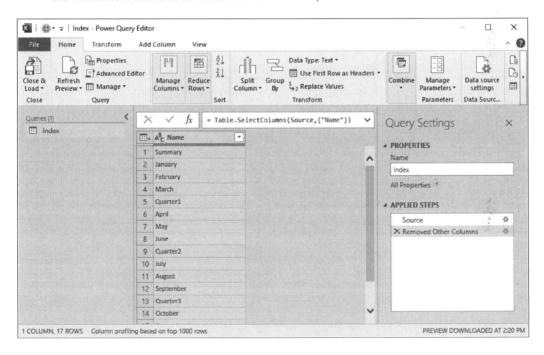

Figure 12.2 – **Power Query** results before loading data into the worksheet

9. Choose **Home | Close & Load | Load To** to bring up the **Import Data** dialog box. As you can see, **Power Query** results can be viewed in several ways:

- **Table**: A range of cells formatted as a **Table** within a new worksheet in your workbook.

- **PivotTable Report**: A dynamic report that summarizes information from a list into rows and columns based on choices that you make. I won't be creating **PivotTables** in this chapter, but if you're new to the feature, a **PivotTable** task pane will appear on the right-hand side of your new worksheet. Drag and drop fields from the field list into the quadrants at the bottom to create a report.

> **Tip**
> I Discuss **Tables** and **PivotTables** in *Chapter 1, Implementing Accessibility* and in *Chapter 7, Automating Tasks with the* **Table** *Feature*.

- **PivotChart**: A dynamic chart that summarizes information in graph form. I won't show you how to create a PivotChart in this chapter, but the process is like creating a **PivotTable**, and inf fact, you'll end up with both a **PivotTable** and **Pivot Chart**.
- **Only Create Connection**: This option enables you to create a connection to a data source without returning the results to Excel. I'll provide an example of this later in this chapter when I show you how to combine data from two or more data sources into a single list.

10. Click **OK** to accept the default choice of **Table**. This will add a new worksheet to the workbook, as shown in *Figure 12.4*:

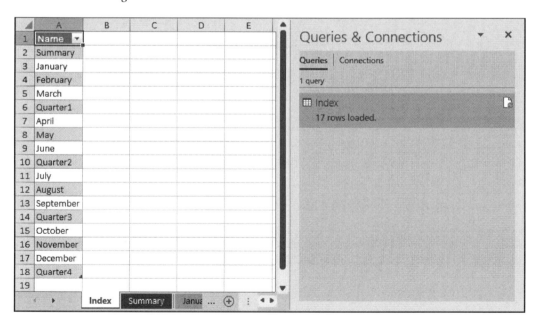

Figure 12.3 – Power Query results returned to a worksheet

> **Tip**
>
> If the **Summary** worksheet was active when you embarked on *Step 1*, the new **Index** worksheet will be the first sheet in the workbook; otherwise, it will appear to the left of what was the active worksheet. Feel free to move the **Index** worksheet to a new position if desired.

The alphabetical file listing shown in *Figure 12.4* could be helpful on its own. However, let's look at the HYPERLINK function so that we can turn this list into an interactive navigation aid.

The HYPERLINK function

Cell **C3** of the HYPERLINK function worksheet of the Chapter 12 - HYPERLINK function.xlsx shown in *Figure 12.5* contains the =HYPERLINK("#'"&B3&"'!A1",B3) formula, which creates a clickable link to cell **A1** of the worksheet referenced in cell **B3**:

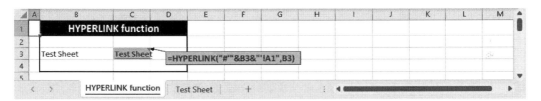

Figure 12.4 – HYPERLINK function

The # operator instructs Excel to reference the active workbook. Ampersands (&) are a form of concatenation, or a way of combining text, in Excel. In this case, we're combining the following components:

- #
- The worksheet's **Name** surrounded by single quotes
- An exclamation mark (!)
- The cell address, such as **A1**

The HYPERLINK function has two arguments:

- link_location: The address or URL that you wish to create a hyperlink for. Here, you can reference a location in a file, or provide a URL to an external document or web page.
- friendly_**Name**: An optional argument that represents text you wish to display in the cell instead of link_location.

Now, let's convert our list of worksheets into a clickable index.

Making Power Query results into a clickable index

We're going to add a new column to the **Table** that **Power Query** created. This will transform our list into a clickable index. Follow these steps:

1. Enter Index in cell **B1**. This will cause the **Table** to create a blank column.
2. Enter =HYPERLINK("#'"&A2&"'!A1",A2) in cell **B2**, and notice how the formula fills the column automatically when you press *Enter*. You can now click on any cell within the second column of the **Table** to navigate to the corresponding worksheet – if the worksheet is visible, meaning not hidden.

> **Nuance**
>
> If you navigate to cell A2 when writing the formula instead of typing A2, your formula will look like =HYPERLINK("#'"&[@**Name**]&"'!A1", [@**Name**]). [@**Name**] is known as a structured reference in Excel, which means Excel is referencing a field **Name** within a **Table**.

Now that you can jump to any worksheet in the workbook with one click, you may wish to create links on the worksheets back to the index. One way to do so is to use the **Group Worksheets** feature in Excel:

1. Activate the **Summary** worksheet.
2. Hold down the *Shift* key and select the Quarter4 worksheet to group all the worksheets between and including **Summary** and **Quarter4**. Notice how the word **Group** now appears in Excel's title bar just after your workbook **Name**.
3. Optional: Right-click on row **1** and choose **Insert** or click row **1** and choose **Home | Insert** to insert a blank row at the start of every worksheet. This will ensure that you don't inadvertently overwrite any data in the worksheets.
4. Enter =HYPERLINK("#'Index'!A1","Index") in cell **A1** if you inserted a blank row, or **B1** if you skipped that step – I happen to know that cell **B1** is blank on every worksheet in this group.
5. Right-click on any worksheet tab and choose **Ungroup** to ungroup the worksheets. It's important to ungroup sheets as soon as possible so that you don't inadvertently start carrying out tasks intended for a single sheet that unwittingly get carried out across the group.

> **Nuance**
>
> A minor side effect of using the HYPERLINK function together with the **Group Worksheets** feature is that the worksheet that you enter the formula on will have what looks like a clickable link. The other worksheets will have an unformatted link that is clickable but may not be apparent to the user. You can use **Format Painter** to copy the formatting to the other worksheets, or you can enter the HYPERLINK formula on a single worksheet and then copy and paste the formula to the other worksheets.

Now, let's see how to refresh the list so that new worksheets you add will appear on the list. This will illustrate how refreshing **Power Query Connections** works in general.

Refreshing Power Query Connections

Refreshing a **Power Query** connection means replacing the existing data in your workbook with a fresh copy from the data source. I'll show you how to both manually and automatically refresh **Power Query Connections**. I'll also show you how to edit queries in case you rename or move the workbook, or simply want to connect to a different data source.

> Tip
>
> **Power Query** results are a snapshot in time and only update when refreshed. In the case of our workbook index, any new worksheets that you add will not appear on the index until you refresh the **Power Query** connection.

You can manually refresh **Power Query** results in several ways:

- Choose **Query | Refresh** (the tab is only present when your cursor is in a **Table** that returns results from **Power Query**)
- Right-click on a **Table** or **PivotTable** and choose **Refresh**
- Choose **Table Design | Refresh** or **PivotTable Analyze | Refresh**
- Click **Data | Refresh All | Refresh** (*Alt + F5*) to refresh the current worksheet only or **Data | Refresh All** (*Ctrl + Alt + F5*) to refresh all the connections in your workbook

You can also instruct Excel to automatically refresh a query, as follows:

1. Click on any **Table** or **PivotTable** that contains results from **Power Query** and then choose **Query | Properties**.

2. Choose **Refresh data when opening the file** from the **Usage** tab, as shown in *Figure 12.6*:

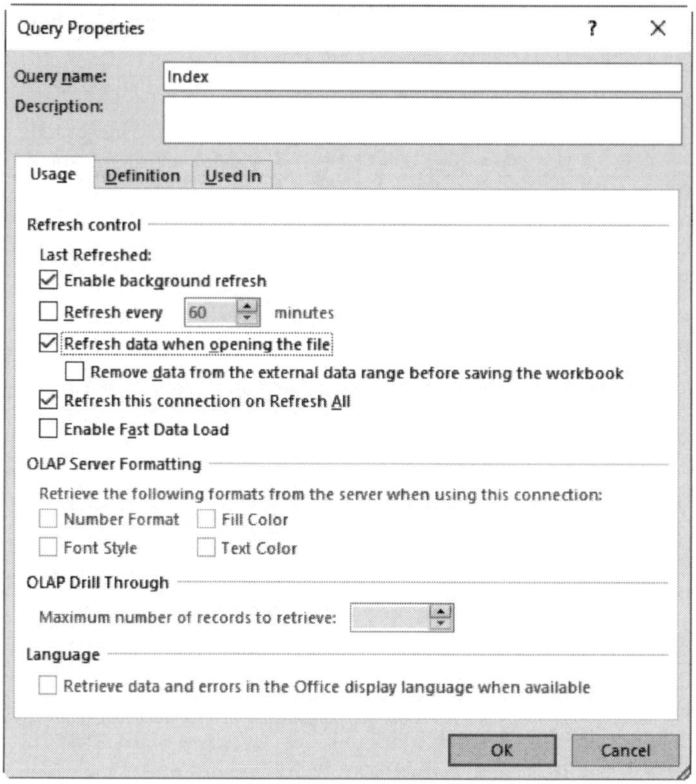

Figure 12.5 – The Query Properties dialog box

When you open your workbook, **Power Query** will refresh the connection automatically. This means that any new worksheets that have been added will appear automatically in the index. This applies to any connection that you create in **Power Query**.

Updating the worksheet index

You may have noticed that the **Index** worksheet doesn't appear in the **Power Query** results. In this case, the **Index** worksheet was created *after* we established our **Power Query** connection, so **Power Query** isn't aware of the new worksheet yet. As you're about to see, for this particular type of query refreshing the list isn't enough to make new worksheets appear on the list:

1. Right-click on cell **A1** of the **Index** worksheet and then choose **Refresh**. Notice that **Index** *still* does not appear. **Power Query** is referring to the *saved* version of our `Chapter 12 - Workbook Index.xlsx` workbook, and *not* the version present in memory.

2. Choose **File | Save** or press *Ctrl + S (⌘ + S)*.
3. Right-click on cell **A1** and choose **Refresh**.
4. As shown in *Figure 12.7*, *now* the **Index** worksheet appears in the list, along with other items, such as those in cells **A20** and **A21**. These stray results are metadata that **Power Query** has captured and automatically create invalid links that will cause a **Reference isn't valid** prompt to appear when clicked:

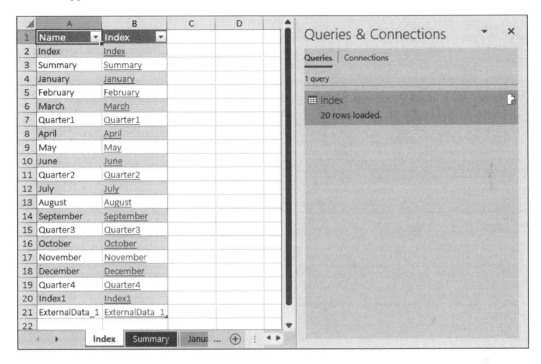

Figure 12.6 – The refreshed Index worksheet

5. We'll need to return to the **Power Query** Editor and filter out the stray results, select any cell within **Table** on the **Index** worksheet, and choose **Query | Edit**.

> **Tip**
> Other ways to return to the **Power Query** Editor include going to **Query | Edit**, double-clicking a connection **Name** in the **Queries & Connections** task pane, or right-clicking a connection in the **Queries & Connections** task pane and then choosing **Edit**. Choose **Data | Queries & Connections** if the task pane isn't present.

6. In the **Power Query** Editor, click the **Filter Button** at the top of the **Name** column in the **Data Preview** window, clear the checkboxes for **Index**, **Index1**, and **ExternalData_1**, and then click **OK**.

7. Choose **Home | Close & Load** to return the results to Excel.
8. Activate the **Summary** worksheet and press *Shift + F11* in **Excel for Windows or macOS** to create a new worksheet or choose **Home | Insert | Worksheet**.
9. Choose **File | Save** or press *Ctrl + S (⌘ + S)*.
10. Right-click on any cell in the clickable index and choose **Refresh** to display the new worksheet in the index.
11. As a finishing touch, right-click on column **A** and chose **Hide** so that only the clickable links are shown.

> **Tip**
> Other ways to hide a column include *Ctrl + 0 (zero) (⌘ + 0 (zero))* or choosing **Home | Format | Hide & Unhide | Hide Columns**.

12. To make the index self-updating, select any cell in the **Table** for the **Index** worksheet, choose **Query | Properties**, click **Refresh data when opening the file**, and click **OK**.

> **Tip**
> A security warning will appear in Excel's **Message Bar** when you open a workbook that contains one or more **Power Query Connections**. In *Chapter 2, Disaster Recovery and File-Related Prompts*, I showed you how to make a workbook a **Data Preview** window so that you don't have to click **Enable Content** each time you open the workbook.

Going forward, when you open the workbook, Excel will automatically refresh the index if you click **Enable Content** when the security warning appears or make the workbook a **Data Preview** window. Now that you can see that **Power Query** only returns results from the saved version of a data source, such as an Excel workbook, let's see what to do when we move or rename a data source.

Updating source data connections

When you move or rename a data source, such as the one you've connected to, **Power Query Connections** will remain attached to the data source – in this case, `Chapter 12 - Workbook Index.xlsx`. Let's give the workbook a new **Name** and then update the **Power Query** connection:

1. Choose **File | Save As**, assign a new **Name**, such as `Power Query Index.xlsx`, and click **Save**.
2. Activate the **Summary** worksheet and press *Shift + F11* to create a new worksheet.

> **Tip**
> You can also insert new worksheets by choosing **Home | Insert | Worksheet**.

3. Choose **File | Save**.
4. Right-click on cell **A1** and choose **Refresh**. Notice that the new worksheet does not appear, even though you refreshed the list. This is because **Power Query** is still referencing the `Chapter 12 - Workbook Index.xlsx` workbook.
5. Select any cell in **Table** on the **Index** worksheet and choose **Query | Edit**.
6. Click the **Gear Icon** next to the **Source** step in the **Applied Steps** listing of the **Query Settings** task pane.
7. Click the **Browse** button to select the updated version of your file, and then click **OK**, as shown in *Figure 12.8*:

Figure 12.7 – Excel Workbook connection dialog box

8. Choose **Home | Close & Load** to return the data to your worksheet.
9. The new worksheet you added will now appear in the list.

This simple example of creating a worksheet index for a workbook covers several common issues that you will encounter in **Power Query** regarding connecting to and refreshing data sources. Now, let's learn how to use **Power Query** to automate cleaning up an accounting report.

Automatic report cleanup

You may find yourself saddled with reports that you need to analyze in Excel that are particularly unfriendly from an analytical standpoint. You may even be manually cleaning up such reports monthly. Or perhaps you're writing macros in Excel to automate repetitive tasks such at this. I will tell you that I write far fewer macros these days now that **Power Query** is available.

As we saw in the workbook index example, **Power Query** offers a code-free approach that is designed to be "set-and-forget." We're going to transform a January accounting report into an analysis ready format, and then save a February report over it. This will illustrate how once you establish **Power Query**, the only repetitive step is to run the new report and save over the previous version of the data source.

First, let's look at some common frustrations that arise in reports that you export to Excel from other software programs.

Analytical obstacles

The Chapter 12 - January Aging.xlsx workbook provided in this chapter's GitHub repository illustrates common frustrations that Excel users can encounter. An **aged receivables report** is an accounting report that shows amounts due by customers and how long the invoices have remained unpaid. The report, shown in *Figure 12.9*, has several issues from an analytical perspective.

	A	B	C	D	E	F	G	H	I	J	K	L	M	N	O	P	Q
1									Aged Receivables								
2									Properties: Riverview Apartments, Tri-County Mall								
3									Current tenants as of 09/22/22								
4		Tenant Name		Property		Unit	Acc#		Type	Date		0-30	31-60		61-90	91+	
5		Clark, Marcia		RIVER		1	143										
6				RIVER		1			RC	9/1/22		90.00	0.00		0.00	0.0	
7												90.00	0.00		0.00	0.0	
8		Apegian, Charlie		RIVER		2	144										
9				RIVER		2			RC	9/1/22		90.00	0.00		0.00	0.0	
10												90.00	0.00		0.00	0.0	
11		Game Stop		TCM		2	177										
12				TCM		2			RC	9/1/22		1,650.00	0.00		0.00	0.0	
13				TCM		2			CAM	9/1/22		128.42	0.00		0.00	0.0	

Figure 12.8 – Typical issues that arise in reports exported from accounting software and other tools

Some issues include:

- Merged cells in columns **B:C**, **D:E**, **G:H**, **J:K**, **M:N**, **P:Q**, and **R:S**
- A total row appear after each tenant, which makes it harder to filter as well as harder to sum without inadvertently doubling some or all of the amounts.
- Tenant and account **Names** only appear on on the first row, but transactions appear on other rows
- Although not shown in *Figure 12.9*, additional report totals unrelated to specific tenants appear beneath the report

Any *one* of these issues can be frustrating enough, much less when multiple issues are present. We will use **Power Query** to transform the ugly report shown in the *Figure 12.9* into the analysis-ready format shown in *Figure 12.10*:

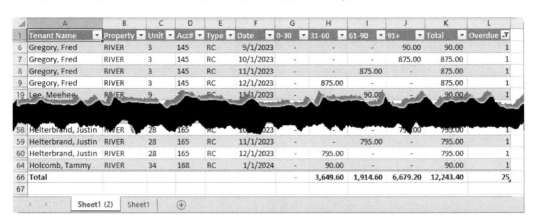

Figure 12.9 – Data transformed by **Power Query**

Let's see how **Power Query** can eliminate frustration and stumbling blocks involved with unlocking data that feels stuck under glass on your computer.

Transforming reports

Hands on experience, such working through this next example, is a great way to conquer the learning curve that comes with **Power Query**:

1. Open the `Chapter 12 - January Aging.xlsx` workbook.

2. Choose **File | Save As** and enter the **Name** `Aging.xslx`. Notice that there is no month **Name** here to avoid confusion in future months. Later in this sequence we'll save the `Chapter 12 - February Aging.xlsx` workbook over this `Aging.xlsx` workbook.

3. Choose **File | Close** to close the `Aging.xlsx` workbook.

4. Press *Ctrl + N* (⌘ + N) to create a blank workbook (or choose **File | New** and choose **Blank Workbook**).

5. Choose **Data | Get Data | From File | From Excel Workbook**, select the `Chapter 12 - January Aging.xlsx` workbook, and then click **Import**.

6. Choose **Sheet1** from the list along the left-hand side of the **Navigator** window. Notice how a preview of the data appears. Click **Transform Data** to open the **the Power Query Editor**.

7. Right-click on **Promoted Headers** in the **Applied Steps** list on the **Query Settings** task pane, choose **Delete Until End**, and then click **Delete**. Tread carefully so that you do not inadvertently remove the **Source** or **Navigation** steps, as doing so can remove your data from the **Data Preview** window, or worse, break the connection to the data entirely. In either case, if you're new to **Power Query** your path of least resistance is to choose **File | Discard & Close** and then start over at *Step 5*.

> **Tip**
>
> **Power Query** sometimes presumes that you want to promote the first row of your worksheet to the column headings, as well as automatically change the **Data Type** property for certain columns. Doing so often converts text-based numbers into whole numbers or decimal values. I prefer to remove any "helpful" steps that **Power Query** adds to the Applied Steps list so that I begin with Source and Navigation in place, and then I add any other steps I need to transform my report. Sometimes the "helpful" steps become unhelpful when they pose a conflict with steps that you add later.

8. Removing columns in **Power Query** is as simple as clicking on a column and pressing *Delete* (*Fn + Delete*). Try the technique out by deleting Column1, which does not have any data that we'll need in the final report.

> **Tip**
>
> **Power Query** does not have an Undo command, but you can roll back your transformation by removing steps from the Applied Steps list. If you carry out a step consecutively, such as deleting blank columns. the Applied Steps list will only have a single Removed Columns step that spans all columns that you deleted. If you remove this step, all of the deleted columns will return, but you can then delete them again.

9. Right-click on **Removed Columns** in the **Applied Steps** list, choose **Rename**, change the caption to `Removed First Column`, and then press *Enter*.

> **Tip**
>
> As the **Applied Steps** list grows, it's easy to lose track of what is happening as the data is transformed. Renaming steps as you go documents the transformation and makes it significantly easier to troubleshoot transformations that yield unexpected results.

10. The first three rows of the report are extraneous, but you cannot delete them. Instead choose **Home | Remove Rows | Remove Top Rows**.

11. Enter 3 in the **Number of rows** field of the **Remove Top Rows** dialog box, shown in *Figure 12.11*, and then click **OK**:

Figure 12.10 – The Remove Top Rows dialog box

12. Right-click on **Removed Top Rows**, choose **Rename**, and then type `Removed Top 3 Rows` and press *Enter*.

> **Tip**
> Notice the **Gear Icon** next to the **Removed Top 3 Rows** (or **Removed Top Rows**) step. You can can click this icon to redisplay the Remove Top Rows dialog box if you want to adjust the number of rows removed.

13. Choose **Home | Use First Row as Headers** to replace the generic **Data Preview** column headings with the titles in the first row.
14. **Changed Type** step appears in the **Applied Steps** list because **Power Query** changed the data type for one or more of your columns. Sometimes this is helpful, sometimes it isn't. Fortunately, you can determine which columns changed:

    I. Click on the **Promoted Headers** step, which causes the **Data Preview** window to present how your data looked *before* the **Changed Type** step was applied.

    II. Notice the **ABC123** icon adjacent to the word **Unit** in the header row, which indicates that the column contains text and/or numbers. This is also referred to as the **Any** data type in **Power Query**, which means a column could contain text, numbers, or both types of data.

    III. Click on the **Changed Type** step and notice that **123** now appears next to the word **Unit**, which indicates that the column has been transformed into whole numbers.

    IV. If you continue clicking back and forth between **Promoted Headers** and **Changed Type** as you work your way across, you'll notice other column type changes as well.

15. Choose **Home | Choose Columns** (if you clicked the bottom half of the command, then click **Choose Columns** a second time).
16. Type `Col` in the **Choose the columns to keep** field to select all blank columns at once.
17. Clear the **(Select All Search Results)** checkbox and then click on **OK**.

> **Nuance**
> You can easily modify a step like this later by clicking on the **Gear** icon and updating your choices. You have two alternatives if you need to update a step that doesn't have a **Gear Icon**: remove the step and add it back again or edit the **M** code in the **Formula Bar** area. **Power Query** uses a programming language called **M** behind the scenes that the **Power Query** Editor mostly shields you from, but also makes available when you're ready.

18. Change the **Name** of the the **Removed Other Columns** step to `Removed Blank Columns`.

19. Select the **Tenant** column, and then choose **Transform | Fill | Down**, shown in *Figure 12.12*, to populate the tenant **Name** on rows where it does not appear:

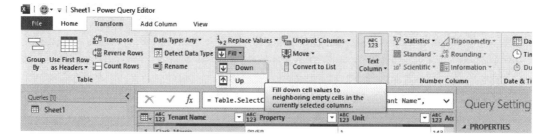

Figure 12.11 – The Fill | Down command

> **Nuance**
>
> The **Fill** command only works when the word *null* appears in one or more cells in a column. If the cells you wish to fill are blank, select the column and then choose **Transform | Replace Values**. Leave the **Value To Find** field blank, type `null` in the **Replace With** field, and then click on **OK**. In this context, the word *null* must be all lowercase. You can then use **Transform | Fill | Down** to populate the missing values.

20. Repeat *Step 24* to fill the **Acc#** column down in the same fashion.
21. Rename **Filled Down** as `Filled Tenant Name/Acc# Down` in the **Applied Steps** list.

> **Nuance**
>
> Notice that **Power Query** only added one **Filled Down** step to the **Applied Steps** list. Consecutive versions of the same task are automatically merged into a single step. In such situations, you cannot remove the task from one column without removing it from the other columns as well. The only way around this is to carry out a different task before then carrying out the task that would get merged with the initial instance.

22. Click the **Filter** arrow in the **Date** column, clear the **Null** checkbox, and then click **OK** to remove the rows that do not contain transactional data.

> **Nuance**
>
> Fields in **Power Query** can be labeled as *null*, or they can be entirely blank. In this case, any row that doesn't contain a date is a row that we want to eliminate. Identifying such patterns within your data helps make transformations painless.

23. Rename **Filtered Rows** as `Filtered Null Date Rows` in the **Applied Steps** list.

24. Select the **0-30** column, and then hold down the *Shift* key and select the **Total** column with your mouse. Alternatively, click on **0-30**, hold down the *Shift* key, and use the right-arrow key to select the aging columns through **Total**, and then choose the **Transform | Data Type: Any | Currency** options to convert the aging columns into currency values.

> **Nuance**
>
> Setting a column to **Currency** in **Power Query** does not apply the **Currency** number format to the cells in Excel, so you'll still need to format the worksheet cells.

25. Rename the **Changed Type** command `Changed Amount Fields to $`.
26. Choose **Home | Close & Load** to return the data to Microsoft Excel.
27. Notice that the **F** column may show the dates in serial number format:

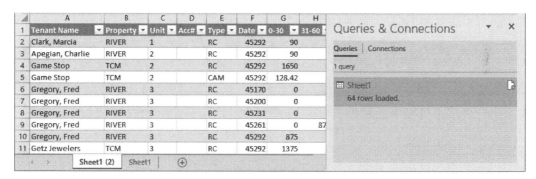

Figure 12.12 – The F column may show serial numbers instead of dates

If this occurs, you could manually format these dates in Excel, or you can make the change in **Power Query**:

1. Choose any cell within **Table** and choose **Query | Edit**.
2. Click the **ABC123** icon in the **Date** column header and choose **Date** from the list, as an alternative to choosing **Transform | Data Type: Any | Date**.
3. Right-click and rename the **Changed Amount Field to $** caption in the **Applied Steps** to needs data entry font since the step now includes two consecutive transformations of the same type.
4. Choose **Home | Close & Load** to return the data to Excel.

> **Nuance**
>
> You won't always be able to tell when you need to change a data type, such as for the **Date** column. In this case, the Data Preview tricked me by showing dates instead of serial numbers.

Now let's see how you can set a locale or region.

Setting a locale or region

I live in Atlanta, which means that in 2024, the *Ides of March* will fall on 03/15/2024 for me, but perhaps on 15/03/2024 for you. Similarly, data that you import into **Power Query** may reflect the locale where the data originated, or the locale of the last person that saved the file. **Power Query** refers to world regions as **locales**. Locales affect how dates, times, and numbers are formatted. Let's see how you can change a locale within your operating system, for a workbook or text file, and for columns within a query:

- **Operating System**: **Power Query** defaults to the **Regional Settings** preferences in Windows and the **Region and Language** settings in **Excel for macOS**. To change these settings:

    - **Windows**: Choose **Start** | **Settings** | **Time & Language** | **Region** and make a choice from the **Regional format** list and then close the **Settings** window.

    - **Mac**: | **System Preferences** | **Language & Region**, make a choice from the **Region** list, and then close the **Language & Region** dialog box.

- **Workbook**: In **Excel for Windows**, you can override the operating system's **Regional Settings** by specifying a locale for a workbook: Choose **Data** | **Get Data** | **Query Options** | **Regional Settings**, make a choice from the **Locale** list, and then click **OK**.

- **Text file:** You can set the locale for text files during the import process or at the query level, which will also override the operating system's settings:

    - **At import**: The steps differ between platforms:

        - **Excel for Windows**: Choose **Data** | **From Text/CSV**, change the **File Origin** field, and then choose **Load** or **Transform Data.**

        - **Excel for macOS**: Choose **Data** | **Get Data (Power Query)** | **Text/CSV**, click **Browse** and select a file, and then click **Next**. Change the **File Origin** and then click **Load** or **Transform Data**

    - **Query settings**: Click the **Gear Icon** for the **Source** step in the **Applied Steps** list of the **Query Settings** task pane, update the **File Origin** field, and then click **OK**.

- **Change Type action**: You can override both the **Operating System** and **Power Query** by specifying a locale on a column-by-column basis:

    I. Click the **Data Type** button in the **Header** field of a query column and choose **Using Locale**, (or right-click on the **Header** and choose **Change Type** | **Using Locale**) to display the **Change Type with Locale** dialog box shown in *Figure 12.14*:

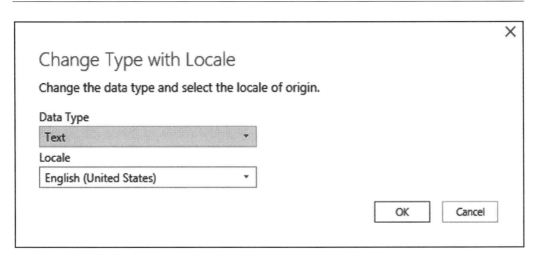

Figure 12.13 – Change Type with Locale dialog box

II. Optional: Change the **Data Type** if needed.

III. Select from the **Locale** list, and then click **OK**.

IV. Now let's see how to enhance data you've loaded to a worksheet from **Power Query** with supplemental formulas.

Adding supplemental formulas to **Power Query** results

Let's create an **Overdue** column so that we can filter the overdue amounts on the accounts receivable aging schedule:

1. Type Overdue in cell **L1**.
2. Enter the =COUNTIF(H2:J2,">0") formula in cell **L2**. Remember, if you navigate to cell **H2** or **J2**, your formula will use the column **Names** as structured references, which means your formula may look like =COUNTIF(Sheet1[@[31-60]:[91+]],">0") The latter is a structured reference formula that returns the same value as a cell reference-based formula.
3. Click on the **Filter** arrow in cell **L1**, clear the checkbox for 0, and then click on **OK**.
4. Optional: Click on the **Total Row** checkbox on the **Table Design** tab. Excel will automatically add a sum to the **L** column, which will give you a count of the overdue invoices. Click on the total cell in the **0-30** column and then choose **Sum** from the drop-down list. Then, you drag the **Fill Handle** in the **0-30** cell across to add totals to the other columns.

You now have an aged receivables report that only display only amounts that are over 30 days old. In this case, the COUNTIF function is counting the number of cells between the **H:J** columns that contain amounts greater than zero.

> **Tip**
> I discuss the COUNTIF function in more detail in *Chapter 5, Data Validation and Form Controls*.

The aging report that we've created shows results for **January**. Now, let's update the report with **February** results.

Updating a Power Query connection with new data

One of the main benefits of **Power Query** is the fact that you can create reusable data transformations. Let's see how to update our spreadsheet with a February aging schedule:

1. Open the Chapter 12 - February Aging.xlsx workbook.
2. Choose **File | Save As**, save the workbook over the Aging.xlsx workbook that you created earlier in this chapter, and then click **Yes** when you're asked whether you want to replace the file.
3. Choose **File | Close** to exit the Aging.xlsx workbook.
4. Right-click on the **Table** that shows January aging, and then choose **Refresh**, or choose **Table Design | Refresh**.

Your workbook should now reflect the **February** aging, which illustrates how easy it is to transform reports on an ongoing basis. Now, let's see how to create an archive copy of a report.

Breaking Power Query Connections

Power Query Connections are designed to be persistent and when needed, such as how we saved the February report version over the Aging.xlsx workbook. Conversely, can break the link if you do not want the data to be refreshed:

1. Choose **File | Save As**, enter a new workbook **Name** such as February Aging.xlsx, and then click **Save**.
2. Click **Table Design | Unlink**, as shown in *Figure 12.14*, and then click **OK**:

Automatic report cleanup 385

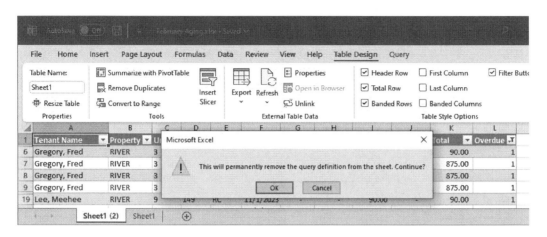

Figure 12.14 – The Unlink command and the confirmation prompt

> **Tip**
> Tread carefully with the **Unlink** command, as you cannot undo this action, nor will you be able to undo any prior actions. If you unlink a query accidentally, you can right-click on the query in the **Queries & Connections** task pane and then choose **Load To**, which will display the **Load To** dialog box. Choose **Table | New Worksheet**, and then click **OK** to recreate the data connection.

3. Click **Data | Queries & Connections** to display the **Queries & Connections** task pane unless it's already displayed.

4. Click once on any query in the task pane and then press *Delete* (or right-click on the query and choose **Delete**), and then click **Delete** when prompted.

> **Nuance**
> Unlike unlinking a **Table**, you *can* undo deleting a connection from the **Queries & Connections** task pane.

Once you remove the connection from the **Queries & Connections** task pane, the workbook can no longer be refreshed from **Power Query** and serves as a permanent snapshot of the data. Now, let's use **Power Query** to extract data from PDF files.

Extracting data from PDF files

Some users purchase third-party software to extract data from PDF files due to a lack of better alternatives. **PDF** stands for **Portable Document Format**, a product of **Adobe Corporation**. PDF files are cross-platform compatible, and can be opened on any device. Extracting data from PDF files with **Power Query** requires **Excel 2021** or **Microsoft 365**. The steps in this section cannot be carried out in **Excel 2019** or earlier. At the time of writing, **Excel for macOS** does not support extracting data from PDF files.

> **Tip**
>
> **Word 2013** and later allows you to open and edit most PDF files if your version of Excel doesn't allow extracting data with **Power Query**. Open a PDF file in Word the same way you would open a Word document, and then copy and paste the results over to Excel. Some PDF documents will transfer cleanly, while others will be a jumbled mess.

Any software that extracts data from PDF files uses **optical character recognition**, so somtimes your data may be misinterpreted. I'll point out two specific instances in our next series of steps. The PDF file that I've chosen as an example is a **Profit & Loss** report from the sample company provided in **QuickBooks Desktop**. Be prepared to handle optical character recognition issues that are unique to PDF files and won't arise when connecting **Power Query** to other data sources.

Let's now extract data from a PDF file. I'm going to move more quickly by not renaming anything in the **Applied Steps** list, but feel free to do so if you find it helpful:

1. Press *Ctrl + N* to create a blank workbook (or choose **File | New** and choose **Blank Workbook**).
2. Choose **Data | Get Data | From File | From PDF**.
3. Select a PDF file, such as `Chapter 12 - Profit & Loss.pdf`, and then click **Import**.
4. As shown in *Figure 12.15*, the **Navigator** dialog box may show both **Tables** and pages. In this context, both **Tables** and pages are subsets of data from the PDF file. You can click the **Select multiple Items** checkbox to be able to see two or more **Tables** or pages. Instead, let's select `Chapter 12 - Profit & Loss.pdf` from the list, and then click **Transform Data**, which ensures that **Power Query** will import all the pages from the PDF document:

Extracting data from PDF files 387

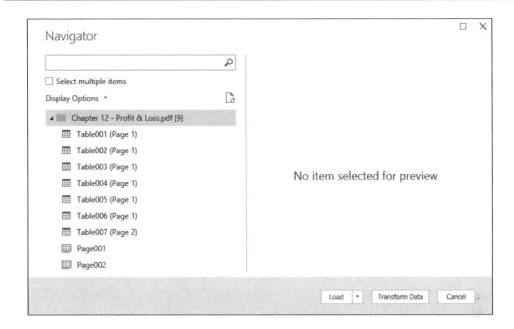

Figure 12.15 – The Navigator dialog box

5. As shown in *Figure 12.16*, a list of the **Tables** and pages from the PDF file will appear. Click the **Filter** button in the **Kind** column, clear the **Table** checkbox, and then click **OK**:

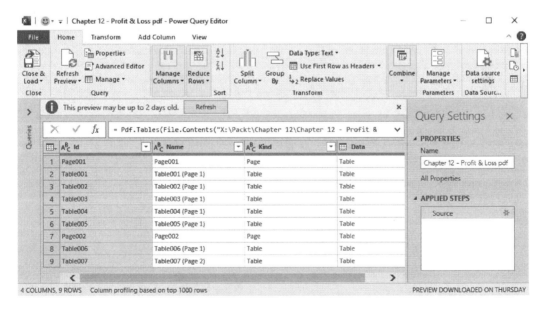

Figure 12.16 – A list of **Tables** and pages

> **Tip**
>
> The **This Preview may be up to X days old** prompt indicates that **Power Query**'s internal cache is out of date. Always click the **Refresh** button when a prompt like this appears.

6. Right-click on the **Data** column and then choose **Remove Other COLUMNS**.
7. Click the double-headed arrow in the heading of the **Data** column, clear the **Use original column Name as prefix** checkbox, and then click **OK** to expand the data to display all the data from the PDF file, as shown in *Figure 12.17*:

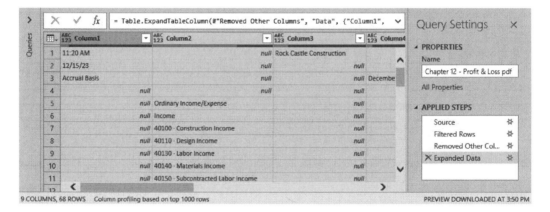

Figure 12.17 – Data extracted from the PDF file

Let's look at some quirks with the data that we've extracted:

- Some account numbers are in **Column2**, while others are in **Column3**, as shown in *Figure 12.18*:

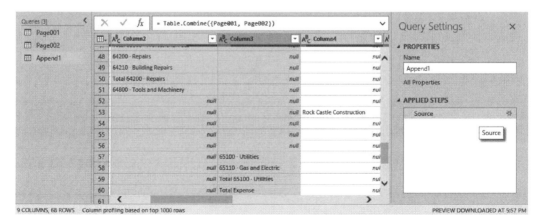

Figure 12.18 – Account numbers spread across two columns

- The letter *N* was dropped from the word **Net** in **Column2** and **Column3** on rows **61**, **66**, and **67**, as shown in *Figure 12.19*. In my testing, I found this doesn't happen to everyone, but it happened on my computer, so I'll show you how to fix it in case you encounter this oddity:

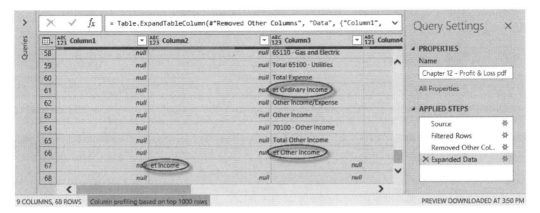

Figure 12.19 – The letter N has been dropped from some words

- Some amounts appear in **Column6**, while others appear in **Column7**, as shown here:

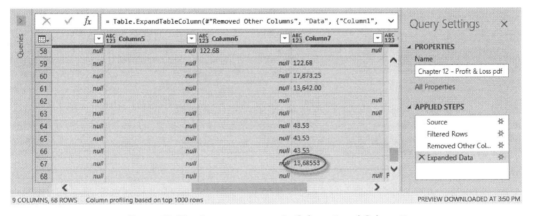

Figure 12.20 – Amounts appear in Column6 and Column7

- **13,68553** appears in **Column7** of row **67** instead of **13,685.53** because the decimal is missing. If you click the **ABC123** icon in the heading for **Column7** and choose **Currency**, **Power Query** will translate this number as **13,685,533**.

Fortunately, we can use **Power Query** features to resolve all four of the preceding issues.

8. Click on **Column1** and then hold down the *Shift* key while you click on **Column5**.
9. Right-click on the selection and choose **Merge Columns** (or click **Transform | Merge Columns**).

10. Type Account in the **New column Name (optional)** box and then click **OK**, as shown in *Figure 12.21*:

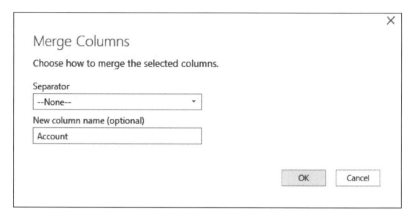

Figure 12.21 – The Merge Columns dialog box

11. Click on **Column6** and then hold down the *Shift* key while you click on **Column9**.
12. Right-click on the selection and choose **Merge Columns** (or click **Transform | Merge Columns**).
13. Type Initial Amount in the **New column Name (optional)** box and then click **OK**.
14. Click the **Filter** arrow in the **Account** field, deselect **(blank)**, and then click **OK**.
15. Click the **Filter** arrow in the **Initial Amount** field, deselect **(blank)**, and then click **OK**.
16. Click the **Data Type** icon, which shows **ABC**, in the **Initial Amount** header and choose **Currency**.
17. Select the **Account** column and then choose **Transform | Replace Values**.
18. Enter "et " without the quotes in the **Value To Find** field, and "Net " without the quotes in the **Replace With** field, and then click **OK**. Make sure that you include a space after both et and Net.
19. The **Net Income** amount on row **41** is **13,368,553**, which we'll correct by creating a **Conditional Column**:

    I. Click **Add Column | Conditional Column**.

    II. Type Amount in the **New column Name** field.

    III. Choose **Initial Amount** from the **Column Name** field.

    IV. Choose **is greater than** from the **Operator** field.

    V. Enter 1000000 in the **Value** field.

    VI. Type [Initial Amount]/100 in the **Output** field.

> **Nuance**
> Field **Names** must be enclosed in square brackets when referenced in custom or **Conditional Columns** in **Power Query**.

    VII. Click the **ABC123** button below **Else** and choose **Select a column**.

    VIII. Choose **Initial Amount** from the **Output** list, as shown here:

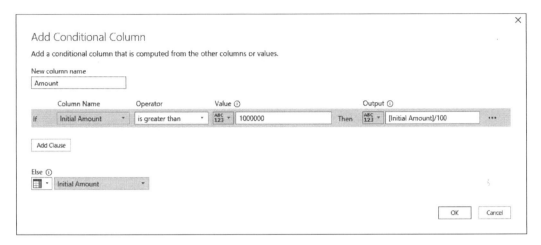

Figure 12.22 – The Add **Conditional Column** dialog box

    IX. Click **OK** to close the **Add Conditional Column** dialog box.

> **Tip**
> Depending on the data that you're working with, there could be some risk in this approach with **Conditional Column**. For this dataset, the *real* numbers will never be anywhere near 1,000,000, so dividing by 100 does not cause an issue. This is by no means an end-all solution, but rather an illustration of just one way to solve the problem when **Power Query** misconstrues some of your data.

20. The **Amount** column in row **41** shows **[Initial Amount]/100** rather than the calculation result. To resolve this, remove the double quotes around **[Initial Amount]/100** in **Power Query**'s **Formula Bar**, as shown in *Figure 12.23*. Click the down arrow in the top right-hand corner if you need to expand the **Formula Bar**:

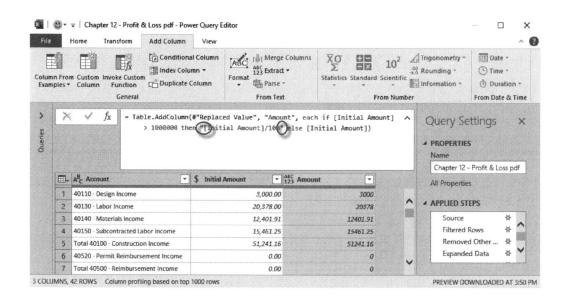

Figure 12.23 – Remove the quotes around [Initial Amount]/100 in the **Formula Bar**

21. Click on the **Initial Amount** column and press *Delete* (or right-click on the column and choose **Remove**).

22. Click the **Data Type** icon for the **Amount** column, which shows **ABC123**, and choose **Currency**; otherwise, in some cases, the numbers may load to your worksheet as text.

23. Click **Home** | **Close & Load** to return the data to Microsoft Excel so that it returns the PDF data to Excel.

24. If I had provided a second PDF file, you could save over the existing PDF file, right-click on **Table**, and then choose **Refresh**, in the same fashion that we did with the aging schedule earlier in this chapter.

Now, let's look at one of my favorite uses of **Power Query**, which is to unpivot data. As you'll see, this means transposing unwieldy reports that may be dozens or more columns wide into analysis-ready formats that are only a few columns wide and easily filterable.

Unpivoting data

Unpivoting data is sometimes referred to as flattening the data, which means that all similar values appear in columns instead of rows. For instance, the *Profit & Loss By Class* report that I exported from QuickBooks Desktop, shown in *Figure 12.24*, spans 123 columns, running from column **A** to column **DS**. It's hard to do much with a report like that since the data is so broadly dispersed. Let's use **Power Query** in **Excel for Windows** or **macOS** to transpose 123 columns of data into three. Once again, I'll move faster by not renaming anything in the **Applied Steps** list:

	A	B	C	D	E	F	G	H	I	J
1							Family Room	Kitchen	Remodel Bathroom	
2							(Abercrombie, Kristy)	(Abercrombie, Kristy)	(Abercrombie, Kristy)	Total Abercrombie, Kristy
3						Ordinary Income/Expense				
4						Income				
5						40100 · Construction Income				
6						40110 · Design Income	0.00	0.00	0.00	0.00
7						40130 · Labor Income	1,111.25	560.00	2,718.00	4,389.25
8						40140 · Materials Income	1,849.80	2,930.00	2,227.50	7,007.30
9						40150 · Subcontracted Labor Income				
10						40199 · Less Discounts given	0.00	0.00	0.00	0.00
11						40100 · Construction Income - Other	0.00	0.00	0.00	0.00
12						Total 40100 · Construction Income	2,961.05	3,490.00	4,945.50	11,396.55

Figure 12.24 – Data to be unpivoted

1. Press *Ctrl + N* (*⌘ + N*) to create a blank workbook (or choose **File** | **New** and choose **Blank Workbook**).

2. Click **Data** | **Get Data** | **From File** | **From Excel Workbook**, select Chapter 12 - Unpivoting Data.xlsx, and then click **Import**.

3. Select **Sheet1** from the list and then click **Transform Data**.

4. Click **Column1** and then hold down the *Shift* key and click **Column6** to condense multiple columns that contain account numbers into one.

5. Right-click on the selection and choose **Merge Columns** (or choose **Transform** | **Merge Columns**), enter Account into the **New column Name** field, and then click **OK**.

6. Click on the **Account** column, which deselects the other columns.

7. Right-click the **Account** column, and then choose **Unpivot Other Columns** (or choose **Transform** | **Unpivot Columns**).

8. As shown in *Figure 12.25*, the data now appears in three columns. You can now build a **PivotTable**, filter the data, use **Slicers**, and conduct any number of other analytical tasks:

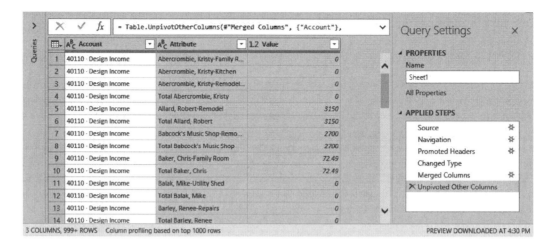

Figure 12.25 – The unpivoted Profit & Loss by Class report

9. Some finishing touches that you could add at this point include:

   - Filtering out **0** values from the **Value** column
   - Renaming the **Attribute** column **Class** by double-clicking on the column heading, typing `Class`, and then pressing *Enter*
   - Renaming the **Values** column as **Amount**

10. Click **Close & Load** to return the unpivoted data to Microsoft Excel.

Now, let's learn how to relate data from two or more sources together. I'm going to use text files as a stand-in for database **Tables** since not everyone has ready access to a database.

Appending and merging data from multiple sources

At this point, we've seen how to extract data from a single data source, such as a PDF file or Excel workbook. In this section, I'm offering you a two-for-one, where you'll not only learn how to extract data from text files but also how to relate data from two or more sources together. The example files for this chapter include six **comma-separated** value (**CSV**) files. *Figure 12.26* shows the data contained within each file, which is also in the `Chapter 12 - Appending and Merging Data.xlsx` workbook. These text files are structured similar to how data is stored in database **Tables**.

You may not have immediate access to a database, but carrying out the steps for appending and merging data from these text files, then you'll know exactly extract data from a database into Excel:

Figure 12.26 – Normalized data

Normalizing data means having as little redundancy as possible. In this example, I have provided transaction files for both January and February. First, we'll append these two files together, which means stack them together into a combined list that has 13 transactions in total. At that point, the data will be combined, but it won't be particularly usable because the vendors and products are represented by an ID number that correlates to the Vendors.csv and Products.csv files, respectively. We cannot directly determine from the Transactions.csv file which **City** or **Region** the transactions belong to, because that data is removed by two or three levels. However, by appending and merging the data in **Power Query**, we can get to a denormalized format, as shown in *Figure 12.27*:

Product Name	Vendor Name	SaleDate	Quantity	Price	Total
Apples	Fruit R Us	1/17/2024	6,079	14	85,106
Bananas	Fruit R Us	1/24/2024	6,868	11	75,548
Bananas	Bob's Fruit	1/19/2024	9,842	10	98,420
Kiwi	Fruit R Us	1/29/2024	6,058	11	66,638
Kiwi	Middle Georgia Fruit	1/26/2024	3,064	15	45,960
Mixed Berries	Orange U Glad	1/12/2024	6,227	15	93,405
Kiwi	Oranges 'n Onions	1/9/2024	1,062	11	11,682
Bananas	Fruitju	2/11/2022	8,442	15	126,630
Bananas	Whistlestop Fruit Stand	2/23/2022	7,994	11	87,934
Oranges	Bob's Fruit	2/15/2022	7,818	12	93,816
Apples	Orange U Glad	2/26/2022	2,605	12	31,260
Kiwi	Whistlestop Fruit Stand	2/7/2022	6,850	10	68,500
Mixed Berries	Mountain Fruit	2/25/2022	3,064	12	36,768
Total					921,667

Figure 12.27 – Denormalized data

As with the last couple of examples, I'm going to speed the process along by not renaming anything in the **Applied Steps** list, to minimize the total number of steps involved in **Excel for Windows** or Mac:

1. Press *Ctrl + N* (⌘ *+ N*) to create a blank workbook (or choose **File** | **New** and choose **Blank Workbook**).
2. Choose **Data** | **Get Data** | **From File** | **From Text/CSV**, select the `Chapter 12 - January Transactions.csv` file, and then click **Import**.
3. Click **Transform Data** to close the **Navigator** window and open the **Power Query Editor**.

> **Tip**
> Typically, you must choose a worksheet, page, or query from the **Navigator** window, but in this context, a text file is treated like database with a single **Table**, so no selection is necessary.

4. Within **Power Query Editor**, click **Home** | **New Source** | **File** | **Text/CSV**, select the `Chapter 12 - February Transactions.csv` file, click **Import**, and then **OK**.

> **Nuance**
> The **Load** and **Transform Data** buttons in the **Navigator** window are replaced by a single **OK** button when you are importing data directly into the **Power Query Editor**.

5. We have two queries that we will append together into a third query by choosing **Home** | **Append Queries** | **Append Queries As New**.
6. Choose **Chapter 12 – January Transactions** from the **First Table** list and **Chapter 12 – February Transactions** from the **Second Table** list, as shown in *Figure 12.28*, and then click **OK**:

Figure 12.28 – The Append dialog box

Appending and merging data from multiple sources   397

> **Nuance**
> You can sort data in **Power Query** in the same fashion as Excel, so that we could just as easily select the February file first and the January file second.

7. Type `Fruit Sales` in the **Name** field of the **Query Settings** task pane and then press *Enter* to give the combined list a more descriptive **Name** than the default **Name** of **Append1**.

8. Now, let's import the vendor list so that we can replace the vendor ID numbers with vendor **Names** in our `Fruit Sales` query. Click **Home | New Source | File | Text/CSV**, select the `Chapter 12 - Vendors.csv` file, click **Import**, and then **OK**.

9. At this point, we're going to merge the data from the `Chapter 12 - Vendors.csv` file into the `Fruit Sales` query, but first, we need to make sure that the ID numbers have the same data type. You can't merge data from two different queries if the fields that you're matching are of different types, such as text and numbers. Here's how to check this:

    I. You should currently see the `Chapter 12 - Vendors` query in the **Data Preview** window, along with the **ID**, **Vendor**, and **City** columns. The left-hand side of the **ID** field has a data type identifier, which in this case is **123**. Click on the icon to display a drop-down menu that indicates that **123** means the field contains whole numbers, as shown in *Figure 12.29*:

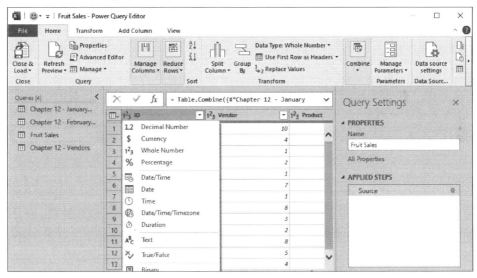

Figure 12.29 – Data types in **Power Query**

    II. Choose `Fruit Sales` from the query list along the left-hand side of the **Power Query Editor** and make note of the data type for the **Vendor** field, which is also **123**, meaning a whole number. We can now merge these two queries since the matching fields in both queries are set to the same data type.

> **Tip**
> If you encounter a situation where one field that you want to match on has a conflicting data type, such as text, you can convert the data by choosing another data type from the list. Errors will appear if you make an incorrect selection, such as trying to convert a column of words into whole numbers, but you won't have any issue changing a text-based column of numbers into a numeric value. Such changes only affect the data in **Power Query** and do not affect the original data.

10. Choose **Home | Merge Queries** and then click on the **Vendor** column in the `Fruit Sales` listing.

11. Choose `Chapter 12 - Vendors` from the list below the `Fruit Sales` listing, and then click on the **ID** field in the `Chapter 12 - Vendors` listing, as shown in *Figure 12.30*. Make note of the status message at the bottom of the **Merge** dialog box, which in this case indicates that 13 of 13 rows matched, and then click **OK**:

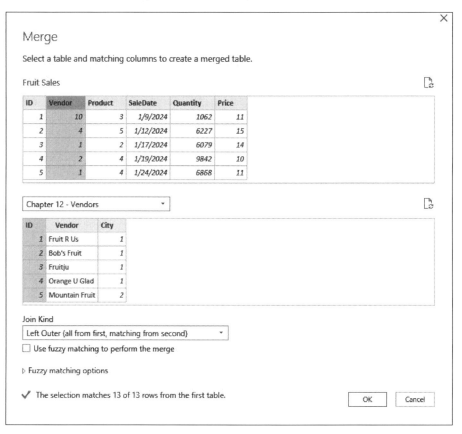

Figure 12.30 – The Merge dialog box

> **Tip**
> A partial number of matches often indicates problems such as merging the wrong **Table**, missing data in a **Table**, or mismatched data types between fields that you're matching on.

12. A **Chapter 12 – Vendors** column will appear in the **Data Preview** window with the word **Table** in every row. This signifies that the `Chapter 12 - Vendors` query has been merged with the `Fruit Sales` query, but the vendor detail hasn't been expanded yet:

    I. Click the double-headed arrow in the header of the **Chapter 12 – Vendors** column.

    II. Clear the checkbox for **ID** to avoid adding a duplicate column since `Fruit Sales` already has a **Vendor** that contains the vendor ID.

    III. Optional: Clear the **Use original column Name as prefix** checkbox. If you leave it checked, the column **Names** for the two fields will become **Chapter 12 – Vendors.Vendor.1** and **Chapter 12 – Vendors.City**. As I generally do, I'll clear that checkbox.

    IV. Click **OK** to expand the columns, which will add two new columns to the query, as shown in *Figure 12.31*:

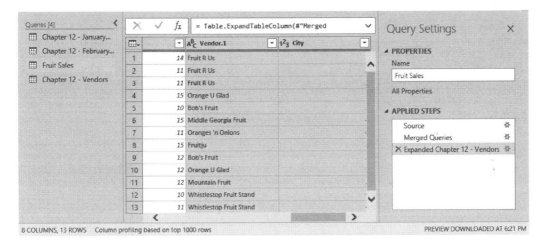

Figure 12.31 – Expanded columns from the Chapter 12 – Vendors query

> **Nuance**
> In *Figure 12.31*, the column with vendor **Names** is labeled **Vendor.1** instead of **Vendor** since the `Fruit Sales` query already had a column named **Vendor**. Each column **Name** in the **Data Preview** window must be unique.

13. Double-click on **Vendor.1** and enter `Vendor Name` (or right-click on **Vendor.1**, choose **Rename**, and enter `Vendor Name`).

> **Tip**
> If you need to rename multiple columns in a query, click on the first column and then press *F2* (*Fn* + *F2* on some keyboards), type the new field **Name**, and press *Enter*. Use the left or right arrow keys to move to the next column, and then press *F2* to rename the next field.

14. Right-click on **Vendor Name** and then choose **Move | To Beginning** to move the **Vendor Name** field to the first column position in the query (or drag the column into a new position with your mouse).

15. Click on the **ID** field and press *Delete*, and then click on the **Vendor** field and press *Delete* to eliminate two extraneous fields from the `Fruit Sales` query.

> **Tip**
> Deleting columns in this fashion only removes the fields from the results. If you click on the `Chapter 12 - January Transactions` or `Chapter 12 - February Transactions` queries, you'll see that the **ID** and **Vendor** columns are still in place.

16. Click **Home | New Source | File | Text/CSV**, select the `Chapter 12 - Products.csv` file, click **Import**, and then click **OK**.

17. Now, let's merge the **Product Names** into the `Fruit Sales` query:

    I. Confirm that the **Product** field in the **Transactions Table** has the same data type as the **ID** field in the **Products Table**, as discussed in *Step 9*.

    II. Select the `Fruit Sales` query from the **Query** list.

    III. Choose **Home | Merge Queries** and click on the **Product** column from the **Fruit Sales**.

    IV. Choose **Chapter 12 - Products** from the second list and select the **ID** column in the **Chapter 12 – Products** list.

    V. Click **OK** to close the **Merge** dialog box.

18. Click the double-headed arrow in the header of the **Chapter 12 – Products** column.

19. Clear the checkbox for **ID** so as not to duplicate the existing product ID column, and then click **OK**.

> **Tip**
> **Use original column Name as prefix** will already be cleared if you chose to do so earlier in this sequence.

20. Double-click on the **Product.1** header, enter `Product Name`, and then press *Enter*.

21. Right-click on **Product Name** and then choose **Move** | **To Beginning** to move the **Product Name** field to the first column position in the query (or drag the column into a new position with your mouse).

22. Click once on the **Product** column and press *Delete* to remove the extraneous field (or right-click on **Product** and choose **Remove**).

23. Optional: To take this technique further, you can import the `Chapter 12 - Cities.csv` and `Chapter 12 - Regions.csv` files and relate their respective columns in the same fashion that we did previously for **Vendors** and **Products**. Remember that you will need to import the `Cities` file first since the **Region ID** column appears in the `Cities` file but does not exist in the `Fruit Sales` query yet. Such sequencing is often a critical part of combining data from two or more sources.

24. Click **Home** | **Close and Load** to return the data to Microsoft Excel.

25. **Power Query** creates a new worksheet for each query that you add, which can result in extraneous worksheets. Right-click on the `Chapter 12 - January Transactions` worksheet, choose **Delete**, and then **Delete** again. Repeat this process for the `Chapter 12 - February Transactions`, `Chapter 12 - Vendors`, `Chapter 12 - Products`, and `Sheet1` worksheets. As shown in *Figure 12.32*, the **Queries & Connections** task pane shows that 13 rows have been loaded from the `Fruit Sales` query, while the other queries indicate **Connection only**. This means that **Power Query** is still attached to the data sources shown, but no results directly tied to those data sources appear in the workbook:

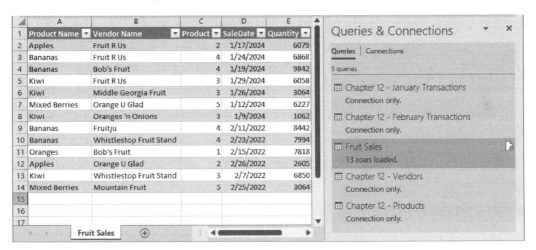

Figure 12.32 – The Queries & Connections task pane

26. As shown in *Figure 12.32*, the city ID numbers appear in column **F** if you did not continue relating the data together. Right-click on column **F** and then choose **Delete**.

27. Right-click on any cell in the **Table** property and then choose **Refresh**. The **City** column will reappear again. Anything that you delete from **Power Query** results in Excel will resurface in this fashion unless you remove the columns within **Power Query**. To do so, follow these steps:

    I. Choose **Query** | **Edit**.

    II. Click once on the **City** column and press *Delete* to remove the extraneous field (or right-click on **City** and choose **Remove**).

    III. Choose **Home** | **Close & Load** to return to Excel.

28. A couple of finishing touches that you may wish to consider are as follows:

    - Enter the word Total in cell **G1** (or **F1** if you deleted the **City** column) and the formula =E2*D2 in cell **G2** (or **F2**).
    - Choose **Table Design** | **Total Row** to add an automatic total to column **G**.
    - Choose **Query** | **Properties**, click **Refresh data when opening the file**, and then click **OK** if you want the query to refresh automatically when you open the file, especially if you use these techniques to connect your spreadsheets to a database.

As I mentioned earlier, the techniques that are used to append and merge data from text files are identical to how you can append and merge data from databases and other data sources. Now, let's take a brief look at how to connect **Power Query** to a database.

Connecting to databases and installing ODBC drivers

You'll notice that this book doesn't have anywhere near 1,000 pages, which means there's simply not enough space to dive very deep into the topic of connecting to databases and installing ODBC drivers. With that said, the examples in this chapter were chosen to give you exposure to using **Power Query** with a variety of data sources. As you'll see, connecting to a database typically only involves a couple of steps, depending on the platform that you're connecting to.

Establishing an Access database and SQL Server connections

Let's start by linking to an Access database in **Excel for Windows** (you cannot connect to Access databases in **Excel for macOS**):

1. Press *Ctrl + N* to create a blank workbook (or choose **File** | **New** and choose **Blank Workbook**).

2. Choose **Data** | **Get Data** | **From Database** | **From Microsoft Access Database**, select the Chapter 12 - Fruit Sales.accdb database from this chapter's example files, and then click **Import**.

3. As shown in *Figure 12.33*, you're now on familiar ground as the **Navigator** window shows you the **Tables** that reside within the database:

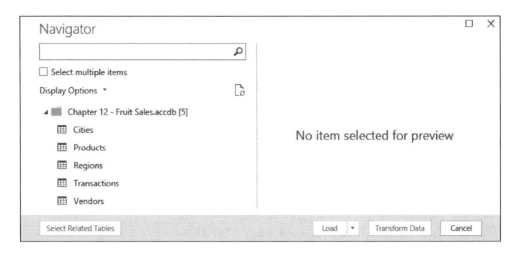

12.33 – Retrieving data from a Microsoft Access database

To take this further, select one or more **Tables** and then use the same techniques that we applied in the *Appending and merging data from multiple sources* section.

> **Tip**
> You can connect to Access databases and extract data even if you do not have Microsoft Access installed on your computer.

Now, let's say that you want to connect to a Microsoft SQL Server database, which you *can* do from **Excel for macOS**:

1. Press *Ctrl* + *N* (⌘ + *N*) to create a blank workbook (or choose **File** | **New** and choose **Blank Workbook**), or open an existing workbook.
2. Choose **Data** | **Get Data** | **From Database** | **From SQL Server Database** to display the **SQL Server database** dialog box, as shown in *Figure 12.34*:

Figure 12.34 – The SQL Server database dialog box

3. Enter the server **Name** or address in the **Server** field, then optionally enter the database **Name** in the **Database (optional)** field, and then click **OK**.

4. As shown in *Figure 12.35*, a second dialog box will appear that requires you to enter your credentials. Whether you choose **Windows**, **Database**, or **Microsoft account** will depend on the configuration of your database:

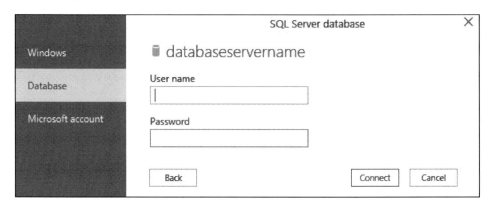

Figure 12.35 – The SQL Server authentication dialog box

5. You may encounter a warning that **Power Query** cannot establish an encrypted connection to the database. Click **OK** to continue using an unencrypted connection.

6. At this point, the familiar **Navigator** window will appear, from which you can choose the database and then the **Tables** or views that you wish to attach to – and have the rights to access.

It was easy to connect to an Access or SQL Server database because the connectivity software, known as a driver, is preinstalled with Excel. You may have a little homework to do if you want to connect to another type of database, such as MySQL or an accounting program.

Establishing ODBC connections

ODBC stands for **Open Database Connectivity** and is an **Application Programming Interface** (**API**) for accessing data within database platforms. Let's say that you want to be able to retrieve data from an accounting software, such as **QuickBooks Desktop**. The **Enterprise** version of QuickBooks ships with an ODBC driver, while the **Pro** and **Premier** versions require you to purchase a third-party ODBC driver. I share this as an example of how ODBC drivers are typically distributed: they may be bundled with your software, or you may have to pay extra.

If you know that the ODBC driver you need is already installed, the steps are going to be like how we connected to a SQL Server database (**Excel for macOS** does not support ODBC):

1. Press *Ctrl + N* to create a blank workbook (or choose **File** | **New** and choose **Blank Workbook**) or open an existing workbook.

2. Choose **Data | Get Data | From Other Sources | From ODBC** to display the **From ODBC** dialog box.
3. Choose a data source **Name** from the **Data source Name (DSN)** list, and then click **OK**.

What appears next will depend on the data source and its ODBC driver. Some drivers allow you to store the database **Name** and credentials within the driver settings on your computer, which means that connecting will be like the steps for connecting to an Access database. Other drivers may require you to authenticate when you connect, much like the SQL Server process.

Installing ODBC drivers and creating data sources

The process of installing an OBDC driver is much like installing any other type of program on your computer. You'll download the setup file and then run the installation process. The remaining steps will occur in the **ODBC Data Source Administrator** window:

1. Click the **Start** button in Microsoft Windows.
2. Type ODBC and then click on either the **ODBC Data Sources (32-bit)** or **ODBC Data Sources (64-bit)** app.
3. Any available drivers that have already been set up will appear in the **ODBC Data Source Administrator** window, as shown in *Figure 12.36*. Simply installing a driver does not make the driver appear in this dialog box. For that, you must click the **Add** button, select a driver, and then click **Finish**:

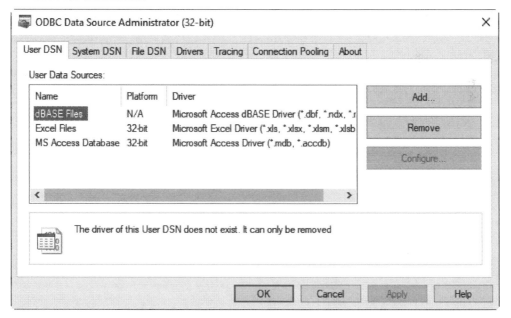

Figure 12.36 – The ODBC Data Source Administrator window

4. From there, the steps involved will depend on your ODBC driver, but you can expect to be able to provide the **Name** and/or address of the database, along with user credentials.

Now, let's summarize what you've learned in this chapter.

Summary

In this book about nuances and quirks in Microsoft Excel, I saved the most nuanced and quirky feature for last. **Power Query** can be a transformational tool for you if you can avoid getting stymied. I've shared several stumbling blocks that I hit during my learning curve. You should now be well prepared for most things that **Power Query** may try to throw at you.

In this chapter, you learned how to create a list of worksheets within any workbook, which you can then transform into an interactive index listing. It's important to understand that **Power Query** does not offer real-time connections to data, but rather provides snapshots of the data that can be refreshed. Then, we transformed an Excel-based report from an accounting program into a streamlined, analysis-ready dataset.

If you've struggled to extract data from PDF files in the past, the ability to do so with **Power Query** may have you dancing in your chair. I know that being able to unpivot reports of the type that we worked with earlier in this chapter makes my day every time I use the feature.

From there, we explored how to append and merge data, which is all part of denormalizing data that has been flattened into a database format to minimize redundancy. Such tasks are necessary to transform data back into a format that is useful to humans, as opposed to a database.

If you've read through this book to this point, then you hopefully have a much deeper understanding of Microsoft Excel's idiosyncrasies. Over the past 30 years, I have spent an unhealthy amount of time watching others use Microsoft Excel, often ineffectively. This book is a summation of the pitfalls and dark corners of Excel because, in my experience, that's where the frustration lies. Most of Excel's features are easy to master, but when something unexpected arises, you might feel like a rank beginner.

This book is far from an an exhaustive list of nuances and quirks. I chose the material for this book based on the webinars that I am requested to teach most often, as well as audience questions that tend to arise repeatedly. I'd like to reiterate the advice that I laid out in *Chapter 1, Implementing Accessibility*. Try to build skyscrapers with your data, meaning orient it vertically up and down columns. Limit horizontal sprawl to the best extent possible, as each avoidable column and worksheet that you add inexorably moves your spreadsheets toward frustration, inefficiency, and ultimately inaccessibility. Thank you for reading my book!

Index

Symbols

#CALC! errors 290
#SPILL! errors
    about 290, 318
    conditions 318, 319

A

Access database
    linking, in Excel for Windows 402, 403
Accessibility Checker feature
    about 25, 26
    errors 25
    tips 26
    warnings 26
Accessibility Reminder add-in
    about 26
    commands 26, 27
ActiveX Controls 153
Advanced Formula Environment 354, 355
aged receivables report 376
alt-number pad nuance 63, 64
Always create backup setting 45, 46
amortization table
    about 313
    arguments 314, 315

Application Programming Interface (API) 404
array 302
array formulas 182
AutoFilter command 69
automatic report cleanup
    about 375
    analytical obstacles 376
    Power Query connection, breaking 385
    Power Query connection, updating
        with new data 384
    reports, transforming 377-381
    supplemental formulas, adding to
        Power Query results 383, 384
AutoRecover feature
    about 35
    Excel for Mac AutoRecover 38, 39
    Excel for Windows AutoRecover 36, 37
AutoSave with OneDrive
    about 39
    disabled AutoSave, resolving 43, 44
    disabling, permanently 44, 45
    files, saving 40-42
    prior AutoSave versions, accessing 42, 43

B

Backstage View 58, 70
base view, multipurpose worksheet
   creating 236-238

C

Calc app 48
calculation argument 344
CELL function
   about 103
   arguments 103
   custom conditional formatting
      rule, creating 103-105
cell icons
   applying 99, 100
   percentile rule 98-100
cell link 154
Center Across Selection
   using 18, 19
center text
   about 65
   keyboard shortcut, creating 65
Chart Range 217
charts
   about 11, 12
   weekend dates, excluding 274, 276
Checkboxes
   about 156
   creating 156
CHOOSE function 327
circular references
   about 279, 280
   iterative calculation option,
      enabling 280, 281
clickable index
   list of worksheets, converting into 370

Close All command 69
co-authoring 78
color scales
   about 97
   applying 97, 98
Combo Box Form Control 154-156
Commands Not in the Ribbon
   commands, with alter-egos 68-70
   exploring 68
comma-separated value (CSV) file 53
Compatibility Checker feature
   about 264-266
   versus Compatibility Mode 266, 267
computers
   Quick Access Toolbar, transferring
      between 74, 75
CONCATENATE function 300
concatenation 300
CONCAT function 300
conditional formatting
   about 85, 86
   troubleshooting 111
conditional formatting rules
   accessible conditional formatting
      legend, creating 109
   Applies to column 107, 108
   conditional formatting legend, creating 108
   conditional formatting, removing 109, 110
   editing 106
   managing 106
Convert command
   versus Save As 267-269
COUNTIF function
   criteria argument 209
   range argument 209
COUNTIFS function
   arguments 313
CUMIPMT function 163, 164

custom data validation rules
  about 146
  COUNTIF function 147
  duplicate entries, preventing 148, 149
  FIND function 146
  names entering in last name, first
    name order 147, 148
custom rules
  about 101
  CELL function 103
  IS functions 101, 102
  logical tests 105, 106
Custom Views
  about 69, 234, 235
  applying, that hides worksheets in
    protected workbook 260, 261
  applying, that unhides worksheets in
    protected workbook 260, 261
  conflicts 255
  removing, from workbook 253-255
  Table feature, conflicting with 257
  used, for applying filters
    automatically 247-250
  used, for hiding worksheets 246
  used, for unhiding worksheets 246
  worksheet, protecting conflicts with 257-260
Custom Views Quick Access Toolbar
  shortcut, creating 240-242

D

damaged workbooks
  excess formatting, removing 48, 49
  repairing 46-48
data
  appending, from multiple sources 394-402
  denormalizing 395
  extracting, from PDF files 386-392
  merging, from multiple sources 394-402
  normalizing 395
  unpivoting 393, 394
data bars
  about 95
  using 95, 96
databases
  connecting to 402
data sources
  creating 405, 406
Data Tables
  about 177, 196
  calculation performance, improving 182
  data table, creating with one input 177, 178
  data table, creating with three
    inputs 180-182
  data table, creating with two inputs 179, 180
Data Validation
  about 119-123
  Error Alert tab 125
  Input Message tab 125
  limitations 150
  removing 129, 130
  Settings tab 124, 125
Data Validation cells
  inputs, auditing 151
  protecting 150
data validation rules
  Any value 131
  custom rules 146
  Date 141
  Decimal 132
  Formula-based Date rule 142, 143
  implementing 131
  List 132
  Text length 145
  Time 143, 144
  Whole Number 131

decision-making functions
    about 325
    CHOOSE function 326, 327
    IF function 325, 326
    SWITCH function 327, 328
Developer tab
    enabling 151, 152
double-click trick
    used, for navigating within worksheets 270
dynamic amortization table 290, 313
dynamic array formulas 302
dynamic array functions 289

E

Enable Content prompt 52
Enter Mode
    versus Edit Mode 271-274
EOMONTH function
    about 142, 316
    arguments 316
Error Alert tab
    about 125, 126
    Error Alert styles 126, 127
    Information style 128, 129
    Warning style 127, 128
Excel
    ribbon, customizing 59
    version, finding 57
    volume calculations 324
Excel accessibility
    charts 11, 12
    color, working with 23, 24
    footers usage, minimizing 19-23
    headers usage, minimizing 19-23
    Help tab 9
    implementing 14
    making 4

merge cells 17, 18
Microsoft Search box 7-9
PivotTables 10, 11
Table feature, using 24
watermarks usage, minimizing 19-23
worksheet function, finding 4
worksheet names, assigning 14-16
Excel for Mac AutoRecover 38, 39
Excel for Windows AutoRecover
    about 36, 37
    interim backups, accessing 37
    temporary files, removing 37, 38
Excel macros
    catch 74
    naming 72
    shortcuts, creating 71-74
Executive Summary view,
        multipurpose worksheet
    creating 238, 239

F

Filter buttons 199
FILTER function
    about 289, 309
    arguments 309-311
filters
    applying, automatically with
        Custom Views 247-250
Forecast Sheet feature
    amounts, projecting with 183-185
Format as Table command 196-198
formatting
    versus conditional formatting 84, 85
Form Controls
    about 119, 152
    Combo Box 154-156
    exploring 152-154

INDEX function 154
  managing 158
formula errors
  handling, with LET function 340
Freeze Panes command 69, 70
full screen feature
  about 75, 76
  restoring 78
Full-screen mode 76, 77
Function Arguments 6
function call 346
Function ScreenTip 6, 7
future value (fv) 163

G

Goal Seek feature 174-177
Group Box form control 157

H

Header Row 200
Headers 192
Help tab
  about 9
  commands 9, 10
hidden Quick Access Toolbar
  restoring 57, 58
highlight cell rules
  about 86
  Between rule 88, 89
  Date Occurring rule 91-93
  Duplicate Values 93, 94
  Equal To rule 89, 90
  Greater Than rule 87
  Less Than rule 88
  Text That Contains rule 90, 91

HYPERLINK function
  about 369
  arguments 369

I

icon sets
  about 98
  applying 99, 100
IFERROR function 341
IF function 325, 326
IFNA function
  about 292
  arguments 292
inaccessible spreadsheets
  example 28-30
INDEX function
  about 289
  arguments 295
INDIRECT function 138
Inquire add-in 48, 284, 285
Insert Function 4, 5
Insert Table command 198
IPMT function
  about 316
  arguments 316, 317
ISERROR function 341, 342
IS functions
  custom conditional formatting
    rule, creating 101, 102
  examples 101
iterative calculation option
  enabling 280, 281

K

keyboard and mouse shortcuts
  for column insertion 225
  for cursor movement 226

for data selection, within worksheet or table 225
for moving columns 226
for row insertion 225

L

LAMBDA formula
  developing 344
  worksheet function, creating with 345
LAMBDA function
  about 344
  Advanced Formula Environment add-in 354-356
  calculations, defining with 345
  conflicts and errors 352, 353
  evaluating 346
  exploring 350
  moving, between workbooks 348-350
  optional parameters 351
  parameters, naming with 345
  XBOXVOLUME function 356-358
legacy features
  about 75
  full screen feature 75, 76
  full screen feature, restoring 78
  Full-screen mode 76, 77
  restoring 75
  Share Workbook feature, restoring 78
  Show Changes feature 79-81
LET function
  about 339
  formula errors, handling with 340
  repetitive calculations, eliminating with 342
  variable name restrictions 342-344
LibreOffice suite 48
list
  assembling 140, 141
  dependent lists, creating 137

range names, assigning 137
self-updating list, creating 136, 137
storing, in Source field 133, 134
storing, in worksheet cells 134, 135
list of worksheets
  converting, into clickable index 370
  creating 365-369
  Power Query connections, refreshing 371, 372
  source data connections, updating 374, 375
logical tests
  about 105
  custom conditional formatting rule, creating 105, 106
lookup functions 289

M

macro
  used, for unhiding worksheets 243-246
macro-enabled workbooks 361
Macro Recorder 72, 243
MATCH function
  about 289, 293
  arguments 293, 294
merge cells
  about 17, 18
  example 17, 18
Microsoft Search box
  about 7-9
  commands 7
Microsoft SQL Server database
  connecting to 403, 404
mixed reference 294
Modify button 73
multipurpose worksheets
  base view, creating 236-238
  creating 235

Executive Summary view, creating 238, 239
Page Layout view conflict 239, 240
Quarters Only view, creating 238

N

Navigation task pane 16

O

ODBC connections
 establishing 404, 405
ODBC drivers
 installing 402-406
Office Online
 URL 80
Office Theme 73
OneDrive
 URL 79
Open Database Connectivity (ODBC) 404
optical character recognition 386
Option Buttons
 about 156
 creating 157
Outline feature 171

P

Page Layout mode 21
Page Layout view conflict 239, 240
PivotTables 10, 11, 195, 393
 integrity 214-216
PMT function 162, 163
Portable Document Format (PDF)
 about 386
 data, extracting from 386-392
 shortcuts 67, 68
Power Query
 about 51, 363

Data preview 367
Query listing 367
Query Settings task pane 367
Ribbon interface 367
technical requisites 363, 364
Power Query, phases
 combining 364
 connecting 364
 loading 364
 refreshing 364
 transforming 364
PPMT function 317
present value (pv) 164
Print Preview 58
Print Preview Full Screen command 70
Print Settings
 applying 251-253
PRODUCT function 325
Protected View 49-51

Q

Quarters Only view, multipurpose worksheet
 creating 238
Quick Access Toolbar
 alt-number pad nuance 63, 64
 exploring 56
 resetting 62, 63
 ribbon commands, adding to 64
 transferring, between computers 74, 75
 workbook-specific toolbars 70
Quick Access Toolbar commands
 removing 61
 repositioning 60
Quick Access Toolbar shortcuts
 naming convention, working 60
 nuances 59, 60
QuickBooks Desktop 404

R

radio buttons 156
RANDARRAY function
   about 290, 319
   arguments 319, 320
Redo command 34-56
repetitive calculations
   eliminating, with LET function 342
reports
   transforming 377-381
Reset All Customizations command 62
reusable LAMBDA functions
   creating 346-348
ribbon
   about 151
   customizing 59
ribbon commands
   adding, to Quick Access Toolbar 64
   center text 65
   PDF shortcuts 67, 68
   worksheet cells, locking 66, 67
   worksheet cells, unlocking 66, 67

S

Save As
   versus Convert command 267-269
Scenario Manager feature
   about 164
   constraints 165
   scenarios, creating 166-168
   scenarios, displaying 168, 169
   scenarios, merging 173, 174
   scenes, setting 165, 166
scenario reports
   about 169
   Scenario PivotTable report 169-173
   Scenario Summary report 169-171

Section 508
   URL 28
SEQUENCE function
   about 315
   arguments 315
Share Workbook feature
   restoring 78
shortcuts
   creating, for Excel macros 71-74
Show Changes feature
   about 79
   workbook changes, viewing 80
   workbook, saving to OneDrive 79
single-purchase version 57, 80
Slicers 393
Solver feature
   about 185-188
   versus Goal Seek feature 188
SORTBY function 289
SORT function
   about 289, 305
   arguments 306-308
sparklines 276-278
spilled range operator 137, 289, 312
structured references
   for formulas 205, 206
SUBSTITUTE function 139
SUMIF function
   about 296, 317
   arguments 296, 317
SUMIF function arguments
   criteria 29
   range 29
   sum range 29
SUMIFS function
   about 296
   arguments 297

Summary Only view
  creating 247
SWITCH function 327

T

table
  about 194
  cells, converting into 196-198
  Data Tables 196
  entire table, copying 223
  entire table, pasting 223
  entire worksheet columns, copying 223
  entire worksheet columns, pasting 223
  PivotTables 195
  portion, copying 224
  portion, pasting 224
  removing 203, 204
  troubleshooting 227-231
table automation opportunities
  about 204
  calculated column 205, 206
  filter feature 210
  PivotTable integrity 214-216
  self-resizing charts 217, 218
  self-resizing formulas 207, 208
  slicers 211-213
  structured references, for writing
    formulas 208-210
table characteristics
  about 199
  automatic changes 199-201
  optional enhancements 201-203
Table feature
  about 24
  conflicting, with Custom Views 257
  using 24

Table Styles
  about 196
  built-in style, customizing 219, 220
  customizing 219
  custom table style, transferring
    to workbooks 221, 222
  default table style, setting 219
table techniques
  about 218
  custom styles, modifying 222, 223
  custom styles, removing 222, 223
  keyboard and mouse shortcuts 225
  tables, copying 223
  tables, pasting 223
  table styles, customizing 219
  table styles, transferring to workbooks 221
Tell Me feature 7
textboxes 21
TODAY function 142
top and bottom rules 94, 95
Top and Double Bottom Border command
  shortcut, creating 65
Track Changes feature 17
troubleshooting, conditional formatting
  no formatting instructions 111, 112
  rules order, changing 113
  Wingdings font 114, 115

U

Undo command 34-56
UNIQUE function
  about 289, 304
  arguments 304
unwritten rule 192, 193
Use in Formulas command 338
user-defined functions 358

V

variable 339
VBA worksheet functions
   about 358
   editing 361
   file, unblocking 359
   testing 359, 360
Visual Basic for Applications (VBA) 71, 358
VLOOKUP function
   about 289, 290
   arguments 291
   constraints 291, 292
volume calculations, Excel
   about 324
   decision-making functions 325
   multiplication, using 324
   PRODUCT function, using 325

W

WordArt 19-21
workbook
   Custom Views, removing from 253-255
   LAMBDA functions, moving between 348-350
   warning prompts 49
workbook-specific toolbars
   about 70
   creating 70
Workbook Statistics dialog box 30
workbooks, warning prompts
   CSV prompt 53, 54
   Protected View 49-51
   trusted documents 51-53
worksheet cells
   locking 66, 67
   naming conventions 328
   unlocking 66, 67

worksheet cells, naming
   Create from Selection command 331
   Define Name command, using 334
   Name Box, using 328-330
   Name Manager area 334-337
   names, using within formulas 338
worksheet function
   finding 4
worksheet function tools
   Function Arguments 6
   Function ScreenTip 6, 7
   Insert Function 4, 5
worksheet index
   updating 372-374
worksheets
   hiding 242, 243
   hiding, with Custom Views 246
   navigating, with double-click trick 270
   protection, conflicting with Custom Views 257-260
   Summary Only view, creating 247
   unhiding 242, 243
   unhiding, with Custom Views 246
   unhiding, with macro 243-246
workspace feature 75

X

XBOXVOLUME function 356-358
XLOOKUP function
   about 289, 297
   arguments 298
   if_not_found argument 298
   match, finding on multiple column criteria 301, 302
   match_mode argument 298, 299
   results, combining into single column 300

results, returning on multiple cells 302
results, returning to multiple columns 301
search_mode argument 300, 301
XMATCH function
  about 289, 303
  arguments 303, 304

Packt.com

Subscribe to our online digital library for full access to over 7,000 books and videos, as well as industry leading tools to help you plan your personal development and advance your career. For more information, please visit our website.

Why subscribe?

- Spend less time learning and more time coding with practical eBooks and Videos from over 4,000 industry professionals
- Improve your learning with Skill Plans built especially for you
- Get a free eBook or video every month
- Fully searchable for easy access to vital information
- Copy and paste, print, and bookmark content

Did you know that Packt offers eBook versions of every book published, with PDF and ePub files available? You can upgrade to the eBook version at packt.com and as a print book customer, you are entitled to a discount on the eBook copy. Get in touch with us at customercare@packtpub.com for more details.

At www.packt.com, you can also read a collection of free technical articles, sign up for a range of free newsletters, and receive exclusive discounts and offers on Packt books and eBooks.

Other Books You May Enjoy

If you enjoyed this book, you may be interested in these other books by Packt:

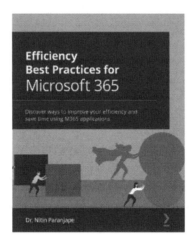

Efficiency Best Practices for Microsoft 365

Dr. Nitin Paranjape

ISBN: 9781801072267

- Understand how different MS 365 tools, such as Office desktop, Teams, Power BI, Lists, and OneDrive, can increase work efficiency
- Replace the content with the following bullet list:
- Identify time-consuming processes and understand how to work through them more efficiently
- Create professional documents quickly with minimal effort
- Work across multiple teams, meetings, and projects without email overload
- Automate mundane, repetitive, and time-consuming manual work
- Manage work, delegation, execution, and project management

Hands-On Financial Modeling with Excel for Microsoft 365 - Second Edition

Shmuel Oluwa

ISBN: 9781803231143

- Identify the growth drivers derived from processing historical data in Excel
- Use discounted cash flow (DCF) for efficient investment analysis
- Prepare detailed asset and debt schedule models in Excel
- Calculate profitability ratios using various profit parameters
- Obtain and transform data using Power Query
- Dive into capital budgeting techniques
- Apply a Monte Carlo simulation to derive key assumptions for your financial model Build a financial model by projecting balance sheets and profit and loss

Packt is searching for authors like you

If you're interested in becoming an author for Packt, please visit `authors.packtpub.com` and apply today. We have worked with thousands of developers and tech professionals, just like you, to help them share their insight with the global tech community. You can make a general application, apply for a specific hot topic that we are recruiting an author for, or submit your own idea.

Share Your Thoughts

Now you've finished *Exploring Microsoft Excel's Hidden Treasures*, we'd love to hear your thoughts! Scan the QR code below to go straight to the Amazon review page for this book and share your feedback or leave a review on the site that you purchased it from.

`https://packt.link/r/1803243945`

Your review is important to us and the tech community and will help us make sure we're delivering excellent quality content.

Made in the USA
Middletown, DE
04 September 2023

37939086R00247